Theories of Planning and Spatial Development

The Built Environment Series

Series Editors

Michael J. Bruton, *Professor of Planning in the University of Wales Institute of Science and Technology*
John Ratcliffe, *Dean of the Faculty of the Built Environment, South Bank Polytechnic, London*

Theories of Planning and Spatial Development

Philip Cooke

Department of Town Planning,
University of Wales Institute of Science and Technology,
Cardiff

Hutchinson

London Melbourne Sydney Auckland Johannesburg

Hutchinson & Co. (Publishers) Ltd

An imprint of the Hutchinson Publishing Group

17–21 Conway Street, London W1P 6JD

Hutchinson Group (Australia) Pty Ltd
30–32 Cremorne Street, Richmond South, Victoria 3121
PO Box 151, Broadway, New South Wales 2007

Hutchinson Group (NZ) Ltd
32–34 View Road, PO Box 40–086, Glenfield, Auckland 10

Hutchinson Group (SA) (Pty) Ltd
PO Box 337, Bergvlei 2012, South Africa

First published 1983

© Philip Cooke 1983

Photoset in 10 on 12 Times Roman by
Kelly Typesetting Limited
Bradford-on-Avon, Wiltshire

Printed in Great Britain by The Anchor Press Ltd
and bound by Wm Brendon & Son Ltd
both of Tiptree, Essex

British Library Cataloguing in Publication Data

Cooke, Philip
    Theories of planning and spatial development. – (Built environment)
    1. Regional planning
    I. Title   II. Series
    361.6'1   HT391

ISBN 0 09 153001 6

Contents

Preface

This book, like many others, has taken considerably longer to write than expected. Putting aside reasons such as involvement with other projects, preferring to play with our new daughters, and laziness, I have found it genuinely difficult to write about urban and regional planning during a period when much of what was familiar when I started writing has since disappeared or been substantially changed. Not the least of what has gone is much of the industrial landscape, the location of which used in part to be the responsibility of urban and regional planners. In parallel, housing investment, especially in the public sector, has all but dried up, and so the other main plank of planning intervention, dealing with residential location, has also contracted. Perhaps these are merely intervals before the pace of spatial development picks up again, but they have marked a new experience for planners and social scientists, and their implications for state intervention are still unclear.

I have been lucky in trying to work out some of the less intractable implications of such changes because of the stimulation to think about them which has come from three sources: the British Sociological Association (Wales) Group; the Conference of Socialist Economists Regionalism Working Group; and the students on my graduate option in Urban Politics. To all friends there I extend general gratitude. I hope the excuses in the preceding paragraph will help placate the long-suffering Hutchinson editors into whose care this volume was taken, especially Rab MacWilliam and Doug Fox. Michael Bruton, as series editor, to whom I am grateful for asking me to contribute, has also been most helpful in numerous ways. As far as the text itself is concerned, I would like to thank John Forester for his critical comments on my version of Critical Theory and Brian McLoughlin for equally constructive suggestions. Gareth Rees I would like to thank for his often iconoclastic approach to conventional wisdoms of many kinds. Special thanks are due to Andrew Sayer and John Urry who read the whole text and helped me improve it substantially but who, unfortunately, cannot be blamed for its remaining faults. Finally, thanks to Mike Hall for trying to teach me how to do an index, and to Myrtle Robins for her speedy and accurate typing.

Philip Cooke
September 1982

1 Introduction

This book is written with a number of objectives in mind. It is, first of all, meant to act as a guide for students to the theoretical framework of urban and regional planning. As such, it may also prove of interest to students in the related fields of development studies, human geography, urban politics and urban sociology. Perhaps a book which speaks to a potentially wide academic audience could be thought lacking in specificity; however one of the strongest intentions behind the writing of this one has been to demonstrate the artificial nature of the barriers that have been erected between the social sciences. This is not to say that an academic division of labour is not both a necessary and a desirable thing, but rather that the point of any division of labour is to create a more productive and useful synthesis than can be achieved by more exclusive methods of production. Urban and regional planning, and the spatial development processes with which it is concerned, is a good vehicle for the inter-disciplinary, co-operative study of a range of social sciences and it is hoped that the book gives some idea of the interesting interconnections which can be made, and remain to be made, between social and spatial processes.

The second objective expresses a narrower aspect of the first, which is to overcome the typical fragmentation effect of social scientific specialization as it occurs within one relatively small area of the study of urban and regional planning. Planning theory has, in recent years, come to be very largely separated from theory of the socio-spatial development processes with which it interacts in the external world. Planning has come to be a paradigm example of McLuhan's famous aphorism about the medium being more important than the message. That is, the ways in which ideas are presented, preferably in as rational, technically sophisticated and glossily packaged a manner as possible, have become of paramount importance to theorists of planning, while the content of plans is often poorly researched, badly understood and socially provocative. This book aims to reintegrate *planning theory* and *development theory* by showing how, at the levels of both theory and practice, the planning system interlocks with certain pressures which are found in capitalist societies, the effects of which are to influence the shape and direction of development. Because of this two further subsidiary aims are more closely approached. The first of these is to formulate a conceptual framework of planning which is capable of yielding testable propositions about planning. This helps to pull development planning theory away from the normative traditions to which it has remained tied for too long. By this is meant that instead of adding more prescriptions about how local or regional planning ought to be conducted, the aim is to present a theoretical description of what the urban and regional planning system does for the spatial development process. It is possible that the resulting description is inaccurate, although the opposite is assumed to be the case, by the author at least, but in any case, in making descriptive statements the ground is prepared for mistakes to be corrected by interested parties. The second subsidiary aim which has been approached by this reintegration strategy is to show, albeit rather generally, how planning policies change historically in tune with changes in the wider political economy. This gets us further away from the idea that planning is somehow a transcendental activity which contains certain principles that are appropriate for all time; in other words it undermines the idealistic[1]* basis of planning which stretches back at least to Geddes, Le Play and similar medievalists.

The third main objective of the book is to move the terrain of debate about the relationship between urban and regional planning and political economy, away from the sterile rut into which it has recently come to rest. Although it will become clearer in subsequent chapters that there are fundamental weaknesses in many orthodox as well as radical theories of development and planning, most of them share an uncritical and unreflective attachment to functionalist and reductionist modes of theorizing. Many of the theorists who have developed a radical critique of traditional theories of development and planning are far worse offenders in this respect than the authors whose work they criticize. Either way, the reader is left with the hopeless feeling, whether reading Lösch, Myrdal, Castells or Harvey that there is an underlying logic to capitalism in which the best the planning system, as part of the state, can expect to do is function according to capital's needs and help to hold the system together for a while longer. It is a little unfair to characterize each of these writers so boldly in this way, especially as the work of some of the more recent among them has developed somewhat to take account of such criticisms. Nevertheless, it is the conscious aim of this book to shift away from the functionalist and reductionist theoretical positions which dominate the field at present. Instead, a more hopeful analysis of the relationship between planning and spatial development is presented, in which both are conceived as objects of struggle, the outcomes of which are partly indeterminate. That is, there are two powerful social forces, capital and labour, each occasionally joined and/or opposed by other less powerful social forces, such as regional, racial or other popular groupings, which pressure each other, and the state, to achieve better material and cultural conditions than they would experience if they did not

* Superior figures refer to the *Notes* on pages 276–285.

struggle. It is the outcomes of such struggles which are important to understand because the state planning system is often part of the solution to
problems posed by them. In the process it helps to produce certain
important spatial effects which keep the acquiescence of the majority for the
continuation of the capitalist system of production.

The last main objective of this book is to seek to push further some of the
more interesting and important findings which have been made in recent
years in urban and regional development theory, and theories of the state
and planning, by writers who have found the observations made by Marx
about the working of capitalism to be worthy of reinterpretation. Put
plainly, this book is sufficiently critical of orthodox development and
planning theory to suggest that both are largely unhelpful to those seeking
an understanding of spatial development, excepting those only concerned
with the surface details of the effects of decisions made by individual
capitalists. However, readers of a Marxist persuasion will probably find a
good deal in the book which smacks of reformism, not to say pluralism in
places. This can be, and is, explained throughout the latter stages of the text
as a desire to get away from the debilitating functionalisms and reduction-
isms of much of this kind of work, and the revolutionary recipes or politics of
despair which are engendered by it. The tradition of Marxism which we
would hope this contribution will be seen as addressing, is that represented
by Gramsci more than any other. In particular, the concepts of civil society,
the city–country division, hegemony and the specificity of locality which
were theorized in his work have been found most useful. It should be added,
though, that the relative clarity with which it is hoped these and other
concepts are communicated owes much to certain contemporary theorists
who have made substantial contributions to the interpretation of Gramsci's
ideas. These authors are copiously cited in the relevant sections of the book.

The book itself falls into two parts: first an exposition and critique of the
fragmentary subject matter of orthodox planning and development theory;
and, second, an exposition, critique and an attempt at synthesis of more
recent radical (mainly Marxist) work in the same broad area. The first part
devotes some attention to showing how standard planning theory is really
composed of adaptations of major theoretical positions found in economics,
political science and sociology. In addition, it is indicated how and why such
adaptations have fitted in with one of two main methodological, analytical
and practical viewpoints found within bourgeois social science and bourgeois society, too. In the second part, the book progresses from an evaluation of spatial development theory, through an analysis of the state and the
planning system, followed by a theorization of planning in which its capacity
to unite land and labour in ways which temporarily resolve the divergent
tendencies between labour and capital is given prominence. Finally certain
deductions and implications for the external and internal structures of the
planning system are drawn from tendencies present and currently visible in

the capitalist development process. In the following few pages of this first chapter a little more detail is given of the content of the following nine chapters.

In Chapter 2 the concern is mainly with establishing certain epistemological distinctions which are of importance subsequently. The first part of the chapter is taken up with an analysis and critique of four important theories of knowledge ranging from positivism to the realist philosophy of science. It is argued that the last of these is a superior method of producing knowledge because it does not limit itself to the counter-intuitive belief that the only things which can be known are those which can be observed. The realist approach, which seeks to identify mechanisms with distinct powers of causation is later used to derive the theoretical linkage between state planning and the spatial development process. In the remainder of the chapter two sets of five distinctions are drawn between approaches to theorization commonly found in the social sciences and planning. The principal division is that between a generally individualist, behaviourist mode of analysis (and, when it comes to policy, practice too) on the one hand, and a more institutional, structural[2] approach on the other. These methodological positions within mainstream planning are described and criticized before more detailed exposition of the theories themselves in later chapters.

In Chapter 3 examples are provided of varieties of planning theory which are substantially informed by two different influences. In the first instance they are heavily individualistic in their methodology and modes of analysis, and secondly they are adaptations, into the public policy and planning fields, of neo-classical economical thought. The combination results in a general approach to planning which is concerned mainly with inducing changes at the margin, and for this reason we refer to them as marginalist planning theories. They are represented first in the work of Downs which dominates the first section. Although his work is firmly in the marginalist tradition, there are certain policy inferences which are made from such a theoretical standpoint which foreshadow many of the experiments of governments influenced by monetarist economic theory in subsequent years. For this reason, if no other, there is a degree of immediacy about aspects of marginalist theory of planning in the UK and USA at least. In the following section attention is devoted to what, in practice, was the dominant approach adopted in planning in most capitalist countries in a period when public sector budgets were increasing at the margin every year. We refer to incrementalism and discuss variants of this approach to planning and public policy-making in the context of the steady growth of the welfare state in the post-war years. The fiscal crises that budgetary incrementalism eventually gave rise to are shown to be an unavoidable consequence of the Keynesian neo-classical synthesis, of which incrementalism represents a form in the arena of public sector service provision and planning. It is also argued that the main variants of marginalist planning incorporated a distinct political theory – pluralism – which is itself an adaptation from neo-classical economic theory. The combination of pluralism and economic individualism is shown to lead to a radical decentralism in planning which borders on the anarchic in the work of one American theorist, Altshuler.

Chapters 4 and 5 represent a shift in emphasis from individualist political economy towards an assessment of more institutional theorizations and criticisms of development planning. In particular we seek to show by illustration, rather than assertion (as has tended to be the case hitherto) that planning theory and practice had a strong structural-functional sociological bias for an important period of its development. Moreover, it is suggested, perhaps somewhat heretically these days (especially so in light of the general criticism of functionalism which this book contains), that the form in which structural-functionalism appeared in planning theory represented an advance from which most subsequent theory has retreated. Prior to this an attempt is made to respond to a certain kind of argument against planning in which planners are presented as having a consensus view of the world while better-informed professionals are less ingenuous. We argue that, far from being alone in assuming there to have been a consensus among the main contending groups in such capitalist societies as the UK and USA in the years when planning was actively being implemented, planners were expressing a more general level of social consensus, which has been referred to elsewhere as the post-war settlement between labour and capital. This consensus was rooted deeply in the political integration which occurred in the pre-war years in both countries after periods of overt class conflict. Planning was part of that settlement. It is concluded that such critiques of planners' consensual ideology miss this materialist point and fall into the functionalist trap of reifying values. On the other hand, it is demonstrable that planning theory came under the influence of structural-functionalism (which itself places great explanatory emphasis upon consensual values) in the 1960s, as what we refer to as 'the Berkeley school' of theorists began to develop their analyses. While it is accepted that many of these efforts suffer in retrospect from the more general weaknesses of functionalism, they nevertheless displayed the foresight of seeking to integrate both the spatial with the aspatial, and the cultural with the physical dimensions of development planning. Moreover, and most importantly, they assigned a central explanatory position to the mechanism of the division of labour in analysing these relationships.

Having picked out the salient features of functionalist planning theory the book moves in Chapters 6 and 7 towards a fairly detailed review and critique of the main currents in spatial theory. In order to evaluate the wide variety of spatial theory which is available, a set of evaluative criteria are derived and formalized, in part from the foregoing discussion of planning theory and epistemological issues. The criteria, which take the form of characteristics which should be avoided to the greatest extent possible if theory is not to be hopelessly unrealistic, are then employed to sift out those spatial development theories which seem to hold the greatest promise for the project of this book, to develop an integrated, realist framework for analysing development planning. The orthodox spatial theories ranging from equilibrium to disequilibrium positions are described, evaluated, and, on the whole, found to suffer unduly from being rooted in a rationalist epistemology. This results in the external world being drastically distorted to fit the theoretical categories which have usually been thought up *a priori* to explain spatial development. In the following chapter attention is devoted partly to small-scale (mainly urban) spatial development theory, most of which suffers unduly from being both rationalist and functionalist, then, at greater length, to recent radical (neo-Ricardian,[3] Marxist) spatial theory. As suggested earlier, much of this is shown to suffer similar problems, often in aggravated form, to those of the more orthodox theories. However, some of the analyses of the contradictions between capital mobility and the immobility of labour, and the spatial effects of developments in the territorial division of labour under capitalism, avoid the weaknesses which are otherwise widespread and thus form fruitful foundations for the rest of the book.

Chapter 8 comprises a review and critique of the relatively recently developed field concerned with the theory of the capitalist state. It is shown how theories of the state can be divided broadly into class, crisis, and capital theories and that the third of these generally meet the criteria established in Chapter 7 better than the rest. However, certain problems of reductionism and rationalism remain even with capital theories of the state. Having established this ground work, attention is directed towards theories of the local state where identical categories are identified which display similar problems to those found in more macro-theories of the state. It is concluded that a theory of the local state is possible because the local state is not merely an agency of the central state but takes its specificity from the local structure of the general spatial division of labour with all that this implies for local civil society, local class structure, and, most importantly, local class relations. The final section of this chapter is taken up with showing how the relationships between the local and central state are expressed in the relations between urban and regional planning within the state. In particular, it is argued that planning interventions do not link directly to the sphere of production but rather to three other spheres which constitute civil society: these are the spheres of circulation, reproduction, and popular-democratic struggle.

In Chapter 9 the mechanism of the spatial division of labour and its connection with the planning system is examined in more depth. Of especial interest here are ways in which labour power represents an important meeting of the spheres of production and circulation and how the market for labour power acts as an important determinant upon the capacity of capital to continue the process of accumulation. In order to explore this argument further a number of theories of dual, segmented and discontinuous labour markets are reviewed and criticized, preference being given to the last category on its performance against the evaluative criteria mentioned earlier. However, the importance of discontinuous labour market theory as far as this book is concerned lies in the degree to which it can be expressed in spatial terms. The middle part of this chapter is devoted to deriving a framework for analysing spatially discontinuous labour markets. Finally the ways in which urban and regional planning connects with the formation of spatially discontinuous labour markets is analysed, and certain strategies are identified which respond to the changing pressures which capitalist development imposes upon the state planning system.

The concluding chapter is concerned with a discussion of certain implications for planning policy which flow from the changing emphasis in the state away from expenditure on labour power reproduction and towards the reproduction of capital and capitalist social relations by means of subsidies to capital in the sphere of circulation. The tendency towards less democratic, discretionary intervention through development agencies, local enterprise boards and Enterprise Zones is explained. Also certain possibilities for planning authorities such as integrated manpower and development planning are discussed. However, an alternative to the process of recapitalization of capitalism is given prominence; this refers to the growing movement towards the production, by shopfloor workers, of Workers' Plans such as those produced by the Lucas Aerospace and Vickers combine committees. Adoption of these initiatives is advocated for local state planning administrations which are sympathetic to the idea that socially useful production is superior to production for profit. Finally, the general argument of the second half of the book is recalled with the assistance of a diagram showing the main connections between the social relations of production, civil society, the state, the planning system and the spatial development process. The key mechanism linking these categories together takes the form of struggles between classes and other social groups over the territorial configurations which emerge from successive recompositions of the division of labour. The planning system is necessary, but not sufficient, to the temporary resolution of these struggles due to its capacity to unite land and labour (and increasingly, though in a limited way, capital) in ways which enable accumulation to continue without massive disruption to labour's defensive attachment to local space.

2 Alternative assumptions of planning theories

Introduction: epistemological considerations

The traditional approach to theorizing planning has consisted of a confused mixture of normative theory, on the one hand, and attempts to develop a positivistic grounding to the subject, on the other. This is most obviously present in work such as that of Davidoff and Reiner (1973) who painstakingly analyse the distinction between facts and values, showing that the former are descriptive truth statements, while the latter possess the wholly separate status of moral statements or assertions of preference. On this basis they derive the planning process as an exercise involving three levels of activity led off by value formulation, followed by identification of means whereby valued ends may be achieved, and the implementation (or as they call it 'effectuation') of policy.

The burden of their discussion is with the analysis of values and it would certainly be unfair to suggest that they are unaware of the complex inter-relationships between fact and value. Nevertheless, having discussed these interactions they conclude that the optimum way to conduct the planning process is one in which although 'disagreement on a value position cannot be resolved by recourse to facts' (1973, p. 20) 'we agree (on) the importance of confronting values with facts in order to make valuation realistic' (1973, p. 21). That is, they prescribe a method of planning which is a curious mixture of rationalism and positivism. The prescriptive element reflects the strong normative theoretical tendency to which we referred. The advocacy of an approach in which a conceptual framework of values triggers off the planning process is both idealist, on the one hand, and rationalistic, on the other (in that it gives primacy to correct principles, rather than material processes, in the derivation of knowledge regarding its object of interest, for example cities). Later, the relationship between idealism and rationalism will be clarified, with the latter being shown to be a sub-category of the former. Yet there is clearly present, also, a belief that positivistic empirical testing of these principles (difficult though this is because of their categorical dissimilarities) is the only sure way to produce valid knowledge on which to base plans.

The tension and confusion to which this admixture gives rise is significant of a more general problem of planning theory. This is that it has a practice orientation which induces a philosophy, even in its theorists, of 'try any-thing', or, 'if it works then it will do'. Such a position is itself not wholly unrespectable in philosophical terms, at least to the extent that it is recog-nized as a viewpoint which is worthy of discussion as an epistemology, or theory of method, entitled *instrumentalism*. However, the position taken in this book is that it is important for planners, and would-be planners who are students, to have a clear picture of what epistemological perspectives are available to them. This is so that they have some way of knowing whether the theoretical approach they may adopt in moving into problem identification, analysis of the object of interest, and advancement to possible solutions, is likely, in itself, to make that exercise more intractable than it may need to be. We would assert from the outset that the congeries of epistemologies which is represented in the Davidoff–Reiner approach, and its many rationalist derivatives (for a collection of such work, see Faludi, 1973a, and for elaboration see Faludi, 1973b) has helped to create insurmountable problems for planners. The worst of these has developed by inducing the assumption that planning solutions should give primacy to the achievement of certain ideal principles rather than being based on thorough knowledge of the mechanisms giving rise to the surface problems which can be empirically identified.

In the next few pages it is proposed that a brief review of the main epistemological positions of relevance to both the development of planning theory, and hence the improvement of planning practice, will be provided. At the end of this section it will be clear that the position which is considered to offer the greatest opportunities for the improvement of planning theory and practice is termed *realist*. Its superiority over other approaches will be argued in preparation for further evaluation of mainstream planning theories in the first half of the book, and the attempt to develop a realist theorization of planning in the second half. We will evaluate four episte-mologies in what follows, starting with positivism then moving on to discuss idealism, rationalism and realism. In this discussion the main references which have been used are Harré (1970); Bhaskar (1975); Keat and Urry (1975); Hindess (1977); Benton (1977); Sayer (1979); Urry (1981b); Sayer (1981).

Positivism

This is the theory of knowledge which philosophers of science have frequently held to be the basis for the enormous developments which have occurred in such fields as physics, chemistry and the various sub-disciplines within the natural sciences. It received its fullest, and most problematic, elaboration by philosophers who adhered to the school of *logical positivism*. Because of the great successes for which this method was thought to be responsible, and the relative simplicity with which it could be described, it

epistomology: study / theory of origins of knowledge

was advocated and adopted by social scientists who sought to found their own disciplines on a more scientific footing. This was supported by those philosophers of science and social science who believed there to be a fundamental unity between all sciences, a belief which was strongly present from the early nineteenth century in the social science of Auguste Comte, and later, Herbert Spencer.[1]

The positivist method is directed at the explanation of events in the natural and social worlds. Explanation is sought by showing that the event which requires understanding is capable of being deduced from certain general statements (or theories) which contain one or more universal laws. Hence, positivist explanation contains a notion of causality, but, importantly, the idea of cause and effect which is normally allowed is one that excludes the possibility of causes being unseen. In other words, cause and effect are treated as observable regularities. To create knowledge involves comparing the event in need of explanation with existing scientific laws, that is, constantly testing the laws to see whether they are verified by the event in question or falsified by it. Where the law is not falsified then the occurrence of the event can be predicted, provided that the initial conditions are met. Thus explanation and prediction are conceived as symmetric and it is on this apparently secure basis that attempts are made to intervene in, control, or plan aspects of the natural and social worlds. In its purest form, *logical positivism*, this kind of method strips away all value judgements from what is to be admitted as valid knowledge. Only those statements which could be empirically tested, or which recorded sense impressions, could be admitted as knowledge since only they had the virtue of incorrigibility. They could be verified, corroborated etc. The subset of statements which were logical deductions from initial premises, and thus true by definition, were also included as valid but all other statements were treated as fundamentally lacking in meaning. This re-emphasis upon observation as the only valid basis for adjudicating truth claims clarified the distinction between science and non-science but also exposed the limitations of positivism as a theory of knowledge as never before.

Three of the main criticisms of positivism, which are of relevance whether its application is in the natural or the social sciences, are given below; they concern problems of induction, theory, and causality. The problem of induction is simply stated. It is that there are no guarantees offered in positivist methodology that past verifications of a scientific theory or law mean that it will necessarily continue to be verified in the future. How, then, can positivist statements justify being designated as true statements when it is possible for past evidence of the validity of a theory to be rendered inadmissible by the arrival of new and different evidence? Furthermore, how are these two bodies of evidence to evaluated, which is the better? The options for positivists, discussed by Keat and Urry (1975, p. 15) and Benton (1977, p. 51–3, 72–3), are to adopt a *confirmationist* or a *falsificationist* position. The former involves arguing that the theory with the greatest amount of empirical support, or the most support in varied contexts, should be favoured. A probabilistic logic is often used to justify such a position. The latter option involves rejecting confirmationism and replacing it with the idea that the objective of science is actually to disprove theories because of the unknowability of the future. In this formulation theories tend to take a lower-order meaning closer to that of hypotheses. These are set up to be knocked down, and cannot be arrived at by a process of induction from evidence. Despite their differences both options continue to share the positivist principle that observation provides the acid test of a theory's validity. The key question is whether this is necessarily so, for as Keat and Urry note, using a quotation from a leading positivist philosopher of science, it seems problematic, to say the least:

It is a remarkable fact, therefore, that the greatest advances in scientific systematiz-ation have not been accomplished by means of laws referring explicitly to *observables* . . . but rather by means of laws that speak of various *hypothetical*, or *theoretical*, *entities* . . . which cannot be perceived or otherwise directly observed by us. (C. Hempel, quoted in Keat and Urry (1975, p. 17) emphasis in original)

This takes us on to a consideration of the second problem with positivism, which concerns the nature of the link between theory and observation. So far, we have spoken, fairly uncomplicatedly, about observations confirming or falsifying theories. Yet the distinction drawn by positivists between science and non-science, on the one hand, and observables and theoretical entities, on the other, suggests that the latter terms in the couples, that is 'non-science' and 'theoretical entities' run the risk of being equated. To avoid this, positivists formulate *correspondence rules*. These take different forms but, consistently, they are used with the objective of defining theoretical entities in the language of observation. This reflects the positivist principle that the latter is capable of more closely representing reality than the language of theory, which contains unobservables. Benton (1977, pp. 65–70) shows how, in the kinetic theory of gases, theoretical terms such as 'speed', 'mass', and 'kinetic energy of molecules' are linked with observa-tional terms such as 'pressure', 'volume', and 'temperature', by correspon-dence rules expressing *quantitative* relations between the statistical properties of aggregates of molecules (such as their specific mean speed, concentration, diameter, and so on), and more general properties such as their rate of diffusion, temperature or pressure as represented in, for example, Boyle's Law. But in this case the correspondence rule depends upon the postulation of the concept 'molecule' which is a theoretical device rather than an observable phenomenon. The probability that its insertion helps to make the theory 'work' does not diminish the fact that it is an arbitrary construct. Correspondence rules are the chosen means whereby an *instrumentalist* position, one in which something which seems to help exposition of scientific theory is retained despite its dispensability to the theory, can be sustained despite the arbitrariness of the attempt it entails to substitute observational terms for theoretical ones.

Finally, there have been criticisms made of the positivist approach to the matter of causality. It will be recalled that this is conceived in terms of a regularity of events occurring in which, wherever one event is always succeeded by another the former is to be understood as bearing a causal relationship to the latter. However, if, as Keat and Urry (1975, p. 12) note, a regularity is detected between, say, the appearance of white spots in the mouth and the later manifestation of a disease, as is the case with measles, then the former can hardly be said to be the cause of the latter even though the capacity to predict is clearly enhanced. This suggests that the positivist symmetry of explanation and prediction requires radical revision. It also indicates a marked weakness in the positivist concept of causation in general. That is, in postulating a merely consequential conception of causation positivism demonstrates the superficiality of its observational principle, on the one hand, while, on the other, getting rid of the aspect which we normally ascribe to the idea of causation, namely that one event or process somehow or other contains the power to influence the action of something external to itself. Perhaps the most telling rejection of this aspect of positivism is that much of science is concerned precisely with identifying the phenomena which bring about such effects as the explosion of gun powder, the occurrence of sounds after the vibration of strings, or the expansion of metal after the application of heat (Harré, 1970, pp. 105–6; Keat and Urry, 1975, pp. 29–30; Benton, 1977, pp. 54–6; Sayer, 1981, pp. 7–8).

Idealism

Owing to these and other problems associated with positivism there has been a marked tendency amongst epistemologists to redirect attention towards the traditionally opposed philosophy of *idealism*. It has been normal to equate positivism with the related, more general approach of *naturalism*, an elision which is by no means necessary, and to equate idealism with an opposite, anti-naturalist standpoint, for which there is rather more justification. Naturalism is here taken to mean the belief in the possibility of an objective science of the external world, anti-naturalism involves the belief that the social world is constituted in a radically different manner from the natural world and must be studied differently as a result. It is the latter tendency which informs the philosophic position of idealism and its many adjuncts. After flowering at various historical stages, the last important one being the neo-Kantian movement of the late nineteenth century which succeeded the Hegelian-inspired German Idealist Movement a century earlier, it seemed that positivism had fatally weakened idealistic philosophy, at least as far as the philosophy of science and theories of scientific method were concerned. This was because of the way in which positivism, and especially logical positivism, invited judges of the validity of claims to knowledge to reject anything which did not match up to the rigorous criteria of empirical verification, corroboration and testing. The intensely metaphysical nature of idealistic philosophy was thus all but dismissed by positivists as the emission of meaningless sounds.

However, as we have seen, positivism itself has been found wanting in certain respects, and the idealistic elements which tend to get smuggled in to positivistic explanation have suggested that the aim of achieving value-free theory is an impossible one. As Sayer puts it:

A common response to this shattering of innocent beliefs in the certainty and neutrality of observation has been the development of idealist (especially conventionalist and rationalist) philosophies which assume that if observation is theory-*laden*, it must necessarily be theory-*determined*. . . . (Sayer, 1981, pp. 6–7, emphasis in original)

We shall be concerned with *rationalist* epistemology in more detail in the following section, so for the moment we will confine ourselves to a brief outline of idealism and its sub-category *conventionalism* with points of criticism where necessary. Philosophical idealism holds that human consciousness is not merely a *tabula rasa* upon which impressions are etched but rather an active process through which the external world is given pattern and shape. Moreover as human requirements change with the development of ideas, reason, concepts and so on, then the understanding of the external world, which has been formed earlier, will itself necessarily be changed. The justification for this privileged world of ideas derives from the fundamental contradictoriness of seeking to reduce the infinite spiritual world which ideas can express to the finite world of observation. Only ideal reason can unify the contradictions of the finite and the infinite through its capacity for the dialectical[2] reconciliation of opposites and for making a philosophical virtue out of the conflicting necessities of reality.

Clearly, such a philosophy challenges the basis of positivistic philosophy by relegating the empirical to a secondary position. However, it is plain that this philosophy cannot be sustained, most obviously because ideas can neither exist without material objects upon which to work, nor can ideas alone, for example logical constructs, create the external world. In other words thought itself consists in the dialectical relationship between subject and object (Benton, 1977, pp. 146–7). Without wading further into these difficult waters it is, nevertheless, important to pay attention to the less far-reaching epistemological argument to which we have referred already as *conventionalism*.

Conventionalism has certain affinities with *instrumentalism*, noted earlier as a philosophical compromise with the failure to create privileged correspondence rules. However, conventionalism is a derivation from idealism rather than positivism. The key characteristic which differentiates conventionalism from positivism is its rejection of empirical testing as the criterion by which truth claims should be admitted or rejected as valid claims to being ascribed the status of cognitive knowledge. This is not to say that empirical evidence is unimportant, just the opposite, but that the evidence cannot determine which of any number of competing scientific explanations for the evidence should be chosen as the correct one. At one extreme this comes close to the full-blown idealist proposition that theories create the external world of interest to science rather than describe it, that observation is theory determined, as Sayer interprets such a position. Or it may mean that there are no socially agreed or agreeable criteria among scientists as to what is to constitute knowledge, because in a liberal society each scientist's different values are to be equally respected. The latter position is taken by Feyerabend, the former approximates that taken by Kuhn (Feyerabend, 1973; Kuhn, 1967). However, while it seems perfectly possible to argue that coherent theoretical statements seeking to explain the same empirical phenomena may contain radically different emphases, that is, that observation can indeed be theory laden and thus not capable of yielding the unvarnished truth, it is a huge and mistaken step to deduce from this that observation must therefore be theory determined. Sayer (1981, p. 7) offers two reasons why this is so: first, however many different theories about certain occurrences may be advanced, each theorist still has to relate his or her theory to the external world for at least some sort of checking; second, while there may be competing explanations they will vary in their degree of fallibility.[3] Thus the overriding weakness of idealistic epistemologies is their failure to come to terms with the problem of relativism, that is if every theory is as good as every other, which should count as valid knowledge?

Rationalism

It has already been stated that rationalism is a sub-category of idealism and, as such, shares the general criticism that in giving precedence to ideas over real processes it is unable to avoid an ultimately hopeless relativism. However, rationalistic explanation is of some interest because it postulates a logical conceptual structure to social processes. Thus, because of the superiority of rational thought in helping humans to figure out the material world – a factor which suggests natural and social processes have an underlying rational structure of their own – there is justification for the process of *a priori* theory formation with a view to explaining material processes. These may later be adjusted in the light of observations, although not in such fundamental ways as to destroy the initial conceptual structure.

In its clearest form, as presented by Descartes, it is the logic of mathematical proof which supplies the criteria by which claims to cognitive knowledge are adjudicated as valid or not. Benton (1977, p. 101) points out that as Descartes assumed the rationalist principles of mathematics to be accessible to everyone then the question of intersubjective agreement upon criteria would not arise, unlike the case with conventionalist epistemology. Thus rationalist thought is tied closely to the level of theory, and is primarily concerned with the relationships between concepts which are defined not by observables but by their logical connections and implications. The rather massive assumption that lies behind this approach to the creation of knowledge is that the rational relationships of logico-mathematical deduction do actually express the relationships between elements and processes in the real world. Furthermore, rationalist epistemology assumes that in the event of a conflict between concept and reality, the former is privileged and that therefore the real can only be properly grasped rationalistically. However, both assumptions are ultimately matters of conviction and commitment rather than being demonstrably true. It may be argued that so are the other epistemologies we have considered and that at least rationalism avoids the relativism of the others by its reliance on universal principles of logic. But if this were the case both theoretical discourse and the external world to which it referred would have to be free of contradictions (problems without apparent solutions), because the point about rationalist epistemology is its presumption of logical coherence to conceptual and real relations. That dilemmas occur in logic and the external world seems to undermine the rationalist standpoint damagingly (Hindess, 1977, pp. 216–20).

Realism

This leads us to describe and evaluate the final theory of method to be considered here, namely the *realist* philosophy of science. Realism takes an important initial step forward from the critique of the positivist theory of causation, which, it will be recalled, postulates cause as the regularity in occurrence of events in which one is always preceded by the other. The realist position holds that positivist causation fails to distinguish, in the way that humans can, the difference between succeeding events and the power of one occurrence to make another happen through the operation of some intervening link. That is, realism is precisely concerned with the identification and descriptive elaboration of the *mechanisms* which make it necessary that a causal force is followed by certain, determinate effects. Realism involves the assumption that objects and/or events are not independent.[4] The extent to which the power of a given mechanism can be activated in fact is recognized as being related to the existence of conditions which, thus, make effects contingent in practice. But that the mechanism is necessary for the effect(s) to occur is inherent to the mechanism, not to concepts which refer to the mechanism. In addition, other mechanisms may be capable of identification which tend to counteract the powers of the first mechanism, as when a virus infection impairs the capacity of a music lover to hear the sound of a plucked string properly. However, the lack of a necessary correspondence between logical relations and real relations does not imply that there cannot be a conceptual derivation of those real relations (Sayer, 1981, pp. 6–8).

There are certain problems with this epistemology as there are with the others, though to the extent that realism does not postulate either a privileged level of conceptual or observational language, but rather a method of successively approximating concepts and real processes, it avoids many of the difficulties of the more established methods. A particular problem to which realism can give rise is that associated with *reductionism*. This means that a certain set of complex interrelationships may be over-simplistically and mistakenly explained by demonstrating them to be instances of a better understood and therefore, more simply presentable, general mechanism or interaction of mechanisms. In other words a complex, detailed process is reduced to the conceptual expression of what has, by ignoring details, been identified as a more general and simplified process. Both Urry (1981a, p. 8) and Sayer (1981, p. 9) point to the problem which reductionism of this kind can pose for attempts to use Marx's theory of modes of production for purposes of relatively detailed empirical work in the social sciences, though the problem is by no means limited to this kind of work. The nature of this problem centres on the possibility that the central mechanism which has been conceptually and empirically identified need not always provide the precise explanation for particular processes for which an explanation is being sought. Some intervening mechanism(s), whose existence may be subject to the constraints of the major one, may be more directly at work in such a case.

In an attempt to show, methodologically, how such a problem might be tackled, Sayer (1981, p. 10) makes the important distinction between abstract concepts and concrete concepts, the former being successfully derived by identifying necessary relationships, the latter being conceived as the resultant of many different determinations that are only capable of identification by empirical research. From this distinction is then drawn up a methodological structure which links the very general, abstract, but necessary, constraining relations of, say, a specific mode of production to the lower level of abstraction which is a specific mechanism. This mechanism then gives rise to certain complex, interrelated tendencies in given conditions (which may be influenced by other mechanisms), which can be described in concrete terms. Finally, the concrete instance is expressed as a particular conjuncture of forces, tendencies and conditions found empirically in certain real-world locations.

This by no means solves all of the problems which exist with realist research, some of which, such as whether mechanisms are verified or falsified by concrete research, are shared with other epistemologies.

Nevertheless, because it avoids the atomism of independent events which fragments the conceptual world portrayed in positivism, and seeks to ground theoretical statements in material processes unlike idealism and rationalism, it offers the best epistemological basis for the present book which is itself concerned to ground theory in material content and to synthesize conjunctural processes with deeper structures than those immediately accessible to empirical observations.

The normative and the positive

Planning theory has tended to be most closely associated with an idealist epistemology in the past. A somewhat desultory effort was made by Faludi (1973b) to shift planning theory more closely towards the positivist standpoint, but relatively little, by way of observables, has emerged to test the validity of certain of the statements about the status of planning which were made therein. The main criticism that tends to have been made, justifiably, of planning theory is that it has remained stubbornly normative (Scott and Roweis, 1977; Scott, 1980). It seems important to ask why planning theory should have become so wedded to the adoption of idealist and normative positions. We can make two points in relation to this question. First, the unquestionable fact that much planning theory has a prescriptive tone has to be seen in terms of the nature of the activity which it serves. That is, professional development planning[5] is fundamentally concerned to prescribe courses of action which range from attempts to stimulate or control the local effects of economic growth to efforts to offset or transcend the local effects of economic decline. In both policy domains planning is invoked to clean up market failures in representative democracies. Planning is, in other words, a political level activity responsible for securing a degree of spatial orderliness to the disorderly forces of the market-place. It helps to secure industrial and commercial efficiencies without dangerously disrupting the social equilibrium. Such an obligation devolves theoretically into questions concerning procedure for modifying existing arrangements. There is a relatively small pay-off in developing comprehensive theories of spatial development planning because planning action is essentially marginal in its impact. Moreover, as the master theories of the economy have, until recently, justified the prescriptive actions of the state, of which urban and regional planning is a part, in matters of development, then the need to rethink the nature of planning activity has received little impetus. This has, of course, changed with the decline of the Western economies, in which forms of state development planning have been practised, and the impetus for concrete analysis of past planning action is now that much stronger.

A second reason for the dominant normative emphasis to traditional planning theory is that, as a subject of study and a basis for practical activity, it has had an inevitably critical tone. That is not to say that theories of planning constitute particularly radical programmes of social action, but rather that they exist as conceptual constructs posed in opposition to the unplanned arrangements of civil society in capitalist economies. It involves the advocacy of alternative methods of organizing living and working conditions from those which occur under the domination of private exchange-relations. This is not unlike the position occupied by eighteenth- and early-nineteenth-century advocates of the superiority of democratic political arrangements over other forms of political system, such as Rousseau, de Tocqueville and Mill. Their task, as they saw it, was to make a case for such innovations as the secret ballot, the extension of the franchise, and freedom of expression. But the case had to be founded upon moral principles which, ultimately, involved the making of normative assertions about the likely improvements democratic institutions would contribute to the self-esteem of the disenfranchised. There could be no demonstration of such improvements until they had been implemented.

However, as Lukes (1977) has shown, once the point had been reached where most of the agenda set by the normative political theorists had been achieved in most capitalist countries, the nature of political theory itself began to change. Normative moralizing was replaced by newer, positivist political science in which, frequently, and mistakenly, what were taken to be the positivistic 'laws' of democracy were 'tested' by the accumulation of survey data on personal and social voting patterns and thought to be falsified by the findings. For example, Mill had argued that giving ordinary people the vote ought to make them more responsible citizens by giving them a greater stake in the running of their communities and states. The voting studies, by contrast, showed high levels of apathy among the electorate, misinformed, prejudiced and even reckless voting behaviour, and the conclusion was drawn that Mill was wrong. An almost exact parallel is found in planning theory where the idea of rational-comprehensive planning was confronted by evidence that planners did not first establish goals, then formulate alternative means of achieving them, and finally evaluate the alternatives against the goals. Rather they sought to achieve what was practically possible and mainly evaluated marginal policy changes against the status quo.

The problem here, which Lukes picks out very clearly, is that the category of 'normative', and that of 'positive' are being manipulated and maltreated. Empirical testing cannot refute a normative assertion except in so far as that assertion contains empirical elements. Hence, the voting studies were wrong in saying that Mill was mistaken in what he thought likely to be the effects of voting upon ordinary people, just as incrementalists are wrong to claim advocates of rational-comprehensive are wrong to recommend their prescriptions. This is because both types of advocate are making prescriptive rather than descriptive statements. However, the interesting, and ironical, factor common to both would-be refutations of what are in fact normative standpoints, is that they then go on to advocate their *empirical* findings as preferred *normative* alternatives. Thus, the form of democracy in which only a relatively small proportion of the electorate is politically interested is often actively supported by political scientists because of its advantages for maintaining system equilibrium. A good example of this approach is Dahl's (1971) advocacy of the *polyarchy*, a system of circulating elites of intelligent and politically-interested individuals and groups as the most rational form of democratic government. Similarly, as will be shown in a subsequent chapter, Dahl's erstwhile academic collaborator, Charles Lindblom, advocates the disjointed-incrementalism which he sees as characteristic of planning policy-making as a preferred model to the rationalism of Herbert Simon's means–ends analysis.

What these examples suggest is further support for our earlier critique of positivism at the level of epistemology. In other words, far from agreeing with criticisms that planning has been normative rather than positive, we would argue that it has been idealist rather than realist. The difficulty of disentangling the normative from the positive in the final analysis is what, as we have seen, caused the downfall of logical positivism. Some studies have shown how it was that logical positivists deluded themselves about the methods of science by their uncritical absorption of the idealistic biographical recollections of retired scientists (for example Cole and Cole, 1973). Others such as those of Kuhn (1967) and Mitroff (1974) have shown that much natural scientific research is far from objective, disinterested, open and impartial, but is, rather, often secretive, prejudiced and elitist. So the value-freedom in science which is assumed in the critique of planning theory for its normative rather than its positive emphases has itself to be questioned. As Myrdal has put it:

Questions must be asked before answers can be given. The questions are an expression of our interest in the world, they are at bottom valuations. Valuations are thus necessarily involved already at the stage when we observe facts and carry on theoretical analysis, and not only at the stage when we draw political inferences from facts and valuations. (Myrdal, 1957, p. 163)

In conclusion then we would wish to argue that it may be no bad thing if planning theory has not moved towards being positivistic or even behaviourist, in the way that many areas of the social sciences have developed. This should not be interpreted as meaning that planning theorists have no interest in the concrete, exactly the opposite is the case. But in this book it will be argued that they should seek to identify mechanisms which cause changes in the nature of planning to be brought about, rather than assuming such changes to be either the creative idealizations of individual minds, or mere regularities in observable events.

Distinctive assumptions for theorizing planning

Having made these points, it is, nevertheless, important to have a clear picture of the kinds of assumptions that act as the foundations for different kinds of theory that are found in traditional planning thought. In the present section an attempt will be made to separate out the main components of two distinctive paradigms in planning theory. These tend to recur in social science theory and in turn can be seen as reflecting corresponding philosophical, pragmatic and value standpoints prevalent in the intellectual world. They cross-cut in numerous ways and any simple classification will inevitably do less than justice to their richness of variety. Their main outlines are sketched below and represented in Figure 1 for brevity.

Methodology: individualist and institutional approaches

There is a basic methodological distinction between analysis of social processes whose prime explanatory focus is the human subject or individual, on the one hand, and analysis whose explanatory focus is located at a conceptual level beyond the observable one of the individual, in macroscopic, supra-individual or organizational and institutional frameworks. The former position, known as *methodological individualism* is one which,

	ATOMISTIC	UNITARY
METHODOLOGY	INDIVIDUALISTIC	INSTITUTIONALIST
ANALYSIS	BEHAVIOURALIST	SYSTEMS
AUTONOMY	VOLUNTARIST	DETERMINIST
CONTROL	DECENTRALIST	CENTRALIST
ORGANIZATION	NATURALISTIC	SOCIALIZED

Figure 1   *Planning frameworks*

sometimes in the face of explicit rejection as a mode of analysis (Faludi, 1973b), recurs in theories of planning. This is traceable to the classical utilitarian notion of rationality, itself couched in individualistic terms but extended willy-nilly to the explanation of organizational behaviour as well as being held up as a normative ideal for planning generally. Such confusion emerges most clearly where the purpose of planning theory is under discussion. Thus Harris (1978) asserts that 'a positive theory of *planning*, it seems to me, cannot avoid talking about what *planners* do' (p. 222 emphasis added). Later he elaborates, rather unclearly upon the functions of planners:

Planners who invent such devices as clean water, boulevards, zoning, workers' housing, suburbs, superhighways and independent jurisdictions are not usually planners but politicians, and they inevitably become so if they are primarily engaged in promoting them. On the other hand, the actual operations of planning systems are manned by individuals who engage in less spectacular professional activities. . . .

Implicit in the above is a muddle stemming essentially from a lack of clarity in distinguishing individual-level action and institutional-level operations. Because of this 'planners', in Harris's formulation, acting as creative individuals are in fact 'politicians'; only when 'planning systems' are invoked are we invited to consider true planners' behaviour. The link between the system and the outputs enumerated is severed and planning and planners are conflated into an abstraction whose form is reduced to that of a computational instrument:

My own outline of such a predictive or diagnostic planning theory would be to accept as a paradigm or pattern for planning organization and procedures the practice of mathematical programming. (p. 223)

This view of planning theory is one which necessarily arises from an uncritical and theoretically ill-informed attempt to conceptualize organizational, *institutional* complexity idealistically. When that ideal is itself formed by a notion of individualistic rationality disembodied from the realistic problems of the external world, then contact with any meaningful theory of planning or theory of planners becomes tenuous to say the least. Even in its own terms a positive theory of what planners do would have to include other forms of human action than those which most nearly correspond to mathematical programming. But more importantly, even such a subjectively-based analysis could tell us little of real value in terms of a theory of planning, for to seek to understand the different forms of planning, as distinct from the individual acts of planners, the *institution* must be seen in relation to the stages of development and associated problems and opportunities of the social, economic and political climate within which it exists, and that sort of task is more appropriately embarked upon from an institutional level of analysis. Otherwise one arrives at the sort of cul-de-sac implied in the following where everything (and therefore nothing of interest) is subsumed under a single, meaningless category:

Holders of an atomistic image of society have a concept of the public interest as the sum of individual interests (its *individualistic* conception); holders of holistic images adhere to the view that there exists a set of ends relating to all individuals in society, even without their explicit consent (its *unitary* conception). Personally I think it meaningful to hold a view of the public interest which may be termed *qualified unitary*. (Faludi, 1973b, p. 295; emphasis in original)

Analysis: behavioural and systems

Associated with the distinction between individualism and institutionalism in methodology is the corresponding focus on *behavioural analysis* on the one hand and systems analysis on the other. Behavioural analysis is closely tied to positivist epistemology. The dominating feature of such analysis is its rejection as explanatory factors of non-observables such as motivations, beliefs, purposes and so on. A great deal of emphasis is therefore placed upon studying problems by observing the actions of individuals in real settings with a view to generating certain propositions about human behaviour. These may, in time, provide the building blocks of behavioural theory. Because of the methodological and technical problems of measuring human behaviour accurately, a great deal of attention is devoted to ways of establishing a reliable basis for quantification. As with other positivist approaches to the process of research, behavioural analysis relies totally upon the establishment of correspondence rules for the translation of theoretical material into the language of observation. One frequently-employed technique is the *operational definition*.

Operational definitions represent a technique, widely employed in the natural sciences, for enabling the measurement of some process, which is not itself directly observable, to be carried out. An example would be the use of meters for the measurement of the power of electrical currents. By this means the theoretical language of conductivity, resistance and so on is translated into the observational language of voltage and amperage units, which are precisely measurable. Hence the unobserved electric charge is rendered in observable form. There are numerous examples of operational definition being employed in the social sciences, especially in psychological research where behaviouralism became a dominant methodological approach. Some of these and their problems are discussed in Keat and Urry (1975, pp. 159–62). An example which may be more familiar to students of decision-making in government would be the work of Dahl, Polsby and other pluralist theorists of community power, whose work is incisively reviewed by Lukes (1974).

The operational definition in question is that concerning the translation of the theoretical concept 'power' into observable, and thus measurable, language. The pluralist theory of power (to which such authors as Dahl adhere) proposes that power is not concentrated in the hands of a minority in democratic societies, neither is it some structural property of social institutions. Rather it is diffused throughout society such that even what may appear to be the most powerless individuals possess at least some power (through possession of the vote, for example). A definition of power is then derived from this perspective. It is proposed that power represents the capacity of one individual to succeed in getting another individual to do something he or she would not otherwise do. So the key to measuring power is to select situations in which there is some disagreement between two individuals and observe which one wins the outcome. Preferably these should represent important issues in which a range of power-holders might be expected to participate. Dahl selected three issues: urban redevelopment, public education and political nominations in his (1961) study of power in New Haven. If the pluralist theory were to be refuted each issue would have to result in victory for the same individual; if power were to be truly diffused then different outcomes should result on each. In the New Haven, and other, studies different individuals won on the range of issues, as measured by the outcomes of political conflicts, hence the pluralist thesis was held to be sustainable.

However, there are certain well-known problems, both with this methodology of research, and with the wider notion of operational definitions, which severely undermine the behaviouralist approach in general. The first of these stems from its methodological individualism. The individualistic orientation clearly determines the nature of the problem studied, and necessarily depends on the assumption that organizational/institutional factors are unimportant in determining behaviour. This is, of course, an heroic assumption to make in the first place, but even if it could be justified in specific cases it would mean that the development of knowledge about behaviour would be limited to precise contexts, and could not be generalized, simply because of the uniqueness of cases being studied. More generally, though, operational definitions of the kind we have discussed require the assumption that there is no intervening determinant between the observable outcome (for example a political decision) and the imputed source of that outcome (for example the exercise of individual power). Yet, as Lukes (1974) shows there are many possible determinants for particular outcomes, ranging from the failure to act by a powerful individual, to procedural rules which constrain possible outcomes to a specific one. The latter need not be the result of any specific individual action but may simply be the institutional accretion of many different historical actions by many individuals. Behavioural analysis, in other words, demonstrates precisely the weakness that was earlier shown to undermine positivist epistemology more generally, namely the tendency to limit research questions only to observables, some of which are, themselves, inadequately exhausted of their theoretical, and thus unobservable, content.[6]

Systems analysis of development processes has reached a plateau after the surge of interest in the application of systems ideas to planning, largely for prescriptive purposes, ten years ago. The somewhat ambitious assumption that there was an objective rationality to the organization of industrial societies which could be comprehended and modified by the technical guidance system of local state planning administrations has evaporated with the onset of the economic recession which punctuated planning's post-war 'age of innocence' (Donnison, 1975). One advantage of this is the demise of the epistemologically confused 'philosophy' that systems have character- istics of 'being, behaving and becoming' (Chadwick, 1971), a classic example of what has been called 'misplaced concreteness'. But the essentialism, idealism and teleology of this sort of view, which seemed relevant when planning in the UK was geared to containing or diverting growth, remains a seductive trap for planning theory. Planning is, after all, goal-oriented, purposive action; it is intellectually derived from the interaction between the chaos of Victorian urbanization and the utopian ideals of philanthropists and social reformers; and in derivation it places a premium on the highest intellectual skill, the synthesis of means and ends through individualistic reason. With such a systematic approach it might be deduced that planners have an appropriate framework through which to exercise control over those integrated systems which comprise urban, industrial societies.

But in spite of the apparent linkage between method and object of interest which the systems perspective has promised, the contributions of urban systems analysis are disappointing. Two basic problems with systems think- ing: arbitrary system closure and choice of system elements, which leave system descriptions open to more than usual analytical bias through emphasis on quantifiable features of reality; and the predisposition to view systems teleologically and harmoniously because available theory is geared to stability, have been documented (Lilienfeld, 1978). Moreover, the further extension of systems concepts to the process of planning, in line with the Faludian separation of procedural from substantive objects of interest has generated little more than descriptions of inputs, procedures and outputs, saying little of meaning about the processes linking these stages together. Thus, for example, programme budgeting and corporate planning in practice seem to exacerbate tensions internally and externally to the local state planning system (Cockburn, 1977). But also, the more general assump- tions of systems theory, which rest fundamentally upon the notion that systems are harmoniously interacting sets of relations, produce trivial solutions to problems. Hence, conflicts are treated as failures of communi- cation. The reader will search the pages of the 'Strategic Choice' school's planning theory (Friend, Power and Yewlett, 1974) in vain if looking for detailed analysis of power relations, conflict generation and resolution, and the nature of dominant coalitions. In typical systems theoretic, organizational-analysis style the planning department is seen as responding in various ways to the uncertainties imposed upon it by various external stimuli. To overcome these uncertainties it is recommended that the level of internal and external information is increased thereby increasing the propensity for system control of its environment; the implicit goal of systems theoretical applications to the study and practice of planning is to increase the level of system control and therefore predictability. The attractiveness of systems analysis for planning, as for other corporate organizational systems, lies in its apparently painless prescriptions for the 'management' of poorly-understood processes.

Scope for action: voluntarism and determinism

The third pair of paradigmatic distinctions of relevance for planning theory is that which distinguishes *voluntarism* from *determinism*. This dichotomy resolves itself into a question of the extent to which planner behaviour or indeed planning *per se* is seen as autonomous. This, in turn, will be a reflection of the degree of acceptance by the planning theorist at a more general level of one of two basic theories of the human condition; on the one hand, there is the view that human action is the result of various aggregations of purposive behaviour freely and creatively entered into. On the other, is the view that human action is conditioned by impersonal forces which stem from human agency but are transformed into organizational or structural determinants of action.

In the former case planning takes on a distinctive appearance consisting of at least four major features. First, it tends to be seen not as a prominent social institution even in the urban and regional spatial ordering sense: rather it exists as one of a relatively small group of necessary or desirable government functions which facilitate the interaction of more important market-orientated social institutions. Examples would be the governmental organization of currency, tariff or weights and measures systems. Second, and implied by this, planning is seen to exist primarily to aid the functioning of private sector and individual decision-making by supplying services which are valuable but unprofitable to private organizations. These would include the provision of basic information about demographic, social and economic trends at various levels or aggregation; the performance of forecasts about labour markets, household formation and mobility patterns; and generally facilitating interaction between private units and relevant public organizations. Third, planning would be seen as aiming to mediate disparate interests by seeking to function as an arena where rational participation and debate produce outcomes reflective of the underlying public will. Lastly, planning is seen as a relatively non-autonomous means of inducing participative involvement by disparate economic and social interests, publicizing and provoking discussion where policy choices are to be made, sometimes in a formal way by arranging the forum, sometimes informally by responding to feedback through the political system.

In all these respects planning may be seen adopting a low profile with minimal interference and a generally low level of autonomy *vis-à-vis* market institutions. The opposite view of the planning function, the deterministic position, adopts a considerably more formal conception of the nature of planning. Although 'determinism' has had a relatively narrow usage within planning theory literature, expressing the idea that social behaviour is in principle alterable given changes in the physical environment (Ranney, 1969, p. 20), it is a common and wide-ranging assumption of all holistic theories of social systems. Its twofold nature is represented, first, in the belief that human behaviour, and the institutions and organizations which express it, are substantially affected by structural factors. Determinists believe that the nature of these basic frameworks should be susceptible to scientific analysis, and instrumental action. Second, the nature of the instrumental action tends to be seen in a particular way. That is, planning is conceived as a formal policy model or instrument whose logic, because rationalistic, is capable of imposing a more orderly set of linkages between frameworks. Planning theory, in its dominant form, has had a strong disposition towards the development of the formal, generalized, deterministic side of the discipline (Faludi, 1973b) by virtue of the stress on procedural, organizational aspects at the expense of substantive analysis. Criticism of this development is strongest from adherents of extreme, that is phenomenological, forms of voluntaristic theories:

Most pernicious of all is the desire for a formal generalized model of planning. Such a model it is argued is formal if its form, alone, represents its content, and interpretations of its form are merely applications of the model. A model is generalized if it refers to no particular persons or situations in its unapplied form. Natural science has 'provided' these models either as mechanistic physics or systemic organismic biology. But if these models are taken formally and dead-seriously, rather than as heuristic guides, they are likely to lead the theorist into some very unhappy dilemmas . . . based on the fact that we lack precise descriptive languages for our planning activity and that people act as persons *in* the situations which they are describing. (Krieger, 1974, p. 156)

The polarization between voluntarism and determinism is clearly wide as Krieger presents it, yet it neatly pinpoints a dichotomy of planning theory. But, in correctly seeking to reject an over-ambitious *goal*, to reduce social complexity to a rational construct, Krieger's proposal for an extreme voluntarism based on symbolic interactionism and ethnomethodology[7] seems, because of the irretrievable relativism thereby entailed, to mark a retrograde step both away from science and socially responsive planning.

Organizational form: decentralization and centralization

At a fourth dichotomous level, a distinction can be drawn between theoretical assumptions which stress *decentralization* and those which stress *centralization* at an organizational level. In the former case this can take two principal forms, neither of which is necessarily excluded by the other: first, it can refer to an authority structure which is multi-nuclear *within* the various levels and spheres of governmental administration; second, it can refer to a form of governmental system which is in itself multi-nucleated, revealing a high propensity for devolved control. Aspects of these forms will be discussed in the following chapters, but at this point the examples of revenue sharing and neighbourhood government would be illustrations of the latter, while the fragmentation of responsibility among governmental departments at different levels, characteristic of American administration, but emerging regionally in the UK, as in Scotland and Wales, exemplify the former tendency.

The reverse tendency in planning theory is to assume that higher levels of efficiency, co-ordination, systematization and equity in the allocation of scarce resources are necessarily accompanied by diminished local autonomy, whether bureaucratic, spatial or some combination of these. For a theory of planning in which the principal function to be fulfilled is that of the planning organization guiding or steering the development of its systems of interest in line with what are conceived to be the goals of the public, this is a necessary corollary. Strategic, goal-based planning assumes a unitary polity, that is, that at bottom there is a fundamental acceptance on the part of members of the public that achievement of certain goals should be sought. It also assumes a unitary command structure where policy initiation follows a thorough, rational examination of planning commitments, choices and prospects, controlled centrally by top-level and key middle-level personnel. Often, inadequacies in the functioning of such a system are due to faults in the communication of information. Consequently there is a premium on the clear portrayal of 'the public interest' to policy-executives and the minimization of internal and external misunderstanding, disaffection and conflict. This is sought by strengthening of the personnel management function internally and the public relations, participative and community development functions externally. Cynthia Cockburn's description of the operation of a budget-led corporate planning system in Lambeth provides a good illustration of the nature and effects of the centralization tendency in local government (Cockburn, 1977).

Planning practice assumptions: naturalistic and socialized

Lastly, it is worth drawing attention to an important distinction between the perspective which stresses that planning, like other human activities takes on a *naturalistic*[8] form, and the assumption that planning is a particularly clear example of human activity which has pierced the apparently 'natural' institutions of society like the market and actively seeks, in a *socialized* way, to overcome the negative effects of a competitive system of resource allocation. Briefly, in the former case planning has no comprehensive, systematic co-ordinating logic which cuts across the 'invisible hand' which controls market relations. Correspondingly, whether operating inside or outside formal governmental institutions its rationale and prescriptions must be fought for in essentially utilitarian ways. That is, the utility of planning expenditure over some other form of either public or private investment requires demonstration *a priori* and in such a way that it is 'naturally' accepted as the 'best buy' in a given context. Planning, and specifically the policies of which it is comprised, must be bargained for in the decision-making process.

In the latter case, where planning is posed antithetically to the naturalistic assumption, this is so because of the inefficiencies and inequities which arise where utilitarian criteria inform decision-making. Even though communities may develop certain pluralistic tendencies in resolving resource allocation problems, especially where economic growth conditions prevail, the extent to which such an increased diffusion of power systematically redistributes real income remains remarkably limited (Lindblom, 1977). When, as has been the case in advanced industrial societies in the 1970s and 1980s, the problems faced by a community are predominantly those of stagnating or declining economic performance, then pressures are generated which demand socialized policies through stronger, increased government intervention. The nature of government involvement under such circumstances is such that if pressures from organized or unorganized labour are to be withstood, concessions of a more socially equitable type may have to be made in the form of public expenditure growth and redirection. The history of planning begins, in effect, as a systematic, co-ordinated and socialized form of government organization of the space economy in periods of economic crisis whether in the form of the American New Deal or British Distressed Areas policy before the war, or French *dirigisme* afterwards.

Though it seems possible to argue in general terms that naturalistic planning predominates under conditions of economic growth with more socialized forms developing during periods of recession, the case is more complex than this simple reasoning would suggest. Actual planning theories employed in different societies will vary according to local conditions. Thus, a strongly naturalistic assumption, as in a buoyant, liberal economy may be reflected in the establishment of a planning organization which is autonomous, thus able to bargain, but which is charged with co-ordinated and socialized planning duties. Nevertheless, the outcomes in terms of implemented policy may be marginal, as happened with the autonomous planning commissions of the USA (Skjei, 1976, p. 325). Equally, economic growth in a more generally socialized context, with established public welfare institutions, may open avenues to large investments of public expenditure, administered in a unitary way to produce, in specific instances, significant development innovations such as the British New Towns or motorway programmes. Contemporaneously, unitary planning organizations charged with relatively vague duties, such as British local authorities were in the 50s and 60s with containment policy, may produce little more than marginal reordering of 'natural' urban and regional growth and development processes consequent upon growth in the economy and its social effects. In conclusion, therefore, it is evident that two broadly definable positions *vis-à-vis* planning and its form of organization can be postulated for analytical purposes but that empirical examples will reflect these differentially at different stages of the planning process and in different institutional contexts.

Summary

Five sets of theoretical norms for planning have been identified: individualism – institutionalism; behaviouralism – systems; voluntarism – determinism; decentralism – centralism; and naturalism – socialization. These constitute the principal distinctive conditions for the rest of social science too, in particular sociology, political science and economics from which planning draws its primary theory. In Figure 1 on page 28 these are located in relation to each other in terms of the following broad categories: methodological scale; mode of analysis; degree of autonomy for human action; structure of control over resource allocation; and the relative centrality of the institution of planning to the overall organization of social relations. This is merely intended as an illustrative guide of the foregoing argument which for ease of communication identifies the relative distinctiveness of the two principal sets of basic assumptions or paradigms which constitute the distinction bases for the two dominant modes of theorizing and practising planning. These are referred to in the diagram as 'planning frameworks', subsequently referred to as unitary and atomistic planning according to extent of objective and subjective orientation respectively. Their role is intended primarily as a heuristic device which clarifies the nature of important distinctions in social science and planning theory, as will become evident from succeeding chapters.

3 Marginalist theories of planning

Introduction

In this chapter reference will be made in passing to the nature and extent of the critique which has developed recently regarding the types of planning based on the unitary framework of assumptions before moving on to an analysis of the theoretical sources of the atomistic alternative. It will be argued that the latter lies in the domain of neo-classical or marginalist economic theory and some general points of contention about that paradigm will be drawn out. In the last section it will be shown first, that marginalist assumptions occur in various planning theories; second, that these theories are subject to heightened forms of the problems of the basic economic theory; and thirdly that, far from supplying a value-free, positivistic exemplar for theories of planning, marginalism is a particular normative ideal which has difficulties of operationalization even for markets, but whose practicability is severely prejudiced in the context of public-sector decision-making.

Unitary modes

The main forms taken by unitary planning are well known: the simple-comprehensive; the rational-comprehensive; the systems-cyclical; and corporate planning. These are the four principal types and all are subject to rather similar criticisms.

Simple-comprehensive

The simple-comprehensive has by now been officially superseded (DoE, 1970) but it retains a considerable attraction for planning authorities since it enables a relatively speedy, clear-cut and easily understood policy document to be formulated. Traditionally it has been the result of the inspirational design work of a small team, sometimes of consultants – especially in New Town development whose consensus upon aesthetic principles enables form to dominate content in a strongly architectural manner. Though the latter precepts have tended to be submerged with the onslaught of social scientific analytical methods, the tendency for a single macro-design to be developed either in the absence of alternatives, or with only a few no-hope 'representative' alternative plans included in the planning report remains strong (Drake *et al.*, 1975). The most salient criticisms here refer to the element of authoritarianism implied in this approach to planning, on the one hand, and the general absence of analysis of social processes in favour of a strongly functional stress on physical integration of land uses, on the other (Hague and McCourt, 1974).

Rational-comprehensive

The officially preferred rational-comprehensive planning form (DoE, 1970) retains the macroscopic view of planning, even re-emphasizing the functionalist approach to space through a strategic concern with structural frameworks of cities and regions. It aspires, though, to a less architectural and more managerial style of plan formation and implementation. Thus ends are related to means synoptically, along *homo oeconomicus* lines and the best value (including 'social welfare' as well as monetary costs and benefits) plan emerges from various degrees of rational argument. Fundamentally similar problems to those of simple-comprehensiveness arise: first, authoritarian centralism, though masked by diluted corporate forms of interest group participation, persists, largely because 'the central problem of corporatist organization is the arbitrariness and partiality of its representation and the unresponsiveness to popular control of its elites' (Crouch, 1979, p. 46). Second, different forms of functionality to those of simple-comprehensiveness, but still physically deterministic in origin, dominate analysis. Thus calculations of social indicators, taken from the Census, transform human qualities into spatial ones. Policies are *ipso facto* constructed in response to areal problems and take the form of providing physical solutions. Such distortions seem unavoidable in the light of the limitations of many of the analytical techniques which have been used in planning exercises (Sayer, 1976).

Systems-cyclical

Systems-cyclical planning is a refined form of rational-comprehensiveness. It seeks to overcome the linear nature of goals-based rational-comprehensiveness which reduced it to only a marginal improvement upon its simple predecessor by systematically integrating the element of feedback. Iterations form the main advance here, and problem-focused plans are constantly worked upon even after selection and implementation. These take account of the system process changes induced by the plan's intervention as well as those generated elsewhere, hence the cyclical nature of the planning process (Boyce *et al.*, 1970). This too, suffers from the key problem associated with burgeoning 'technostructural' (Galbraith, 1970) expertise.

It is noted by Silverman (1970) how frequently the posing of new questions about aspects of social organization reflect the concerns of those who have most to lose when change occurs, namely the occupants of positions of authority. Such concerns tend to produce a desire for the prescriptive treatment of symptoms rather than root-and-branch analysis of a conceivably more disruptive kind. The ideology of systems-thinking has fitted into such a predisposition with remarkable facility. This approach to the organization of knowledge into ordered layers and compartments which is systems theory's main contribution encourages certain kinds of questions to be asked of the systems of interest. These tend to have an inherently tautological bias, meaning that they lead to answers which add up to re-statements of the original question.

There are three main kinds of questions posed in the systems perspective according to Silverman. The first is concerned with system relations between the various system units and sub-units that have been identified, and the answers to this kind of question take the descriptive form of specifying inputs, throughputs and outputs, an exercise of limited utility to developing understanding of the nature and determinants of the processes being des-cribed. Nevertheless, such system description leads to the next kind of question, which is concerned with system effectiveness. To what extent can the system which has been distinguished be said to be producing a satis-factory performance in terms of the needs of, for example, urban or regional systems? The systems-cyclical approach represents an improvement upon the rational-comprehensive planning model in that it appears to move beyond the uninteresting conclusion that what the system needs is what will allow it to survive. Since it is surviving at the time it is examined the presumption of that approach is that needs of the system are already being met. Analysis of effectiveness does allow consideration of alternative system profiles but this, in turn, requires answers to questions about system dynamics.

So the third question inquires about the forces making for system change. The most general answer to this question (reflecting the biological origins of the theory) is that systems change to meet their need for survival; they adjust rather like thermostatic devices allow heating systems to adjust (Faludi, 1973b, p. 43). In adjusting in this way the system in question is held to undergo a process of evolution towards a higher order of greater internal consistency as elements which may act counter to the long-term survival of the system are gradually modified or eliminated. However, the key ques-tion, namely how this process is held to occur, is left unexplained as the product of a black box, or 'hidden hand' which adjusts the system auto-matically. The tautology of the systems approach lies precisely in the assumption that systems have the capacity to fulfil their needs for survival and that this attribute is what gives them their systemic character. This makes the role of the planner as an agent of system intervention somewhat redundant,[1] and helps us understand why so much systems-theoretic research and systems-inspired planning represents a descriptive reaction to effects rather than a thoroughgoing analysis of causes. The inevitably cosmetic treatment of 'problems' to which such an approach to planning gives rise puts the systems planner squarely in the position of salesman selling a dubious package rather than someone concerned with the quality control of the product (Healey, 1979, p. 58).

Corporate planning

Lastly, one of the more recent reformulations of the unitary approach to the organization of planning systems appeared in the form of corporate planning. The interesting feature of this approach was the way in which the logic of systems analysis was turned in upon the internal management of, especially local, government administration. The exercise revealed, perhaps most clearly of all, the superficiality and expediency which systems analysis (at least as applied to social organizations) entails. Moreover, it underlined the demand for heightened control over local state budgets by increasingly cost-conscious central state officialdom. Well before its implementation following the recommendations of the Maud (DoE, 1967) and Bains (DoE, 1972) reports the experiences of planning departments in following decision-theoretic principles (as in the previous sections) suggested that this style would be adopted if local government was to function effectively in its new role as disburser of large public expenditures, since it was, as PPBS,[2] the only practicable and tested alternative. However, theoretically-informed critiques of PPBS were already available (Williams, 1971) before local authorities adopted it as the underlying corporate planning model. It is remarkable how similarly the weaknesses materialized in different contexts. Williams noted how for political, technical and structural (organizational) reasons it had been dropped by most of his sample in the USA. Cockburn noted political and technical problems in Lambeth too, such as the *de facto* demotion of councillors *vis-à-vis* officers and the poor performance of the management system in improving information flows and implementing plans. But in organizational terms a new dimension of administrative 'Taylorism'[3] is alluded to in her discussion of the functioning of Community Planning, that is the means of integrating the community more closely with the local authority. Cockburn suggests that the participatory joint committees established for this purpose entailed the socialization and manipulation of the target system (the community), thus enhancing the potential control of that system. The reciprocal danger to the control system of the integration of hypothetically disruptive groups, as noted by Cockburn, could only be offset in two ways: first, by the socialization process, or second, as happened in fact in Lambeth, the disengagement of community representatives and the abandonment of the joint committee experiment (see also Haines, 1981).

The widespread disenchantment in theory and practice with the traditionally British unitary mode of planning organization, itself rooted in Keynesian precepts of state intervention by a cultured elite charged with the management of the political economy,[4] has proved a signal for reconsideration or perhaps discovery of alternative modes. The strength of these critiques, coupled with a more far-reaching epistemological scrutiny of the knowledge foundations of such planning approaches, especially their technical and methodological aspects (Batey and Breheny, 1978), following the earlier and often penetrative critiques of functionalist ideology in planning (Orlans, 1952; Bailey, 1973; Simmie, 1974), have dealt severe shocks to the fundamental assumptions upon which much of traditional planning theory has been constructed.

As disaffection with Keynesianism has grown (Skidelsky, 1979) the theory which underpins the management of complex state–market interconnections has itself changed. Around the mixed economies of the world serious attention has been devoted to a less unitary form of economic management, namely that based upon the quantity theory of money (Friedman, 1970). Urban development planning already possesses a range of cognate theories, already being drawn upon to complement the state's adoption of monetarist economic policies. In the rest of this chapter we will give an exposition and critique of the principal forms which these theories take. This is done as a prelude to the attempt in subsequent chapters to draw attention to the need for radically different foundations to be provided if the failures of past planning practice are not to be repeated.

Atomistic modes

It was noted above that in conditions of economic buoyancy the latitude for a more responsive governmental attitude to plural interests, a tendency to apply planning controls in a mildly restraining or containing way, and, if the presence of state intervention is marked, opportunity for further innovatory growth-promoting activity by state institutions, is considerable. This will depend upon the politico-economic context of the society in question: however, it is clear from the already mentioned rejection of Keynesian demand management largely because of its inflation-generating effects, that in periods of serious economic recession resort may be made to what may be thought to be a reliable alternative mode of political economic management, to Keynesian state intervention, that is, some variant of *laissez-faire*. This has been happening in Britain since the mid-1970s, and the form which has emerged is one rooted in the belief that a tight control of the money supply and balanced budgeting can succeed in controlling inflation where Keynesianism cannot.

While there is no plainly 'monetarist' theory of planning available – the terms are almost mutually exclusive – there are at least four non-unitary, atomistic modes available which would be appropriate to Friedmanesque government economic policy. These are: Downs's economic theory of planning; incremental budgeting; decentralism and adjunctive planning. These will be considered in the above order.

Downs's economic theory of planning

With the publication of his first book (Downs, 1957) Anthony Downs challenged traditional normative political theory with a positive theory of political behaviour developed from marginalist economic theory. In brief, the latter postulates the following:

1   The individual evaluates all feasible courses of action in terms of the value he attaches to them as satisfying wants (or their 'utility' for him).
2   Two individuals thus only engage in exchange relations (a market) if their utilities, measured in terms of subjective preference, differ for the same good.
3   Value, thus, is the degree of utility an individual places on goods. Transactions in markets rest on the exchange of goods such that individual benefits are perceived to be maximized.
4   Returns to individuals from these transactions are determined according to the market value (supply and demand) of their contribution (Gamble and Walton, 1976).

Downs's interpretation of marginalism (which should not be confused with the theses connected with the quantity theory of money, or 'monetarist' position, despite their compatibility) began with an application first to the democratic political process, second to bureaucracy and subsequently to the problems of urban planning. The basic theory in the first case stressed that political behaviour could be usefully understood as representing a voting market. Here politicians sought to maximize *their* utility by supplying relevant decisions and policies to individual voters who would cast their vote in favour of the politician who offered to or succeeded in maximizing their – the voters' – utilities. Failure to maximize voter-utilities was explained as the result of distorted perceptions by voters of their own interests, culminating in a miscast vote. Some hypotheses which derive from this theory refer to the effects of such utility-maximization upon the configuration of government policy. Three of these are noted by Toye (1976): first, 'government fiscal favouritism'; second, 'government redistribution of income'; and finally, the 'size of the government budget'.

With regard to the first, it is held that utility maximization carries high information costs and that producers are better able to sustain these than consumers. However, since consumers are more sensitive to government manipulation of incomes than prices, politicians will tend to vary the latter more than the former. This results in producers being favoured over consumers. As for the second, it is proposed that owing to the distributive inequality characteristic of democracies, politicians may maximize their benefits, that is votes, by implementing redistributive policies since they are thereby improving the economic situation of large numbers of people at the expense of the rich minority. Thirdly, Downs has argued that government budgets tend to be undersized, resulting in an increasingly serious mis-allocation of expenditure as differentiation develops in the economy. This is because, once again, of misperceptions by voters of the nature of their utilities owing to the costs of information.

Before considering some fairly obvious criticisms that can be or have been directed at these hypotheses (which Downs claims are, because tested successfully, predictions) it is necessary to link in his analysis of bureaucracy in the first place, and that of urban planning in the second. The central idea in the work on bureaucracy (Downs, 1967) is that large bureaucracies are change-resistant. However, this commonplace observation is the basis for a prescriptive analysis of how to bring about a transformation. Change, it is postulated, can be effected by pressure from bureaucracy's erstwhile supporters: the most conclusive form of pressure is to treat bureaucracy exactly as trusts or monopolies are under neo-classical economic theory, that is introduce competition to restore market efficiency. Competition for bureaucracy makes its organization more adaptive to consumer wishes without consumers having to perform a watchdog function *vis-à-vis* bureaucratic organizations.

It is clear that this view of bureaucracy equates at a general level with that expressed of the political process in one principal way. In both cases the maximization of utility by consumers dictates the production of policies in the interests of consumers. This form of consumer sovereignty is prejudiced only by those phenomena which prejudice the existence of perfect markets; uncertainty, high information costs and inefficiency resulting from infringement of market conditions.

However, at a lower, more detailed level this consistency disintegrates since bureaucracy presumably results either from politicians' attempts to fulfil vote-maximizing promises such as redistribution of incomes and wealth, or despite them and despite the predictions of undersized government budgets, or price rather than income manipulation. If politicians were to behave as Downs suggests then bureaucracy should always be, on balance, undersized too, and therefore not be prone to attacks for its excessive absorption of public expenditure in manpower expenses. However, it seems less the size than the conservatism of bureaucracy which is Downs's main concern and it is this aspect which he clearly sees as most vulnerable to his brand of radical individualism. To this end he quotes the work of Milton Friedman, especially with regard to the desirability of an educational voucher system to introduce competition in the production of education, with enthusiasm (Downs, 1970, p. 289).

In similar vein he turns his attention to the problem of change in advanced urban complexes. He sees the structure of existing institutions charged with containing the most serious urban pathologies as central to the problem. Their reluctance to change, other than to make marginal accommodations to public opinion, is underlined as the cause. Institutions thus focus and intensify conflicts already visible in the effects of technical, economic and cultural transformations. Downs's approach to analysis is comparably irreverent to that adopted for his other subjects of interest, politics and bureaucracy, though he stresses that comprehension of the nature of urban systems is not possible to the same degree as for those more bounded social institutions. Principally, this is because of the much greater relative complexity and instability or dynamism of cities. This is why Downs's analysis is limited to institutional analysis, and government institutions at that; the irreverence appears in an iconoclastic perspective upon those institutions.

The method of analysis and prescription which Downs adopts is close to Dror's (1964) 'normative-optimum' model of planning whose main stages involve:

1 Operational clarification and definition of planning norms.
2 Generation of alternative strategies in accordance with these norms, emphasizing innovative ideas.
3 Limited estimation of expected strategy pay-off.
4 (i) If a minimal risk strategy has high pay-off pursue marginal-increment policies.
(ii) If not, perform limited rational planning combining forecasting, intuition and systematic monitoring.

Downs speaks in terms of:

1 clearly and critically defining basic planning concepts;
2 generating preferred and alternative policy 'futures';
3 performing a wide-ranging 'coarse' evaluation, applying limiting[5] criteria to justify more detailed 'fine' evaluation;
4 employing intuition to make simplifying judgements in policy formulation and at least crude analyses of redistributive effects of policy.

This method is then applied to a diverse range of urban problems such as urban growth, racism, low income, housing, transportation, and educational choice. It is clear in all these cases that Downs's belief in equality of opportunity through market relations structures his approach. This in itself is, as we have seen, a fundamental element in marginal utilitarian economic theorization which enables the precept of 'returns in accordance with sacrifices made' to, on the one hand, define the nature of equality under market conditions while on the other, giving the appearance to the theory of scientific neutrality. To some extent Downs is aware of the tendency for this approach to discriminate against the indigent by overemphasizing economic efficiency in the selection of public policy, at the expense of income redistribution implications. But as can be seen from what he considers his best solution, namely, a policy for solving the 'sink' effect of ghettoization, he swings a long way towards evaluating policy more in terms of likely redistributive impact but in such a way that it discriminates in favour of individuals whose motivations and behaviour patterns most resemble those of *homo oeconomicus*. In this way a basic weakness of marginalist theory of planning is revealed. This is its underlying attachment to a markedly idealist view of the human subject, an attachment which is basic to the supposed objectivity of the neo-classical economic method.

Briefly, the four stages of Downs's theory of planning are applied to the urban problem of ghetto-formation and development as follows:

1   'Ghetto' as a concept is examined, distinctions in meaning are drawn between its economic and racial dimensions. Given the American context to which his analysis is applied the latter is taken as more reflective of reality since ethnic concentration is seen to cross-cut socio-economic stratification.

   Conventional wisdom regarding the nature of ghetto-residents' socio-economic characteristics and attitudes is critically analysed and explanations for the inadequacy of current policy initiatives and analysis are sought.

   Suburbanization of job opportunities, racism by service-sector employers, poor public transportation, and local government fiscal crises resulting from the combined effect of these and associated disadvantages of advanced urbanization, are seen as causing and exacerbating ghettoization.

2   Then, employing a decision-framework based on the methods of disjointed incrementalism (Dahl and Lindblom, 1953) social strategies are formulated. These comprise combinations of choices among dichotomous policies for dealing with non-white populations. They include: concentration versus dispersal; segregation versus integration; and low-welfare versus high-welfare expenditure.

   After eliminating the internally inconsistent strategies, a simple choice is left between preserving present policies of concentration, segregation and low-welfare expenditure, and a policy of integrated dispersal emphasizing dispersal, integration and high-welfare expenditure.

3   Each is examined in coarse terms for estimation of goal-achievement, internal coherence, political salience and economic and social rationality. A set of strategies favouring dispersal is selected because it alone provides 'negro Americans with real freedom of choice concerning housing and school accommodations' (Downs, 1971, p. 48). From this basis, attention is directed at the finer detail of a broad dispersal strategy. Segregation and integration are evaluated as modes of successfully

achieving the dispersal objective and the latter is chosen. This is for three reasons: whites must be reassured that non-white dominance will not occur in suburban areas; new ghetto-formation would have the effect of restricting real freedom by leaving presently discriminatory housing access laws unchallenged; and the suburbs, with their low-density structure are less susceptible to educational segregation than high-density inner cities, a feature which is underlined given a dispersal strategy.

4   Finally, Downs's solution recommends the formulation of a policy with a variety of implementation tactics, some of which are fairly conventional, others of which are innovative in an individualistic way. In the latter respect, incentives play a key role. Thus to encourage voluntary migration of ghetto-households to suburban locations incentives, in the form of cash payments to movers, would be established; these would be administered by metropolis-wide 'quasi-private bodies able to co-operate directly with existing local governments and other geographically limited organizations' (Downs, 1971, p. 65); and positive discrimination via educational and residential grant-aid, as well as occupational training subsidies to individuals, would be established. The receiving communities would also receive individual cash incentives, educational priority status would be assigned to host schools, and cash bonuses would go to local governments participating in the servicing of in-migrants. All of this would occur in the context of a wide-ranging legitimation exercise in which political and business interests would be persuaded of its benefits to them, thus eliciting compliance.

The relationship between this plan for overcoming a highly complex nexus of problems through radical theoretical and practical critique of existing institutional arrangements and the economic theories of democracy and bureaucracy is apparent. The reduction of complexity is effected to a considerable extent by concentration upon the utility-maximizing individual. Rational calculation is proposed as the central intellectual device assisting change to occur, whether engaged in by producers or consumers. And conversely, it is interference with this central principle, reflected in bureaucratic and institutional ossification, which contributes to misunderstanding of the nature of social problems. These are more clearly understood by marginalists as supply and demand bottlenecks, solvable by restoring the hegemony of the market.

The particular problem with the planning solution, present though in more submerged form in the economic theories of democracy and bureaucracy, is that its basic assumption is unconvincing. In other words the thesis that social change can be effected and social problems overcome by the creation of a climate for individual utility-maximization is not validated theoretically or empirically. It is clearly an ideology masquerading as a fairly commonplace truth, and if the assumptions on which it rests are questionable then prescriptions based upon their validity must be the more so. Quite clearly the central problem of this kind of theorization is its restrictive nature. An idealized individual is hypothesized whose choice processes are conditioned by a particularly abstract mode of theorizing economic relations. The abstraction consists in the treatment of individuals as fundamentally asocial, acultural and ahistorical atoms whose self-interested, rational calculation produces an ordered and stable form of social organization because each individual is rewarded according to the nature and extent of his contribution.

In the sphere of politics it is by no means clear either that in theoretical terms a utility-maximizing conception of politicians', or more to the point, voters' behaviour captures any very important part of the total political process, or that in empirical terms, predictions based upon the propositions derived from that theory bear a convincing relation to real politics.[6]

First, the level of information necessary to enable politicians to influence voter-intentions through detailed exposition of policies would have to be very large. Then there is the problem of the extent to which such exposition is effective. That is, the impact of policies upon voters may be considerably less than politicians' perceptions of that impact with the result that false conclusions about voters' attitudes to policy may be drawn.

Second, for a range of well-known reasons, voters, marginally more than consumers, appear to behave far from rationally in making political choices. This is explicitly included in the Downsian model as a function of information costs though as Toye notes: 'Introspection alone should alert us to the extent of inconsistency, myopia and miscalculation in the pursuit of ends, even under conditions of comparative certainty' (Toye, 1976, p. 443). The findings of the American voting studies (Lukes, 1977, pp. 30–51) show that strong elements of apathy, ignorance and even recklessness must be taken into account in consideration of voter behaviour. It seems clear that the utility-maximizing politician or voter is something of an idealistic abstraction invented to allow a reasonably coherent theory of economic behaviour (albeit one of dubious validity) to be extended into new areas. Such reductionism mainly serves to undermine the claim that this kind of theory is somehow neutral and scientific and thus does not have any particular preferred value position contained within it.

While, theoretically, there are problems with the economic theory of politics it is possible that its predictions may nevertheless be accurate, and to a considerable extent this is made explicit by Downs who enjoins his readers to concentrate upon the predictive qualities of the theory rather than its necessarily simplifying assumptions (Downs, 1957, p. 21). But, on the one hand, it is clear that predictions about public finance may not work in democracies outside the advanced industrial countries, and, on the other, that even for the developed democracies some of them are not only difficult but impossible to test, such as the notion of the undersized budget (undersized by comparison with what?).

There are also problems of a rather similar nature connected with the economic theory of bureaucracy. There is an initial ambiguity about the nature of the change-resistance of bureaucracy and indeed, the nature of the change itself. Is it resistance to change in the *environment*, such as shifts in the employment structure of a nation or region, which lies at the heart of the problem with bureaucracy? Or is it resistance within the bureaucracy to demands that it performs its duties differently? If it is the former, then it is not immediately clear how introducing competitive organizations or 'non-bureaucracies' can have any point to it. This is because unevenness in spatial development is a basic and systematic characteristic of market economies. Most forms of state intervention exist in some form of contradictory relationship with the ideals of perfect competition because they usually involve activities for which markets are inappropriate but from which markets may benefit. If it is the latter, the above also applies *a fortiori* but it is not clear that any organization operating in the real world can be expected to adapt to ideal, atomistic, utility-maximizing individuals in a coherent manner anyway. Bureaucracies and especially government bureaucracies are charged with administering, and to some extent generating, policy on the assumption that uncertainty exists in democracies but that enough of that uncertainty can be absorbed so that policy is rendered workable. And, if pressure emerges against policy, either bureaucracy is well-enough informed, through its power and communications linkages, to be able to resist, or if pressure causes power holders to begin to seek change, it has the resources to bring about slow but relatively smooth adaptations to policy.

This positive aspect of bureaucratic institutions is precisely what is underplayed and represented as rigidity in Downs's analysis. This, and the alternatives to it, are exposed most clearly in his planning theory where in at least three major ways the tautological nature of utilitarian marginalism produces fatal effects for both theory and prescription. In brief, the marginalist tautology derives from the assertion that preferences of consumers determine the nature of markets. But, since price is a constraint, then in practice markets actually determine preferences. This means that utility or preference is actually measured by price which in turn determines preference. Clearly this does not get us very far. The first sign of this circularity in the case of the ghetto concerns the processes of in- and out-migration. Though the explanation of migration is highly complex, it is probable that occupational and cultural factors are primarily responsible for household movements of this type. Each kind of migration then, can profitably be viewed as a process associated with: occupational, social and physical mobility increases; changes in labour markets; availability of homes and house finance in suburbia; and cultural change signals as inner-city ethnic or class tipping-points are approached and passed. Ghettoization represents a stage in the spatially uneven development process (Tilly, 1968). Hence, the relatively wealthy, culturally homogeneous class of suburbanites is maximizing utility by migrating to new, low density districts; equally the underclass of poor non-white migrants is maximizing its collective utility in line with market constraints. The calculus of utilitarian marginalism is the source of the ghetto, rather than the solution to its problems.

Second, the marginalist tautology is apparent in the definition Downs adopts to clarify the meaning of the word ghetto, that is a racial rather than a class one. Relatively affluent non-white individuals with the *relatively* wider span of choice that such a designation implies clearly choose to live in the ghetto for cultural or other social reasons. The abstractions of marginalism, though, discount this criterion, presumably because it cannot be assigned a monetary value. By abstracting the individual from the social context in one-sided fashion, the utility-maximizing approach reveals not only the narrowness of its value-price equivalence, but also the unrealistic assumptions which such limitations require of it. Where *social* utility-maximization is already occurring in ways which the calculus cannot cope with, Downs blandly continues to prescribe *abstract* utility-maximization of the restricted, atomistic, kind.

And finally, it is interesting to note that the complex policy solution advanced takes the classic welfare state form of semi-governmentally organized disbursement of public funds. That is, in order to secure a market-like structure of freedoms and opportunities for equivalent individual utility maximizers, a bureaucratic organization is required to administer the system. This is in addition to the existing legal and administrative structures which retain partial responsibility for dealing with various aspects of the problem. In order for the incentives system to work there needs to be a substantial system of transfer payments, not, however, on the familiar pattern of rich to poor, but on a spatially selective basis to both rich and poor, a proposal which takes the idea of Pareto optimality (the marginalist scales of justice) to its strange limits.

In conclusion, therefore, it is apparent that Downs's theory of marginalist planning constitutes a scarcely veiled ideology, a normative statement of the preferability of a system of social and economic arrangements which appears to treat all members of that system as atoms of rational calculation whose utilities are measured and satisfied by the price they pay for what they value. The effect of this ideology is a massive evasion of, on the one hand, the unevenness of individual ability to maximize utility in the terms that marginalism itself defines that criterion, and on the other, the extent to which the mythical qualities of market relations have to be bolstered by the very sort of non-market agency of which marginalist theorists are so critical. Underpinning this is the problem of idealistic abstractionism which excludes from consideration those basic social utilities which the market cannot measure. Nevertheless, from Downs's treatment of social problems we do gain an insight into the ways in which the nature of individuality is distorted by a mode of analysis which reduces the complexities of social and cultural reproduction in capitalist societies to a simplistic 'economics of politics' (Tomlinson, 1981). This problem of reductionism is not, however, confined to neo-classicists such as Downs, it is a characteristic feature of a good deal of contemporary social scientific and planning thought of both orthodox and more radical persuasions, as will be shown. However, before discussing reductionism and related problems, it is necessary to examine a few more examples of marginalist 'economism' in theories of planning and public policy-making to further illustrate the inadequacies of atomistic theories as these have been used in planning discourse.

Varieties of incrementalism

The general approach to decision-making known as *incrementalism* has certain marked affinities with Downs's economic theories, although it predates the latter in its original formulation (Dahl and Lindblom, 1953). More recent elaborations and critiques have made it a widely understood mode of analysis and prescription in the field of public policy (Braybrooke and Lindblom, 1963; Lindblom, 1968; Dror, 1964; Faludi, 1973a and b). The basic idea can be explained quite simply. It is that policies are not made *de novo* each time but are, rather, marginal additions to prevailing policy. There is little wide-ranging generation of alternative strategies, or evaluation of consequences, because choices are constrained by pragmatic considerations. If incremental remedies provoke opposition they can be opposed by pluralistic interests and, if necessary, changed at no great economic or political cost. Three points can be made to indicate the similarities, and certain differences, between incrementalism and utilitarian marginalism.

First, where utilitarian marginalism eschews the concept of a strong, influential and interventionist state, incrementalism rejects 'the notion that institutions can consciously formulate policies that express the collective "good"' (Etzioni, 1976, p. 86). The difference at this level between the two philosophies is an empirical one. For, whereas marginalism is a theory of how private transactions occur in markets, incrementalism is a theory of how public policy is made within the state. Inevitably, therefore, there is a strong hint of contradiction contained in the quote from Etzioni, since some estimate of the collective good clearly has to be made within institutions for policies to emerge at all. The incrementalist compromise is to describe and prescribe a fragmentary and competitive array of institutional sub-systems, including non-public ones, as an optimum arena for correct decision-making.

Second, marginalism postulates utility-maximizing individuals evaluating feasible alternative strategies, exchanging, and adjusting their relationships in markets according to differing individual levels of utility. In incrementalism, the equivalent process is referred to as 'partisan mutual adjustment' (Lindblom, 1968). The public interest is served by protest and pressure groups bargaining over policy inputs in an openly partisan way. From this system of adjustment something equivalent to the order-giving properties of 'the invisible hand' emerges to guide policy towards a greater wisdom, with greater benefits all round, than would be the case if a centralized elite were to attempt to comprehend the collective good.

Finally, as in the case of marginalism each participant or contributor to a market transaction reaps advantage in accordance with the sacrifice, or contribution made, so in the incremental mode participants in the 'decision-market' reap benefits according to the vigour and effort with which they pursue their interests. Those who are slow off the mark are not thereby debarred from influencing the outputs of policy since they can, in pluralist fashion, participate *post facto* to seek to effect marginal alterations in policy to accord with their interests. However, those who do not participate in the policy-making process must be assumed to be apathetic or satisfied with decisions taken for them, in which case they cannot expect to gain the same sort of policy return as can those who participate wholeheartedly.

Incremental expenditure budgeting

Most analysts of public policy-making agree that incrementalism is the dominant model both for the practicalities of policy-making in the public sector and the academic analysis of public sector expenditure profiles. In the latter case there is a mass of research (for example Wildavsky, 1964; Sharkansky, 1970; Crecine, 1969; Anton, 1966; Sullivan, 1972) which purports to show that budgeting in the state sector follows a clearly definable path of marginal annual increments overall, though within the overall budget there may well be large leaps, stagnations or cuts. More recently, fairly elaborate algorithms have appeared (Crecine, 1969) which aim to predict expenditure. Some important and useful descriptive and predictive analyses of public expenditure have thus added considerably to our knowledge of the structure of public sector budgets.

However, several serious caveats must be borne in mind in considering these findings, some of which, in fairness, are mentioned by incrementalist authors. The first, and most important of these is that the focus upon relatively easily measurable cash outputs almost certainly gives a distorted picture of the processes involved in producing incremental profiles. That is, simply because public sector budgets appear to fit incrementalist predictions it cannot be assumed that policy-makers follow Lindblom-type decision rules. Second, the definition of what actually constitutes an increment, that is a ratio to the previous year's expenditure small enough to qualify as a marginal increase, is not entirely immune from criticism. Factor values lying between +0.3 and −0.3 have been proposed as the range limiting the definition of incremental change (Wildavsky, 1964). Such a large range casts doubt upon the confidence with which incrementalists present their predictions, since even the fairly substantial cuts in public expenditure in the UK in recent years come nowhere near to denting the lower limit on an annual basis (see Else and Marshall, 1979). Caution on this scale produces results which point to all budgeting as being incremental, a profoundly uninteresting conclusion which cannot be refuted.

Thirdly, certain interesting variations which occur to upset predictions of incremental stability (that is a smooth progression in expenditure levels from year to year), suggest that policy-making in certain sectors which are high spenders and thus more affected by national state policy, can swing around quite violently. Thus Sharkansky (1970) has noted that USA highway construction displays marked short-term increases and decreases, and that these changes correlate more closely with changes in federal subsidy levels for highway building than with the annual expenditure level for the previous year. Danziger has found a similar phenomenon to occur in Britain (Danziger, 1976). But in both cases overall allocation levels across an administration's expenditure were more stable in their incremental rate than was generally the case for specific departments within an administration. Once more, this offers a glimpse of the extent to which the method of estimating policy change in terms of budgetary output masks the processes by which those outputs are achieved. A further problem with the method is that it offers little or no guidance for the analysis of the policy process in departments which may have high policy impact, particularly in policy formulation, but have low budgetary output; land-use planning being almost a classic case in this respect.

Incrementalism and demand management

But the more fundamental problem with budgetary incrementalism as a mode of both policy analysis and policy performance is that it is most closely associated with, on the one hand, a period of growth in Western economies and, on the other, a general acceptance of a more-or-less Keynesian attitude to public finance on the part of governments generally. Both of these features are, as we have seen, substantially less prominent a component of the public policy scene now than hitherto.

Throughout the post-war years, until the 1970s the general trend in public expenditure in the advanced industrial societies has been an upward one. In the UK it rose from around 40 per cent of GNP in the 1940s to around 45 per cent in the 1950s. During the 1950s it dropped back to about 40 per cent but from the early 1960s to the early 1970s it had risen to over 50 per cent. The level finally approached 58 per cent before dropping back again to around 54 per cent in 1977 (Else and Marshall, 1979). These levels do bear some relation to the slope of the GNP curve until the early 1970s (though expenditure begins to rise more steeply than GNP in the early 1960s). However, there was a substantial gap between the two more or less throughout the 1970s, though significant and sharp actual reductions in expenditure, as distinct from reductions in the rate of increase, only began in 1976. Clearly, while GNP is rising, and to some extent even after it ceases rising, for a time, expectations that public expenditure can also rise, though in a controlled, marginal, way are reasonable. However, once GNP ceases to rise wild fluctuations occur. In the UK this was represented by a sharp rise for a short period, followed by a levelling off in the rate of increase over a similar period, and the most recent sharp cutbacks with magnified effects in different sectors. The marginal increments of the 1950s and 1960s in the UK are distinctly not echoed in the 1970s.

Why should there have been this expectation that public expenditure could rise incrementally with economic growth? Why also should a policy-making mode whose affinities rest with marginalist economic theory prosper under a system of economic management premissed upon a critique of marginalism, that is Keynesian demand management? The answer to the first question is relatively straightforward compared with the second. Growth in public expenditure is simply an integrated component of the process of Keynesian demand management. That is, under this theory of the role of the state in economic affairs it is recognized that as well as 'normal' sources of expenditure such as private consumption, industrial investment or export sales, government expenditure has a crucial role to play in influencing the level of total expenditure. Upon the latter depends the level of employment, so, as governments can control public expenditure to a considerable extent this mechanism is used to bring about stabilization in the economy. Following the post-war successes in securing growth and full employment without inflation, the objective of maintaining economic growth was seen to be a feasible one given progressive increments of government-induced public expenditure. Thus spending departments in both central and local government got used to competing for a marginally larger share of a growing cake, especially in the USA where fragmented government bureaucracies which engage in policy-bargaining are prevalent and where the incrementalist model was first generated. In Britain's more unitary system there are, as indicated, later signs of incremental growth in public expenditure but there are also surges and declines which seem to be closely associated, more so than in the USA, with central government spending plans. In the USA equivalent surges are more closely associated with the wars in South-East Asia (Fenno, 1966).

The second question is more complex, and to answer it attention must again be focused upon the unique institutional structure of American government. For, even though broadly Keynesian federal economic management had been adopted consequent to the 1930s depression, meaning that an increasing proportion of GNP was taken up by public expenditure, the strongly individualistic, utilitarian approach to bargaining and negotiation with its traditional 'log-rolling' and 'pork-barrelling' style[7] of political mediation clearly remained a prominent feature of state and local policy-formulation. It is essentially this sort of process which Lindblom succeeds in formalizing in his model of disjointed incrementalism. At a more general, theoretical level, it is of great importance also to note that while marginalism was clearly failing, and indeed making matters worse, at the time of the economic crisis of the inter-war years, Keynesianism, though conceived as having radical overtones in that it brought state management to the heart of market relations, can be interpreted as simply a variant form of marginalism. It 'only added special assumptions reflecting "institutional factors", in particular the notion that wage rates were generally inflexible downwards' (Gamble and Walton, 1976, p. 46). Though this interpretation is controversial (Gamble and Walton themselves in fact reject it), nevertheless it seems clear that there is a sufficient degree of compatibility between demand management and incrementalism *under economic growth conditions* for incremental outputs of public expenditure to be fairly common. Of course, the extent to which the internal policy formulation process reflects Lindblom's classic description outside American institutional contexts remains unclear.

In summary then, an important theory of planning and one which has been posed as a realistic alternative to the idealism of rational-comprehensiveness can be seen to be a highly contingent approach, dependent upon relative success in the operation of market relations. In the sphere where incrementalism appears strongest, that is the scholarly analysis and practical process of public expenditure policy-making, it appears to have limited value and applicability. This is because its operation is historically constrained to periods of economic growth and institutionally constrained to political systems characterized by a high level of bureaucratic fragmentation, a relatively weak central-to-local government command structure and a strong commitment to the hegemony of the market in ordering economic and social relations.

Crisis management and incremental corporatism

Finally and interestingly, given the changing nature under economic crisis of the structure of expenditure patterns in Western economies and academic theorization about the political and economic processes which give rise to them, Lindblom's recent work (Lindblom, 1977) signifies a distinct shift away from a marginalist and strictly pluralist theory of planning. Following his close collaborator Robert Dahl's (1971) concept of 'polyarchy', developed to meet, half-way, criticisms of the more optimistic propositions of pluralism, Lindblom now more clearly sees the centrality of government to the continued existence of markets. Where Dahl postulates a political system managed by a circle of elites responsive to public pressure as characteristic of democratic societies, Lindblom reformulates this 'polyarchy' as the first of two pressures acting to constrain government, the second being the demands of the private sector. In combination these pressures constrain government to generate policy responsive to a wide range of interests, but particularly so to business interests. This is because it recognizes the centrality to the continuation of liberal democracy of a private productive sector (for slightly different reasons this is reminiscent of Downs's 'government fiscal favouritism' and 'government redistribution of income' hypotheses). However, Lindblom stresses that it is a mistake to assume that:

the vast productive tasks performed in market-oriented systems could be motivated solely by exchange relations between buyers and sellers. . . . What is required in addition is a set of governmentally provided inducements in the form of market and political benefits. And because market demands themselves do not spontaneously spring up, they too have to be nurtured by government. (Lindblom, 1977, p. 173)

This analysis leads Lindblom to advocate a role for planning very different from that it played in the incrementalist mode and much more akin to the sort of crisis-management entailed in full-blown Keynesianism. He terms this a 'planner sovereignty market system' (p. 98) in which government uses its economic and legal powers to constrain business to pursue government-set policy goals. Skidelsky (1979, p. 83) equates this with what has been referred to elsewhere as corporatism (Winkler, 1977) though there are differences to the mechanisms by which the state would control the private sector between the two approaches. There does, however, seem to be a notable inconsistency in Lindblom's argument since if the business sector is powerful and privileged in liberal democracies to what extent can the state expect to exert the requisite pressure upon it? Urban planning provides a good illustration of this problem in a number of ways, not the least of which has been the failure of the various policies to socialize the profits from development land, but also more generally in its inability to seriously control the development process, which is largely dependent upon private initiatives and investment.

The incrementalist alternative to centralized planning looks to be dubious both empirically, if the Wildavskian definitional criteria are relaxed as they have to be if the theory is to sustain interest and credibility, and in theoretical terms if the shift in its originator's position is any guide. No convincing replacement to this hitherto dominant mode of analysing and performing the process of policy formulation in the public sector is in sight at present, and with public sector finance in a fluid relationship with unstable market conditions it seems unlikely that such a theory will emerge in the short term. More likely is the development of a variety of pragmatic analyses resulting in empirical descriptions of, on the one hand, the effectiveness of policies made when expenditure was more freely available, and on the other, the techniques and procedures by means of which resources are obtained from a parsimonious exchequer. This will inevitably require analysis of processes of policy-making and policy-bidding as well as the calculation of budgetary outputs.

Decentralism: rolling back the frontiers of the state

Associated with the revived interest in the virtues of marginalist prescriptions for introducing efficiency in the disposition of public budgets is another which questions the need for large parts of the state's apparatus. Decentralism (which carries with it the corollary of debureaucratization) is a radical individualist form of managing the consumption of necessary public expenditure. It is, in principle, an ideal shared by political thinkers of all persuasions but, interestingly, in the West it has tended to be appropriated by the right. This stems from the ease with which those institutions intended by the left to liberate the mass of ordinary people have been transformed into oppressive, statist, monoliths. Freedom has, temporarily at least, become defined as freedom *from* the welfare state, planning controls and public ownership.

Decentralism in the management of local urban affairs has a liberal-pluralist source in antipathy towards the strong, potentially arbitrary, state. It finds modern expression in enthusiasm for neighbourhood control, advocacy planning and revenue sharing, all of which aim to grant greater power to local communities to act in the ways they see fit. It has been most lucidly described by Alan Altshuler (1968) who, building upon an earlier (Altshuler, 1965) empirical critique of rational-comprehensive planning, sought to found new planning institutions. The basic weakness of centralized planning in the cities of the USA revolved around the claim of the planning authority to possess special expertise in comprehending the public interest, thereby enabling a representative set of goals to be set for the city. Altshuler cited numerous instances of the failure of this expertise, ranging from apathy to confusion on the part of the public whose interests the goals purported to articulate, and loss of status for planners whose general expertise could not match that of specialists in particular functional areas.

Nevertheless, in his later paper Altshuler recognized that, on the one hand, the tide of governmental sympathy was running towards the sort of integrated, corporate form of planning which he had criticized, especially in such sectors as: the regulation of privately-induced negative externalities; politically-determined resource allocation; and the application of a systematic planning discipline to social problem-solving. On the other hand, and in contradiction to the latter trend, he noted the movement at the popular level towards the liberalization of the mechanisms of social control represented in requests for: greater participation and diffusion of power;

increased individual freedom and choice; and limitations upon government activity and power. The question to be answered concerns the extent to which the implementation of collective goals can be achieved non-bureaucratically. The solution is reminiscent at a general level of the Downsian prescription for overcoming pathological aspects of bureaucratic organization, involving resort to market-type relations, a utilitarian calculus, and disaggregation of centralized functions.

Three main features characterize the decentralist prescription for diminishing bureaucratic organization and control. First, disaggregation of the planning function would reduce the authority's responsibility for the direct production of planning policy. Experimentally, special studies in particular substantive and functional areas could be contracted to private sector consultancies, and simultaneously most middle priority issues could be expedited without reference to chief planners, thus speeding up policy processing. Second, the institution and implementation of rigid and deterministic bureaucratic regulations could be markedly curtailed. Instead, flexible rules allowing some degrees of freedom for both planning officers and the public are advocated as guidelines for action, but wherever possible persuasion of the validity of policy should be sought through structuring of incentives and prices and stimulating self-sufficiency. Third, to minimize bureaucratic attachment to programmes and prevent planning goals becoming self-perpetuating, regular resort to public scrutiny as well as competition from the private sector for technical planning solutions would be required.

Before considering the limitations of debureaucratization it is necessary to outline the main ways in which the gaps left are to be filled. This is to be achieved by strengthening metropolitan and neighbourhood councils, which — means at least the following: shifts in the location of power; devolution of financial control; and development of public–private sector partnerships. In terms of rearranging the power structure the proposal involves an assumption that institutions which perform important social functions tend to be administratively large and remote from consumers, hence let such functions be devolved from central to metropolitan level and nurture neighbourhood-level influence and responsibility. Moreover, these institutions would be the main levels at which the nature and scale of expenditure would be negotiated, with block grants and authorizations to tax being administered by neighbourhoods. Finally, neighbourhoods would be serviced in technical expertise by metropolitan or private agencies, and joint schemes between neighbourhoods and local businesses would be encouraged as ways of improving conditions in complex problem areas such as the inner-city.

Now, at both main points of this scheme there are elements advocated which are difficult to disagree with, notably those urging flexibility and speed upon bureaucracy and less remote government generally. But the key issues devolve, as they must, to questions of practicality on the one hand, and equity on the other. Clearly, balkanization has its attractions during an era when the homogenizing effects of rational-legal administration increasingly impinge upon daily life. The state, which is the more pervasive, though when compared with business not necessarily the most penetrative, of the forms taken by this rationalization of everyday affairs is, in principle, tractable to reform by human agency through processes of political control. However, the state in particular, charged as it is with organizing social relations into an ordered pattern by managing the pursuit of a diverse range of interests, necessarily operates according to a logic at variance with that of individualistic utility-maximization. Traditionally, this logic has taken the form of the generation and application of regulative instruments whose chief source of acceptance resides in their universality, though 'the monopoly of the legitimate use of physical force' (Weber, 1948, p. 78) provides the solid base for this facility. More recently, as the scope of state involvement in social and economic affairs has increased, requiring of government departments a more recognizably rational mode of decision-making than mere authority, a form of utility-maximization, though much distorted, has emerged as planning. But here again the requirements of legitimate global planning exert pressures upon planners in democracies which are precisely those which Altshuler identifies, namely those of squaring rationality and efficiency with democratic participation. Clearly, if Altshuler's argument is to be sustained, then decentralism implies conflict, and processes for its resolution at different hierarchical levels. A slow, sometimes non-rational, inefficient (in the economic sense of cost-minimization) and thus impracticable form of planning seems to be adumbrated in Altshuler's analysis.

The reproduction of atomistic market relations within the public sector also has deleterious implications for the degree of equity with which the social wage may be expected to be distributed. Altshuler gives his imprimatur to the kind of decentralized planning, self-help and committed action envisaged under the system of 'advocacy planning' (Davidoff, 1973) except that in so far as Altshuler's system is more formalized, some of the fundamental practical problems of advocacy, such as finance and credibility, are largely overcome. Nevertheless, a basic weakness of advocacy planning and decentralism, reflecting that to be found in political pluralism and economic marginalism as well, is underlined. Just as marginalism diverted attention away from questions of distribution and initial endowment, assuming 'that the capitalist market system did maximize utility, and that it gave everyone – labourer, entrepreneur, capitalist, and land-owner – exactly what his contribution was worth' (MacPherson, 1972, p. 23), so pluralistic advocacy offers the similar promise of equity of treatment, but takes no account of:

the problem of market perfection: even if you get your economic equilibrium it may not be at anywhere near full employment. The political variant of this would be equilibrium at something far less than an acceptable level of participation, or satisfaction, or even 'public interest'. (Lowi, 1969, p. 51)

Furthermore, even where this problem is understood by disadvantaged but willing participants, the extent to which their best interests are served by engaging in planning exercises rather than formal political organization is unclear, as Fox–Piven (1970) has observed from studying the effectiveness of this sort of planning.

Adjunctive planning: towards planning brokerage

Adjunctive planning is the last variant of marginalist planning theory to be considered here. Its originator, Dennis Rondinelli (1971) argues in mainstream pluralist fashion that rational-comprehensiveness is inadequate because first, it pretends to exclude politics from the planning process, and second, it is a normative rather than a descriptive theory. In contrast, it is argued, planning policy emerges from a pluralistic and fragmentary process of political interaction. Though Rondinelli's experiences are American, a report of the policy-making process in British structure planning (Drake *et al.*, 1975) reveals a rather similar set of problems to those pinpointed by Rondinelli. In both cases inter-organizational conflict is endemic; uncertainty leads to incremental policy steps; problem-identification tends to oust goal-orientation; and low environmental control associated with participatory demands result in continuous policy adjustment. In both cases the authors recommend that planning should trim to meet these constraints – in Britain by following a pluralistic 'mixed-scanning' (Etzioni, 1968) strategy; in America, by adopting a low-key, supportive function. There, however, the similarity stops, since in the British case mixed-scanning is merely advocated as a methodological improvement to strengthen the existing institutional functions of urban and rural development planning, whereas Rondinelli is advocating a different kind of institutional role for planning. Here, clearly, the divergent institutional contexts of the two countries, reflecting distinctive philosophies of government, impose constraints upon the nature of theoretical solutions to similar problems.

But because of these linkage and dependency problems in a context of multifold pressure from interest groups, planning, according to Rondinelli, necessarily conforms with the pattern of power-diffusion by adopting the role of another pressure point. It becomes an adjunct to the market process with the specific function of mobilizing disparate interests and lubricating the process of mutual adjustment between them as an honest broker. This co-ordinative role facilitates the achievement of marginal change towards desired strategic policy-outcomes because information and analysis are exchanged for support from different interests. The planning function thus becomes a research and intelligence resource mediating in the key interrelationship between private and public sectors. In real terms it consti-tutes a more effective function than the idealistic rational-comprehensive form of planning could fulfil. As an intermediary a planning authority can, lists Rondinelli: initiate policy innovations; mediate policy conflicts; com-municate information, and facilitate interaction among private and public organizations.

The analysis which leads to the development of a concept of planning as adjunctive contains some interesting and useful points. It is clear that deference to authority has declined sufficiently for policy-making to be a markedly more complex problem now than hitherto (King, 1975) and, as the American experience of this kind of policy arena is longer than the British, so Rondinelli's separation of the principal sources of difficulty is helpful in that it tends to confirm those which have been identified in the British context. But the flaws emerge in the interpretation of the nature of the problems, and prescribed means towards their solution which follow; three may be identified.

The process of policy formulation is presented as being performed in an environment made complex by the different appreciative systems of groups and individuals whose interests are brought into play by the policy initiative. But this policy arena is equally conceived as one in which interests are reconcilable given a willingness on the part of contributors to the process to be shown the advantages which can accrue from co-operation. However, the bulk of this burden falls, in Rondinelli's scheme, upon the analytical and informational capabilities of the honest brokerage of the planning authority. Now clearly to the extent that the desired expertise is possessed and deployed by the planning authority to a qualitative level which gives this facility the status of a desirable resource, the sort of system envisaged is likely to be effective. The mediative information function is obviously a crucial element, taken on by private agencies or sectors of private firms, in the maintenance of market relations in free enterprise economies, and the addition of a facility for supplementing market intelligence with that con-cerning market-effects, and public sector policy proposals in response to those effects, is an extra bonus. However, a number of questions must be posed of such a scheme which in themselves cast doubt upon its likely practical effectiveness. First there is the question of basic *recalcitrance* on the part of single or multiple groups in the face of information and analysis which they conceive as prejudicial to their interests. Information is not value-free and it can be refuted by counter-information composed within different frameworks of assumptions, as frequently occurs around issues such as the effects of smoking on health, the safety of nuclear power-generation or the benefits of comprehensive education. Second, and to some extent the reverse of the previous point, were a planning authority to devote its main attention to research and intelligence functions, that role in itself would confer a degree of *influence* upon planning derived from the observed association between possession of information and acquisition of authority (Pettigrew, 1972). Given Rondinelli's assumption that planning policies should still to some extent be formulated so as to gain support from the plurality of interest groups, this influence would place planning in a privileged position *vis-à-vis* those interests, thus compromising the mediative function foreseen for the planning authority. Finally, and importantly, the preceding discussion has assumed a high *standard* of research output from a planning authority. But this is, to say the least, a questionable assumption given the scepticism frequently found in the literature addressed to the question of policy research (Coleman, 1972; Etzioni, 1971). The problems tackled, the pressures (especially in terms of time and finance), and the political sensitivity of findings all contribute in making policy research very much more difficult than academic research, and high standards the less likely.

At a more general level, however, it is clear that, developing from some of the difficulties associated with a strong emphasis upon research and intelligence, there is a more thoroughgoing paradox in Rondinelli's scheme raised, ironically, as an element of pluralist critique of corporate planning (Wildavsky, 1973). It centres upon the question of *co-ordination* which, it will be remembered, was seen as a fundamental aspect of adjunctive planning, in which disparate interests are meant to be reconciled. Wildavsky notes four contradictory implications which can legitimately be associated with the concept: it stands for efficiency, but its measure is goal-achievement and this is prejudiced by pluralism; it also implies reliability but true reliability is inefficient since contingency resources must be set aside; co-ordination requires coercion because without it decisions need unanimity, implying the privilege of ultimate authority residing with the co-ordinating agency; and if coercion is passed over then consent must be sought, itself implying compromise and, possibly, lower efficiency in turn. Co-ordination, therefore, to be efficient and effective can be held to require powers above those proposed for adjunctive planning.

Lastly, adjunctive planning simply ignores what has become a large collection of activities which are performed by governments because they cannot be fulfilled by the private sector in market economies. Though there are political controversies regarding the fringe of public sector activity, especially where this overlaps the productive aspects of private sector activity, most advanced industrial societies have a large framework of substantive responsibilities because, for a variety of reasons, the private market economy cannot or will not seek to make them subject to the criteria of profitability. In the planning of cities and regions this function is controversial in some areas, such as control and reallocation of profits from land dealing but largely not so, especially in areas such as infrastructural investment, disbursements to industry in industrial blackspots or the protection of valued environments. While it makes sense for planning authorities to consult and, where appropriate, be guided by interests legitimately concerned about the effects of policy it is unrealistic and contradictory to assign planning authorities to primarily mediative roles in areas where, were it not for public intervention, there would be little to mediate. Moreover, Rondinelli's prescription seems to confuse mediation and initiation in a contradictory way. The function of mediation is to transmit; it is essentially a responsive role, yet through mediation it is expected that planning authorities will have the capacity to initiate policy innovations in the adjunctive mode. Quite how these two functions will link is never made clear in Rondinelli's scheme. Rather as with the glossing of the issues raised by his faith in co-ordination, one is left wondering about the extent to which the implications of a pluralist and marginalist analysis of planning have been thought through in practice.

Conclusions

It has been shown that the aspirations for planning theory to become more scientific by becoming more positivistic and thus objective, impartial, neutral and so on, are partly undermined by the model of applied social scientific objectivity upon which that aspiration is based. Marginalism, as an example, proves to be apologetic for a particular, historically specific, set of social arrangements. This point is considered worthy of being spelt out because planning is principally a practice-dominated discipline which uses theory generated elsewhere somewhat indiscriminately for purposes of problem identification, analysis and solution. For this reason planning theory has traditionally been composed in a rather dangerous context of uncritical eclecticism. The main effect of this, it can be argued, is further to devalue the contribution which theory can make to the successful pursuit of planning, by causing practitioners to become disillusioned with theories before they have been adequately scrutinized prior to reinterpretation into a planning framework.

In order to attempt to clarify the underlying nature of some distinctive theoretical modes which have been developed in planning it has been found useful to identify a range of assumptions common in social science theory, which themselves help form the foundations of two philosophies of planning. On the one hand there is what can be referred to as the *unitary* framework, displaying clear tendencies towards: institutionalism; systems; determinism; centralism; and socialization when assessed against a range of scale, level, emphasis and control criteria. On the other hand, measured against the same criteria, an *atomistic* framework can be adduced. The characteristic conditions of this framework are: individualism; behaviouralism; voluntarism; decentralism; and naturalism.

Both of these frameworks are represented as theoretical markers in the literature of planning theory, but for practical purposes the unitary mode has dominated most planning practice in one or other of its forms, especially in Britain. Rationalist planning modes which overtly and consciously adhere to formalized intellectual constructs of the logic of human reasoning have been advanced by theorists of planning, and cognate fields, and adopted on a significant scale as management and planning systems in local and central government. In either their early, relatively crude forms or the more refined recent forms, these unitary planning modes have proved disappointing in their implementation precisely because of their emphasis upon formal structures and their neglect of substantive issues intrinsic to the processes of planning and public policy-making generally. Central to the understanding of these substantive issues would seem to be some theory of the relationship between organizations conceived in terms of strategic relations between levels of power. It seems likely that policies emerge from struggles, especially over key resources, notably finance, manpower and authority. Above all, the constraints of the material world upon these processes would need to be given greater prominence than tends to be the case with the rather idealistic unitary modes of planning.

While it can be argued that the intellectual origins of unitary planning lie with the Keynesian critique of neo-classical economic theory, atomistic planning theory owes its inspiration to the object of that critique, particularly its utilitarian marginalist philosophy. Just as there is a decline of faith in Keynesian economic prescriptions and the exploration of hitherto rejected economic theories, especially 'monetarism' which has affinities with marginalism, so the failures of rational-comprehensive or corporate planning allied to a financial environment of tight budgetary control may lead to closer examination of ideas which have yet to be tried seriously as planning modes. One source of alternative theories that profess to be both empirical and prescriptive regarding the planning and policy-making processes falls squarely within the atomistic framework; some aspects of them take their substance from monetarist ideas.

Despite the occasional helpful insights into the problems entailed by the adoption of the decision to plan, these theories, which are all to a considerable extent formed in the mould of marginalist economic theory and its political correlate, pluralism, suffer from the same basic weaknesses. They seem to be more scientific in the sense of being more positivistic, concerned to demonstrate the nature of empirical reality, and thus to form a sounder base from which normative propositions may be developed. But they are in fact apologetic for a particular set of socio-economic arrangements which favour individualistic utility-maximization while ignoring both the issue of distribution and the question of the extent to which pure efficiency criteria comprehend the definition of rational behaviour. Even then, the claim that individualistic judgements of utility determine the structure of market prices is eroded in the tautological method by which preferences are measured, that is in terms of preparedness to pay the market price. More practically, marginalist predictions about the nature of public expenditure profiles are so bolstered by exaggerated definitions of marginality as to be virtually irrefutable. This means that changes which it may have seemed reasonable to designate 'incremental' during the period when Keynesianism ensured marginal annual increases to the public sector budget can continue so to be designated even when budget profiles are markedly more volatile.

Then, each of the theories considered assumes that market-type relations and institutions are optimal for all individual and organizational goal-achievement. Markets distribute fairly in proportion to the marginal productivity of contributions, and the application of market methods to the public sector will similarly produce greater efficiency and fairness by rewarding those whose efforts to influence outcomes are, directly and indirectly, the greatest. What is lost in the zeal with which the deliberate fragmentation and reduction of the public sector is sought, is the recognition that state intervention exists, on the one hand, to ameliorate the effects of market failure upon the workforce and its dependents, while on the other, and increasingly, to help maintain the extensive weaker parts of the private sector.[8] That is, precisely because of the socially unacceptable characteristics of market organization, socialized, centralized though relatively market-responsive economic management, physical and social planning were introduced. The inherent viciousness of the business cycle makes it improbable that the state can ever be displaced from a substantial unitary presence in the management and planning of social and economic affairs in the advanced industrial societies. This does not, however, mean that the state must necessarily exercise these functions according to the older forms of institutionalized determinism associated with traditional authoritarian bureaucratic rules, or the newer, subtler forms of institutionalized determinism associated with the extension of systems control through community manipulation under corporatism.

Finally, the marginalist theories of planning divert attention away from the analysis of processes and problems occurring in the institutional structures which we have inherited. By offering as a panacea the return to some factually unhistoric system predating the entanglement of the state in private affairs, or advocating that small is beautiful, democratic and efficient while bureaucracy is inescapably monolithic, inefficient and arbitrarily rigid, marginalists are ascribing to ordinary exchange relations a harmonious and co-operative gloss which is difficult to sustain given what we know about the exploitative nature of social relations in the early industrial period. And, second, they are simultaneously offering a restricted and abstract view of the nature of individual motivations. In this, all actions are the product of rational calculations of economic efficiency, and those which are not are either trivial or incomprehensible and therefore not to be treated seriously as policy considerations. Much more positive and realistic from the viewpoints of both planning practice and the scholarly analysis of planning would be attempts to formalize some of the aspects of policy-making behaviour which *are* captured in the marginalist analyses. These include the varying extents of responsiveness, accountability, quality of information, influence, discretion, types of resources, bargaining capacity, and policy networks characteristic of unitary planning organizations. Finally, in times of economic stringency questions of policy-value per unit of expenditure have arisen which are of great importance to the future of the public sector. For, the centralist model with which planning is associated in capitalist and socialist societies, has been less attractive economically and politically than its supporters wish. The key question, of course, is why this should be, and what might be done to rectify matters. These issues are broached more fully in the final chapter.

4 Planning and consensus: a review of the critics

Introduction: scientific management and rationality in planning

Planning theory has, as may be seen, been heavily influenced by theoretical developments in other academic disciplines, notably economics, politics and sociology. The reason for pointing to this is not to suggest that this is in some way undesirable, for it is normal that ideas developed in one sphere of activity should migrate to other areas (Mulkay, 1979). Rather, it is important to recognize the common theoretical origins which often underlie what can appear to be opposed frameworks and to understand the nature of the interests served by their appearance upon the scene. The planning theory which first began to be widely discussed in planning education in the 1960s was almost exclusively American in origin. Although it contained many different facets which, as in the case of the disagreements between rational-comprehensive planning theorists and incrementalists or the later rejection of the former by adherents of advocacy planning it shared certain key assumptions (Simon, 1955; Lindblom, 1973; Meyerson and Banfield, 1955; Davidoff, 1973).

The three principal assumptions were, firstly, that whatever form planning took it should strive to be rational in the sense that clear objectives should be identified and then achieved, either by large steps (comprehensive plans), small steps (incrementalism) or popular will (advocacy). Secondly, it was accepted that planning should seek social goals by assisting market processes to function more smoothly. Thirdly, it was accepted, even by the most centralist of comprehensive planners, that plans should primarily provide opportunities which individuals and organizations could exploit without transgressing basic principles of a capitalist society. These assumptions, to a large extent, map out the limits of the underlying consensus about the relationship between planning and capitalist society. Of course, to speak in terms of 'capitalist society' is both correct and yet diverting because while it is scarcely a distortion to refer to the USA as a capitalist society, it is scarcely archetypal. More importantly its institutions are different in important ways from those of most European countries including Britain. In particular it has been a society with a considerable fascination for European socialists, as Gramsci (1971) makes clear in his discussion of 'Americanism and Fordism'. Thus 'Americanism' was seen as holding out a concrete example to the old European societies, with their accretions of parasitic *rentier* classes, of the form which post-revolutionary society might take. Of especial interest were the productive techniques pioneered through the theories of Frederick Taylor's 'scientific management' and Henry Ford's applications on the assembly-line at Highland Park, and even the apparently democratic nature of American enterprise.[1]

These changes in the relations of production marked the first stage in a new phase of the development of industrialism which was perceived as the beginning of capitalist planning. Gramsci saw this particularly clearly:

In generic terms one could say that Americanism and Fordism derive from an inherent necessity to achieve the organization of a planned economy, and the various problems examined here should be the links of the chain marking the passage from the old economic individualism to the planned economy. (Gramsci, 1971, p. 279)

As he saw it, there was no opposition in principle from either the interests of labour or capital to Fordism, rather the increased productivity ensuing meant greater returns to both. Where opposition would be at its severest would be in the sphere of social reproduction, for the new social relations at the point of production required the enforcement, through authoritarian cultural repression, of new forms of social life. Thus, associated with the gearing up of the mode of production was an extension of factory rules into the personal lives of workers through the agency of the Ford Sociological Department. For instance, in 1914 a wages deal of revolutionary impact was implemented which doubled the going rate in the vehicle industry. It became known as the Five Dollar Day. It was the function of the Sociological Department to assess the appropriateness of particular workers for admission to the Five Dollar Day. This was fulfilled by a probationary system in which participants were required to meet certain social criteria according to a programme:

The paternalism of the Sociological Department's programme was deeply influenced by Henry Ford's assumptions about both the 'common man' and 'the good life'. Ford neither smoke nor drank. He believed in the value of the open air and long walks. Hard work and cleanliness. It had been good for him so it was good for everybody. 'Nobody smokes in the Ford industries.' (Beynon, 1975, p. 25)

At a higher level, that of the state, this kind of ethic was unsuccessfully being promulgated, most notoriously through Prohibition which placed alcohol in the luxury category beyond the reach of the Five Dollar workers, but also the numerous controls upon sexual morality under a more wide-ranging ideology of puritanism, associated with the Wilson–Coolidge era. What the state was being pressured to do during the period when Fordism was becoming deeply rooted, was to ameliorate its most extreme effects while, nevertheless, creating the basic conditions in which the new productive technologies could prosper. And this complex process involved both ideological manipulations to replace the baser precepts of *laissez-faire* by the ideal of an orderly social system where benefits were shared, and a reformed business ethic in which co-operation between labour and capital replaced the conflicts between classes.

Hence, it is the transmission of the ideological consensus formed in the 'Progressive Era' from 1900 to 1918 into the community by means of the planning of new environments in the inter-war years, that Herbert Gans has in mind when he speaks of the manner in which:

The ends underlying the planners' physical approach reflected their Protestant middle-class view of city life. As a result the master plan tried to eliminate as 'blighting influences' many of the facilities, land uses, and institutions of working-class, lower-class, and ethnic groups. (Gans, 1972, p. 76)

Here is one pole of the consensual planning theory which survived from before the New Deal through to the next stage in the restructuring of American capitalism with the beginnings of the next, primarily electronically based, phase of industrial development in the 1950s and early 1960s (Mandel, 1975). And, of course, for somewhat different reasons it was the bedrock of British city and regional planning during the same period. However, before reconsidering the bases of the British consensus from a materialist rather than a functionalist[2] (Foley, 1973) viewpoint we must complete the delineation of the influential American theoretical consensus.

The post-war succession to the Taylorist–Fordist tradition of rationalizing human actions to maximize human efficiency was secured by the management theories of Herbert Simon.[3] His 'models of man' provided a link with 'scientific management' from factory floor to office desk. They generalized the requirement for 'explicit stable roles which make for a high degree of predictability and co-ordination in organizational behaviour' (Silverman, 1970, p. 12) to all organizations. The similarity of approach between March and Simon's (1958) explanation of organizational attachment on the part of workers and Taylor's (1913) analysis is moderated by the latter's stress upon economic motives and the former's emphasis upon social as well as economic considerations. Moreover, where Taylorism is non-empirical, that is it is wholly devoted to the reproduction in the worker of an ideal, mechanical form of rationality, and is thus intensely normative, the work of Simon seeks to humanize the norms by respecting human constraints as these are to be observed behaviourally. But none the less, Simon's expressed aim is to conceptualize rational choice to reflect 'the actual properties of human beings, and at the same time retain some of the formal clarity of the economic (that is rational) model' (Simon quoted in Mouzelis, 1975, p. 122). Hence, we can see the basis of a theoretical concern with problems, decisions, and decision makers in planning. Their task is to identify ends and the means of achieving them in the face of limitations on expertise, resources and, ultimately power, to decide.

This pole of the consensus is always in partial tension with another which questions the scope of the ends which this mode of decision analysis opens up. In epistemological terms it is equally individualistic, behaviourist and voluntarist but stems from the political rather than the administrative side of the policy sciences. It is therefore more prone to stress the uncertainty with which decisions are made, the capriciousness of policy-making, the retractability of policies, and above all, the constraints placed by what is possible upon what is desirable. Underpinning this uncertainty are the political and institutional structures of American society. Each individual expects to share in the various benefits of a liberal society, and, in exchange, contributes to its social orderliness. The political philosophy is that of *pluralism* and the policy method is that of *incrementalism*, or more radically, *advocacy planning* (Dahl and Lindblom, 1953; Wildavsky, 1964; Davidoff, 1973). Above all, it echoes the individualistic and democratic principles which are central to the American constitution. These were even thought, notably by Gramsci, *inter alia*, likely to be reproduced in the giant joint-stock enterprises which Fordism spawned. Rationality tempered with democratic participation was thus the essence of the planning theory developed in America to square the circle of free enterprise and the planned economy. And the puritanical ideal could be shown to be furthered by the imposition of this method upon corrupt, Tammany Hall practices such as those found by Meyerson and Banfield in Mayor Daly's Chicago. Finally, with the promotion of these ideas to the level of a process of societal guidance for the achievement of consensual goals (Friedmann, 1969), planning was established as a dynamic instrument for legitimizing change, easing transitions, and lowering obstacles, *in the abstract as a totally formal exercise*. The medium had become the message, and the message was that planning embodied reason, a virtue to which all classes, political parties and interests could subscribe. As well as being the product of a broad consensus it was a means of reproducing it. Thus, in Britain with the onset in 1958 of an unanticipated recession even the Conservative party could espouse it[4] as could the technically inclined Labour government shortly to follow (Jessop, 1980).

Planning had thus become a respected element of the process by which capitalist development could be secured. The influence of a Keynesian economic theory had brought the idea of a managed capitalism into acceptance in even the most liberal of economies. The relatively trouble-free passage in the USA from wartime production to a peacetime economic regime showed that limited planning of economic and physical development was not inconsistent with the ultimate hegemony of the market. Also, it could help in securing a level of consensus between classes, provided that economic growth continued to prevail, through the apparent redistributive effects of higher quality social services provision and housing redevelopment for the worst-off.

However, although similar discoveries had been made even earlier in Britain, the means of their implementation was not informed, initially at least, by the more rigorous theoretical planning knowledge which had been adapted from the experiences of planned production within the firm under 'scientific management'. Planning in Britain had a more ideological ring to it initially, due to its close association with the socialism and centralism of the new welfare state and nationalized industry ministries. The early post-war blueprints typical of the local authority development plans of the time are also examples of this approach to planning. And it was criticism of these, and in particular of their rigid and authoritarian characteristics, which helped to herald what appeared to be the more rational and democratic American planning methods which had been shown not to be inconsistent with the objective of sustaining economic growth under market capitalism.

Undermining the consensus in British planning

Initial reservations about the nature of British planning principles were expressed mainly in terms of substantive criticisms of, for example, the concepts of community or of social balance that they seemed to contain. Hence, the main criticism was aimed at what was thought to be an over-rigid adherence to the organic analogy in the planning of New Towns. This type of criticism was picked up subsequently from time to time, mainly by urban sociologists. For example, Ruth Glass identified what she considered to be a tendency for 'anti-urbanism' in much planning thought, a feature which it would perhaps have been more surprising *not* to find given the permanent tension between the country and the city in capitalist society (Glass, 1968; White and White, 1964; Williams, 1973). This derived, it was argued, from the 'utopian' origins of planning which were closely associated with Victorian reforming ideals which affirmed the salubriousness of rural community life. Later, Ray Pahl mildly reiterated the criticism of functionalist planning in offering an explanation for the widely publicized alienation effects suffered by New Town immigrants. In contrast to the rigidly-defined functional separation of social activities and social space in ways which left little room for personal expressions of individuality, Pahl argued for a more liberal provision of undefined spaces where expressions of individuality might find an outlet (Pahl, 1968).

However, none of this criticism directly questioned the nature of the class-interests served by planning, preferring rather to point out the illiberalism of centralist planning in theoretically indistinct ways.

Planners had become a legitimate target for sociological inquiry but were given no real inkling, despite promises from Glass (1973), as to the problems with their underlying theory. It is probably not stretching the point to suggest that the vague unease which urban sociological critics induced in planners helped usher in the American rationalism which promised both greater social scientific rigour in analysis, as well as elements of public participation and even limited neighbourhood control in practice.

It was in the early 1970s, as the first fruits of the legislative liberalizations of 1968, notably the Skeffington Report and the 1968 Town and Country Planning Act, were being borne that the more thoroughgoing critiques of planning theory began to emerge. Each, for different reasons it will be argued, missed its target when considered in hindsight but each at the time came as a refreshingly *theoretical* counterblast to prevailing dogmas. Two of these critiques sought to expose a *functionalist* bias which had long been embedded in planning thought; a third, the solider, critique questioned the liberal-democratic consensus within which planning had been formed, and sought to develop an alternative Marxist theory of space and planning. The first pair, J. Simmie's *Citizens in Conflict* (1974) and J. Bailey's *Social Theory for Planning* (1973) will be considered initially, then D. Harvey's *Social Justice and the City* (1973) will be discussed separately.

Simmie, Bailey and sociological conflict theory

These two critiques may be taken together as, in terms of the particular subject matter of this chapter, namely the question of functionalism in planning theory, they largely coincide even though in other respects the books are different. In the matter of criticism at least four characteristics unite their content.

Functionalism

First, the critiques are marked by a somewhat cavalier lack of differentiation among at least four separate theoretical categories: functionalism; structural-functionalism; systems theory; and the consensus or co-operative view of society. Now while it may be argued that these share certain fundamental propositions, it is a wholly different matter to equate or, as Bailey does, conflate them. Functionalism is probably best defined as an over-arching epistemological position in which teleological as distinct from causal explanatory forms are stressed. Within the various social scientific disciplines this form of explanation has enjoyed some popularity, most notably in sociology. Thus for example the work of Merton (1968) might more appropriately be termed functionalist due to its focus on the middle-range theoretical interdependence of single institutional areas.[5] We would distinguish this from a structural-functionalist approach as follows. The latter has the professed aim of producing a theoretical account of a total social system, itself represented as a structured whole, each of whose institutional parts is integrated to the others to meet the functional needs of survival and evolution for the system as a whole. Central to the methodology of explanation in this project is a functionalist teleology employed both to account for system and sub-system integration and for linking individual motivations to system requirements.

Moving to an even more abstracted level, we come to the analysis of the nature of systems themselves, as distinct from the content which may be circumscribed with the label 'system', as in social system, economic system, organizational system etc. Here in systems theory, a crucial assumption, namely that 'systemness' is a characteristic of all known interrelationships, leads to the study of the processes by which these interrelationships are constituted, irrespective of content and context. Given the universal language of mathematics to perform the relevant analysis of process, it becomes a matter of relative indifference as to the nature of the particular kind of system characteristics under inspection for:

Whether one is dealing with a machine, an organism or an organization, it is fruitful to use the idea of a supply of resources ("input"), a conversion process ("through-put"), and the production of an object or objects ("output"). (Silverman, 1970, p. 27)

Finally, the consensus and/or co-operative view of society which tends, especially in criticism, to be associated with all of the foregoing, can by no means be reduced to any one of them. For example, it is not entirely the case that 'one of the unexpressed assumptions behind the systems and function-alist models of society is that society is fundamentally consensual' (Bailey, 1973, p. 73) as the work of Lewis Coser (1965) testifies. Hence, although it may be argued that Coser is a 'false' conflict theorist because he argues conflict is functional for social order, it can hardly be insisted that he takes an implicit view that society is fundamentally *consensual*. Even the more abstracted structural-functional theory takes as its point of departure the task of explaining why the 'Hobbesian war of all against all' is transcended so that society is made possible and is enabled to persist. It has often seemed strange that some sociologists have criticized this kind of work more for what it did not set out to achieve, that is to explain social conflict, than for what it did, that is to explain social order.

Of far greater importance as points of criticism of structural-functional-ism, in particular, are its overemphasis on values, its failure to consider the historical sources of ideas and institutions, and its neglect of the importance of the analysis of power for purposes of explanation. We will return to these issues below; suffice it to say for the moment that concerning the dominance of a consensus/co-operative view of capitalist society it can be understood as existing for fundamentally material reasons. These arose because of the dangers to the continuation of a capitalist order posed by class conflict in the USA and Britain in the first quarter of the twentieth century. Conflict was resolved by class settlements[6] in both countries, and these were fully sub-scribed to by most social scientists in the post-war years. As urban and regional planning was one of the institutional outcomes of those settlements, informed by Keynesianism and Beveridgism, on the one hand, and an emergent technicism, on the other, it is perhaps unsurprising that the conflict perspective remained unconceptualized for so long.

Organicism

The second feature common to the sociological critiques of planning thought is fairly closely related to the first. The main differences are that it is both sharper and more accurate, but also that it is more centrally an observably *sociological* insertion into the planner's technical apparatus. We refer to *organicism*.

The crisis of rapid industrialism provoked an ideological split within the nineteenth-century bourgeoisie. Those who advocated the expansion of the scientific and rational modes of discourse which had induced large-scale industrialism represented one faction, while those who sought to undermine the hegemony of scientific-technical rationality and stress the advantages, primarily those of humanistic harmony, associated with nature and community, formed the other (Stedman Jones, 1977). The second faction is the one in which organicism, in the sense of the belief in the possibility of a compromise between the advantages of capitalist and pre-capitalist forms of life, finds its intellectual home. Since, overwhelmingly, town planning has traditionally been a central vehicle through which the reform of dehumanizing industrialism has been sought, then, once again it ought not to surprise us that the organic community has featured strongly in the ideals of its leading visionaries.[7]

What is remarkable, however, is the particular strength of criticism which this ideal gives rise to on the part of the sociological critics, given that their discipline is largely responsible for its absorption into planning (a point normally overlooked).[8] However, the burden which organicism, and planners' espousal of it, is forced to bear, seems out of all proportion to the reality of planners' control upon the development process. What surprises here is the power assigned to consensual norms, albeit professional, which carry all before them, including trade cycles, agricultural depressions and industrial migrations (of both plant and labour). Thus Simmie (1974) indicts the organic analogy in British town planning for, promoting *inter alia*: static town plans; the flourishing of paternalism; the garden city movement; the green belt and the green wedge; city park systems; nature reserves; national parks; recreation areas; limited town size; the satellite city idea; regionalism; the spread of the garden suburb; low density housing developments; urban sprawl, and the anti-urban animus of British town planning.

Hence a substantial part of what comprises the contribution of planning to the use of space in Britain is being subsumed under a single, intellectual concept. But, in direct terms, the entries in the above list scarcely relate to the definitions of organicism offered by Simmie, that is an attempt to explain the world or even the universe as a kind of organism (p. 7) . . . in which individuals and groups in a society are likened to the parts of a mechanical system or the organs of an organism whose specialization contributes to the functioning of the whole (p. 17); . . . (the) planners' traditional, feudal and organic view of society in which each member had his allocated, understood and accepted place (p. 21).

With the possible exception of 'paternalism' each of the remainder can be ascribed equally to a mixture of simple reformism and the effects of economic depression. With reference to these we can differentiate the reforms which gave greater access to recreation space to the *urban* poor, itself an intensely political process paradoxically tied in with the efforts of the Country Landowners Association and Council for the Preservation of Rural England to protect urban fringe estates from the ravages of the inter-war agricultural depression. While, simultaneously, as a result of the cheap land and labour deriving from that slump,[9] suburbia sprawled into the English countryside (Hall *et al.*, 1973). Finally, regionalism, garden cities, and satellite cities represent the practical, as distinct from philosophical response of the town planning movement to the anarchy of capitalist development. The unreflective pragmatism of this movement is typified by its leader, Abercrombie, who was both a leading light of the forces of reaction, having helped form the CPRE in 1925, and those of reform, through the Town and Country Planning Association. That some form of organic analogy may be traced through to these concrete forms of development and planning intervention is of far less importance than the identification of the historical processes which produced them. By stressing the value standpoint of planners to the relative neglect of the material forces which formed the constraints upon their action, this line of criticism itself tends to offer a functionalist analysis in order to make its case.

Idealism

This emphasis upon the level of ideas in seeking to explain the twentieth-century spatial restructuring of Britain is replicated in other ways in these critiques to a point, indeed, where one can say that they are generally characterized by their idealism. By idealism is meant the explanation of material processes as if ideas alone are principally responsible for social processes and actions.

  Hence, in discussing the application of systems theory to planning the rationale for this development is explained in terms of its ideological utility for planners. This includes its potential for mystifying the public due to the incomprehensibility of the associated language, its prestige value to the 'self-image' of planners *vis-à-vis* politicians or other experts, and the power it gives them to generate system goals, thus augmenting the status of planners even further (Bailey, 1973, pp. 68–71). Now, while careerism may have played some part in the *extension* of systems thinking once the relevant professionals had discovered these unanticipated by-products, it seems unlikely that these might be reasons for its adoption in the first place. Available research on professionals in organizations suggests they are normally confronted with severe bureaucratic inertia in the face of efforts to gain the adoption of innovatory initiatives. The case for change has to be argued with exhausting reference to efficiency and other economic criteria against interests which are particularly sensitive to the impact of such changes upon their own and other career-structures (Benson, 1973; Heydebrand, 1977).

We may be forgiven once more, therefore, for suspecting the critic of functionalism in planning of fabricating a consensus in order to point to its limitations. Moreover, even a cursory glance at the professional planning literature of the relevant period would demonstrate the far greater applicability of the sociological conflict theory which Bailey advocates as superior to functionalism in explaining the uneven adoption of the new technology. On the last point, the little evidence we have on take-up of innovations in planning authorities suggests that it was the metropolitan authorities with the greatest incidence of urban deprivation who were in the forefront in trying out the new systems techniques, and that this was done in what, retrospectively, was the naïve belief that anything was worth a try in aiding local planners' understanding of ways to overcome massive problems (Jefferson, 1973).

Much the same general criticism can be advanced in consideration of the alternative to the planners' co-operative view of social relations proposed by both Simmie and Bailey, that is, a conflict perspective. In the case of the former, at least a clear theoretical position is adopted throughout whereas Bailey (1973) openly states from the outset that his aim is to offer planners an education in social theory so that their dimly perceived constructs of social reality may be sharpened by exposure to new thinking about the social world. To this end the planner is offered perspectives ranging from interpretative sociology – symbolic interactionism, phenomenology and ethnomethodology – through the sociology of knowledge, to Weberian institutional theory, systems theory, structural-functionalism and historical materialism at the other extreme. In some ways this is to perform a useful function at the risk of giving little or no guidance to the reader on which is the best 'theory for planning' (p. vii) and conceivably increasing his or her level of confusion. But the lack of an explicit reference point is evidently at the heart of what is intended as a 'critical philosophy' to enable planners as *social controllers* to be more *reflexive* in their work. Clearly, it would be myopic to dissent from this as an ideal but we must also be clear that educating planners about 'man as a meaning-creating being, and society as a structure of rival power groups (p. 148) is one thing, but getting them much further than 'the description of alternative goals and utopias' (p. 149) is quite another. And the reason for this is that the conflicts which are held to characterize the system in which town planners operate are not adequately grounded in terms of the interests served and the limitations imposed upon action in such a system. Without such specifications even idealism simply degenerates into a hopeless relativism.

This problem, which is partially one of abstractionism, is also a feature of Simmie's (1974) critique of planning ideology. By abstractionism is meant a predisposition to focus study upon society in general rather than theorizing an historically specific form of society. The effect is to theorize an *idea* of what social relations are formed by, for example conflict, in preference to examining actual processes. Abstractionism is the corner-stone of idealism therefore. The key abstraction in Simmie's book, is that of 'modern industrial societies' (p. 57), a useful descriptive phrase that, however, does not allow of a distinction between capitalist and socialist societies. This immediately suggests that, despite discussing the concept of mode of production, Simmie does not intend this to be a basic analytical category in his subsequent discussion of the nature of conflict, classes and planners' ideologies. And this turns out to be indeed the case when, following a useful discussion of liberal critiques of Marxism, Simmie opts for one of these, namely John Rex's (1961) essentially Weberian theory of group conflict, that he proposes to employ in his institutional analysis of town planning.

In this theory conflicts are endemic because of plural values, aims and interests represented through classes, one of which becomes a ruling class which seeks to legitimate its rule, against opposition, ideologically. The most likely outcome of these conflicts is a balance of power reflecting compromise and reform as with the post-war settlement of the British welfare state. Now, there is much to commend this conceptualization to those who seek an *a posteriori* explanation of welfarism, but questions must be posed about the extent to which *ideological* factors should bear the burden of explanation, as Simmie seems to argue. Thus, in empirical terms it is well documented that representatives of leading segments of labour and large firms in the inter-war years were happy to submerge their *ideological* antagonisms to preserve capitalism in Britain, not because of any ideological rapprochement but because of the *material* effects of the General Strike, itself called over precisely material wage-cuts, initially to coal-miners prospectively to all industrial workers. The profound change of strategy among the Labour party, the TUC, and large corporations such as ICI, and hence the Conservative party, which produced among other things the strongly centralist welfare institutions and nationalized industries of post-war Britain, was certainly reflected ideologically, but was stimulated by real experiences (Jacques, 1976). To suggest otherwise, is, once again, to risk occupying precisely the functionalist ground that the conflict theorist is seeking to cut away.

The principal theoretical question therefore is the extent to which the kind of conflict theory proposed by Simmie, Rex and Weber advances our understanding of the relationship between planning and the wider structure of society beyond that which is being rejected. On the surface, the Weberian tradition with its focus upon rationality, bureaucracy, class, power relations, and the capitalist state seems a fruitful avenue for the institutional analysis of planning. Yet, as others, notably Pahl, who have employed its framework seem to have found, this promise is less than easily fulfilled. The reason lies in the ultimate *idealism* of the Weberian perspective. For central to its form of analysis is the concept of a process – rationalization - which is held to be an immanent tendency in human society, characteristic of both individual thought and institutional structures. In the most advanced societies rationality is most fully extended throughout their institutions in the form of bureaucratic organization, developed most fully in the administrative apparatus of the capitalist state. In social relations the influence of the state's administrative techniques results in a power structure in which an administrative rather than an economic (capitalist) class dominates. For, under the guise of extending rational principles of organization to the multiplicity of economic and social interests of capitalist society, it comes to serve its own interests. Or, it should be said, its bureaucratic elite becomes responsible only to itself, becoming the class *primus inter pares* with all other interests.

Unfortunately, the keystone to the argument is missing. That is, no explanation is provided of the essential inner organizing principle, that is rationalization. This is because, in the tradition of German idealism, Weber ultimately assumes it to be a theological rather than a scientific matter.[10] Because of this it is not clear why power should accrue to the bureaucratic elite; the argument becomes circular. Put another way, the class in power becomes powerful because its skills coincide with the structural requirements of the society; but why does the society have *those* as distinct from some other, structural requirements? This circularity foreshadows that present in structural functional theorization to a considerable extent although in other respects, notably the treatment of power and class, the analysis offered is superior.

Simmie's argument about the relationship of planning to the wider society is similarly constructed. Thus, planners belong to a profession whose principal function has been to further its own interests in the market-place. The planning profession is able to do this because of its monopoly over the technical skills which were seen to be necessary if successive social democratic governments were to improve the quality of life in cities and regions. In this process of re-ordering spatial structures there are two key factors with which the planning system must come to terms. These are politics on the one hand, and the market, on the other. With regard to the former, it is the planning profession in its formal sense as a representative institution that legitimizes planning solutions by its appeal to the deceptively neutral concept of *the public interest*. But the ensuing policies conceal real outcomes which reinforce the distributional patterns and hence the class structure of the *status quo ante*. Planning is thus a conservative force using democratic politics as an instrument to control the market allocation of resources to different classes of consumers.

Unfortunately absent from the account, however, is a satisfactory explanation of the reasons why the form taken by social democratic planning is one which emphasizes technical expertise and rationality so strongly. In the absence of a rationale for social democratic gullibility to the charms of city and regional planning the logic of the argument points to a Machiavellian planning profession in possession of privileged knowledge of the requirements and workings of modern society which it uses to further the interests of its members in a wholly partisan way. Without a questioning of the place of institutionalized reason in advanced industrial societies what results is a rather unlikely picture of important social forces being manipulated by what, without being unduly dismissive, remains a relatively insignificant professional interest group.

The relationship between planning and the market is, by contrast, rather more firmly grounded. As we have seen, the point at which planning intervenes in social relations is at the level of the distribution of the product. Hence, scarce and desired resources are allocated through market mechanisms and the resulting pattern of unevenness in income distribution is the basis of the class structure. Planning interventions help sustain this by various policies such as green belts, housing redevelopment and highway alignments which have income regressive effects. The main problem with this analysis derives from the Weberian idea that the market allocates resources in ways which create the resulting class structure of capitalist societies. This idea is shared by neo-classical economic accounts of income gradations found in market economies in which differential rewards accrue to individuals according to the sacrifices which they make in their market engagements. So an entrepreneur is morally justified in anticipating and receiving large rewards from market transactions because of the large amount of postponed satisfaction that is entailed in investing capital in productive enterprise, and the scarcity of the entrepreneurial skill which makes unsuccessful investment possible. The labourer is morally unjustified in expecting large rewards because he or she is only selling, say, physical strength or endurance, the rewards for which are mostly consumed immediately, and such skills are not normally in scarce supply. What is left out of presentations such as these are the historical preconditions which are necessary for markets to become the dominant form of exchange in societies. Clearly, in the absence of a widespread money economy they cannot become dominant as, indeed, they cannot where a majority of the population is able to live without substantial recourse to the purchase of market commodities, as occurs in peasant societies. The preconditions necessary for market relations to dominate must be secured, normally by means of threat or actual performance of violence, as occurred at the time of the enclosure movement or with the colonization of territory. This process of creating a dominated and dependent class whose members have to sell their labour power to an entrepreneur or starve because their means of subsistence have been removed is a key condition for the emergence of the kind of class structure found in market-dominated, or capitalist societies. Moreover, it is the various restrictions, placed through the position of dominance enjoyed by entrepreneurs over government policies, upon the capacity of the lower orders to modify these *production* relations that maintain the system.

In other words it is not adequate to present the formation of classes as being solely a matter of the distribution of resources in the market-place. It should not, however, be thought of as somehow wrong to speak of the influence of differential rewards in the market as having an effect upon the details of class composition. Clearly, it is possible for individuals to alter their class position[11] by means of engaging in an occupation which provides them with a better income than they previously enjoyed or than their parents received. However, such movements occur upon a terrain which is already fairly clearly mapped out beforehand, and the underlying structures are given by relations of production before they are elaborated by relations of distribution.

The relationship of city planning or regional policies to class structure is an interesting one which is by no means well understood. Certainly it would be inaccurate to present planning as intrinsically tending to work against the interests of the weakest in capitalist societies, though it should not thereby be assumed that the weakest necessarily benefit greatly from the attentions of city and regional planners. But the analysis which Simmie provides contains a strong element of determinism as a result of the particular version of bureaucratic elite theory which is employed. It makes the elite a self-seeking and self-serving one which benefits from the continuation of the unequal class structure in which it comes to exert a dominant influence. The implication of this is that planning systematically discriminates against poor people. However, this is to ignore the capacity of working people to organize themselves politically into parties which represent the interests of the worst-off. Periodically, these become the government of the day which, in turn may implement policies, including urban and regional ones, which improve the material conditions of the lowest classes, albeit not enormously. This analytical weakness is a result of Simmie's adoption of an elite theory which unnecessarily boxes-in the treatment of planning, politics and class.

Functionalist planning

It is noticeable that although both Bailey's and Simmie's critiques aim to expose functionalism in planning, clear and convincing evidence in support of their case does not appear strongly in their accounts. Bailey gives a historical account of functionalism, exemplifying its weaknesses with reference to its failure to yield a satisfactory theory of social stratification, before moving on to describe systems theory and *its* application to planning, as though the two were the same. However, as we have argued earlier, this is to neglect important distinctions between these sets of ideas, as well as to neglect the actual history of the emergence of systems concepts in British planning thought – as distinct, importantly in this instance, from American thought. For, in the work of the early proponents of systems ideas in British planning J. B. McLoughlin and G. Chadwick, the stimulus for the development of systems perspectives in planning owes more to the examples offered by transportation engineering, ecological studies, and operations research than sociological theory of any kind. This is stated with one qualification regarding a school of theorists who clearly did, tangentially, supply a sociological stimulus, which, for convenience, we will refer to as the Berkeley school of planning theorists. Their work features in both McLoughlin and Chadwick's systems views of planning, and will be considered more fully in the next chapter.

Simmie's approach tends to follow Bailey's line though more carefully in that he picks out more important distinctions between structural functionalism, social ecology, and systems analysis, but nevertheless tends to run them together in developing a chronology of functionalism in planning. Thus in a section entitled 'The application of structural-functionalism in town planning' (p. 20) the whole is given over not to a consideration of the influence of Parsonian sociological theory upon planning thought but to an exposition and critique of the organic analogy in planning thought. This is followed by a discussion of ecological theories of the city, which seems only tangentially relevant to a consideration of what theories actually motivated planning action. For, as Gans (1972) noted, planners' policies were more disposed towards breaking up the various zones which were claimed, it now seems rather dubiously, to have been identified by the Chicago school. Moreover, in Britain, the inherited class structure, patterns of land ownership and the relative success of those interests representing labour in pressing for state housing provision had produced a social and spatial structure which bore little similarity to the sectoral/zonal, ecological patterns hypothesized for American cities anyway.

Although it is argued by Simmie that planners have been concerned to promote social segregation or at least to have done very little to prevent it, the evidence suggests that they would have been relatively powerless to induce change either way. This is because of the enormous land-assembly problems which the existence of private land-ownership entails. Even with the existence of compulsory purchase rights, the decisive power of large private landlords, in particular, makes substantial restructuring of residential space a hugely expensive undertaking. This was a particular problem in the early years of state intervention in housing provision, where the defensive strength of the landed lobby forced the state to pursue similarly large-scale land-purchasing policies to get housing programmes underway, with the result that large single-class estates have been the norm (Hall *et al.*, 1973). Ecological considerations seem, then, to have been distant from the thoughts of planners seeking to meet the land assembly requirements associated with successive government house building commitments as is only too clear from the destructive effects which redevelopment has had upon working class communities in the post-war years (Lambert *et al.*, 1978).

In conclusion, therefore, the evidence that planning thought and action have been consciously, or even unwittingly informed by structural functionalism does not really appear. The tendency to ascribe largely non-existent ideas to the motivated actions of planners has a blinding effect upon both critics. It results in important material constraints being largely ignored in the effort to establish the basic argument. This is not to deprecate the intention but rather the execution. For if there were a case to be answered to the effect that planning, far from bringing about changes in the quality of life of poorly-housed, unemployed or otherwise disadvantaged citizens, had cemented the conditions of disadvantage more securely, it should be clearly enunciated. Furthermore if it were demonstrable that this flowed from the uncritical adoption of a planning theory which counteracted established objectives of planned intervention in the development process, then important questions could be posed about the purpose, nature and limitations of this contradiction. The interests served by maintaining a form of planning which appeared to meet the demands of disadvantaged neighbourhoods and regions while simultaneously reproducing the conditions which gave rise to the demands initially, could be studied, and the untenability of the position could be shown. But as it is, the sociology of planning has not achieved this because the analysis has remained at the level of ideas. The danger inherent in the kind of analysis adopted is that the functionalist methods which are the object of criticism are themselves reproduced in the process of demonstrating the homogeneity of planners' beliefs and the ease with which these are transformed into spatial structures. It is possible to show in precise ways how structural functional theory came to inform planning thought and, more importantly, planning action without an undue stress upon the consensual norms of planners. It can also be shown that this influence has not been wholly bad either in intention or effect, and this is done in the next chapter.

Harvey and the critique of liberal pragmatism

Before undertaking that task, however, it is necessary to assess the contribution of Harvey's (1973) major critique of mainstream geographic and planning theory. This moves us on a stage because it offers criticism from, on the one hand, a liberal democratic or managed capitalist viewpoint and, on the other, an historical materialist perspective. It is the former critique rather than the latter which will concern us in this chapter. The managed capitalist critique is developed under the general heading of 'Liberal formulations', that is varieties of analysis and prescription about spatial differentiation and planning intervention which, nevertheless, do not question the broad framework of the market economy. Thus basic conditions such as private property rights, freedom of contract, mobility and association, and democratic representation via the ballot box form the parameters of both the problems of, and the solutions to, the contemporary city.

Fragmentation in social science

The most telling part of Harvey's critique is his attack upon the abstractions of neo-classical *marginalist* land-use theory. Here, the dependence upon the unrealistic concept of utility as a basis for explaining location preferences, by authors such as Alonso (1964) and Muth (1962), is exposed as a scarcely veiled apology for the maintenance of status quo patterns of production and consumption of space, especially housing, and one which geographers and planners have uncritically sustained in their policy recommendations. The essence of the critique is that to focus solely on the demand side of market processes is to ignore all of those powerful social forces such as finance capital, developers, the construction industry and the local and central branches of the state apparatus which massively constrain and filter supply. In the context of such one-sidedness in analysis, even the tautology of utilitarian marginalism is only partly responsible for the inadequacies of the plans which result.

This kind of critical insight is a facet of a general theme which is sustained in what is, in many ways, a quite disjointed book. Despite this, Harvey is often at pains to expose and undermine the typically fragmentary structure which characterizes mainstream social science and to criticize the ways it fragments our understanding of reality. Hence, not only are social sciences split up into disciplines which scarcely interact, although theories do filter through from, for example, economics to geography, but within the disciplines only certain parts of reality are selected for research and analysis, in a highly abstracted way. The result is even more elaborate descriptions of small parts of initially real processes which, through abstraction, become idealistic conceptual frameworks, models and so on. These not only purport to describe but also, through frequent recourse to the notoriously conservative Pareto optimality criterion,[12] appear to have normative content as well. Thereby, bourgeois society, itself predicated upon the atomistic and fragmentary principles of possessive individualism and subjective rationality, is replicated and reinforced in bourgeois social science with profoundly conservative effects. So deeply-rooted is idealism in the academic world that even when a new theory of the way knowledge grows and is transformed in science is advanced (Kuhn, 1967) the explanation for these 'scientific revolu-tions' remains at the level of 'a leap of faith' rather than the more obvious materialist explanation which would pay at least some attention to the control and organizational structures of the academic world. As has been argued often in this book, the effects of idealism resonate throughout planning theory and even inform the main critiques of planning, and credit must be given to Harvey for opening up the discussion of this important question, as well as drawing attention to the miasma of fragmentary know-ledge which social science produces, often with the effect of mystification rather than illumination.

A second side of the critical analysis developed by Harvey is that which addresses two kinds of necessary *rapprochement*. The first, and most impor-tant, of these is the one which seeks to turn geographical analysis from its fetishization of space and its locational determinism, by integrating it more centrally with those important aspatial sociological categories of subjective meaning, culture and – crucially – social classes. The second relationship is stressed less overtly than the first but is no less important. It involves seeing different forms which may be taken by planning as representations of social processes in interaction with spatial structures. Once more the importance of a grounded concept of planning is raised. This situates it as a material part of the control system which advanced and complex capitalist urban aggre-gations require in order to function. Thus the activity of planning is expressly *not* conceived by Harvey as a transcendent formula unbridled by historical context or substantive focus. It is recognized, by contrast, that forms of planning action represent specific, determinate perspectives on the nature of urban problems. However, planning having, as it were, been subsumed under analysis, the problem of what is to be done and in what ways is not thereby dissolved. For as Harvey says, planning can only modify spatial form in order to affect social processes for the better if its prescriptions are measured against some coherent social objective. Planning is therefore a moral act.

Flaws in liberal integration

But it is precisely in seeking to establish the moral basis of planning that Harvey resorts to a type of idealistic analysis which he himself has been so careful to identify as the source of acquiescence in bourgeois social science and planning. And in order to specify the moral basis of planning, which is identified as residing in its capacity for reflexive action stimulated by values present in the urban system, he uncritically employs a functionalist metaphor which leads to eventual inconsistency. Perhaps the clearest way of demonstrating this is by briefly running through the basic argument of Harvey's liberal formulatiohs. Harvey relies considerably on Melvin Webber's thesis that new social norms give rise to changing spatial forms and that the planner is the servant of the social processes underlying these transformations. As we shall see in the next chapter this argument is a functionalist reification of technological development but it does have the virtue of unifying socio-spatial structural relationships. However, Harvey is more perceptive in his treatment of the implications of this argument than Webber. He sees the banality of trend-planning which is necessarily associated with it. He therefore substitutes for Webber's acquiescent goal for planning, which is that it should fit system needs, a goal of reforming the real income distribution consequent on economic growth, to produce a greater evenness of allocation between social groups. This goal is then constituted in a form suitable for urban planning to be a means of achieving it. Analysis, it is argued, has to be focused on the identification of the hidden mechanisms which increase inequalities, and this will necessarily mean rejecting general equilibrium models of the urban system in favour of one based on the cultural and political diversity of values typical of the city.

This is the point in the argument where the view becomes somewhat clouded. For location, as a source of physical and social environmental stimuli, is presented as, independently, a key means of value-implantation, the effect of which is to reinforce a culture of poverty within inner-city communities. Moreover, the urban political system is seen as controlled by oligopolistic elites representing city centre commercial, and suburban interests who manipulate the allocation of physical and social environmental stimuli to these communities. These stimuli contribute to cultural evolution and, as they vary over space they can generate cultural divergence rather than a kind of subtopian value-convergence as envisaged by Webber. But because middle-class norms dominate the planned provision of welfare investments there is great potential for conflict from communities requiring more sensitive consideration of their welfare needs.

Now, above and beyond the crude behaviourism inherent in Harvey's use of an almost Pavlovian stimulus-response model of action-motivation, there are two crucial problems here which stem from functionalist ways of thinking, albeit aimed at analysing potential sources of class conflict. The first of these concerns the argument that environmental stimuli are key sources of cultural values. If it is the case that a bourgeois political elite, operating through the medium of middle-class planners, controls the production of these so that they in turn take a bourgeois form (whatever that might be), and are in themselves important socialization agents, then it seems paradoxical that middle-class values are not coming to dominate inner-city community culture. As Harvey argues, against Webber and even Herbert Marcuse, that this is not the case then, either the environmental stimuli do not perform the function allotted to them by Harvey, or elite values are outweighed by inner-city locationally-derived norms.

The second problem involves the precise capacity of the manipulating elite – a problem which, incidentally, is carried over into the second part of

Harvey's book, as well as his subsequent work. For the image given is of an alliance of the various agents of supply: financiers; developers; builders; landlords and so on, using the city council as an instrument for furthering its own class-monopoly interests. However, the logic of this kind of analysis is that scarcely any resources are allocated to inner-city residents, an argument broached by Harvey as a speculative rationale for urban class-conflict as follows:

By the constant rearrangement of stimuli in the urban system we are provoking a gradual process of cultural evolution. Evolution towards what? One way of making sure that a sub-culture places no value upon urban open space is to deny it all experience of it. . . . In the long run, therefore, we must evaluate decisions about the growth of the city against a set of overriding cultural values which we wish to preserve or augment. If we do not do this, we may see the emergence of new sets of cultural values and, if present trends are anything to go by, these may lead to violent conflict and, perhaps, to an ultimate social self-destruction. (Harvey, 1973, p. 85)

Now, at one level this is clearly a most prescient remark, foreshadowing the social conflict of the British inner-cities of the 1980s as well, of course, as those of American cities a decade or more earlier. At a different level, however, it fails to take account of the fact that pressure from interests sympathetic to the plight of inner-city residents in British cities had produced planning policy initiatives and resources which, while clearly being insufficient, nevertheless had the effect of preventing the communities in the inner-cites from explosive self-destruction for some time. While it is clearly far too complex an issue to pass judgement briefly on the precise causes of violent urban disorder, some of the questions which will have to be answered if understanding and therefore policies, are to improve will concern *inter alia* the availability of employment opportunities, the quality of education and training available, and the sensitivity of the social control mechanisms in such areas. It may be possible to trace profound inadequacies in each of these and other areas of social policy back to the local state and the nature of its power bloc, but to do so would be to miss the crucial point that recent developments in the capitalist production processes, notably in its changing division of labour, are being played out on a world scale and, momentarily, effective opposition to its worst effects is muted.

Subsequently in the book, Harvey moves into a deeper consideration of the forces which underlie the spatial development processes of capitalist society and his concern with elite cultural values becomes less salient. Nevertheless, despite some of the weaknesses which have been noted, these early sections of his book do have the virtue of opening up for fuller consideration some of the advantages and disadvantages for the development of planning thought to be found in the work of Webber and others of 'the Berkeley school' for whom the structural functionalist concern with culture and values in social processes was central to the understanding of urban and regional development.

Conclusions

Three main points have been argued in this chapter. In the first place it has been proposed that urban and regional planners operated according to a broad set of shared assumptions about the spatial development process in the post-war years. The consensus may be plainly stated as one in which it was assumed that rational intervention by an educated elite could produce modifications to the development process which would improve the welfare of all members of society. It was further assumed that there were no serious disagreements between the main social groupings in the liberal democracies, all sharing the belief that there were substantial welfare gains to be achieved from social democratic planning. Moreover, this consensus was widespread within especially US and British society and was not simply a view taken only by planners.

The second main point to be made was that while planners have been criticized for their co-operative view of society, much of this critique has been misdirected. The critique rested upon a supposed adoption by practising planners of a functionalist social theory. However, no evidence is adduced in support of this line of criticism and, in view of the heavy stress laid by such critics upon planners' shared ideas (derived from shared professional assumptions) as the source of this consensus, the critics leave themselves open to the accusation of a functionalist reification of values.

Finally, it was argued that this kind of ideological critique has been far too common in social science, and in planning theory, as the criticisms by Harvey have made clear. It is part of the mystifying effect of much conventional social science which places a great stress upon individual valuations as motives for action and understates the constraints of social forces. One of the most valuable contributions in the work of Harvey, and some other urban theorists in the 1960s and 1970s was to seek to more fully integrate areas of intellectual activity which, under the atomizing influence of bourgeois social science, had become fragmented. The most notable synthesis for development planning is that connecting social and spatial forces and structures. In the following chapter a period of renewal in the effort to reintegrate these categories is reappraised.

5 The Berkeley school: structural-functional planning theory

Introduction

The main source of consciously structural-functional planning theory is to be found in Webber's (1964) collection. Each of the academic contributors was at the time a member of the City and Regional Planning Faculty at the University of California, Berkeley, and each in their different ways was concerned to bring planning into the mainstream of social science from the architectural ghetto. The key theoretical contribution is made by Donald Foley though the more celebrated essay is Webber's paper, somewhat grandiosely entitled 'The urban place and the nonplace urban realm'. A useful critical summary is supplied by John Dyckman who questions the unitariness of conventional descriptions of urbanity given by planners, criticizing the ways in which administrative boundaries are treated as sacrosanct, and points out that 'The functionalist view which is ascendant in these essays finds this distinction of activity by place of occurrence exaggerated' (p. 226). This means that urbanity is to be conceived as a matter of social process in space rather than land use bounded by space.

In Foley's schema social process is connected to space according to the hierarchical framework established by Parsons and Shils (1951) and elaborated by Parsons (1955).[1] In this framework social life is conceived as structured according to four systems: the social system; the cultural system; the personality system; and the physical system. The last of these, the physical system is analytically unimportant except in so far as it imposes *functional prerequisites* upon the other systems. The functional prerequisite it imposes on the social system is one of *adaptation* of social organization such that system maintenance is ensured. In ordinary language this constitutes the economic sphere of activity. The social system in its turn gives rise to a functional prerequisite of *goal attainment* which poses problems regarding the mode of social organization to be adopted to maintain an ordered process of social interaction. This problem is solved within the political sphere. The cultural system is confronted with the functional prerequisite of *integration*. This means that the normative order and cherished values which are established in a given social system must be legitimized so as to maintain social co-operation despite the societal strains which arise through the processes of goal-attainment. This may be equated with the ideological sphere of normal social life, managed through communication from the various religious, legal, mass media, and state ideological institutions. Finally the personality system, conceived at the level of the individual rather than the collectivity, imposes the functional prerequisite of *latency*, or the problem of the unsocialized individual. The problem is to ensure that individuals have the required motivation to move the social system towards its goal by participating in the appropriate activities. It is tackled through socialization, or imprinting of socially desired norms, in the family and the education system, with corrective institutions such as prisons available where socialization has proved faulty.

Clearly, norms play a central role in this analysis of the mechanisms which bring about ordered social relations. Conceptually the norm is the kernel of order since it emerges first, from the recognition by the individual of the role he or she is expected to play by other individuals or institutions, and, second from *conformity* to that expectation so as to gain *approval* from others. This acquiescent conception of the nature of norms is masked by the insistence that roles and expectations are voluntaristically arrived at, and that norms themselves are a doubly-contingent product of interaction. But it is quite clear from subsequent elaborations of norms into what are called *pattern-variables*, that the choices are between antiquated and modernistic, pre-capitalist and capitalist, and perhaps proletarian and bourgeois values, with the latter appearing the more rational and more common-sense norms to which to adhere. Thus deferment of gratification, specialization of role, universalism, recognition of merit, and unselfishness are characteristics of modernization, industrialization and Protestantism (Gouldner, 1971). Their identity with the norms informing scientific management and Fordism should not be underestimated either. For though it has been conventional to explain value pattern variables as modifications of the contrast between mechanical and organic solidarity or *Gemeinschaft/Gesellschaft*, we should not forget either the period when Parsons and his associates began their studies, which coincided with the inter-war revolutions in industrial pro-ductive technique, or the emphasis throughout their project on the explan-ation of order within industrial society, and the functionality (rather than – as with Durkheim – the anomie) of modern institutions for social life. The social system, then, is the system of inter-functional roles prescribed by shared norms and underpinned by culturally-determined values.

Values, functions and spatial structures

Because physical structures such as cities are wholly man-made and are conceived as more directly malleable in response to stated values and subsequent actions, they are given a special status as the representation of centrally-accepted values by the Berkeley theorists. Foley conceptualizes a relationship between cultural values and the spatial form of the city which is more reflexive than that of Parsons. That is, cultural norms may be understood as receiving partial expression in the built environment, but they are themselves modified by the cognitive feedback offered to the cultural system by the resulting physical system. In this way abstract but fundamental social values receive spatial expression and the link between the sociological and the geographic spheres is forged. But this link is, importantly, mediated by the social system. This is composed of functionally interacting institutions and organizations producing, consuming, controlling, authorizing, influencing, deciding and so on, which themselves are spatially located as well as constituting elements of social structure. And it is into the social system that the institution of planning is interposed. It '. . . facilitates or impedes the achievement of stated values . . . which reflect the fundamental values that are agreed upon or taken for granted' (Foley, 1964, p. 23).

Because planning is correctly perceived as an institutional rather than an individual level activity and because the object of analysis is metropolitan socio-spatial structure, there is no place in this schema for the personality system. Rather, the important triggering device of planning, namely goal-formulation, is taken as being a normative, cultural level activity, equivalent to the functional prerequisite of *integration*, while the *goal-attainment* or formulation of means stage is performed at social system level, though as an administrative rather than a political act. Thus planning, in the structural-functional schema, is effectively depoliticized, it merely becomes one more facet of the process of authoritative expression of consensual values. Where demands for goal-attainment at social system level are not met with goal-formulation at cultural system level, *cultural lag* is said to occur. This implies that where the needs of the overall system are for more progressive, modernized, technologically-sensitive norms and the central value system is backward in responding, the onus is on the latter to accommodate the former rather than vice versa. It is at the 'functional-organizational', or social system level that the functional prerequisite of *adaptation* is complied with as a response to demands placed upon the social system by the physical environment. Here '. . . the structure by which diverse functions are allocated and integrated within a community' (Foley, 1964, p. 25) is to be found, in the form of activities, activity systems, spatial linkages and the differentiation of specialized tasks and roles. The role of planning is theorized as smoothing the adaptive prerequisite by identifying key structural elements of the social system and their interconnections, and guiding their interactions to improve the capacity of the system to achieve its goals. *Physical lag* occurs when the built environment fails to respond to social system needs – hence the need for land use planning.

In its dynamic form, that is, where these merely formal relationships between system levels are transformed into representations of a structured process, this schema underpins Webber's conceptualization of 'community without propinquity' as foreshadowed in the 1964 collection. The theory is employed to demonstrate how technological change, occurring at the social system level in response to the physical constraint traditionally exerted by local space, has freed members of society into social interactions centred upon interests rather than upon mere contiguity. The key to this change is the widespread availability of private mobility in the form of the motor car. Expressed in a different form the spread of communications-based technology is also seen as presaging a post-industrial society in which transactions in information and communications-related services come to dominate the traditional manufacturing industries of capitalist societies. This again frees spatial structuring from the locational constraints exerted by localized linkage patterns and heralds the emergence of formless spatial development in 'nonplace urban realms'. Much of Webber's subsequent research has focused upon the spatial and social structures which post-industrial planning needs to create in response (Webber, 1968; 1973).

Lastly, but not locationally a member of the Berkeley school, the structural-functional analyses of residential activity systems of F. S. Chapin (1965; 1968) should be noted. Here too a basic values → activities → spatial patterning sequence is adopted, though Chapin incorporates the personality system into his analysis. Thus, the basic concept of 'the needs of human interaction being the key to the spatial organization of cities' (p. 12) is logically prior to the 'value-system' against which choices are evaluated. Needs are conceived as being *fundamental* (for example security) and *supplemental* (for example status and achievement) and for each individual the social system supplies a set of norms which for purposes of personal well-being the individual must measure up to. Recognition of progress in this role compliance is accorded by peers, and the process of socialization is completed when individual needs-satisfaction and societal norms move into congruence. Chapin moves on next to use this model as an explanation of residential mobility. The behaviour of households in moving their location from one position in the housing market to another, better, one is to be understood in terms of rational action. This fulfils, first, the fundamental needs such as job security, social security and mental security, and, second, supplemental needs such as prestige or status. These motivations are presented as the 'energizing phenomena behind human activity' (p. 13) to which all persons are subject *in whatever social stratum they are positioned*. In this way competition in the housing market results from rational households struggling to measure up to internalized norms of appropriate behaviour and locate in the optimal spatial location. Hence social structure reveals itself in spatial structure as the outcome of a game in which those who adhere most closely to the rules win the best prizes.

It is strange, to say the least, that in this explanation of residential mobility the only constraints upon behaviour which are given prominence are those which relate to certain energizing forces of human motivation, the deep limitations of which may be traced back to the quality of different personalities. Some are clearly 'survivors' who learn the rules of the game quickly and gain their just deserts, the rest, who have deviated for some reason from the established norms, pay the penalty of being also-rans. We are invited to understand the functioning of the housing market not only as the working out of the principles of social Darwinism but of the more deeply-structured results of natural selection. This is the heart of the matter in functionalist explanations, for despite their apparent lack of interest about the individualistic level of analysis, embodied in the essential view of human action upon which functionalism rests is an idealized, entrepreneurial, possessive individual. The segment of the social structure for which this kind of explanation is least of a caricature is occupied by the minority for whom choice in the housing market, as in all other markets, is relatively unconstrained by financial considerations, by questions of race or of educational experience, and by the policies of the institutions which control the production of housing. The households theorized in Chapin's activity systems are the same as those in Webber's non-place urban realms: they are clearly not the residents of Watts, Harlem or Brixton.

Functionalist principles in planning practice

It is not enough to show that planning theorists of some influence internationally have espoused functionalist ideas in the recent past. In themselves, as ideas, they need have attracted no special attention from planners seeking to reorganize the use of space in cities and regions. Moreover, they might have been considered and later rejected following argument between practising planners about their feasibility as the basis for plan-formulation, or between planners and interest-group representatives regarding their assumptions about societal values. However, these possibilities do not seem to have been realized, at least in so far as the more advanced experimentation in planning during the decade after the Webber collection first appeared was concerned. In Britain in particular, some little time after the trend got under way in some of the early US Community Renewal Programs (Robinson, 1973) and later inter-state regional planning exercises (Rothblatt, 1971), there was a strong move towards the production of plans which explicitly aimed to maximize on specified statements of desired goals. These goals were frequently generated not so much by local councillors as their local planning officials and for a number of years were the subject of much philosophical debate, especially in the professional planning house journal (Gutch, 1972; Needham, 1971; Faludi, 1971; all appearing in the *Journal of the Royal Town Planning Institute*, as did many others). It would be interesting to know how many of the thousands of goals which were generated in the aftermath of the 1968 Town and Country Planning Act, in which their centrality to the plan-making process was formalized, were approached, let alone achieved, by subsequent planning action. They represent a great professional outpouring of energy, released by the functionalist requirement that purposive action should be seen to be in pursuit of collectively-held ideals which it was the responsibility of the planner to identify.

A properly-designed piece of research into this movement would need to take a representative sample of development plans produced at the time in question (mainly the 1970s) from which a distillate of the planning profession's collectively-held beliefs and desires for the different areas of the United Kingdom could be drawn. This is not the place to perform that kind of exercise (but see Drake *et al.*, 1975, for some preliminary insights). However, what may be more useful in the space available is to take a detailed look at one of the first and most influential of the goal-seeking plans produced and implemented in the UK, although not one that should be taken as necessarily representative of what came later. The reasons for this are, first, that it was a plan for a New Town, and, second, that the New Town, Milton Keynes, is unique in being very large in target population (250,000) and being the only green field scheme of its size to be built. It does have certain advantages from the viewpoint of this chapter, however, which is to demonstrate the nature of functionalist planning theory in practice.

Milton Keynes was not only to be a new concept in New Town construction from the viewpoint of scale, it was to develop further the rather limited social objectives of earlier British New Towns, social balance and social mixing. In the words of Llewellyn Davies, its design chief, Milton Keynes's

. . . main social purpose . . . is to assist in breaking down the urban poverty syndrome – the vicious centrifuging of population by social class – which has created the urban ghettos of America, and could do in Britain. (It) must be designed to attract, accept, and tolerate every social and racial group. (Llewellyn Davies, 1972)

This aspiration was expressed in the form of six major goals, the first explicit New Town planning goals, in themselves not untypical of much of the goals-seeking planning which was to follow in New Towns plans, such as that for Telford, the sub-regional studies, and country structure plans. The goals were:

1 opportunity and freedom of choice;
2 easy movement and access, and good communications;
3 balance and variety;
4 an attractive city;
5 public awareness and participation;
6 efficient and imaginative use of resources.

A number of points arise immediately when these goals are contemplated in the light of the main social purpose identified above. The first concerns the extent to which any of them would appear at all on the list of priorities of the target population suffering from the urban poverty syndrome.

The second point is that each goal constitutes a platitude to which there is no hard core of meaning. Each could be agreed to by individuals holding the gamut of possible attitudes or opinions about what constitutes a desirable form of society, because each individualized concept of freedom, balance, or attractiveness appears capable of being accommodated. The third point to note is that there are certain obvious contradictions, between elements of the different goals. Thus, 'freedom' of choice and 'balance', or 'variety' and 'efficiency' while, on the surface appearing not to be in opposition, are sharply contrasting criteria once they are set against concrete policy proposals, such as those which refer to education or housing services (Harloe, 1970). The problem of transforming vague goals into detailed policies can be examined with reference to the plan's recommendations for these two services.

In keeping with the aspirations furthering freedom of choice and balance, that is, offering residents the greatest possible range of opportunities while achieving a wider spread of social classes than the earlier New Towns, the education system is given central importance in the task of meeting the needs of the future city. In particular it is stressed that the city is being built for a future where transactions in knowledge rather than transactions in goods may well be the major activity of its residents. This far-sightedness owes a substantial debt to the academic work of the special consultant on 'urban society' who was commissioned by the New Town design team to advise on the social future open to Milton Keynes, Melvin Webber.[2] However, as we have seen, Webber's information-rich, non-place, urban realms are the spatial structures created by an unencumbered, relatively wealthy, technical-academic elite. It has by now become apparent that the kind of footloose, high-technology industry which no doubt prompted Webber's theorizations, located on the doorstep of Berkeley, in the Santa Clara county semiconductor industry, has resulted in massive and unsatisfied demand for unskilled, low-wage labour, severe bifurcation of the local class structure, and chaotic urban development processes[3] (Saxenian, 1981).

Hence it is unlikely that education for the high-skill occupations in the knowledge industries of the 1980s and 1990s could ever have been a mass requirement. However, even if it had been the case that there would be a large and unfulfilled demand for highly-skilled labour to work in local high-technology industries, this would almost certainly not have been overcome if the aspiration towards social balance in education were to be adhered to. This is because of the peculiar social structure which characterizes all New Towns despite the best efforts of New Town planners to produce in the first place, a mixture of social classes which might, later, develop into an eventually classless society. New Town social structure is normally over-represented in skilled and semi-skilled manual, and unskilled non-manual occupations, while typically being under-represented in professional, managerial and unskilled manual occupations. Social mixing in this context does not yield the best results, measured in terms of reading-age levels, with respect to educational attainment, because the advantaged children from professional backgrounds are necessarily too thinly spread either to effect improved attainment among less-advantaged children or to maintain their own initial attainment levels (Mabey, 1973). In other words, the social mix criterion is at variance with the freedom of choice criterion particularly where a key objective for the education system is to give everyone the grounding for future employment in the higher-order skill range in local high-technology industry.

If, as is clear both from an assessment of low-level skill demands of a great deal of high-technology industry and the evidence of the influence of social mixing upon educational attainment, such a prospectus could never be fulfilled by the county education system then, plainly, it was misleading to offer it. However, the problem arose not because these analyses were performed then overlooked. Rather, by relying upon a functionalist theoretical statement of what are feasible aspirations and values for a narrow band of the population, then generalizing from it, Milton Keynes's planners were able to construct an attractive town plan without apparently referring to much empirical research at all. The most likely outcome of the contradiction between freedom of choice and balance would be a segregation of children of professional parents. This could occur either because they would be sent to schools outside Milton Keynes, or because parents would exercise their right to send children to the school of their choice in Milton Keynes, leading in turn to segregation between schools. The latter could occur despite the aspiration for balanced school populations because the Milton Keynes plan anticipated that schools would develop separate identities, specialisms and administrative structures.

A similar criticism can be applied with respect to another important concern of the plan: its housing proposals. It was intended that a balanced population should be achieved by means of a social mix policy in housing allocation. This policy was pursued despite the evidence, partially acknowledged in the plan, that it was unlikely to succeed:

the Corporation has accepted the fact that status distinctions will persist in housing as in other fields and to plan against it would inhibit upper income groups from moving to the city, or hasten their departure to other areas. (Llewellyn Davies Ptnrs 1968, vol. 2 Para. 540)

In response to this, the housing objectives included proposals for: 50 per cent home-ownership (high by New Town standards and remarkably so for a plan aiming to break down the urban poverty syndrome); quality and variety of housing provision whether for rent or sale; attractiveness for all income groups with wide price-range availability to allow the relatively poor as well as the relatively wealthy to move to the city; and social mix, with no large areas to be developed with houses of a similar type, size or tenure. It is not difficult to see that the social mixing which is proposed in Milton Keynes is of an intentionally mild kind. Indeed, so relatively weak are the constraints upon social segregation for the higher income groups that it seems difficult to justify its retention as an objective at all.

The research which has been carried out into the effectiveness of social mix policies (see, for example, Evans, 1976) shows a rather monotonous tendency on the part of higher income groups to segregate from those individuals and households which are economically less well-endowed. The reasons are straightforward and are a combination of income, social class, and institutional effects. Variations in the first of these imply the greatest choice of optimal location for higher income groups, though this is modified to some extent by family size and environmental factors. The social class of households adds to the segregation effect by constraining the possibilities for friendship formation outside the particular class-band in which given higher income groups are located. And the institutional effect comprises a range of constraints from the personal predilections of housing managers to the lending policies of building societies and other sources of housing finance, all of which act to refine the process of segregation of social classes into separate spatial locations.

The somewhat tame counter-mechanism to the 'vicious centrifuging', referred to earlier, which is proposed for Milton Keynes is the standard New Town ice-breaking device:

. . . activity centres have been located so they have convenience value to a given area of the city, and in so far as a choice of these is available, patronage need not be allied to social distinctions, nor develop in a way which will limit the opportunities open to less privileged groups, but will encourage the meeeting of a wide range of social groups in one place. (Llewellyn Davies Ptnrs, 1968, Vol. 2, Para. 541)

However, to the extent that housing segregation does occur, then such activity centres are likely to promote further segregation, even in terms of shopping activity. This is due to the process whereby activity centres in close proximity to high-income areas, in catering for the needs of the dominant clientele will attract a similar clientele from more distant areas. Because of the purchasing patterns of high-income households, retailers have initially to stock expensive lines as well as those more commonly purchased. This increases overall cost to the retailer who will incline towards the elimination of low-profit basic lines. The cost of the remaining lines, even where these remain basic, will be higher in such centres, thus discouraging low-income groups even further (Evans, 1976). In other words there is an absolute contradiction between freedom of choice and the achievement of balanced, socially-mixed communities in an economy which is based upon the institution of private property.[4]

Problems with structural functionalism as a planning theory

These examples point up a basic weakness of the structural functionalism which has been applied as a normative model for planning. From its earliest adaptations by Foley, Webber and Chapin to its more general diffusion into the planning process as unreflective goal-setting of the kind which was represented in the Milton Keynes plan and other contemporary planning exercises, it has represented narrow, particular interests as generalizable ones. In this way some of the underlying biases of the structural functionalist method and findings are revealed in new ways. For it should be borne in mind that, fundamentally, it is a theory and method for analysing and explaining the bases of social order, of orderly sets of relationships between institutions and persons and the norms which mediate them. Theoretically it is assumed that any functioning institution, social sub-system or set of norms has some useful purpose otherwise it would have ceased to function. Its usefulness to the continued functioning of the social system is therefore taken as a justification for its continuation, and, by implication, its reproduction in parts of the system undergoing renewal. Thus if two sets of values co-exist in a system, even where they are contradictory, they are seen as functionally important to its continuation. The two main value-systems in capitalist societies are some form of socialism, or at least in an American context liberal interventionism, and some form of anti-collectivism or possessive individualism. The point about their co-existence is that they are supported by interests antagonistic to one another and are in conflict with each other. It is because of the dominance of some version of the latter value-system over the former that capitalist societies retain their essential features, in the final analysis.

An analysis which sees both as functional for the maintenance of social order is not mistaken. The system of social democracy is a most refined institution for sifting out and reprocessing economic, political and social issues in ways which restrict the various sub-institutions of capitalist societies to limited spheres of competence and responsibility. Thus the workplace is the preferred location in which direct conflicts between labour and capital are best resolved (though in recent decades the state has incorporated parts of this function too). By contrast, it is considered unconstitutional for strikes to be used as a political weapon – though it is not as yet illegal for that to occur in many capitalist countries. The community, on the other hand, is the basis of political constituencies and branches of political parties. From here, issues to do with the social wage, housing, broad economic policy, defence and so on take their impetus. Now, because of this division of functions typical of capitalist societies, it is possible for antagonistic value-systems to co-exist, in part because the supporters of the different value-systems are, largely, spatially segregated, but also due to the adversarial, party-basis of the standard liberal political system. Because social democracy has these

effective mechanisms for absorbing social tensions and redirecting potentially explosive ones into fragmented parts of the general society then the
existence of antagonistic interests, and methods for their political and
economic representation, can appear functional in the aggregate.[5]

However, in taking certain key elements of these opposing value-systems
and recomposing them into a series of aspirations which will guide the
development of a new community, through their appeal to its individual
members, planners have misunderstood the nature of the theory with which
they have experimented. There is a strong parallel here with the criticism,
directed especially at New Town planning, that in seeking to decompose the
elements of the organically developed city and reassembling them in
spatially functional patterns, planners have created environments lacking
variety and interest (Alexander, 1968). Both kinds of problem have their
origin in the same basic tendency, which structural functionalism emphasizes. It is the tendency to neglect *the political nature of social processes*
which, it should be added, Alexander's alternative to abstract planning is
even more subject to than the plans which he criticizes. What is meant here
by the political nature of social processes is the way in which power relations
are systematically expressed in and through the everyday interactions of
individuals, social groups and classes as particular kinds of outcome favouring one kind of interest over another. In the planning of Milton Keynes we
see that despite the appearance that the scheme will contribute to amelior-
ating urban poverty, in reality that will occur in ways from which those
experiencing that condition can scarcely benefit. Because the ultimate aim
of structural functionalist analysis is to describe how the dominant values in
capitalist societies operate to structure those societies into orderly and
integrated wholes, any forces which come into conflict with this process must
either be shown to contribute to it or must be treated as irrelevant.

This important characteristic tends to be left out of many of the major
critiques of structural functionalism. In standard accounts of the reasons
why this kind of theoretical analysis should be rejected a number of basic
criticisms are usually offered (Rex, 1961; Cohen, 1968; Gouldner, 1971 are
fairly representative). It is argued, for example, that functionalism is teleological in nature, which means to say that phenomena are explained by
showing that they are necessary to bring about some consequence. This is
unacceptable because in normal scientific discourse causes precede effects,
whereas teleological explanation allows effects to be treated as causes.[6] But
this is only a problem for those who seek monocausal explanation of a
particularly narrow kind. It may be preferable to some epistemologists to
seek historical explanations for events or phenomena while for others who
are indifferent to historical effects a functional explanation may suffice,
while for still others who prefer a dialectical mode of explanation neither will
be satisfactory. These preferences, too, are political in the sense that
different modes of explanation will yield different ways of seeing the world.

One which, as in the dialectical mode, is predicated on the belief that conflicts between opposing forces are the primary source of occurrences in the natural and social worlds will conceivably appeal more to the student of processes of change than one which postulates, as with teleology, some final cause with which present arrangements are in conformity (Benton, 1977).

This leads us to a second criticism of functionalist explanation that is often made, which is that it contains a particular limiting concept of the capacities of individuals. This is held to be because it encourages an oversocialized view of the individual (Wrong, 1961). The implication is that societal norms, rather than rational choices, induce conforming behaviour from the majority of society's members. The corollary of this is that non-conforming behaviour can largely be labelled deviant with the practical implication that such wrinkles may be ironed-out institutionally. The problem here is two-fold. On the one hand such a theorization of social relations, even when only the mechanisms producing social order are under investigation, is profoundly neglectful of the processes by means of which important cultural transitions can come about, for example the prohibition of slavery or of capital punishment. On the other hand, a basic inadequacy of underlying theory seems to be highlighted by the need to introduce designations which relegate conflicting value-systems to the status of residuals. In both cases the capacity for the creative penetration of hegemonic value-systems by individuals and groups is simply assumed away.

However, these are clearly not problems for most practising institutions in all kinds of societies which exist to re-integrate deviant or dissident opinions and behaviour patterns with some more normally acceptable set of values. Neither is it obviously the case to most international or regional aid agencies that the problems of underdevelopment do not stem from some complex of culturally-lagging values which modernity has left behind. Functionalist explanation is in some ways, and for all its arcane language and concepts, a common-sense way of understanding the world, in which social processes are unencumbered by historical contingencies. And for those whose intellectual aim is to understand orderliness rather than change, the neglect of actual historical contingency is both methodologically important, because of the requirements of teleology, and theoretically necessary because of the need to explain the functionality of present institutional arrangements.

It is the latter constraint which has given rise to the most vociferous rejection of structural functionalism in the broad range of social sciences. This is because, it is argued, the functionalist stress on the harmonious nature of social systems and the use of a concept of order as a criterion with which to distinguish better or more advanced societies from less developed ones, produces an inherently conservative bias to the theory. It is not clear how theory can in itself be either conservative or radical as theory is only a formalized explanation of processes which theorists seek to understand. As we have argued above, the political decision is taken prior to the commencement of theoretical analysis. This derives from the particular interest which the theorist has in a subject, which in turn will supply the conditions for the adoption of one theoretical perspective rather than another. Structural functionalism as a theory is principally a representation of a concern to explain how the mechanisms making for orderly sets of relationships between social groups, institutions and values actually operate. What allows this to be treated as conservatism are, of course, the interpretations and deductions derived from those explanations of the functioning of integrative mechanisms. Thus if it is deduced that the master institutions are given and unchangeable, or that the theory postulates no better future than the present, or that the whole social system is self-equilibriating rather than simply those mechanisms which are concerned with social order having that tendency, then it is likely that conservatism will be inferred. This is made even more likely when key figures such as Merton make the mistake of trying to refute the criticism by pointing to the applicability of functionalist explanation to the social system of the Soviet Union. For the point of the theory is that it is quite successful in explaining any relatively stable social system because its focus is on those forces which act to produce stability, irrespective of the ideological leaning of the value system of the dominant elite.

We would wish to argue, in conclusion, that the structural functional analysis which planning theorists have developed to the point where it has become the basis of the theory of society embodied in many official plans, is an inappropriate vehicle for city and regional planning for the following reasons. First, it is unproductive to assume a homogeneous central value system which frames the goals which planned social action should seek to achieve. This is because the sleight-of-hand which allows plans to appear to accommodate divergent priorities and norms into a harmonious code does nothing to discourage the idealism, in the sense of a pre-occupation with ideal recipes for complex problems of development, which has remained an important source of weakness in many planning strategies. The notion that by establishing a series of desired goals, this in itself will bring about the consensus which will enable these to be approached quite closely, if not achieved, is demonstrably an inadequate approach to planning action. Functionalism has often been criticized for being archetypally armchair theorizing, and although much of this criticism is misplaced in the light of careful empirical studies which have been performed from within its perspective, nevertheless there is in this approach to analysis, as with other idealistic modes, notoriously in utilitarian marginalism in economics, the possibility that in the hands of harassed policy-makers the idealism will displace empirical analysis. This clearly occurred in the Milton Keynes planning exercise and conceivably in many others also.

The second reason for rejecting structural functionalism as a planning theory lies in the circularity of argument which arises once the analysis is extended into prescriptive planning. This can best be illustrated by reference back to Foley's (1964) schematic analysis of the interconnections between culture and spatial structure. The main relationship is a cyclical process in which the dominant cultural values of a given society are represented first in the ways in which functions are allocated among persons and groups (as for example in the division of labour between higher-order managerial functions, middle-order skilled design functions, and lower-order production or assembly functions in an industrial enterprise). There is, next, a representation of these in space as locations of activities, linkages between them, and so on. And last there is the detailed physical form which the combinations of differentiated activities take as cities, conurbations etc. The latter, by encapsulating the dominant social values in built form, reacts upon the cultural level and is reproduced through the same endless process. In this way, even though progress occurs in the technical sphere such that the division of functions does not take precisely the same form from cycle to cycle, nevertheless the same basic principles of the development process continually operate. Hence the division of labour may become less spatially concentrated in some respects and more spatially centralized in others, but the same underlying values which result in individuals being destined for different functions in the system of social relations, and different locations in the process of production, are nevertheless reproduced.

At one level this is an interesting analysis in that it achieves a considerable understanding of the processes of cultural and social reproduction, nominally applicable to any society, although clearly constructed with capitalist society and cities – indeed specifically American metropolitan structure – in mind. But it is seriously flawed none the less owing to its failure to take account of the constraints upon the capacity of the system as described to reproduce itself in the simple manner outlined schematically. Of central importance here is the generalized pressure exerted by those classes which do not accept the implication of the dominant value system that substantial inequalities in income, wealth and power are an acceptable feature of the resulting system of social relations. This pressure has gradually eroded some educational segregation, secured increased social welfare expenditure, and reduced managerial autonomy in the workplace. It continually modifies the forms of physical environment and cultural values which characterize particular cycles of development in ways which cannot simply be anticipated as the scheme suggests. City and regional planning is another institutional outcome of the pressure to organize the forces which give rise to intolerable inequalities in urban and regional systems more rationally and humanely. It is on precisely this point that the extension of functionalist analysis into the area of prescriptive planning produces the clearest of inconsistencies.

For the deduction drawn from the analysis is that planned intervention should involve creating a system which functions more efficiently but in other respects no differently. In defence of Foley's argument it is important to recognize that he was advancing this technicist alternative in preference to the mainstream methods of planning of the time, one of which was the production of static master plans, the other being unco-ordinated responses to piecemeal market pressures. However, the point of planned intervention in the development process is not simply to increase the efficiency of, for example, the functional division of labour. It may be argued that in most capitalist societies that has been one of its main effects, although the criticism which development planning has suffered in the less successful capitalist societies of late suggests that such an argument would be contentious, to business interests, at least. Planned intervention in urban and regional development processes in mixed economies has the twin objectives of improving income disparities between cities and regions which are differentially favoured by the normal workings of those processes, and doing so in ways which, minimally, do not result in welfare disbenefits (the Pareto criterion). That these objectives may have been achieved at the expense of recomposing the spatial division of labour so as to produce new forms of inequality is an argument with some force but one for which further discussion must be delayed until a subsequent chapter. But planning which was openly committed to meeting only the needs of capital and not the demands of labour and its allies would be unlikely to survive the necessarily pluralistic responsiveness of the state under social democracy. The peculiarities of social democracy have already been commented upon but they do not include the systematic failure to acknowledge important, albeit dominated, interests. *This means that development, far from being a circular process as is implied by a structural functionalist analysis, is better understood as a fairly indeterminate process, guided by certain essential requirements but, spatially, relatively unconstrained. In particular, it is unconstrained by the fact that it may at one stage have given rise to metropolitan concentrations.*

The third reason for rejecting this approach to planning theory and practice concerns its inability to deal realistically with the question of power in social decision-making. Because of the assumption that there are agreed values which can be transformed into planning goals that are then sought through the application of technical means, the whole apparatus of adversarial bargaining, negotiation, compromise and deadlock which normally surround the planning process is undervalued. This is surprising because the apparatus is itself one of the crucial mechanisms which contribute to social order in democratic societies. Instead, planners have found themselves spending substantial periods of time decomposing often vague goal statements into a multiplicity of more concrete objectives, then generating numerous comprehensive plans and selecting the one which most closely fulfilled the goals and objectives initially set out, only to find that their political leaders would not accept the results because important political considerations had not been attended to. Some of the most notable instances of this gap in thinking occurred when the structure plans for those local authorities which had earlier been selected as the subjects of experimental sub-regional studies were published (Leicester, Leicestershire, 1969; Notts Derby, 1969; Coventry, Solihull, Warwickshire, 1971). The corridors of growth which, for example, the Leicester and Leicestershire sub-regional study had identified as an optimal development pattern were taken as initial assumptions by the Leiestershire structure planners, yet, despite the wealth of technical reasoning, complex analysis and human and financial resources associated with the preferred option, the final plan distributed small bits of growth to existing small and large towns. The reasons are simple and are implied in the final document. Local politicians would not support a policy which allocated all the growth to a minority of the county's communities because their responsibility was to represent the interest of their own electorates. This kind of constraint is ubiquitous in local and regional development planning and is one with which functionalist planning theory seems ill-fitted to cope.

The importance of an understanding of power relations in planning has been widely argued in recent years, and interesting and informative accounts of planning and local politics are now available (Saunders, 1979; Dunleavy, 1977, 1980, 1981; Goldsmith, 1980). Each points, in different ways, to the problems posed for rationally formulated, best-choice planning decisions by the structures and networks of local political organization. Planners in the 1970s appeared to be receiving advice to bypass this system of local democracy because of fears that low councillor-calibre (Dearlove, 1979) was restricting the capacity of local authorities to produce efficiently-managed services. More business-like methods such as corporate planning with their own separate links to the community were advocated, above all by central government ministries keen to increase the level of control they could exert over local administrations. This latter tendency has continued at an accelerated pace under the budget-cutting policies of recent Labour and Conservative governments in Westminster. It is more likely now than hitherto that local authority planners will seek to understand work far more closely with their local political system in order to counteract the substantial reductions in autonomy which are occurring in local government and to seek to maintain a realistic level of local democracy. This in turn will signify a tendency to look further than the simplistic goal-setting exercises of an earlier period of theoretical development in planning.

One final point requires to be made regarding the influence of structural functionalist thought upon planning theory. In this review of the sources and nature of its influence upon the subject there has not been an outright attempt made to dismiss the approach out of hand. This is in contrast with most of the scholarly literature in planning which is concerned to evaluate its contribution. As we have seen the strong inclination has been to point to the negative qualities of that contribution and leave it at that. There are three reasons for identifying positive aspects of those adaptations into planning thought made from a structural functionalist perspective with which we have been concerned here. The first is that the work represents a genuine *theoretical* enterprise which subsequent planning theoreticians have diverged from. That is, it does have explanatory intent rather than simply providing normative recipes, although as we have seen, it is difficult for Foley to resist making prescriptive deductions. Nevertheless, the aim of understanding the relationship between the planning system and the main forces which stimulate urban and regional development, which is what planning theory has to be concerned with in the final analysis, is present in this work.

Second, and developing importantly from the latter observations, the planning theory which has been discussed here seeks to integrate theories concerning processes which can be conceptualized aspatially with those whose prime concern is to explain processes which occur in space. This link is one of the most important for any successful planning theory yet it is one which has been deliberately severed by leading planning theorists.[7] We need not enter into a discussion of the rationale for this procedure at this point, suffice it to say that the aim of producing an abstracted yet still relevant planning theory capable of application to any substantive sphere of interest is now probably further from fulfilment as a result of experiments in city planning practice than hitherto. What many of the goal-setting exercises and corporate planning experiments of recent years appear to have shown is that inadequate attention to the nature of the local socio-economic and political systems and, hence, inappropriate attempts to link policy to elements of these systems can result in a great deal of wasted effort and unnecessary tension both within the local state and between it and its intended policy-recipients. Future developments in planning theory and practice will be emasculated without a serious reappraisal of the past lack of integration between social processes (including planning decision-making) and spatial processes.

Finally, the insight into the crucial connection between the analysis of non-spatial processes and their spatial representation centring upon *the division of labour* made in Foley's structural functional analysis of metropolitan systems, is valuable. This is because it identifies a key mechanism of the development process in capitalist societies. It is also fundamental to understanding development in pre-capitalist and socialist societies but these are not under consideration in this book. The centrality of the division of labour to an understanding of the development process stems from the fact, recognized by Adam Smith, that it was the transition from craft production, in which a single individual performs all the tasks involved in the process of creating a commodity, to manufacture, in which individuals specialized in repeating the same part of the production process, which ushered in the industrial revolution. Subsequent stages of industrial development have normally been associated with more refined divisions of labour, increasingly dominated by more and more advanced levels of mechanization, as with Taylorism and Fordism, and more latterly semiconductor technology. Urban and regional inequalities in access to income, resources and welfare services are largely comprehensible in terms of the increasingly complex divisions of labour in modern societies.[8] An attempt will be made in subsequent chapters to demonstrate the importance of this latter concept, and to move towards an integrated theory of planning which may have relevance for praxis, though not limited solely to praxis for planners but rather for popular planning of a more wide-ranging kind.

6 Theories of development processes I

Introduction: evaluation criteria

We have seen thus far that standard accounts of the ways in which planning is theorized in relation to processes of urban and regional development are flawed in numerous ways. These flaws can be summarized under the following headings: rationalism; essentialism; idealism; functionalism and abstractionism. To clarify the meaning of each of these in order, then it will be recalled that the first problematical characteristic, that designated *rationalism*, arises from the assumption that the logic of processes operating in the real world can be equated with the logic of concepts employed to represent those processes. It was shown how adopting a rationalist view of planning imposed impossibly rigid criteria for what should constitute real world planning action, the effects of which were to mystify the planning process and to reduce it to a hopelessly relativistic construct of the theorists' mental processes. As a result an adequate theorization could not be forthcoming since there is no way of knowing which of any number of theorists' personal constructs is preferable and why. The rationalist theory of planning cannot begin to address the indeterminate ways in which planning policies emerge and are implemented since it is only coterminous with those aspects of planning which conform to the model of pure rationality. Since this is, by definition, unachievable planning rationalism must be relegated to the position of a normative but meaningless ideal.

The second and to some extent quite closely-related problem with standard planning theory refers to its *essentialism*. By this is meant the implicit notion that there is an essence to whatever planning exists to realize, a single core of purposiveness attached to the conduct of any form of planning. In other words it is assumed that there is some general, theoretically ubiquitous structure to the planning process in the same way as there are thought to be general theoretical structures founded upon the essential laws of other social processes. The ultimate essentialism is that all social processes have the same essence, or, more probably, that all social and natural processes do. This is problematic because it either means that whatever forms and results planning reveals must of necessity represent the essence in some way even when these representations are obviously contradictory. Faludi (1973b) exemplifies this with the notion that the essence of planning is the furtherance of 'human growth'. Or, if this is not the case then some forms of planning must be in conflict with their own essence, in which case the idea of there being some essence is incoherent. It would seem preferable for theoretical discourse to avoid this kind of problem from the start, and not only in planning, if the variability of real world processes is to be explained to any meaningful degree.

The problem of *idealism* is another which has come under discussion at various points so far. Here the concern has been to show that planning theory, planning action and some critiques of these suffer from explaining material processes as if they were the unproblematic outcome of ideas alone. Now, in a trivial sense this must be true in that human action is, for all but the most automatic of responses such as the avoidance of danger, preceded by thoughts. However, it is now accepted that notions of the ideal city, which have until recently been of great importance to the formation of plans, have generally resulted in unusable paper exercises or inappropriate physical structures. Furthermore, even when rather more sophisticated idealizations have been translated into implementable planning objectives, the resulting outcomes have failed to take account of material diversity in social processes, mostly notably in the New Towns. Nevertheless, even though some kinds of planning have been characterized by a perhaps obsessive concern with translating a set of ideas of social process into built form it is inadmissible for some critics of planning to treat the bulk of the activity of urban and regional development planning as though it were homogeneously informed by a single set of ideas such as 'organicism' to which all its practitioners were wedded. This is to run the risk of practising what is being criticized, and is equally open to the criticism of failure to take into account the constraints, diversions, conflicts and retractions to which planning policy and action are subject when proposals come into contact with material forces and interests.

The fourth weakness of planning theory is its characteristic *functionalism*. By this is meant a reliance upon the belief that there is a dominant value-system or ideology to be found in general acceptance among the members of a society, and that this informs the patterns and processes which operate in the social system in a thoroughgoing way. It is reflected in the morphology of cities and regions which, in turn, reacts back through the social system to stimulate the activation of cultural norms towards further cycles of development. Furthermore, this ideology is taken to be the basis from which the various goals which plans are intended to achieve, or at least approach, are derived. In consequence, the questions of whether or not there are such norms, whether, if they are identifiable they are sectional rather than general, and whether, if they are not sectional, they are mutually inconsistent and hence are poor guides for planning action, are not considered. A particular problem of both planning theory and certain sorts of planning action of a strategic kind is posed by the combination of functionalism with rationalism which often results in plans which both generate substantial conflict through representing only particular interests or through representing conflicting interests as the general interest, and which are hopelessly unachievable. One effect of this is that at a popular level planning is severely mistrusted and devalued, and since it has a basis in law which allows the planning authority considerable latitude to implement policy in the face of massive opposition, it frequently appears as one of the more oppressive agencies of the state. That is not to say that popular opposition does not sometimes succeed in preventing plan-implementation, since it clearly does on occasions. However, this further serves to devalue the institution of planning by demonstrating that even within the state, of which the planning system is an integral part, there are disagreements about the quality of some, if not all, planning strategies, goals and the interpretations which planners make of the values which underpin them. These problems stem, fundamentally from weaknesses of theory.

Finally, planning theory labours under an all-embracing *abstractionism*. By abstraction is meant a process of focusing upon single facets of an activity or range of related objects and treating those as the only elements of importance. Clearly some form of this is a prerequisite of theorizing but if it is performed unconsciously and uncritically it can have disastrous effects for the resulting theory. The dominant abstraction which planning theory has laboured under in recent years is one which equates it to the subject of engineering, in particular that part of the subject dealing with servo-mechanisms. Hence, the way that planning operates in society is equated to that of a thermostat in a domestic central heating system, as a metaphor for more general societal guidance.[1] This of course is consistent with rationalistic notions concerning goal-achievement as well as idealizations which characterize planning as merely functionally rational – hence politically indifferent – rather than substantially rational – the sphere of politics. It is nevertheless inconsistent with notions of indeterminacy, diversity, conflict between popular groupings and social classes, and of ideological divergence. These material forces act in ways which make the particular metaphors of abstractionism in planning – thermostats, guidance systems, servo-mechanisms and the like – wholly inappropriate. This is because they refer to a limiting case, almost never found in planning, where there is no disagreement over the desirability of a given course of action.

Because of these inadequacies of existing theories of planning, it is clearly important that any preferred alternatives to them should not display these characteristics. In the chapters which follow the foundations for such non-rationalist, non-essentialist etc. theory will be discussed. However, as the major aim is to go rather further than that by developing a theoretical analysis of the material links between planning processes and processes of development, including their social, political, economic and cultural-ideological dimensions, it is important first of all to evaluate theories of development against the same criteria. In this way we will begin seeking to bridge the gap which has typified planning theory of late, between theory which addresses the abstracted planning process and theory which deals with the processes of urban and regional development. The latter has tended to remain outside the ambit of much mainstream planning theory although there are already signs that this is changing (Scott and Roweis, 1977; Scott, 1980). But for there to be the all-important element of consistency between the two bodies of theory which eventually come into combination as planning theory is reintegrated with its material basis, the relevant development theory must compare favourably against the five evaluative criteria which are the obverse of the five problems which were shown to have undermined the validity of standard planning theory.

First, theory will be appropriate to the extent that it avoids relying only upon the logic of conceptual relationships in order to explain real world processes.[2] In other words theory must be capable of addressing the mechanisms which cause material processes to operate rather than simply assuming that there is a logic to real world processes which has identity with conceptual frameworks. This is not to say that concepts and their logical relationships will be unimportant to theory-building but that as merely logical constructs they are likely to divert attention away from the real, material practices, with all their indeterminacy, which are instrumental to processes of development as well as all other social processes.

Second, acceptable theory will not be founded on the premise that the phenomenon to be explained will represent the working out of some essential underlying purpose or design. An example of this, at the expense of leaping ahead to the next section of this chapter, would be a theory which sought to explain change in any social process as being a stage in the gradual unfolding of a general principle as the parts of the system which are in some way lagging behind other parts move towards some more advanced condition. Modernization theory, with its implication of the inevitable diffusion of greater rationality in the organization of society, bringing under-developed countries closer to the level of the advanced industrial societies, would be a case in point.

Third, appropriate theory is required to avoid the pitfall of assuming that the level of ideas unproblematically motivates action.[3] This problem is exposed on those occasions when events in the material world are seen to diverge markedly from the limits imposed by the system of ideas being postulated. If the idealization is not to be rejected, as it cannot be since for idealists that is the only way in which material processes can be understood, then the phenomena under inspection must be relegated to a position of unimportance if they do not appear to express the system of ideas. Or, as with essentialism, if contradictory expressions are to be allowed then the idealization is incoherent and the idealist has no obvious means of explaining events other than to resort to a relativist position which denies logical contradiction (Hindess, 1977). So we should prefer a theoretical account of development which both allows for contradiction and is not wedded to the notion that real world occurrences are to be understood only as the expression of idealizations. To the extent that theories of development display categorical affinities to the Weberian notion of 'ideal type', for example, they will tend to fall foul of the problems discussed here. Correspondingly, appropriate theory will explain development by reference to specific material characteristics of given societies or types of societies rather than seeing in development some transcendent expression of a generally applicable set of ideas.

Fourth, theories which depend upon functionalist explanation are unlikely to be useful in assisting the development of an integrated planning theory.[4] It has already been shown how the aspects of structural functional planning theory which assume the existence and universality of a dominant value system, postulate a circular theory of development, and exclude from consideration questions of power and interests in social decision-making, severely weaken its explanatory force. Equivalent instances in development theory whereby it might be argued that a particular form or scale of development is functional for the maintenance of a central place hierarchy, or that regional underdevelopment is a necessary by-product of industrial concentration and functional specialization, would have to be the subject of the closest scrutiny. And in so far as such theories were unable to accommodate questions of cultural diversity, power relations, and the processes of interest-mediation and divergence in their explanations, they would have to be rejected.

Finally, the problem of abstractionism would, with all the difficulties this entails, have to be avoided. Hence, it will not be possible to engage in theoretical discourse without some element of abstraction but in that process we should be critical of those abstractions which are comprised of 'chaotic conceptions' (Sayer, 1981). The latter arise from the uncritical, and, therefore, untheoretical process of isolating particular facets of phenomena under investigation, perhaps for instrumental reasons such as data availability, for example, or an overwhelming concern with a single, technically tractable dimension of a complex structure of material relations. By contrast a mode of theorizing which aims not to rest upon 'chaotic conceptions' in the process of abstraction will recognize that material processes and the visible effects of these are the outcomes of perhaps unique combinations of social, cultural, political and economic forces. Nevertheless, recognition of the inappropriateness of simply describing unique situations will be present in the concern with identification of mechanisms which prime these processes. These in turn will be theoretically given, a result of successively approximating conceptual abstractions with empirical instances to the point where certain underlying tendencies, which in particular circumstances will trigger the relevant mechanisms, are understood. In this way the abstractions which are necessary to theoretical discourse will be constructed in ways which are neither rationalist, because of the search for mediating levels of causality between tendencies identified by abstract concepts and empirical outcomes, nor essentialist, because it is not a single mechanism that is being sought but a diversity in which contradiction as well as consistency is conceivable.

In the following section attention will be given to a selection of theories of the regional development process which is representative of the range available. The theories to be considered will be evaluated against the criteria discussed above, and, to the extent that they avoid the problems which characterized mainstream theories of the planning process, they will be retained as a basis for further theorization of the connections between planning and development, in keeping with the main aim of this book. Although theories of the urban development process are not considered in this chapter (except in so far as development is assumed to occur in urban concentrations) some critical attention will be devoted to them in the following chapter.

Theories of regional development

Although we are concerned here with theories of regional development it is perhaps worth noting that some of those to be discussed first are primarily devoted to explaining regional location or, more accurately, industrial location patterns. In the brief space available we shall be concerned initially with three sets of theories: regional equilibrium; disequilibrium theory; and Keynesian applications. Despite the qualification made regarding the relatively constrained focus of these theories they are clearly of relevance to a consideration of processes underlying regional development since it seems reasonable to argue that one of the key motivations of change in the regional system is likely to be that which is found in the sphere of industrial development.

Regional equilibrium theories

In this section we will draw attention to the work of two of the main progenitors of spatial equilibrium economics, Alfred Weber[5] and August Lösch and then consider some relatively recent literature couched within this broad perspective. In the work of the former theorist three aims were pursued. The main aim was to explain the process of rapid urbanization which was observable in his native Germany as a belated process of industrialization got under way there in the late nineteenth century. The other, contributory, aims were to assess the contribution of transport costs of commodities to the variations in development which were observable in regional space, and to examine the possible modifying effects of variations in labour costs upon the agglomeration process. In order to perform the necessary analysis assumptions were made which allowed the isolation of the two prime factors, transport and labour costs, which were hypothesized as being the key determinants of the agglomeration process. It was assumed that the cost of labour did not vary over space and that there were no limits upon labour-supply. Next it was assumed that distance rather than any other variable determined costs of transport.

Thereafter, all institutional factors such as the modifying effect of political or socio-cultural influences and the spatial impact of the banking and finance sectors, were excluded from consideration. However, despite these restrictions it was not the case that a homogeneous regional space was assumed for either the location of raw materials or for the equivalence of their cost in all locations. And, although analysis was centred mainly upon the behaviour underlying decision-making at the micro-level of the individual enterprise, it was set in the context of the regional field of forces which governed ultimate locational choice. Nevertheless, to simplify one of the elements of variability allowed in the schema, an element of substitutability between differential raw material costs was introduced by absorbing these differences under the category of transport costs. Transport costs are thus loaded with the basic explanatory elements for agglomeration because the other hypothetically crucial variable, labour costs, is held constant. The deductions for locational behaviour made from these premises and assumptions were that a rational location for a new plant would be one which maximized on proximity to raw materials where there was substantial weight loss in production – hence minimizing on transport costs, and one which maximized on proximity to the market where production resulted in a gain in weight – thus maximizing on transport costs.

Weber was conscious of the hugely restrictive effect of his assumptions upon the capacity of theory to address real world processes especially with regard to the efficacy of his main explanatory variable of transport costs. For instance, he recognized that locations would frequently be less than rational judged by the criterion of minimizing transport costs, owing to the likelihood that variations in labour costs (which for purposes of analysis were assumed away, it will be recalled) would exert a determining effect upon location, in practice, which would modify the optimum location to be derived solely from transport-cost accounting. He also made it clear that technical factors other than those affecting transport costs substantially, were a major force in bringing about spatial concentrations of production, especially in industries involved in complementary areas of production. Moreover, and importantly, he was conscious of the contradictory effects of this for the spatial patterning associated with the technical division of labour. This can be seen in the recognition that as well as there being an advantage for enterprises engaged in related areas of production agglomerating, and thus concentrating an increasingly specialized and differentiated workforce in local space, these could nevertheless function efficiently if located in a deconcentrated pattern, provided there were other advantages, notably those associated with reduced transport costs, resulting from such spatial decomposition. Hence, despite the obvious limitations which followed from Weber's reliance upon what was effectively a monocausal, transport-costs explanation of urban agglomeration in regional space, the various elaborations and awareness of institutional factors (despite their absence from the analysis) which are mentioned made important contributions to regional development theory. However, as we shall see later, these were not taken up by subsequent theorists to be fully worked through conceptually until very recently indeed (Holland, 1976).

Having made these points, however, it is important that we do not overstress the theoretical contribution made by Weber, particularly when it is measured against the criteria laid out at the beginning of this chapter. For this theory performs badly against each of the tests which have been mentioned. Some of the problems with which the theory is confronted are obvious and require little lengthy discussion. It is clearly an explanation rooted in rationalism as is noted by Holland (1976) who stresses that 'Weber's analysis was intended primarily as a technique of explaining rational behaviour, not as a description of reality' (p. 7). In order to do this Weber relied heavily upon a concept of the motivation for action which fully substituted for the practices of real-world actors and to that extent can be said to have adopted both a rationalist epistemology and a rationalist conception of action. The distinctions between these is that in the former case the logic of conceptual relations and real relations is assumed to be symmetrical, while the latter postulates human action as uniquely informed by certain kinds of ideas, in this case rationality. This means that Holland's stricture above is only partially correct because in seeking to explain locational decisions Weber was presumably seeking to describe some portion of human action, that is, rational behaviour, which is a part of reality but which is by no means the whole of it.[6]

For the reasons mentioned it should be clear that this theory of development is idealist in the sense that it is rooted in a symbolic view of the development process which is scarcely related to the world of experience except in so far as one important real-world category, namely that which refers to the cost of movement and which varies in both theory and reality (although in curious ways in the former due to its absorption of raw material cost-variations), is addressed. The emphasis upon the latter as a major mechanism with reference to which rationality is largely identified, and hence the tendency to agglomeration is set in train, means that the theoretical account is also essentialist. This problem was revealed in the qualification that although agglomeration was the logical outcome of this kind of rational decision-making, it was also possible for spatial decomposition of activities to occur according to the same essential logic. The latter theoretical inconsistency would tend to suggest that Weber's abstractions, which seem to be based to some extent on a gravitational analogy, are chaotic conceptions, a feature which is unavoidable given the weaknesses already identified.

Finally, to the extent that the resulting system is the manifestation of both a single, central valuation, namely rationality, expressed in space, and produces a result whose final purpose is agglomeration (despite the counter-tendencies) then the schema also displays functionalist characteristics. However, the extent to which Weber's formulation can be said to have exhibited the weaknesses which have been identified is somewhat less pronounced than much of the regional equilibrium theory which was to follow his seminal work. This was in some measure due to the fact that he sought only to develop a partial rather than a general equilibrium model and the restrictiveness of the assumptions necessary to carry out the former is, although as we have seen, formidable, less so than for the formulation of the latter. The step towards formulating a spatial general equilibrium model of regional development was taken by Lösch. As will be seen below the assumptions of the model are immensely restrictive upon real-world conditions.

The model is derived by, first, defining a theoretical region in which even less unevenness of resources is postulated than in Weber's model. It is assumed that the distribution of raw materials, population and accessibility is uniform for each; that the conditions for perfect competition, including uniform preferences, technical knowledge and opportunities for market entry are also present; and that each region is isolated from all others, and self-sufficient in raw materials. Second, upon this uniform regional space Lösch proceeded to demonstrate the effects of the full working out of profit-maximizing market competition for the range of economic sectors. The analysis rested on the condition that a producer who was able to earn a profit by producing a surplus in a given commodity would first maximize the number of local sales then simultaneously expand the market spatially in all directions. This is the spatial expression of the decentralized pricing which is held to apply under conditions of perfect competition, and, because under these conditions markets cannot overlap, the resulting market pattern is one in which markets for the same product abut one another to fill up the regional space. The circular expansion of markets evenly distributed in space results in the nearest geometric shape to a circle for each market, which is a hexagon.[7] These hexagons satisfy Pareto-optimality criteria in that they minimize overall distance between production locations, maximize the level of local sales while maximizing profits so long as no abnormal profits could be earned from a producer being fortuitously located close to centres of above-average purchasing power. Hence, and this is the third point, Lösch was able to derive a model of general equilibrium for location in regional space for which it was possible to solve: the price of production of a given commodity, its sales area, the number of production points and their location, and the boundaries of the product market, provided that certain equilibrium conditions held. These mainly referred to such conditions as there being no unused space, no locations which are not profit-maximizing, but equally no locations capable of yielding super-profits, and no large market areas. The model was valid for both producers and consumers and for the agricultural as well as the industrial sectors.

The most intriguing feature of this theory of regional development is not so much the extreme forms of rationalism, idealism and functionalism which it displays, to which we will return later, but the clarity with which it portrays the precise reasons for its own inapplicability to material processes. It also, on the other hand, pinpoints certain key characteristics of the functioning of a pure capitalist model of production which can be instructive in showing why it is that abstractionism of such a heavily economistic kind as we see practised here has to be transcended if planning theory is to progress. There are at least four questionable areas of logic within the theory itself. First of all there is a problem surrounding the basic argument that the system results in spatial equilibrium. This is made problematic by two of the model conditions, for, in the first place it is a condition that profit-maximization is fulfilled in the production location sought by the producer but it is also a condition that surplus profit should not be an outcome of the process of competitive profit-maximizing behaviour by producers. Moreover, it is a crucial assumption that competitive behaviour will result in the tendency for the profit rate to decline to an even level as between sectors – this is the nature of the equilibrium towards which the system develops. In other words the processes of competition between producers seeking the most favourable location logically result in the removal of the basis, profit, upon which the system is founded.

However, second, it might be objected, as is frequently the case in response to criticisms of the equilibrium approach, that it is never intended that equilibrium should be reached, merely that the system in question should tend to move towards that condition. But if this is the case then clearly additional model specifications need to be included to show why the apparent goal of the system cannot, even in theory, be achieved. There is, though, no indication as to the nature and extent of these counter-tenden-, cies in Lösch's discussion of the properties of his model. The single reference to any disturbances to the final expression of the model's implications arises when the relationship between theory and reality is under consideration and mention is made of irregularities which might modify the spatial pattern which is derived theoretically. The irregularities in the availability of resources and markets are not elaborated beyond the statement that they are the result of personal and political factors, however.

The third problem again involves the profit-maximization criteria, but this time in relation to the condition that because a system of perfect competition requires no barriers to entry into the competitive market, the resulting market areas for each product remain small. For this to occur it would seem necessary either for the profit-maximizing criterion to be suspended fairly soon after market entry has been effected, which would seem not to be particularly rational entrepreneurial behaviour, or alternatively, for market areas to remain small would seem to imply the relatively rapid arrival of the equilibrium condition in which profits have reached the point where each producer decides simultaneously to cease trading and start up again, or sacrifice his share of the market to a new entrant. In either case it seems strange that in order for the equilibrium solution to the problem of regional growth to hold, the fundamental motive force of the system, economic rationality in the competitive pursuit of profit-maximization, must cease to obtain either in the interests of keeping market areas small or because the existence of small markets quickly erodes the basis for profit-maximization. In other words it is surely an oddity for a theory which postulates the theoretical existence of an equilibrium solution to require that the state thus described depends upon permanent disequilibrium, not to say economic crisis. The fourth problem seems to be partially an outcome of the previous one in that the theory produces a central place hierarchy of differentially-sized production centres which presumably implies an uneven distribution of population employed in these centres, and yet one of the model assumptions is that there is an even distribution of consumers despite the obvious overlap between the two categories of population.

These problems are one result of a particular kind of chaotic conception in which, on the one hand, space has been introduced to an aspatially constricted theoretical framework, general equilibrium theory, without the constraints intrinsic to the operations of economic processes in space being adequately attended to, notably the effect of distance upon conditions of perfect competition. But on the other hand this seems a particularly good example of another form of chaotic conception in which the indivisible, in this case the complex structures associated with the processes of regional development, is arbitrarily divided up. As a result even basic requirements of the model cannot be justified by its own internal logic as we have seen in the discussion of the contradictions arising between profit-maximization and the scale of market areas.

From what has been said it is clear that, as with the previously-considered partial equilibrium theory, the Löschian model is founded upon the premises of a rationalist epistemology. This is made clear in the glorification of the capacity of rational economic man to structure space in accord with the basic harmony which pure reason imparts to human action. But rationalism in this case is heavily overlain by an extreme and conscious idealism. For the Löschian system is plainly less affected by the constraints of the material world than that which Weber constructs, it is a severely idealistic construct. Even when the real world is addressed it is only brought into discussion in order to be uncompromisingly ejected immediately afterwards as is made clear in the following:

'. . . whoever anxiously submits the result of his thinking to the existent shows little confidence in his own reason. No! Comparison now has to be drawn no longer to test the theory, but to test reality! Now it must be determined whether reality is rational. This, and not verification of theory, is the purpose of the following investigations.' (Lösch, quoted in Holland, 1976)

In philosophical terms this is an almost perfect inversion of the Kantian doctrine that understanding could not go beyond experience because for it to do so would be to transform knowledge into merely theoretical constructs which themselves were the representation of the idle fancies of the brain. The Löschian system seems to represent a spatial manifestation of the speculative metaphysics which were revived by the German Idealist Movement in the early post-Kantian era.[8] And when to this is added the teleology of spatial equilibrium in which an end-condition is postulated towards which each part of the space-economy is functionally predisposed, it is not surprising that some critics have wondered whether the Löschian system refers to inter-planetary rather than inter-regional space.[9]

Regional equilibrium theory, at least in its early formulations, appears to have a good deal in common with mainstream planning theory, therefore. Neither appears to be much wedded to the notion that theory should explain reality, rather it seems that both share the same predisposition to formulate ideal systems to which reality, to the extent that it is considered at all, may come to conform in due course. This conclusion is confirmed when we consider more recent spatial equilibrium theory which seeks to transcend the problems found in the earlier formulations. It is impossible to do more than devote attention to specific aspects of the vast corpus of the work of the major contributor to this field in modern times, Walter Isard. To do so would in any case be superfluous to a considerable extent since in a definitive work (Isard *et al.*, 1969) many of his earlier findings are renounced.

Briefly, Isard set out initially to produce a synthesis of the two spatial equilibrium theories which have been discussed above. In particular he sought to introduce to the static Löschian system an element of dynamic process by employing the principle of substitution. This meant that by applying Weber's technique of subsuming location costs under transport costs the theory of regional development could now take account of such irregularities to the ideal regional surface as the effects of scale economies upon the distribution of production locations in regional space. However, unlike Weber he did not begin with assumptions of irregularity and examine the implications for regional development of economies of scale upon an unevenly endowed space economy. Rather, he assumed the Löschian premises of multi-uniformity with all their limitations, which were recognized by Isard, and sought to show the effect of scale economies on uniform space. The resulting pattern of development is one which concentrates industrial production at locations determined by proximity to two separate sources of two raw materials. Basically these are initially evenly spread in concentrations which resemble the pattern formed by iron filings around magnetic poles, with each pole representing one of two raw materials. This pattern is then skewed by the existence of the important counter-magnet of a single large cheap labour supply such that those production fields closest to the latter become bloated while those furthest away are attenuated. The boundaries of the production fields are identified by substitution points determined by transport and labour costs. However, with the introduction of scale economies the smallest production field disappears and concentration of production and market areas occurs in the larger remaining areas. Economies of scale now allow greater mobility of production location within these areas as various trade-offs are now possible which minimize the limiting effect of transport or labour costs.

Isard himself recognized the weaknesses of this formulation in his later work, pointing out that among other things it failed to address problems involving the location of industry, unemployment and income distribution, marketing and distribution for individual firms, and problems of urban decline and their associated social effects. In consequence Isard draws on other branches of social science in an attempt to reintegrate the complex structural relations which economic abstractionism has dismantled. But in so doing the fundamental problem is reintroduced since the social science theory employed itself derives from precisely the same utilitarian marginalist assumptions regarding human behaviour that are present in the economic theory which has proven so ineffective for improving understanding of processes of regional development. Hence, social, political and administrative, as well as economic, actions are conceptualized in terms of incremental changes which maximize individual utilities following limited evaluation of alternative options. The main difference from Lindblom's incrementalist theories is that Isard ascribes perfect information and constant preference rankings to individuals which enables a game-theoretic approach to be taken to the analysis of decision-making behaviour in regional development. It is well known that there are massive problems which have not been satisfactorily resolved in the application of the fully utilitarian and individualistic assumptions and techniques of game theory to social decision-making. Not the least among these is the Arrow paradox of voting where, fairly indisputably, it was shown to be impossible to secure a socially consistent preference-ranking in a three-person, three-option constitution. Moreover, in the theory of second-best, it is shown that where there are constraints preventing utility-maximization this, in itself, constitutes another constraint which requires the establishment of a new set of conditions for utility-maximization. Such constraints will include many institutional and market factors such as taxes and subsidies or imperfect product or factor markets. These are, in part, a product of government intervention which in turn depend on further legislation or policy to allow first-best utility-maximization to occur. The latter point demonstrates that a constraint such as space which is not subject to legislative neutralization in all respects must severely undermine all of the assumptions associated with utility-maximization. It is only by assuming that it is not a constraint that the conceptual system can work. This is, to say the least, a strange premise for a theory purporting to explain the attainment of spatial equilibrium.

Thus, the more recent developments of spatial equilibrium theory remain trapped in the logic of initial assumptions which, in turn, make it virtually impossible to break out of theory to compare it with reality. In consequence progress has been largely confined to the elaboration of techniques which, as with game theory, bolster these assumptions while purporting to address rational human behaviour. Occasional attempts have been made to relax some of the more outlandish assumptions with, for example, the introduction of monopolistic competition, transport cost variation and differential industrial composition assumptions. But attempting to introduce them simultaneously massively obfuscates the theoretical model. Hence, rather than dispense with spatial equilibrium theory, researchers have relaxed single assumptions to a limited extent at the expense of tightening others. The resulting spatial development patterns have in some cases produced little improvement upon the original Löschian configuration.

To conclude this discussion of regional equilibrium theories of the development process it seems that, if anything, the more elaboration that has been added to the early theoretical systems, the more the approach diverges from an explanation of material processes of regional development. It is clear that Isard's attempts to ground his theory with a fuller recognition of the real complexities of structural relationships by adding social and political dimensions to the initial economic abstraction only yield a multi-dimensional ideal system. Moreover, all behaviour is boiled down to the purest of rational utility-maximization. On this essentialist principle, firms and individuals are unproblematically conflated despite their obvious differences, even at the level of theory, as was shown in our earlier discussion of individual-institutional distinction in Chapter 3. The rationalist epistemology inherited from the Löschian tradition and Weber's original formulations is nowhere transcended in regional equilibrium theory which has been more recently constructed. Moreover, as the whole edifice remains committed to the description of, albeit theoretical, processes by means of which a regional system attains the position of spatial equilibrium through its own internal interactions, it constitutes a wholly teleological and functionalist account of the development process.

Regional disequilibrium theories

The three main theories predicated on the observation that economic well being is not evenly spread over regional space and that in consequence regional development processes tend to be characterized more by disequilibrium than by a tendency towards spatial equilibrium are: Myrdal's theory of cumulative causation; Perroux's growth pole theory; and certain derivatives. These can be fairly briefly outlined and criticized, starting with cumulative causation theory of regional development. This by now very well-known formulation can be summarized in five main points.

1   The development process unfolds in characteristically uneven fashion. Development does not start up and spread simultaneously in all regions, rather it begins in some parts of the space-economy ahead of others because not all regions are endowed with the same initial advantages in terms of resources, skills, capacity to meet demand, and so on. Furthermore, to the extent that development does occur in a particular region that fact will of itself attract further growth in the developing region.

2   When development takes the form of industrialization rather than improvements in agricultural output there will be a transfer of capital generated in agricultural regions to the more profitable areas of industrial development rather than the whole of that capital being, potentially, re-invested in agricultural production. Hence, development in one region is associated with increasing wealth disparities as between the regions undergoing industrialization and those which are not.

3   Once set in train this process becomes cumulative as trade in the less developed regions comes to be dominated by the commodities marketed from the development centres, labour migrates away from the non-industrialized to the industrializing regions to maximize on the interregional wage-differential, and firms in the developing areas begin to reap the benefits of increasing internal and external economies and improved welfare and infrastructural services. These tendencies are referred to as 'backwash' effects by Myrdal for their capacity to drain off resources from backward regions.

4   Correspondingly these tendencies are countered by the diffusion of growth potential outwards from the developing into the less developed regions. This can occur initially in terms of increased demand for agricultural or other primary sector products and it may lead to the industrialization of these activities as with, for example, mechanized food-packing or extraction of minerals. Conceivably the regions experiencing these 'spread effects', as Myrdal terms them, may begin to expand industrially following the cumulative developmental path of the more advanced centres of production.

5   Nevertheless, the overall tendency in cumulative causation is for superior regions to continue their upward growth spiral at the general

expense of economically less-advanced regions. This is because of the initial impetus which works its way through the various levels of the regional economy in a systematic fashion and feeds back into the main triggers of growth in a circular and beneficial manner.

This theory of regional development by no means performs as questionably as regional equilibrium theory with respect to the evaluative criteria with which we are concerned. It is not especially prone to the criticism that it postulates a final end state towards which the system is progressing and towards which all system-variables are functionally contributing. This is overcome by allowing for the important element of indeterminacy whereby growth may or may not be diffused as the various counter-tendencies are brought into play, although it is difficult for Myrdal to resist the temptation to postulate imbalance as a permanent condition. Nevertheless, since imbalance may take an indeterminate number of forms it seems difficult to argue that Myrdal is postulating the ultimately ordered relationships with which functionalist explanation tends to be associated. However, it does seem that the concern with imbalance as a basic characteristic of regional development processes marks Myrdal's theory out as being essentialist, as indeed does the stress on the process of cumulative causation which explains development.

Furthermore, there does not appear to be any mechanism which actually brings forth the development process in Myrdal's account; it is, rather, assumed to start spontaneously from some endowment within a region of an initial advantage. This seems to signify two things, first, the presence of a chaotic conception of the regional growth process which rests uneasily on the unclear notion of the more advantaged region exploiting the less advantaged regions. This seems to attribute a feature characteristic of humans to abstract spaces. And, second, it signifies an over-rigid commitment to a system of ideas which yield what is in fact only a part-theorization of regional development. For, without explaining the origins of the process under discussion we are not provided with any means of knowing whether what follows the beginnings of development is either cumulative upon what precedes it, or indeed whether the latter even causes what follows to occur at all. This suggests the cumulative causation thesis is a particularly clear example of the way in which, even when an inductive rather than a deductive method is being followed, a rationalist epistemology leads to the tendency for explanation to be constructed by reading-off the logic of a material process from the logic of a conceptualized series of relationships, rather than exploring the nature of those processes themselves.

In outlining the second main area of regional imbalance theory we can, perhaps controversially,[10] include a radical version as advocated by Holland (1976) and an orthodox version, which has many similarities to 'cumulative causation', Perroux's 'growth pole' theory of regional development. We shall briefly consider and criticize the latter before going on to discuss the former. Growth pole theory begins with the premise that growth neither occurs ubiquitously nor spreads out evenly, but rather, it occurs at key points and at different intensities within a region. In another version of the magnetization analogy the concept of attraction by polarization is used to explain how factors of production and exchange concentrate at these points. It is then argued that the cause of growth in the growth pole is the presence there of a specific growth industry which belongs to a sector in which there are prospects for sustained and high levels of demand, and in which there are substantial internal and external economies to be enjoyed. Next, it is held that the effects of growth may be diffused outwards to areas contiguous to the growth pole as factors continue to be attracted to the expanding centre and trade, in turn, increases over a wider area, rather along the lines of Myrdal's 'spread effects'. Also, however, expansion at the growth pole can equally deprive contiguous areas of factors of production, especially labour, but also capital, and of markets in a manner not dissimilar from the afore-mentioned 'backwash' effects. Finally, the growth pole concept is extended from being merely descriptive to having a prescriptive intent by the policy conclusion that planned intervention to establish counter-magnets to the initial growth poles should be undertaken to effect reductions in income and other disparities as between growth regions and those remaining less developed.

Before briefly considering the extent to which growth pole theory improves upon or diverges from cumulative causation in the light of our evaluative criteria, it is worth commenting upon the policy experiences of governments which have implemented growth pole policy. By and large these have been disappointing, especially in Italy where there have been attempts to establish them in the Mezzogiorno but also, on a more limited scale in parts of Britain. A major problem seems to arise from confusion between the geographical and sectoral meanings of the term, for most growth centres do not in fact receive industries in leading growth sectors in the relevant national economy. Hence, motor vehicle production and associated components industries have often been established in growth centres, though scarcely ever in combination, but since they are well-established technologies with little room for innovation they tend not to stimulate growth except in so far as the firm concerned may benefit from marginally lower labour costs. These savings are, of course, absorbed in the whole enterprise and do not benefit the receiving region. Thus the established internal and external economies of many of the firms locating in planned growth poles outweigh the imputed polarization effects of their being there, and it is possible that this would be equally the case for high-technology industries. For, although the growth pole concept appears to apply with reasonable accuracy with respect to, say, the growth of the semiconductor industry in California even to the extent of its dependence on state financing, if not state planning, nevertheless attempts to induce similar phenomena elsewhere have resulted in disappointment and/or the repetition of the familiar branch plant syndrome often associated with less advanced engineering enterprises.

This kind of confusion need not arise, of course, because it is quite a simple matter to specify whether a geographical or sectoral intent is implied by the growth pole concept. However, it does signify substantial weaknesses in theoretical analysis which stem from an inadequate basis for theoretical abstraction. There, once again, appears to be little detailed theoretical analysis of the mechanisms which bring the growth industry to its pre-eminence. For example, the role of the state is considered mainly as being confined to planning the counter-magnet rather than, perhaps, being seen as crucially important to the development of growth industries which *appear* to be the effect of the pure operation of the free market. The theoretical account is similar in its rationalistic connection of rather simple surface features of, admittedly real, economies to that of Myrdal, as indeed is the essentialism of the emphasis upon the single factor of growth in an advanced industrial sector and nothing else as being the only cause of regional development. The sole purpose of regional space appears to be to supply centres for a rather narrowly-defined concept of growth. The account is clearly also somewhat idealistic in that a specific concept resting on a highly specific abstraction is taken to be the *Deus ex machina* of the process of regional development. Growth too seems to be presented as an all or nothing process, although it should be stressed that to the extent that the concept is taken from observable material processes the idealization is less extreme than those found in regional equilibrium theory. Finally, although there is mention of the importance of growth values within the culture associated with growth pole development, as to some extent there is in Myrdal's account, it is difficult to argue that these are presented as the functionalist, dominant value-system, the diffusion of which will result in some final, ordered state in which inequalities have converged at the mean. Both Perroux and Myrdal appear to remain sceptical of the prospects for the development process to spread out evenly over space, although growth poles, to the extent that they are successfully implanted, at least imply some reduction in the asymmetry of development, at least in the inter-regional aggregate.

Before moving on to consider Keynesian demand models of regional development it is interesting to look into a relatively recent disequilibrium approach which seeks to weld together elements of cumulative causation and growth pole theory with aspects of the Marxian critique of classical political economy. This occurs in Holland's (1976) useful critical appraisal of existing regional development theory, on the basis of which he then develops an alternative explanation for regional disequilibrium, and a framework for policy intervention which will overcome its income and welfare effects. The argument can be presented in five main steps:

1   The effects of inter-firm competition over space result in regional divergence in the level of economic development principally because of the higher mobility of capital over labour. Economies of scale quickly allow the penetration of less developed markets by monopoly firms which subsequently exercise their economic power over state legislatures to maintain certain privileges.

2   Cumulative divergence is set in train by the capacity for firms in developed regions to exercise monopoly advantages not only in production, but also over distribution, financial sourcing, technical innovation and management of consumption patterns. These advantages exert backwash effects on smaller competitors but introduce spread effects for satellite industries with possible benefits for less developed regions.

3   Unequal competition is further established by the capacity of multi-regional firms to erect barriers to entry for new firms by techniques such as short-term price-reduction to eliminate competitors, monopsonistic[11] control over factor inputs, and the ability to shuffle investments to low-wage locations in other nations where opportunities for transfer-pricing and tax-avoidance are substantial.

4   The spatial impact of these tendencies in developed economies takes the form of a regional dual economy in which the production, distribution and consumption patterns in the developed regions are different from those in less developed regions. The former are dominated by the 'meso-economic sector' of multinational firms while the latter are increasingly characterized by small, peripheral enterprises.

5   The only way in which this pattern of regional concentration along core-periphery lines can be broken is for the state to intervene, not in traditional ways by incentives to firms locating in less developed regions, but through control over investment by means of planning agreements. The latter would enable the state to require fuller mobilization of meso-economic investment towards problem regions in exchange for which multinationals would receive regional assistance.

Numerous criticisms have been made of the policy implications of Holland's analysis, ranging from the obvious concern that multinationals would simply invest in locations which did not require such conditions to the scepticism that state intervention of the kind outlined would result in a markedly less divergent inter-regional configuration anyway since regional assistance has increasingly become a subsidy to capital rather than labour. However, it seems possible to divorce the debate about meso-economic power with respect to the state from the notion of meso-economic concentration with respect to regional development because as we shall see the one does not in fact follow from the other even in Holland's own analysis. For, although this specific account of regional disequilibrium theory seems to avoid many of the theoretical problems which the others which we have considered come up against, there is one important difficulty which is not overcome and which causes analytical inconsistency separate from the issue of whether or not the state can or should control the multinationals.

This difficulty arises because Holland remains closely wedded to the Myrdal–Perroux abstraction whereby regions are presented as exploiting other regions, or more specifically large firms exploit small ones. This is not only a poor abstraction which ascribes power of an ultimately social kind to inanimate objects but it suggests a continuation of the essentialist notion that only the kind of core-periphery dualism implied in this form of imbalance theory can emerge from the workings of imperfect competition. That is, regions can be either developed or in some way less developed. Clearly this is not a particularly helpful categorization even when it is based upon the large-firm/small-firm dichotomy which Holland discusses. What is absent from this account of regional development is some means of separating out the different ways in which different kinds of multinational and multi-regional firm in different sectors use regional space differentially, and their variety of resultant effects.

The effect of this is to imply that the activities of all meso-economic enterprises are tarred with the same brush. This means that the notion of concentration in a single exploiting region may be sustained. Even *a priori* it seems unlikely that multinational mining enterprises will structure space in the same way that clothing or electronics companies are prone to do, even ignoring intra-sectoral variation momentarily. Similarly, it seems unlikely that all meso-economic enterprises will organize production in terms of the structure of satellite-suppliers to which Holland refers, many seeking to control components production, for example, internally, by purchasing subsidiaries or establishing branch-plants. In other words the thesis as advanced lacks the flexibility to cope with the possibility of indeterminacy in spatial structures even within production let alone distribution and consumption.

The result is an overemphasis upon the concentration effects of meso-economic activity within favoured regions and a relative lack of attention to decentralizing tendencies which, as Holland notes, are also characteristic of multinationals. The question then becomes one concerning the quality rather than the quantity of regional employment in meso-economic enterprises. This in turn may or may not require legislation and heavy state intervention to induce multinationals to create more higher-order decision-making occupations in problem regions, for example. As it is, Holland's belief that the state can make multinationals do things which their controllers believe not to be in the interests of their shareholders seems rather academic. This is principally because the methods proposed merely seem to replace private corporate capitalist management structures with state-influenced or state-controlled corporate capitalist management structures. So long as there are constraints on the extent to which equity and profitability can be assimilated to one another then the latitude for the state, even assuming it is able to tame meso-economic power, will inevitably be marginal. When, as seems to be the case here, this limited manoeuvrability is directed towards solving a misconceived and inadequately formulated problem, the concept of planned intervention may be severely undermined even for those who, as residents of less developed regions have frequently been enjoined to see in the state the only means of reducing the asymmetries of regional development.

Thus, although Holland's work does seem to avoid being wedded to an ideal system since it is clearly rooted in an analysis of material processes and practices pursued by certain kinds of corporation, and equally it avoids postulating some functional prerequisites which the current system exists to fulfil, nevertheless it does contain features which seem questionable theoretically. These stem from inadequate abstraction and an essentialist commitment to core-periphery relationships which suggest that the rationalism of Myrdal's and Perroux's accounts of regional development, in which the logic of the relationships established theoretically is recounted as the logic of real processes, has not been sloughed-off. Because of this, the effectiveness of Holland's version of state intervention to remove regional imbalance seems unlikely to be any more successful than those upon which it is intended to be a theoretical and practical advance. In the final section of this chapter we shall examine certain Keynesian models of development which have been the mainstay of state intervention to offset regional disparities in the post-war era.

Keynesian regional development models

For purposes of simplicity and brevity three areas of theory can be identified which are predicated on the Keynesian insight that factor demand and variations in the methods of managing it were of central importance to the processes underlying economic growth. However, it should be noted that none of the models to be described could realistically be called purely Keynesian in their application to the analysis of regional development. Rather, each is in some way reliant upon frequent recourse to assumptions common to the spatial equilibrium theories discussed earlier. Nevertheless, in seeking to explain how conditions of imbalance which result from the working of the free market may be subject to interventions leading to the possibility of equilibrium being achieved, these models display some of the concern with material processes which were found valuable in regional disequilibrium theory. The three categories to be considered are: the Harrod–Domar investment models, the export-base model, and synthetic, factor-export models.

In the Harrod–Domar models the explanatory emphasis for regional development is placed upon the migration of factors such as capital, labour and technical innovation over space in response to demand from a given centre of production. However, for inter-regional equilibrium conditions to be satisfied the following restrictive assumptions are required: a constant propensity to save, equal capital to labour ratios, a constant rate of growth in the labour force (taken as the rate of population growth), a single-good economy, constant returns to scale, uniformity in cost and skill of labour, and no technical progress (Richardson, 1969, p. 47). Clearly, taken together, these assumptions require a formidable degree of inter-regional homogeneity to start with. Nevertheless, it is possible to modify some assumptions where a change can be offset in a reciprocal direction by changes in others. Hence, equilibrium conditions can be maintained even if capital-labour ratios are unequal, provided that there are counteracting variations in regional propensities to save. The likelihood of such arrangements being approached in practice, is, of course, even more remote than the initial assumptions of inter-regional uniformity.

This is shown by consideration of another modification which may be made in the equilibrium assumptions where if there is inequality in regional incomes it is then assumed that there will similarly be variation in the propensity to save. As the region scoring lower on these two indices will be a deprived region, then for equilibrium to be maintained, capital should flow in from higher income regions. But this is unlikely to occur unless investment capacity has been reached in the latter and good investment opportunities exist in the former. This would seem to apply *a fortiori* with regard to labour migration. Since low income and low saving regions tend not to offer good investment opportunities, except in the case of natural windfalls such as oil or other minerals, capital may not follow an equilibriating path but rather flow in such a way as to intensify the disequilibrium.

It is because of these divergences from the equilibrium that this development theory contains obvious policy implications. These are that state intervention should seek to return the faltering regions to spatial equilibrium by returning the level of regional investment to the region's capacity. This can either follow the path of direct state investment in construction, nationalized industries or whatever, or it can take the form of incentives to private investors such as regional assistance or allowances. To the extent that these also increase the level of adoption of technology where capital to labour ratios vary, there are always possibilities of further disequilibrium in the market for labour which have repercussions upon the initial move back towards equilibrium conditions. Hence, there is a constant role for state intervention implicit in Harrod–Domar models. This arises from Harrod's interpretation of Keynes's equation of economic growth with an excess of investment over saving, and vice versa. In effect this leads to a not dissimilar conclusion from that of other disequilibrium theorists that if the above equilibrium conditions are not found regional divergence will be cumulative, centrifugal and self-reinforcing (Holland, 1976, p. 71).

The export-base models of regional development place the explanation for regional development in inverse relationship to that of the Harrod–Domar approach. That is, whereas the latter explain growth in terms of the movement of factors towards regions diverging from equilibrium in relation to capacity, the former suggest that growth is a function of the effect of demand external to the growth-region exerted upon its export industries. Regional income rises as a direct effect of demand for exports and indirectly through local multipliers, while over the longer term continued demand will attract labour and capital which will sustain the growth process while further weighting the structure of the regional economy towards the successful export-industry configuration. The exporting industry is of key importance in shaping the patterns of secondary and tertiary sector development, the scale and location of residential development, and hence the patterns of urbanization to be found in the growth region.

However, the assumptions which are required in order to sustain the export-base thesis are highly restrictive. For example it is assumed that exports alone account for regional development and that the level of exports is set by demand in the rest of the world. This further assumes that a region can unproblematically develop an export-base which complements the export-bases of other regions and the national economy. Finally, it involves the assumption that technical progress and other devices making for improved efficiency in production of goods and services do not exert a material effect upon the tendency to development in an exporting region. Subsequently some of these assumptions have been modified, as Richardson (1969) shows. Influences other than growth in exports have been admitted as stimulants of regional development. Some of these include the effects of state expenditure, labour inflow for other than economic reasons, intra-regionally generated technical and other improvements in efficiency of satellite industries, and the growth of a regional import-substitution strategy by indigenous industry. None the less, these developments are themselves assumed to be determined by the increased income received by the region as a result of the expansion of exports.

On the basis of these assumptions and modifications it is predicted that income expansion will be directly proportional to growth in a region's export-base, subject to exports continuing to be in surplus over imports. Moreover, this will occur straightforwardly if a region has underused capacity or unemployment although where there is full employment and continued export surpluses, increased consumer demand would reduce indigenous savings and lead to a lowering of the rate of expansion. But continued export expansion under such circumstances would mean the continuation of labour in-migration. Thus export-base theory does not postulate the achievement of inter-regional equilibrium, except in so far as less developed regions embark upon an expansion of their exporting industries. On this point the assumption of regional export complementarity becomes problematic for the same reason that the equilibrium assumptions of Harrod–Domar models are. A less developed region may simply not be sufficiently attractive for the capital investment which would enable an expansion in exports to occur. This may remain the case even where the modified assumption that state expenditure may stimulate growth is admitted. Nevertheless, the policy implications of export-base theory point to the importance of stimulating the export performance of less developed regions although in the light of the previous point the form taken by intervention often necessarily results in an industrial diversification policy. To that extent it is evident that much state regional policy in advanced industrial economies is influenced by the propositions of export-base theory as part of a broad Keynesian management strategy.

The third regional development theory to be discussed in this section can be interpreted as a synthesis of the two preceding approaches. In the Keynesian international trade model an economy experiencing increased demand for its exports would suffer price inflation, monetary growth, and an increase in imports leading to a trade deficit. This is predicated on the assumption that there are no compensating capital and labour flows. However, in a regional system this need not occur precisely because of the absence of barriers to factor flows. Hence, in an economy in which demand for a region's exports increases where that region is already experiencing growth and inflationary pressure, the following can be expected to occur. An export surplus will attract capital towards the expanding sector from a less developed region. The effects on the developed region will include a multiplier effect causing increases in regional income through higher wages and reduced unemployment and a consequent increase in the flow of labour away from the less developed region. The effect on the latter will include a decline in exports, a reduction in capital stock, negative multiplier effects and the consequent unemployment which is the condition for labour outflow. The divergence between the regional incomes will become cumulative as capital flows improve the capital to labour ratio in the growth region bringing about productivity increases and more competitive pricing of exports. In other words an increased demand for exports with associated capital and labour inflow to a more developed region produces an anti-inflationary effect due to the creation of greater labour availability and the increased capacity ensuing from larger capital stock. However, this is achieved at the expense of permanent trade deficit for the less developed region with effectively indefinite surplus for the growth region. There is, therefore, no spatial equilibrium as between regions but rather, as with the disequilibrium or imbalance theorizations of regional development, a cumulative regional divergence (Borts and Stein, 1968; Holland, 1976).

Again, it is important to be aware of the assumptions upon which this theoretical account is conditioned. Clearly it stands or falls by the extent to which the factor mobility assumptions are fulfilled. In this respect there is clearly a comparison to be made with the limiting nature of equivalent assumptions in neo-classical equilibrium theory. As we have seen already, there are considerable problems attending upon assumptions of factor mobility of the kind employed here, not least with respect to labour flows from less developed to more developed regions. In addition the assumption that the regional system is closed to international trade means that undue stress is almost certainly placed upon the 'backwashing' effect of trade between divergent regions since both would develop links with less and more developed regions outside the system which would alter the levels of divergence between the original regions. Both of these weaknesses of assumption imply that the further assumption that a full employment ceiling is initially reached, then breached, in the more developed region must also be treated with caution. In other words, the synthetic approach seems if anything to induce an overestimation in the extent of divergence between regions on account of its reliance upon certain neo-classical assumptions regarding the relative simplicity of inter-regional factor flows in a closed economy.

To conclude this section on Keynesian models of regional development it remains to comment upon their performance against the evaluative criteria elaborated at the outset of this chapter with a view to assessing their usefulness in helping to move towards an integrated theory of development planning. It is evident that, although each does offer some interesting insights, nevertheless the overall impression given is that they display many of the characteristics which are to be avoided for our purpose. Thus, on the positive side it is noteworthy that each clearly implies the necessity of state intervention in the inter-regional system if the inherent disequilibrating effects of the development process under market conditions are to be overcome. It is also a matter of some interest that even where equilibrium assumptions are employed there is an underlying recognition of the reality of the development process, which is that growth produces uneven develop-ment.

However, the models which have been described share an apparent functionalism whether it takes the form of explaining the functional pre-requisites for ultimate equilibrium conditions, including the role of the state in that process, or, conversely, showing the reasons why equilibrium is not achieved. In either case there is a strong tendency to assume that equilib-rium is the final purpose of the system but one which is obstinacy itself to achieve. There is too, a pronounced idealism about the processes which are described as characterizing economic activity in regional space, notably in the factor-mobility which is a central element of each model. This is a consequence of the fully-fledged rationalism which informs each variant as the conceptual logic of stimulus and response is inscribed upon the forces which yield material changes in regional structure and well being. The stress on exports in the second and third models considered displays a predeliction on the part of respective theorists to seek, as it were, the essence of the growth process in a single cause, although as we have seen, there is a willingness to recognize, albeit at a secondary level, the importance of multiple causation to development. The overriding weakness in these approaches to explanation is the form of abstraction which they are based upon. While we have seen that a place is allowed for state intervention in the otherwise idealistic developmental processes which are conceptualized, it is a peculiarly instrumentalist agency stepping in at the behest of a teleology of equilibrium, divorced from the material mechanisms which indeterminately affect the nature of regional development planning, which must ultimately be social groups and classes seeking to further their material interests.

Hence, we have seen that a number of different theories of the development process leave much to be desired in the light of the criteria which were established to help move towards a theory of development planning capable of engaging with real-world development processes. In varying degrees it was found that these theories displayed characteristics of rationalism, idealism, essentialism, functionalism and abstractionism which are also characteristic of the otherwise distinct group of theories of the planning process. Clearly, not all theories considered were without value, and those which found even an attenuated space for the state in our understanding of the development process were marginally closer to engaging with reality than those which did not. Similarly those which explained the development process as tending towards spatial disequilibrium had an obvious advantage over those which postulated equilibrium as the final purpose of market competition. However, it was shown that there was an apparent predisposition by disequilibrium theorists to see a process of cumulative divergence between regions which itself has begun to lose touch with reality. This failure flows from an attachment to rationalistic explanations in which a logical conceptual apparatus, in this case a core-periphery model, is ascribed material status. But by exhausting material processes of their human content, which is what spatial exploitation theory of this kind implies, the possibility of counter-tendencies to an ultimate disequilibrium being mobilized by social groups and classes is closed off. In the following chapter it will be shown how this closure-effect can also be applied to many of the more radical urban and regional development theories which have been advanced in recent years to seek to ground explanations more squarely in material processes.

7 Theories of development processes II

In discussing the processes of development so far we have concentrated upon theories which are set at the regional level of resolution. This tends to be problematic for at least three reasons. First, it is unclear what is being referred to in the designation 'regional' in these theories. We do not know whether they are intended to refer to, for example, areas defined in the way that planning regions are, or administrative units such as states as in the USA, or whether they are perhaps defined in the process of analysing development patterns in space. Second, it seems difficult to abstract regional processes from urban, in the sense that since all regional growth is theorized as occurring in urban concentrations of some kind, every regional development theory offers some, albeit general, rationale for urban development too. And third, and most importantly, designations such as 'regional' and 'urban' clearly reflect a particular, spatially-dominated, way of thinking about processes which are not themselves primarily spatial, but social (Anderson, 1975; Massey, 1978). They tend to divert attention away from the mechanisms which lead to space being consumed in variable ways, and, as we have seen in the case of disequilibrium theory, can result in a misleading causal analysis which endows space with capacities which are, in reality, social. Some of these problems are clearly recognized in attempts to reproduce the variety of spatial scales of development in terms such as city-region, sub-region, conurbation, urban realm, megalopolis and so on, but these verbal containers obfuscate rather than clarify distinctions, a feature which stems from a reluctance to relinquish the initial spatial categorization.

However, while keeping these problems to the forefront in attempting to move towards a better theorization of development and planning it would be pointless to overlook the fact that the different designations 'urban' and 'regional' have stimulated qualitatively distinctive kinds of theorization. To generalize, work done at the urban level is more detailed in its focus, tending to be concerned with individual decision-making to a greater extent than is the case with regional theory, much of which, as has been seen, includes only the vaguest abstraction of humanity in the form of profit-maximizing rational economic man. In what follows, the first section will be concerned with examining major theories of urbanization or urban development to establish, once again, the extent to which they may potentially assist the process of theorization of a non-rationalistic, non-idealistic etc. kind. At this stage there will be something of an epistemological break in that mainstream urban theories will be confronted with the critiques and proposals of theorists professing a materialist focus. Once again space limitations will only allow a limited consideration of urban theory. The next three sections will be devoted to the evaluation of a range of theories of the development process which are all more or less critical of the work which has been considered in the preceding chapter. Some of these are pitched at a very broad level of spatial resolution, others are adaptations of these or related theory set at the intra-national level; for simplicity they will be subsumed under the following section headings: core-periphery theories; unequal exchange theories; and capital logic theories.

Urban development theories

The dominant theory of urban development has been that founded upon the idea that cities are the outward manifestation of processes of spatial competition and adaptation by social groups which correspond to the ecological struggle for environmental adaptation found in nature. Building upon the original formulations of members of the Chicago school, such as Park, Burgess and McKenzie (1925), subsequent researchers have accumulated an impressive catalogue of ecological descriptions of the processes of change occurring in cities in the light of interrelationships between key system variables (Berry and Kasarda, 1977; Herbert and Johnston, 1976). Much of this latter work has moved beyond the fairly unrefined basic categories which the early human ecologists introduced, yet it is surprising how indefatigable concepts such as 'invasion' and 'succession' are shown to be even in contemporary accounts of, for example, modern ghetto-formation. Words such as these are of fundamental importance in the apparatus of ecological accounts of urban development because they designate some of the biotic processes upon which this approach was originally founded.

Hence, in the earliest Chicago school models of the urban development process, it was suggested that urbanization involves the development of an equilibrium system, the maintenance of such a system, and the capacity in the system to return to a condition of stable order following any disturbance to its overall operation.[1] This ordered state was arrived at through a process of struggle for survival by different communities in which the most powerful groups acquired the best locations and the weaker then adjusted to the space which remained. This element of dominance is fundamental to the structural form taken by the city. It is represented in the force which the fulfilment of the needs of industry and business exerted upon the developing urban form. This, in turn, is followed by fulfilment of the residential requirements of the population attracted to the opportunities available and constrained by the need to survive in a competitive environment. The spatial development of the urban system is marked by the processes of invasion and succession as new interests come to dominate particular parts of the city, forcing those whom they have succeeded to invade new areas in turn. A static picture of the process is given by the celebrated concentric ecological rings inscribed upon the city of Chicago. The centre of the city is dominated by the business function; this is surrounded, in turn, by the zone of transition where small businesses intermingle with recent immigrants; there is next the working-class zone in which second generation immigrants are found; beyond this is the middle-class residential zone; and finally on the fringe of the city and beyond it is the commuter belt. As a refinement to this basic pattern various ethnic and functional communities are superimposed on the concentric pattern, identifying some of the distinctive districts of the city such as Chinatown, the Black Belt and the bright lights areas etc.

It is important to take note of some of the assumptions which are contained in what on the surface can appear as a fairly accurate, common-sense account of the structure of Chicago which, of course, need not be accurate for any other city. Thus this ecological form is representative of a very specific kind of city. It is plainly one which is a major business and industrial centre rather than being predominantly either one or the other, or, say, a city dominated by government employment or some mixture of business and government functions. Also, the commerce and industry are assumed to be centrally concentrated. Moreover, it is clearly assumed that there is a socially and ethnically heterogeneous population of which a substantial portion is composed of new immigrants seeking low-cost, temporary accommodation. These are also seen as having been preceded in time by a similar wave of migrants to a rapidly expanding city. Furthermore the arrangements under which space is rented in this system are entirely unaffected by government intervention, dominance is a synonym for wealth which, in turn, determines the amount and location of the space acquired by individuals and households. Finally it is assumed that all locations are equally well served in terms of accessibility and that transport costs are equal in all directions. Only with the assumption of a uniform transport surface of this kind can the concentric pattern of development be justified.

More recent research within the framework outlined here has questioned the concentric ecological structure and proposed an urban development process in which sectors based on rental values of land dominate, the highest value sectors exerting the most influence on the resulting development patterns. This in turn has been modified by the observation that there is not a single dominant area but, rather, most large cities display multiple nuclei. These were determined by proximity to areas free of polluting industrial activity and, as the most desirable areas, these were also locations of high-status housing. Low-status residential areas were to be found closest to noxious environments. Subsequently a good deal of effort has been expended in mapping social differentiation within the residential areas of the city. One of the main conclusions here has been that changes in the social composition of city districts is a function of increasing social differentiation as industrial societies become more complex and wide-ranging in their organizational scale. Hence residential areas were differentiated and segregated according to the changing economic status, the extent of acculturation to urban ways of living and the ethnic status of individuals and households in the city in question. Criticisms of the tautological nature of much of this work have since led to greater and greater elaboration of the dimensions of social differentiation but without in any fundamental way altering the underlying ecological theory. This, as we have seen, is fully informed with assumptions which conceptualize spatial differentiation as the realization of utility-maximizing behaviour. Successful competition in the residential market-place confers status upon individuals which is, in turn, a reflection of their skills in operating within the complexities of modern society. Exactly the same framework is also used to show how those who are unsuccessful in exploiting these complexities are to be found in ethnic ghettos (Dicken and Lloyd, 1981).

The most overt characteristic of this theory of urban development is plainly its overwhelming dependence upon a functionalist mode of explanation for the changes which occur in the urban system. In the early formulations no secret was made of desire to present an explanation of the evolving city in functionalist terms as the emphasis upon final state equilibrium, the organic analogy, and the functions of diverse activities in the ecological structure testifies. What must be considered a failure is the patently extreme picture of stability[2] that is forced upon what must have been one of the most disorderly and unstable cities of the time, which grew in population at a rate of 500,000 per decade between 1900 and 1930, became an internationally celebrated centre of criminal activity, and was the location of some of the most exploitative industries and explosive labour relations in American social history (Harvey, 1978a).

These are empirical points, however, and it is the theoretical absences which ultimately condemn this approach. These include the failure to explore the nature of the factor of 'dominance' in the system, the neglect of the mechanisms of change in the system, and most importantly the failure to explore factors other than the superficial 'urbanism' and its supposed value-system, which Wirth subsequently discussed, as the cause of the particular social and spatial relations which Chicago displayed. These absences are carried over into the latter-day human ecology research where there is little consideration of the impact of power relations upon socio-spatial structure and change except in so far as devices such as 'exclusionary zoning' have to be described. Moreover, the static concept of modern industrial society which informs the explanation of spatial differentiation seems only to produce the circular reasoning whereby, ultimately, social status is both cause and effect of segregation. Without a concept of substantial cultural divergence predicated upon the material asymmetries in access to power in the market and the state, human ecology will remain a cul-de-sac in the search for explanations of urban development processes. Yet it seems likely that such assumptions would destroy the functionalism upon which the approach is fundamentally dependent.

The basis of ecological theory is the rationalist notion that biotic processes pursue a particular, competitive logic and that these processes can be conceptually mapped on to human residential behaviour in the city. Because this idea, or system of interconnected ideas, is so restrictive, allowing relatively little part to be played in explanation by, for example, institutional factors, it makes for a severely deterministic attempt to understand socio-spatial development. Thus, idealized forces, drives or whatever, cause individuals to conform to particular kinds of residential locational behaviour. Hence, ultimately, what is being described can be expressed as utility-maximization or its cognate, status-fulfilling activity. It is, in consequence, an essentialist approach to theory because the essence of the urban development process is conceived as an ecological competition for status and position in the urban system. Having grasped the code, as it were, the essential struggle for survival, the invasions and successions can be clearly perceived in real urban life. Once more, and at the risk of tedious repetition, we see the problems for theorization that arise from abstractionism of an inadequate kind. For whether or not it is the case that plants and animals find their accorded niches in the natural order through competitive struggle, they have the distinct advantages of not having to negotiate with the local council for accommodation as recent migrants, not having to convince building society managers of their credit worthiness, and not having to cope with the booms and slumps of the construction industry or the effects of changes in state monetary policy, in their quest for somewhere to live.

Before moving on to consider theories of urban development which do take at least some account of the institutions which differentiate social from natural modes of existence, it is necessary to devote some attention to the other major urban development theory which has been advanced to explain individual locational decision-making in cities. This brings us full circle in our evaluation of the major theories of spatial development since it is an urban application of neo-classical micro-economic theory in the tradition of Weber and Lösch, which also contains assumptions in common with ecological analysis, such as the concentric-zone pattern of urban development. Perhaps the clearest exponent of neo-classical urban theory is Alonso (1964) although more recent elaborations include Solow (1973) and Evans (1973).

Making the full neo-classical assumptions of perfect competition in the land, housing and other markets, profit maximizing behaviour by rational individuals, the existence of a preference schedule to be maximized, which in terms of the urban land market is based on high utilities being ascribed to space and low utilities to daily travelling distances, and full employment throughout the economic system, the following predictions are made. Each individual will locate at the point which maximizes overall utility within the constraint of their available budget. This optimum location will be one in which land rent and other expenditures consume total income and compared with which all other locations fail to maximize overall utility. Because of the inverse relationship between the level of land rent and distance from a central point in the city, the individual indifference curves (graphical representations of the point at which an individual is indifferent to the extra utility associated with increases in a specific commodity at the cost of decreases in a different commodity) reflect the desire to trade-off increases in transport costs against lower land rent costs by taking a left-to-right slope. Where this slope intersects the land-rent curve for a city, which reflects the decreasing cost of peripheral locations, the individual will be maximizing utility, hence his or her location can be predicted. Similarly, an industrial locational decision will be one which maximizes profits, hence maximizing utility, by minimizing on costs, which include land rent and transport expenditures. These trade-offs are what underlie the concentric development pattern found in most cities. This is because, say, commercial decision-makers placing a premium on accessibility to the city centre will concentrate near the centre, paying high rents for relatively small plots of land. Similarly, residential decision-makers, whether wealthy or poor, who have reasons for locating close to the centre will be found in areas adjacent to the central business district, and so on. Therefore, those who value abundant space and for whom distance from the city centre is ranked high on their preference schedule, perhaps because transportation costs are only a small part of income, will be found in the outermost locational 'ring' of the city.

To the extent that this theory shares practically every assumption that the equilibrium theories of regional development display then it is subject to the same negative judgement in terms of our evaluative criteria. It is, first of all, an equilibrium theory in which a final end-state is postulated for the urban system based on high densities and rents in the centre and low ones towards the periphery. The values of actors in the system for some balance between space and minimal daily travel distance are ubiquitous and functional for the achievement of that equilibrium. Hence, in common with other functionalist accounts of the development process it reifies a small part of social consciousness and raises it to an artificially high level of determinacy. In common with all neo-classical economic theory Alonso-type models are idealist as is suggested in the following criticism:

. . . the doctrine of consumer sovereignty that is enshrined in neo-classical theory bears a disconcerting resemblance to Hegel's idealist philosophy of history in which the World Spirit (appearing out of nowhere) is supposed to make itself manifest in material reality. In the same way, the doctrine of consumer sovereignty is idealist in the sense that it presumes that objective socio-historical conditions are simple matters of subjective decidability . . . neo-classical urban models, despite the fact that they are frequently highly elaborated as symbolic and mathematical statements, represent a largely emasculated social logic. (Scott, 1980, p. 77)

Neo-classical models are good examples of the rationalist mode of thought in operation since, as we have already seen, they postulate a narrowly rational logic for action at a conceptual level and transcribe it unproblematically upon real-world processes. Moreover, in its reliance upon the protean concept of utility and its propensity to stimulate action, it is perhaps the fullest instance of an essentialist epistemology to be found in the social sciences. Humans are conceived as existing to express this fundamental, utility-maximizing quality and little else. But, finally, attention must be drawn again to the inadequacy of even this over-restrictive abstraction. For, as Sayer (1978), Scott (1980) and others back to Dobb (1972) have shown, while appearing to establish that economic processes are initiated by individuals acting to maximize their utilities on the basis of their preference rankings, as a result of which urban development, for example, takes its particular form, it is only by assuming that preferences are, in fact, as they are revealed to be in the actual land-use pattern which emerges that the neo-classical edifice can be maintained. The tautological nature of such a 'proof' casts severe doubt upon the validity of the abstractions upon which this kind of theorizing is based.

Clearly both of the main theories of urban development so far discussed are inadequate to our project, more so than, for example, the regional disequilibrium theories or even, possibly, the synthetic regional theories discussed in the previous chapter. As there are no real equivalents of the latter at the urban level which are not written from a materialist viewpoint, we can move on immediately to consider only three examples of what seems now to be becoming a major body of theoretical work on the urban development process. The first contribution to be considered is the structuralist-Marxist theory of Castells (1976a, b; 1977a; 1978); the second will be the neo-Ricardian theory advanced by Scott (1980); and the third will be the 'value and motion' version of capital-logic theory applied to the urban system by Harvey (1973; 1974; 1978a, b; 1981).

In the context of this discussion it is important to point out that each of these writers is to some extent aware of the failure of the regional and urban development theories we have been discussing, to offer a satisfactory explanation of the processes in which they are interested, for the reasons we have given. However, the relevant question to be asked is whether or not their alternative formulations avoid the weaknesses which we have identified in those earlier theoretical exercises. Hence all three theorists are critical of the philosophical idealism which characterizes the bulk of mainstream urban and regional theory. Castells castigates the Chicago school and more recent urban ecologists for their idealization of 'the urban' and their reification of spatial relations as determinant forces arguing that the word 'urban' merely connotes an idealization of processes operating widely across modern society. The concept of 'the urban' thus becomes an ideological representation of particular phases in the development of liberal-capitalist society, especially American society, as the final state of a long progression towards modernity. And this representation, Castells further notes, is fully equipped with the integrative devices of functionalism (Castells, 1976a, b, pp. 38, 72). It has already been pointed out that one of Harvey's (1973) main criticisms of the fragmentation of the social sciences concerned the idealism and abstractionism which this process served. Finally Scott's strictures on idealism in urban theory have also been registered, but these are subsequently extended to apply to planning theory in general. This is described as having reinforced its 'idealist-utopian' origins as 'oriental mysticism' and 'paranormal mental powers' have been advocated as aids to planning thought (Scott, 1980, pp. 236–8; Friedmann, 1974; Michaels, 1974). As criticisms these parallel earlier well-founded points concerning the empiricism of mainstream approaches to urban analysis and their reliance upon chaotic conceptions based on inadequate abstractions from real processes (Scott, 1980, p. 8).

Castells wishes to transcend the fallacies of ecological development theory in a formal model which is not prey to the uncritical assumptions of 'the urban ideology'. To do this he relies initially upon the structuralist theory of social formations (Althusser and Balibar, 1970) which conceives society as consisting of three main 'levels'. The lowest of these is occupied by the economy. This is dominated by the capitalist mode of production in connection with fragments of past and future modes such as feudalism (for example peasantry) and socialism (for example state industry). The main elements are relations of production, represented in the class system of owners of capital, on the one hand, and labourers, on the other, and forces of production such as technology, the way the division of labour is structured, machines, buildings and so on. The latter are controlled by the class of owners who purchase the labour power of non-owners, set them to work with other productive forces, and as a result are able to produce and sell commodities. Because the wage paid is less than the value of the labour in the commodity on the market, owners of capital accumulate more and more in the form of surplus value if the commodities are successfully marketed. In other words the basic economic relation is an exploitative one.

The middle level is occupied by the state and associated elements of the political system. It is where, for Castells and other structuralists, the struggle for power between the two principal contending classes occurs. But it is also the sphere in which the main force for the integration of the contradictory system, namely the state, is found. The exploitative relations of production produce class antagonisms as each class strives to reduce the power of the other. To stop the system flying apart the state must formulate and implement policies which meet the demands of both classes. But, as a capitalist state, it must do so in ways which further interests of owners of capital at the expense of the working class. Nationalization of industry and health services are examples of aids to labour, while tax reliefs and grants on capital investment exemplify aids to capital. The practices of members of different classes and segments within classes are largely determined by the structural relations of capitalist production. The uppermost storey of the theoretical structure is that referring to ideology. The structuralist theory of ideology identifies the requirement for reproduction of capitalist relations of production if the system is to continue. This is conducted under the control of the state through its various ideological apparatuses, such as the education system. It is not, therefore, simply a device for mystifying persons, rather ideology creates persons as subjects to the given social order by for instance, under capitalism, emphasizing individuality as separation from rather than contribution to class-membership. Importantly, each of these levels has a degree of 'relative autonomy' from the others such that at any particular stage of development one or other may be temporarily dominant, although even when economic conflicts are not directly governing political or ideological struggles they are always the determining force in the final analysis.

For Castells, the important feature of these relationships is how they influence the development of urban structure. Each of the three levels makes an appearance in this process. The economy is expressed spatially in terms of: *production space*, occupied by offices and industry; *consumption space*, containing elements in the reproduction of labour power such as housing and welfare services; and *exchange space*, devoted to flows of goods and information. A fourth category *administration space*, which covers local government, urban planning and so on, floats uneasily in economic space and can be subsumed under exchange space without undue damage to the conceptual framework. The level to which it largely refers institutionally is the second, political, level. This is composed of two basic relations: *domination-regulation* whereby capitalist interests are expressed in the segregation of communities and their administrative organization; and *integration-repression* which is the means whereby the state appears to confer a degree of relative autonomy upon communities in the form of neighbourhood committees or public participation, but with repressive intent. This politicization of space isolates communities further by increasing their vertical dependence upon central administration.

Lastly, ideology structures space through two devices: *legitimation*, which is the effect of making particular interests appear to be general ones; and *communication* which allows recognition of commonly-understood meanings. Hence, urban renewal, for example, communicates an ideology of consumerism, modernity and social status by legitimating these particular bourgeois aspirations as having universal appeal. Neighbourhood centres communicate an ideology which underlines the legitimacy of social integration; central business districts communicate the particular interest of the captalist class in exchange, authoritative co-ordination of diverse activities, and divisions of labour, as commonplace and unexceptionable. In these ways the fragmentation of space and the social relations which are conducted over it in disjointed and individuated ways are received as normal aspects of spatial structure.

Having conceptualized the main processes by which the dominant mode of production structures space, Castells proceeds to derive a definition of 'the urban' from the logical relations of the structuralist framework. Taking as his reference point the present monopoly stage of capitalism he shows how the domination and determination of social life by economic relations, which is characteristic of this stage of development, segments space in particular ways. The organization of the production process under the influence of large multi-regional and multi-national enterprises extends over large geographic areas, discounting the effects of space. Because of the concentration in favoured locations of the more advanced production complexes and the concentration in less favoured areas of lower-order functions such as extractive or first-manufacturing stages of production, there is a segmentation of production space on regional and even international scales with associated regional inequalities. This process is assisted by state intervention to plan complex regional industrial agglomerations in favourable locations. Hence the organization of production is largely, though not exclusively, conducted at the regional scale (Castells, 1977a, p. 444).

By contrast, the spatial organization of the reproduction of labour power, the basis upon which the everyday life of the labour force is conducted, their residential activities, consumption of commodities, use of welfare services and so on, is signified by a more urban scale of activity. This is a developing feature of urbanized, industrialized societies where the state intervenes increasingly to supply the collectively consumed housing and welfare services associated with greater concentration of ownership and organization of production. Collective rather than individual consumption is the main force structuring urban space in advanced capitalism. Because the state is the main supplier of collective consumption services the element of concentration is underlined by the centralized units of provision with which it is most convenient to administer supply. But this greater power of control allows the state to plan consumption in ways which fragment the bases in the urban structure for popular organization.

The distinction between a regional production scale and an urban consumption scale leads to the last two stages of Castells's framework. First, Castells identifies the process by which collectively consumed services are supplied, with *urban planning* in the broad sense. Second, and in contradiction to it, are the politicized struggles which occur as dominated groups come into conflict with the urban planning policies of the state to form *urban social movements*. The interaction between these two categories thus defines the field of *urban politics*. Specifically urban struggles develop in response to the state's efforts to break through the bottlenecks created by the development process. As concentration proceeds in the organization of production, the demand for socialized, state, provision of appropriate services comes into conflict with the atomized property relations of the private land market in which many different groupings can be shown to have their *stake*. Because these stakes are not necessarily tied to class positions of consumers, collective consumption struggles, unlike individual consumption issues, have a degree of autonomy from class conflicts based on the relations of production. Hence the element of relative autonomy between structural relations and the actual practices of classes in the urban system allows 'the urban' itself to be defined as relatively autonomous (Castells, 1977a, p. 449). The resulting urban groupings may bring about real change in the power relations between state and dominated interests but this will only occur to the extent that they align with other movements whose conflicts are rooted in production relations. Otherwise they have been integrated or repressed into mere protest or participation and do not qualify for the ascription of *urban social movements* in consequence (Pickvance, 1976, p. 201).

The dynamics of urban development are therefore given by the network of interactions which connect the drive to accumulate capital within the production process with the state's function to maintain the social relations which allow this to continue. Under advanced capitalism the development process is expressed in the conflicts between urban planning, which functions to secure the economic, political and ideological conditions for development, and groups whose interests are adversely affected in the sphere of the reproduction of labour power as a result. The growing socialization of production and consumption, with increasing state involvement most evident in the latter, signifies the emergence of a political terrain with the potential of producing not merely quantitative but qualitative transformations (in association with other mass movements) in the relations between the contending classes of capitalism.

This theory of urban structure and development clearly has a good deal in common with the structural-functionalist models of the Berkeley school, a point whose irony is underlined by the fact that Castells is currently a faculty member there. There are parallels in the ways in which reality is divided up into ideological, economic and physical structures. Also both approaches stress the importance of interaction between all three of these levels in forming urban structure. Finally each postulates a central role for urban planning in meeting the needs of the developing mode of production with its recomposition of space into different production and consumption patterns and divisions of labour. Obviously there are differences too, for whereas the Berkeley school theorize only dominant values and their unproblematical diffusion throughout industrial society, Castells founds his analysis upon the contradictory social relations which are a necessary accompaniment of the dominance of these values in capitalist society. As a consequence, there is in Castells's theory a potential mechanism for explaining development and change which is absent elsewhere, although as we shall see there are confusions in his theorization which mean that the mechanism is underdeveloped. Such failure occurs because although Castells's approach does not set out to be idealist, it does in fact end up by being so. Despite an apparent materialism in the attempt to found theory upon real processes in capitalism rather than the reverse, Borja (in Castells, 1977a) points out that the dynamic aspects of the theory suffer difficulty from the clash of two contradictory theoretical aims present in Castells's work. On the one hand, there is the aim of explaining how urban structure is formed, sought by elaborating a theory of reproduction. But, on the other hand, there is the aim of explaining the way in which urban social movements come into play which is a theory of change. These are only reconcilable because of the allowance made for relative autonomy between structures and practices, between the social relations of production and urban relations of consumption. This device is inserted subjectively on the basis of an idealization of how conflict must emerge rather than from theorizing actual processes. If the account were fully materialist the structures could not be conceived as rigidifying but rather as being themselves processes in continual change, or structuration,[3] a point which Castells, in admitting to the formalism of his urban theory, accepts (Borja quoted in Castells, 1977a, p. 452).

This tension is repeated in two related areas, the first dealing with the specification of 'the urban', the second with the identification of 'the urban' with consumption. Both of these rely upon the conceptual device of allowing relative autonomy to account for their specificity. But with regard to the former it can only arise as a semi-autonomous category because, first of all, a rationalistic conceptual grid (structuralism) is employed as the means of expressing real world processes,[4] and second, in order to induce correspondence between the two an escape clause is added. Thus a rationalist explanation for exceptions to structural causality has to be provided because of the constraints of the initial conceptual logic, otherwise the theoretical system must fail. The designation 'urban' seems thus to be a matter of analytical convenience rather than being derived from a study of the ways in which space is distorted by the contrasting strategies of capital and labour.

However, once an urban sub-structure has been established it requires justification as a semi-autonomous object. This is achieved by making the urban area the spatial field *par excellence* for the organization of collective consumption services. Splitting consumption from production in this way has been criticized for its arbitrariness by Harloe (1977; 1979) and for its neglect of production relations in the urban context in ways reminiscent of Weberian and other bourgeois urban theory by Lojkine (1977). Contrariwise it has been supported as a valid distinction by Dunleavy (1980) since it points to the centrality (though not the exclusivity) of collective consumption among other processes in cities, and by Saunders (1981) for its usefulness in helping the analysis of urban problems. As most of these criticisms and justifications rely on empirical rather than theoretical reasoning they miss the important point which is that there is a mutual dependence between production and consumption wherever they occur (Marx, 1973, pp. 90–4). However, as baldly stated this is not all that helpful, but, taken in conjunction with the related concepts that production consists also in part of distribution, consumption and exchange, each of which takes its form from the social relations of production and the ways these are represented in town and country (Marx, 1973, pp. 95–100), it is clear that Castells's abstractions is a chaotic rather than simply an arbitrary conception. The difficulty arises from beginning with a concept of 'the urban' rather than of the social relations of commodity production as these are represented in space.

Finally, the problem which undermines Castells's theoretical approach most of all is, as we noted earlier, its affinities with structural functionalism. As Mingione (1981) puts it, Castells:

. . . disregards essential social connections and relations and, worse, he reduces some important social relations to mechanical roles and functional links. The dominating interests of the monopolistic sector of the bourgeoisie appear to determine every social event. . . . Thus the ghost of functionalism, which Castells explicitly throws out of the window, comes back through the door. (Mingione, 1981, p. 68)

Thus in the discussion of the determinants of urban structure, spatial segregation is the planned fulfilment of the state's function to maintain social cohesion by isolating potentially solidary communities from one another. If this is successful then 'the urban' cannot interfere to change capitalist social relations; yet urban protests exist. However, these protests cannot function as urban social movements without connecting to wider class movements.[5] Hence, even solely urban protest is functional for ensuring the maintenance of equilibrium conditions. This is further sustained by the various political and ideological devices by which the state maintains its essential function of dominating, regulating, integrating, repressing and legitimating antimonopoly expressions of dissent into oblivion. Finally, the presumption that the state functions in the interests of the monopolizing fraction of the capitalist class results in the assertion that the interests of the latter lie primarily in the spatial agglomeration of collective consumption. Yet even Castells notes a reverse tendency towards the 'de-localizing' of production across space which, at a theoretical level, would exert a powerful countertendency to spatial concentration even on Castells's own limited assumption that the state acts in the interests of the monopolies. Once again, the urban focus blinds Castells from perceiving the real complexity and diversity of which concentration is only one aspect.

We must now briefly turn to more recent theories of urban development written from perspectives which are critical of the structuralist rigidities of which we have spoken but which demonstrate similar characteristics at the end of the day, albeit for different reasons. The first of these theories is developed by Scott (1980) building on earlier research by Scott and Roweis (1977) and Roweis and Scott (1978). This work has the aim of establishing a broad theoretical framework to explain the nature of the urban development process within capitalist society and the ways in which urban planning is a necessary element of urbanization. Of central importance to urban development is the concept of the *urban land nexus*, 'the essence of the city as such' (Scott, 1980, p. 134), which is the system of differential locational advantages offered by the intersection of variable land rent with the spatial requirements of firms and households. The latter are seen to be the objects of structural causality in the Althusserian sense that the logical relations of the two main social classes, capital and labour, are determined by the logical relations of the underlying mode of production. These in turn are conceived along neo-Ricardian lines as characterized by conflict over the distribution of profits to capital and wages to labour.

The capitalist state functions to stabilize relations between the contending classes by reproducing the basis for capitalist civil society. It modifies class conflict by legitimizing capitalist social and property relations and assisting capital accumulation through welfare and other subventions. Urban development is essentially a function of changing capital to labour ratios among firms as they engage in technical switching to maximize profits. Increased capital intensity associated with investment in technology is accompanied by increased decentralization of location from the urban core. Many labour-intensive firms remain tied to city centre labour supplies, however. A similar logic underlies office location decisions although technical switching is not so well-developed as in manufacturing industry. These changes in production space stimulate responses in reproduction space as households seek suburban locations closer to employment centres where wages are higher due to the lower overall labour content of the enterprise. The state is heavily involved in unravelling the spatial knots to which this process gives rise, especially in the spheres of reproduction and circulation, to overcome market failures in the provision of housing and transportation facilities. This is the point at which urban planning performs its main functions by resolving land use dilemmas, eliminating infrastructural overloads and bottlenecks and smoothing the dynamics of land development. Planning is especially involved with bridging the public-private interface between the state and civil society and as such occupies a contradictory position of being functional for and yet refractory to the social and property relations of capitalism. It thus appears as a locus of decentralized, fragmented decision-making and a lightning-rod for popular protest rooted in the contradictions of the urban land nexus.

Scott's attempt to integrate planning and urban theory is important for the ways in which it situates the origin of planning in the contradictory material processes of late capitalism, for the rigorous theorization of the peculiarities of the land market and its role in focusing spatial development unevenly, and, not least, for introducing, albeit inadequately, the crucial concept of *civil society*[6] into the explanations of the development process, the delimitation of the state, and the ambiguities of urban planning. However, there are serious problems with the account as it stands. The most obvious of these is its thoroughgoing functionalism whereby the needs of capital bring forth institutional arrangements whether in terms of the state which engages in a mystifying legitimizing function *vis-à-vis* the working class, urban planning which always responds to the disorganizing spatial effects of capitalist development, or even the family which serves to socialize labour into fulfilling the requirements of capital (as indeed do urban neighbourhoods). This is a functionalist account because it allows no space for the *agency* effects of workers, that is their capacity to successfully cause the state or private institutions to implement policies or take forms inimical to the interests of capital. Thus it would not be unreasonable to theorize aspects of state action in the sphere of reproduction as victories for workers in achieving better housing, universal education or unemployment compensation, though Scott does not allow this. Similarly, it is theoretically valid to argue that the family unit is a survival from an earlier mode of production fought for by working people as a source of security against the atomizing effects of the freedom of contract, movement and so on which are fundamental to the maintenance of capitalist social relations.[7] But familism, too, is one-sidedly conceived as functioning in the interests of capital alone (Scott, 1980, p. 120).

This feature in which state and other institutional functions are read off from the imputed needs of capital is characteristic of neo-Ricardian theories of capitalist economies (Holloway and Picciotto, 1978, pp. 10–11). These abstract from the sphere of production in their analyses, concentrating upon the spheres of distribution and exchange. The former is revealed in Scott's location of the basic antagonism between capital and labour in the issue of distribution. The latter is shown in the emphasis on technological switching as a stimulus to development. This is treated not as an effect of changing relations of production but as determined by exchange-based categories such as variations in wage rates and profits.[8] Changes in these, in turn, are unexplained. Concern with the common-sense categories of wages, prices and the rate of profit is precisely the characteristic feature of the neo-classical theories of urban development of which Scott is critical for their abstractionism and idealism. As Fine (1980) has put it:

Both schools begin with given production possibilities with the object of deriving price, wage and profit equations from the conditions of individual profit maximization and perfect competition. Both also share a form of axiomatic logic. (Fine, 1980, p. 135)

In our terms the nature of that logic, in which propositions are deduced from assumptions which abstract[9] one-sidedly from real world processes and are then used as explanations of these processes, is rationalistic and counter-productive.

The result is a kind of state essentialism[10] in which the contradictions which capitalism creates for itself brings forth unproblematically and without apparent limits, other than its functional congruence with the social and property relations of capitalism, planned state intervention. This notion of the state as an ideal capitalist solving the problems created by the real capitalists because it is outside and separated from civil society, managing dangerous monopoly undertakings, supplying use-values which private firms cannot or will not, and planning the urban system rationally, is too shallow. It does not come to grips with the ways in which different branches of capital themselves may compete for or against state support, or with the impact of different branches of organized labour upon state intervention where capitals have become monopolistic or have failed to sustain profitability. The state and urban planning are simply asserted to be ever-present functionaries acting in the interests of capital. The basic concepts employed are revealed to be chaotic concepts because the analysis begins not with production upon which the classes, the division of labour, distribution, exchange, civil society and the state are established, but with superficial categories whose relationships, for example the inverse relationships between wages and profits, labour and capital, are assumed rather than demonstrated.

Similar problems attended the initial materialist analysis of the development of the urban system in which Harvey (1973) engaged. It has been pointed out (Breugel, 1975) that the concepts of surplus value, labour power etc., which appear there seem to be employed primarily as synonyms for more familiar concepts such as profits, wages and so on rather than being rigorously derived from more fundamental concepts such as capital accumulation, commodity, relations of production. This tendency has subsequently been corrected as Harvey's later work has come to focus precisely upon the processes of capital accumulation and, in particular, the interaction of finance capital and the reproduction of the built environment in the general accumulation process. However, in pursuing this project the main emphasis is, rather as with Castells's, concentrated upon a semi-autonomous urban entity the problems of which arise from the importance which the urban built environment has for the maintenance of capitalist social and property relations. Hence, pursuing a particular theorization of the tendency towards recurrent crises in capitalist societies, in which the explanation is based on the problem of underconsumption, a theory of urban development in late capitalism is derived. The problem of underconsumption, or too many goods chasing too few buyers, is held to arise because of the growing concentration and centralization of ownership of productive capacity by monopoly interests. The latter are in a sufficiently powerful position to be able to manage the markets in which they operate, thus replacing the mechanism of price competition with price fixing. The result is the generation of a massive economic surplus composed of super-profits earned on top of the normal rate of profit to be accrued in the market-place, a position which was held to have characterized the American economy, in particular, in the post-war era. In order to prevent economic stagnation and to encourage the further growth of productive capacity, the state induced finance capital to stimulate a huge wave of new construction of the built environment. The two main effects of this were the massive expansion of suburban housing and the concomitant disinvestment and regressive redistribution of real income in the inner cities.

The state was involved in this process at all levels, from creating the conditions where suburbanization could become a demand capable of satisfaction through fiscal and monetary policies at the level of the central state, down to highway construction and the local provision of the other infrastructures necessary for development (Harvey, 1977, p. 124). In this way a whole range of new consumer goods became the objects of further, enhanced demand as households came to occupy suburban space with its concomitant status-conscious ideology. This meant that a further stimulus was provided to the manufacturing sectors of productive industry, and capitalist social relations were reproduced at a heightened level. At the level of individual cities this process resulted in the class fragment of financiers, mortgage companies, landlords and construction entrepreneurs having sufficient power to manipulate metropolitan governments into passing exclusionary zoning ordinances and other statutory devices which diverted the profits from 'class monopoly rent' (Harvey, 1974) into their pockets. Furthermore, the continued diversion of funds away from areas of need in the inner cities encouraged a widening bifurcation of the class structure as precisely urban forces worked against the prospect of social justice through public expenditure and in favour of the already powerful logic of profit maximization. This in turn could be understood as the basis for expressly urban class conflicts between the state and the appropriators of class monopoly rent on the one side, and deprived inner city residents on the other.

More recently Harvey (1978) has formalized this connection between finance capital and the built environment into what he calls secondary and tertiary circuits of capital which parallel the primary circuit devoted to the production of commodities. The secondary circuit is peculiar in that its output lasts over a long period and acts as a material condition for production rather than as a consumed raw material. As over-accumulation (or underconsumption) occurs in the primary circuit, capital switching can occur towards the secondary or even a tertiary circuit temporarily. Investment in the built environment results from the former, investments in education, health and welfare which improve the quality of labour power characterize the latter. More recently still it is apparent that Harvey has become greatly concerned with the function of the dead capital of the built environment within the overall laws of motion of the capital accumulation process. In particular Harvey (1981) explores the ways in which the logic of capitalist development is founded on the contradiction between the flexibility of money and commodity capital to move to the point of highest return and the immobility of production capital and labour rooted in the built environment. The result is:

> . . . a terrible tension within the geographical landscape of capitalism between the requirement for perpetual shifts in technology and location in search of both absolute and relative surplus value, and the dead weight of past investments, the value of which can be realized only through use *in situ*. (Harvey, 1981, p. 26)

These tensions, in turn, give rise to territorial conflicts in which labour seeks to defend the value of existing built environments sometimes in alliance with capital, or parts of the capitalist class. At some point the rate of return on continuation of the value of that investment becomes sufficiently less than that to be gained from new investment possibilities in other regions or nations for a radical restructuring of the social and spatial relations of production to be effected. In this way, and with different and complex variations across sectors, the laws of value and capital accumulation engender the process of spatial development under capitalism.

Although there appears to be a broader focus to Harvey's more recent writing, there is relatively little difference in his situation of class conflict around the issue of the reproduction of the built environment from that found in his early studies of inner city conflicts. Clearly the analysis of the role of the built environment as a special form of fixed capital with contradictory effects for capital accumulation is of the utmost importance to the study of development processes. But by situating the source of the social problems which occur in the urban, or more latterly the regional, system in the built environment first and foremost, the analysis runs the risk of overestimating the importance of 'the urban' as a determining influence upon what are really problems of accumulation, while underestimating the class dimension at the point of production as the source of those problems. This was particularly evident in the earlier employment of the 'underconsumption' thesis as an explanation of the crisis to which suburbanization was the solution. The thesis itself rests fundamentally on the notion that effective demand for goods is not forthcoming due to a maldistribution of income because profits have entered a massive surplus over wages. This is consistent with Harvey's early substitution of wages, price and profit by a more Marxian terminology but without fundamentally altering their meaning in the process. It is also consistent with an overtly functionalist view of the state whose essential responsibility lies in furthering the interests of the monopolies at the expense of inner city residents, most of whom are members of the working class. By failing to identify the cause of the deficiency in demand, of which underconsumption is the symptom, this explanation of crisis, state intervention and urban development displays comparable conceptual chaos in its mode of analysis to that of Scott's neo-Ricardian formulation.

It has been suggested by Mingione (1981) that these problems stem, as they do for Castells (and, we might add, Scott also), from taking the urban unit and its built environment as the delimiting object of study rather than conceiving it as an important part of understanding the nature and the problems of social reproduction and the accumulation process in capitalist development. Doing this leads to an inevitable functionalism because it requires the making of assumptions regarding influences external to the delimited object, to which it responds in mechanistic ways, whereas observation demonstrates both the indistinctness of the chosen object from its material background and the ambiguity of its relationship to problems of social reproduction, which cannot simply be read off mechanically (Mingione, 1981, p. 70). The tendency towards mechanistic accounts of the accumulation process is carried through to the work on the various capital circuits which Harvey himself admits appear structural-functionalist (Harvey, 1978, p. 98) and the more recent theorizations of the restructuring process in which capital switching appears relatively unproblematic, as indeed does the echoing class conflict in response. These problems seem to go hand in hand with the rationalist conceptual logic which Harvey seems reluctant to eschew in studying accumulation.

In conclusion, therefore, we have seen how difficult it has proven even for critics who are clearly aware of the rationalism, idealism, functionalism, essentialism and abstractionism of a chaotic kind which characterizes mainstream urban development theory to avoid degrees of precisely the same qualities in their own work. Each of the radical theories which we have examined is replete with the most thoroughgoing functionalism of a kind which we found severely weakening in the work of the early Berkeley school of theorists, albeit coming from a conflict rather than a consensus perspective. This is especially apparent in the often strikingly weak and essentialist theorizations of the state which are contained in these theories of development, and *a fortiori* the inadequate theories of planning which they advance. Each theorist too, displays a marked reluctance to distance his account from a rationalistic conceptual logic which succeeds mainly in producing ideal systems devoid of the agency and ambiguity of struggling groups and classes in capitalist society. We have seen, finally, how the failure to situate analysis in the basic categories of materialist analysis; production relations, the commodity form, capital accumulation, the division of labour and so on has often resulted in a conceptual chaos of modes of production, structural determination, wages, prices, profits and the problematic of the urban *inter alia*. Despite this, these theories are closer in intent to the project in which we are engaged than the neo-classical orthodoxy against which they have been formed, and some aspects are, we have seen, of great importance, not the least; the integration of state planning and development, the vague awareness of the importance of labour in development, and the similarly vague concern with civil society found in Scott's work especially. These and related concepts will be elaborated in subsequent chapters, but before that we wish to review a few more theories of development in order to clarify precisely the pitfalls to be avoided in reintegrating planning and development theory in the light of the evaluative criteria which we have set ourselves.

Core-periphery theories

To some extent the idea of a core-periphery relationship has been touched upon in the discussion of regional disequilibrium theory. However, it is more fully developed in sociological development theory, and it is three forms of this that we propose to outline and evaluate next. Each has in common the fundamental distinction between a core, not necessarily spatially defined, which is a centre of the mechanisms making for change in social relations, new ideas, cultural arrangements, modes of organization and so on, and a periphery which exists in some secondary, possibly dependent relation to it. The first version to be discussed can be referred to for convenience as *diffusion* theory, a formulation having close affinities with theories of modernization (Lewis, 1955; Rostow, 1963). Here, development spreads outward from a core region or country which contains the most modern economic sectors to reach those regions at the periphery which are still at the first, or pre-industrial stage of development. The connections made between the core and the periphery smooth out the economic and cultural distinctiveness existing between them, such that a second stage of development is reached. This is characterized by industrial interdependence and the diffusion of core culture and functional organiz-ation to the periphery. The third and final stage of development arrives with the establishment of homogeneous and uniform standards in terms in income, access to collective and private goods and services, political accul-turation and industrialization between core and periphery. In this latter stage the role of the state is crucial in securing the necessary conditions for uniformity.

A more radical variant of core-periphery theory of development is that which is founded upon the idea of *internal colonialism* (Hechter, 1975). He rejects diffusion theory because of its failure to explain the persistence of peripheral underdevelopment and cultural distinctiveness in most countries despite the massive power of core institutions in the contemporary world. The alternative approach can be stated in the following sequence of points:

1   The process of industrialization spreads in a spatially uneven wave which advantages social groups in core locations. These groups seek to stabilize the emergent system to their continuing advantage.

2   This is achieved by crystallizing the emergent social stratification system as it comes to be represented across space, into a cultural division of labour. This fixes an ethnic distinctiveness to the dominant core and dominated peripheral social groups.

3   The industrial diversification associated with modernizing tendencies within the core distorts the form of development occurring in the periphery. The latter is forced into specialist, complementary functions by the external control mechanism, notably into primary export activities.

4   Continued monopolization of peripheral trade, credit and employment patterns by core institutions prevents equalization of wealth between core and periphery. This relationship is further strengthened by state allocations of resources and systematic ethnic, religious and linguistic discrimination which combine to produce permanent backwardness in the 'internal colony' (Hechter, 1975, pp. 9-34).

Clearly there are substantial differences between the uses to which the dualistic idea of core and periphery are put in these two accounts. The first optimistically postulates an underlying teleology to the development process in which the fruits of the (market) economy, first enjoyed by one privileged core group, are generalized to the underprivileged in Lösch-like fashion. The second pessimistically foresees the entrenchment of the inequality upon which modernization necessarily depends by systematic, institutionalized forces of exploitation. The second version seems theoretically the more satisfying in that it does not require the acceptance of economically irrational behavioural assumptions on the part of the endogenous sources of modernization within the core, which is clearly necessary for the notion of 'catching-up' by peripheral areas or groups to have any real meaning. It is also the more empirically satisfying at a causal level of inspection since the kind of equality postulated by diffusionists is nowhere approached in practice, although as we shall see later, the validity of a principally ethnic basis to exploitation would appear to be somewhat dubious.

In advance of further discussion of core-periphery theory, however, it is worth considering one final version which has recently appeared, and which elaborates significantly upon the basic dualistic conceptual apparatus. We are referring to what, again for convenience, can be termed *world-system* theory, the main proponent of which is Wallerstein (1974; 1979). Arguing that in order to trace the processes by which capitalist development emerged and matured it is inadequate to focus on any analytical unit of a lower order than the world, he goes on to theorize the ways in which the core areas in which great bursts of industrialization occurred are related to the periphery. Thus the characteristic feature of core development is that it consists of a complex variety of economic activities such as mass-market industries, commerce of both a local and international range controlled by an indigenous bourgeoisie, and a relatively progressive agricultural middle-class. Through the twin mobilization of accumulated capital on the one hand, and a working class formed by the release of labour from advancing agricultural productivity on the other, first a core-zone comes to be dominated by capitalist development and subsequently the rest of the world assists in the fuelling of the industrialization process. The latter process arises from the colonial expansion undertaken by the core region which has the eventual effect of structuring the relations of world regions with one another according to an international division of labour. The core is characterized by free labour engaged in skilled tasks, while at the periphery, which is characteristically involved in monocultural cash-crop or mining production, are the countries in which coerced labour, repressed under colonial state power, is found. Between the core and the periphery is what Wallerstein calls the *semi-periphery*, composed of countries that have regressed from core status through undergoing a process of deindustrialization and those heading for core status as they experience rapid industrial development. The designation core, semi-periphery, periphery arises from the position a country or region occupies in the hierarchy of allotted tasks under the international division of labour. The international division of labour itself is a series of exploitative relationships based upon the trading links of the capitalist world-system in which: '. . . production is for exchange, that is . . . determined by its profitability on a market' (Wallerstein, 1979, p. 159).

Despite their obvious differences each of these theories suffers to a marked degree from their overt functionalism. Diffusion theory postulates an ideal system of evolution towards an essential goal already achieved by the core, with the latter acting out a functional role for the development of the periphery. It abstracts weakly from social processes in stressing the logic of spatial relations which are then imposed rationalistically upon real developmental processes. The internal colonialism model is functionalist in the reverse direction, that is, by stressing the functionality of the periphery for the core it condemns the latter to a structurally-determined and un-changing fate. This stems from an idealization of the nature of economic exploitation which is conceived, strangely, as being primarily ethnic in origin rather than rooted in relations between classes. This formulation seems, therefore, to be based on a conceptually incomplete analysis of the nature of regional inequality. It is further compromised by a failure to move beyond an explanation of inequality rooted in the market exchanges between colonial core and colonized periphery. A rather similar criticism can be made of Wallerstein's approach which also theorizes the origin of inequality in the sphere of exchange rather than the class relations of production. This, in turn, allows him to impose an idealized system of divisions upon the world in which the international division of labour reflects the functionality of different areas for particular types of production. Nevertheless, the world-system theory of development is less deterministic than the internal colonialism model in that it allows for the possibility of a change in status, for which the concept of the semi-periphery is of crucial importance. However, despite constituting a marked improvement upon earlier core-periphery theories, world-system theory fails fully to escape the rationalism which is inevitably entailed in the conceptual apparatus of core-periphery relations. Where these are, in turn, founded upon the limited and essentialist abstraction of development (or exploitation) arising through exchange relations and not new modes of class relationships (Brenner, 1977, p. 57) the more interesting aspects of this perspective are seriously undermined. The further weaknesses entailed by a focus on exchange rather than production relations in development theory are explored in the next section of this chapter, and some of the problems in trying to overcome them are discussed in the last section.

Unequal exchange theories

The emphasis upon the sphere of exchange as the mechanism responsible for the exploitation by core of periphery is examined much more profoundly in the work of theorists who, although concerned to identify the importance of international economic relations upon national and sub-national underdevelopment, are less immediately interested in the justification of functionalist schemata than core-periphery theorists seem to be. In addition it can be shown that there is a greater awareness of the role of production relations and, to some extent of the relevance of the class dimension in the processes giving rise to unequal levels of development. Nevertheless, it will be argued that serious problems remain with these theories which make them inappropriate, as they stand, for the purpose of bringing together the important dimensions of capitalist systems in an order representative of their relationships in reality. The integration of planning and development theory which is our specific task is more likely to be impossible without an appreciation of the nature of some of these problems and possible solutions to them. Because of a degree of overlap in the main areas of unequal exchange theory we will provide a global account of the basic propositions pointing to important individual elaborations in the process: the main ideas are derived from Emmanuel (1972) and Amin (1976; 1978) and we include, possibly controversially, the work of key *dependency* theorists such as Frank (1979) and Cardoso and Faletto (1979) for partial contrast upon a similar theme.

The basic propositions of unequal exchange theory are fairly straightforward. In the labour theory of value it is assumed that exchange takes place on the basis that the commodities in question have equivalent labour time content. Because the commodities which are the object of exchange are produced by equally rewarded labour they have an equal value, assuming technology, labour productivity and transport costs are held constant. However, in practice, and for reasons having to do especially with the differential costs of reproduction of labour power, commodities do not in fact exchange at equivalent amounts of 'socially-necessary' labour time. Because in some countries the level of reward which is socially necessary to reproduce labour power is lower than in others, the exchange of commodities which may have taken the same number of hours to produce is unequal because wage levels are unequal. As real wages are higher in the advanced industrial economies than those which are less developed, then the value of the same commodity is higher in the former than the latter. Hence, the differential exchange of purchased labour power, and thus value, produce an exploitative relationship which works to the advantage of high wage areas and against the interests of low wage areas, notoriously as between Western economies and Third World economies.

Emmanuel (1972) notes that it is because low wage regions of the world specialize in the production of primary and intermediate goods which command low prices that there is a flow of value towards advanced countries.[11] Profit equalization, which occurs as capital moves to seek out the sources of highest profit, then acts as a constraint upon any prospect of increasing wage levels in low wage countries thus locking such economies into an international system of exploitation located within the sphere of exchange (or circulation). Because of this mobility of capital across international boundaries, a factor which operates even more smoothly within national boundaries, it has been tempting to apply the theory of unequal exchange to the analysis of regional inequality. However, Emmanuel is clear that the important distinguishing feature between the intra-national and the international levels which makes this practice inadmissible is the high degree of intra-national mobility of labour and the low international level of labour mobility. Thus he argues that:

. . . if Guinea were a part of France like Brittany . . . with free circulation of capital and people to and from other parts of France, with the same legislation and the same relationship between social forces as elsewhere in France, and a unified labour market embracing Guinea and the rest of France unequal exchange . . . would vanish. (Emmanuel, 1972, p. 161)

Unequal exchange in the broad sense after Emmanuel may be contrasted with unequal exchange in the narrow sense (Massey, 1978). In the latter, the focus of analysis is more upon wage level differentiations than upon differences of productive structure. Amin's (1976) identification of unequal exchange with the bifurcation of wage increases and productivity in peripheral countries is a good example of this distinction. He argues that low wages in the advanced countries, or 'centres of *autocentric* accumulation', would be a problem for continued capital accumulation due to the under-consumption problem, therefore real wages must rise in line with productivity increases. But continued capital accumulation requires the reverse of this relationship between wage levels and productivity in peripheral areas where '*extraverted* accumulation' and, hence, unequal exchange occurs.

The main problems with these accounts of unequal development are their inherent functionalism and rationalism which can be traced back to an incomplete abstraction of the determinants of the processes to be explained. The functionalism derives from the same source as was identified in core-periphery theory (with which, of course, unequal exchange has similarities). That is, the underdeveloped areas stand in a functional relationship for the areas which are economically advanced or capable of autocentric accumulation and their development or lack of it can be read off from this relationship. But as Brewer (1980) has pointed out this is to ignore both the variable conditions under which wage struggles necessarily occur in the core, and the influence of wage struggles and production conditions in establishing the going rate in the periphery (or peripheries). This problem can be traced back to the over-rigid use of the sphere of exchange as the source of exploitation which, in turn, rests upon a mainly technological explanation of the sources of increased productivity and, hence, wage increases.[12] But to impose an apparently logical conceptual relation such as this upon what is clearly a far more complex process is to discount the impact of conditions such as levels of unemployment, rate of profit, state intervention, and production relations in a rationalistic manner. Amin (1978) seems aware of this in wishing to argue that wage levels are a direct outcome of class conflict but this clearly contradicts the technological argument. By abstracting from exchange rather than production relations in association with exchange relations neither Emmanuel nor Amin can satisfactorily explain the phenomena which they undoubtedly observe.

The power of forces external to underdeveloped economies in imposing upon such economies a *conditioning situation* of dependence was stressed in the early writings of Frank (1967; 1972) and Dos Santos (1970) among others. Production was seen to be controlled by international enterprises centred in the core of advanced industrial societies whose growth required that economic organization in the periphery should be biased mainly towards extractive industry. Where secondary-sector industries were implanted these were typically to be found in low wage *enclaves*. The commodities produced were for export and, due to associated profit repatriation, the recycling of obsolescent core-economy technology, and the levying of technological rents, peripheral economies were prevented from achieving indigenous capital formation and so could not break out of their underdeveloped status. In other words underdeveloped economies were conceived as being locked in to a permanently asymmetric economic relationship with developed economies because of the requirements of the latter for low raw material and production costs. However, despite a certain superficial plausibility, the argument that exploitation occurred via international asymmetries in exchange explicable solely in terms of external control has been roundly criticized by the thesis *of associated-dependent development* (Cardoso, 1973).

By contrast with the static and deterministic assertions of the previous thesis, what Cardoso advances is a theory of changing forms of dependency in which factors internal to dependent economies are as important as those external to them in establishing a relationship of dependency. Of great importance among these factors are the prevailing class structure and the role of the state in seeking a coherent development programme. Pressures for development in lagging economies coincide with the trend towards the internationalization of capital and the consequent restructuring of the international division of labour led by multinational corporations. These are increasingly keen to open up underdeveloped economies as markets for their offshore production while continuing to enjoy production advantages in the form of low labour costs, strict control of work practices, and weak unionization in dependent economies. Under such a regime development is possible, as is shown by the experiences of the Newly Industrializing Countries (OECD, 1979) but the new occupational structure is dominated by low-skill employment, especially for the cheaper female labour force. Exploitation is thus a product of the association of the state with the multinationals in establishing a new division of labour in which the low-wage part of the production process of, often quite advanced, commodities is centred in the periphery. This remains dependent because the centres of corporate control are externally situated and can, through mechanisms such as transfer-pricing as well as profit-repatriation and so on, engage in intra-corporate practices which work against the processes leading to self-sustaining growth.

The newer dependency theory thus overcomes the functionalism and determinism of the theory of dependency as 'development of under-development' which Frank and others espoused and seem from recent work (Frank, 1979) reluctant to relinquish. The functionalism of the earlier work derived from a rigid adherence to the notion of imbalance implicit in the core-periphery metaphor in which the underdevelopment of the periphery was imposed by the core because it was functional for its survival. And because of the necessity of this relationship the deduction was deterministically made that so long as unequal capitalist exchange continued, the condition of underdevelopment would be permanent. This example thus replicates many of the problems of the core-periphery rationalism of Hechter or Wallerstein and reveals some of the weaknesses of abstraction which have already been seen to be characteristic of the focus upon exchange in unequal exchange theory. Cardoso's formulation, in allowing that development can occur and that underdevelopment is not functional for core institutions, overcomes the first problem but does not fully escape the problem of focusing mainly upon exchange. For although there is an important and interesting introduction of internal factors such as the influence of classes and the state upon dependency, and a concern to identify labour supply advantages for multinational enterprise in dependent economies, exploitation is still conceived as occurring in the sphere of exchange. This occurs through the internal trading arrangements of multi-national corporations and through the exploitative wage relations in the labour market. Now, while these, and perhaps most importantly the latter, are highly relevant to the analysis of imbalance they need to be situated more firmly in production issues such as the changing organization of pro-duction, the need for greater control by capital over the labour process, the importance of weak unionization for corporate strategies and so on to be more than superficial theoretical abstractions of the development process.

Capital logic theories

The last group of development theories to be examined specifically seek to overcome the limited nature of the abstractions which characterize even the better of the previous group of theories by theorizing the laws of motion of capital over space to establish the extent to which a general theory of spatial development can be derived. The first, and quite influential, of these attempts to be discussed here combines a structuralist method of analysis with the theory of unequal exchange in seeking to explain the unevenness of development across space (Lipietz, 1977; 1980a; 1980b). Unlike most of the core-periphery and unequal exchange theories which we have considered, Lipietz's work represents an application of certain concepts such as mode of production, extraverted and introverted accumulation, dominance and dependence which have no specific spatial delimitations, to the regional level. This signifies that Emmanuel's stricture regarding the inapplicability of the unequal exchange idea to that level is either wrong or can be accom-modated in an analysis which starts from a study of different modes of production (rather than unequal exchanges of labour power). For it is in the ways in which different modes of production connect across inter-regional space that Lipietz derives his unequal regional exchange. Taking as an example the ways in which a region dominated by peasant and artisanal petty-commodity production relates to one dominated by fully capitalist commodity production, Lipietz shows how the former is forced into unequal exchange with the latter by means of, say, its agricultural products being sold at cost price in exchange for industrially-produced goods whose price includes a capitalist profit element. This acts to interfere with capital accumulation in the petty-commodity producing region and leads to its *external articulation* or dependence upon the capitalist region.

From this point, the logic of capital accumulation in the dominant region, which is to drive out the least profitable and most labour-intensive economic activities and replace them with more profitable and more differentiated and efficient capital-consuming activities, takes a phased course. First, control of the petty-commodity production process passes to financial institutions as credit is extended to enable producers to purchase the means of more intensive production. The processing of agricultural output also passes into the control of centralizing capitalist industries. The emergent spatial division of labour, based on unequal exchange between regions with different levels of technical development provides the setting for unequal exchange in terms of differences in wage levels. Underpayment and the consequent squeeze upon living standards stimulates rural depopulation and migration to urban-industrial agglomerations. External articulation has been transformed into a relationship between the less and the more advanced region which Lipietz terms *integration-domination*. The binding connections of ownership and control further the capacity of the capitalist region for *introverted accumulation* (equivalent to Amin's *autocentric* accumulation) leaving the transitional region capable only of *extraverted* accumulation. Second, as capital seeks out areas from which further accumulation may be secured, the integration of the dominated region is tightened by the transfer of branch plants which engage in low skill, labour-intensive production and assembly work where wages are low. The economic structure of the dominated region loses its internal cohesiveness as capitalist industry develops regional space to accommodate what Lipietz terms the *branch circuit*, the uneven regional division of labour based on external control, polarization of functions, and exploitation of the periphery. Finally, this inter-regional polarization develops in the tertiary sector as well as the manufacturing sector as depopulated rural areas become centres for tourism and military services, while intermediate regions receive *feminized*, low-skill office-work, and headquarter regions intensify their level of higher order service functions (Lipietz, 1980a).

The criticisms that can be made of this theory are comparable though less pronounced than those to which Castells's work on urban structure and development is subject. They stem mainly from the rationalism and functionalism which accompanies explanations founded on the concept of structural determination. For the structuralist treatment of the mechanism which makes for change, namely the articulation of different modes of production, produces a logical grid for organizing real historical processes but the grid is itself derived from a narrow and particular abstraction of material processes. Hence, simply as one example, the accession to dominance of capitalist regions over pre-capitalist ones is presented as a logical outcome of the capital accumulation process, thus leaving class and popular initiatives and responses towards the development process, the ways in which government and the legal system assisted or hindered the process and the contradictory nature of historical change reduced to the juggernaut of structural determination. The functionalism in Lipietz's account derives, not from its structuralist method, at least not directly, but rather from its reliance upon the unequal exchange mechanism as an explanation of uneven development between regions. Hence, Lipietz is conscious that different branches of capital will exploit regional inequalities in different ways, but in whichever way they do this it is always determined by an earlier stage of unequal exchange, based on unequal technical and organizational development between regions. The latter keeps backward regions in a permanently functional relationship for introverted accumulation at the centre. This seems both theoretically and historically dubious given the early history of British accumulation in peripheral regions, and contemporary spatial restructuring in the USA and, to a lesser extent, European countries.

The attractions of structuralism and unequal exchange theory are resisted by Carney *et al.* (1976; 1977; 1980) although some work has drawn upon Frankian dependency theory to show how depressed wage levels controlled by a regional bourgeoisie allowed the latter to realize huge profits when output reached markets elsewhere. However, as economic control has passed from the region in question (North-east England) so a new dependency based on external technical control of industry under direct or indirect state-intervention and profit-repatriation out of the region has deepened its underdevelopment. More recently though, the point of emphasis has shifted from the sphere of exchange to the study of the ways in which the requirements of capital in production create uneven spatial effects. The contradictory process of capitalist development is represented in two processes, one, the stronger, towards spatial concentration based on the reproduction needs of modern industry (cf. Castells's thesis) while the other tendency is towards spatial decentralization along the lines described by Lipietz. Because of the instability with which accumulation proceeds, different regions come to meet various requirements of capital in overcoming its own internally-generated crises.

Under contemporary monopoly capitalism the state's industrial and planning resources are crucially important in supplying conditions for cheapening the component parts of capital and thus enabling accumulation to continue. This occurs with regard to variable capital (labour-power), circulating constant capital (raw materials and fuel) and fixed constant capital (buildings, infrastructure). Historically, rural areas have specialized in the reproduction of cheap labour power but past concentration and consequent rural depopulation have exhausted this source. However, the capacity of the state to cheapen the cost of energy, first, by depressing the market price of nationalized coal production, and second, by shifting to a cheaper oil-based energy strategy in the 1960s, resulted in both the requirement for lower circulating constant capital costs and the provision of a new source of cheap variable capital (in redundant mining communities) being met. In the meantime large amounts of fixed constant capital have been scrapped as a condition for future restructuring in which the state, through regional policy, performs an important role by cheapening new fixed constant capital investments. One effect of this crisis-ridden process in culturally distinctive regions is to provoke regionalist political movements to defend their community against accumulation imperatives, an intervention which leads to new rounds of state involvement to secure the general accumulation process.

The principal criticisms of this theory of uneven development and spatial relations must be directed at its tendencies towards economic reductionism, in turn a product of inadequate abstraction, and an overwhelming function-alism. With regard to the latter, everything that occurs in space appears to be conducted at the behest of capital, whether it is coalfields being closed, labour power being cheapened, or the state intervening to perform the functions generally necessary for accumulation in a generally unproblematic way. There is little reference, for example, to the role of class mobilization and political action in bringing about the crisis of accumulation for indigenous coal owners, neither is the question of the class impact upon subsequent forms of state-intervention explored. Rather, class and political behaviour tend to be read off from what happens at the level of the economy and what is in the direct interests of capital. This leads on to the second point of criticism, which is that because the main focus of abstraction is upon the logic of accumulation, the question, for example, of whether or not there are substantial cultural, political and social forces which influenced specific outcomes, is subsumed into relative unimportance. Hence, the possibility that by making it hard for variable capital to be significantly cheapened (unionization, national wage bargaining) or, via nationalization, preventing the earlier scrapping of inefficient private fixed investment, the working class may have countered the imperatives of capital accumulation, and that political regionalism is a recognition of this too, is not faced. Similarly, though less palatably, the possibility that restructuring of the kind theorized can appear, to some extent, on the agenda of political demands of working class parties is not considered.

Despite these problems it is clearly correct to begin the analysis of regional uneven development with a theorization of the effects of differ-ential spatial relations upon the capacity of firms to secure conditions of production which enable capital accumulation to proceed, rather than assuming these to be predetermined by unequal exchange. This is because unequal exchange, to the extent that it may be found to exist, is itself contingent upon a previous, asymmetrical relationship which yields up the surplus value available for exchange in the first place. The latter occurs at the point of commodity-production where the capacity for capital accumulation depends upon labour, despite its countervailing efforts, commanding wages, the value of which is less than the exchange value of the commodities produced. Such an inequality of *exchange* is crucial to the analysis of capital accumulation and spatial variations in its occurrence, but it is secondary to the existence of the social relations whereby capitalists control all the means of production and workers can only gain access to these by selling their labour power on the terms set by the former. The importance of an assymetry in social relations of this kind lies in the relative ease with which capital investments, whether fixed or circulating, may be shuffled over space to take advantage of variations in the reproduction costs of variable capital.

The interaction of periodic changes in the requirements of firms towards the organization of production and the specific, spatially-differentiated qualities of sub-national labour markets has been recognized in the work of Massey (1978; 1979; 1980). Regional development is not theorized as necessarily occurring in a series of pre-existing spatial containers but rather as emerging through the complex workings out of the accumulation process and its distinctive productive configurations. The first phase of capitalist development resulted in accumulation centres being polarized on the basis of sectoral specialization – textile manufacturing, ship building, coal and steel producing regions and so on. A later phase brought further, but concentrated sectoral specialization in previously underindustrialized regions – motor vehicles, domestic appliances, pharmaceuticals etc. The most recent phase is signified by concentration of ownership of capital and, on the one hand, spatial concentration of complex production units, but on the other, spatial decomposition of different parts of the production process in some sectors. The latter can occur either within the organization of a single large firm through the establishment of branch plants or between a large firm and its (semi-) autonomous suppliers. Developments in productive technique mean that the labour-intensive parts of the production process do not require high skill levels on the part of the workforce, hence deskilled jobs tend to be made available in areas of highest unskilled or semi-skilled labour concentration. These are often, though by no means exclusively, found in former polarized centres of accumulation for which state regional and local planning and investment agencies act as suppliers of infrastructure, investment capital and information to firms wishing to decentralize or relocate. One result of this is the superimposition of different and historically specific *spatial divisions of labour* (see also Dunford, 1977; 1979), the most recent of which assimilates low-wage workers in problem regions into the routine assembly work, skilled workers in semi-peripheral regions for stages of production requiring craftsmanship, and managerial, technical and research workers in a central metropolitan region. This is not a predetermined pattern, however, and as in some sectors, standardization of production deskills the workforce to an increasing extent, a new polarization of productive organization between metropolitan headquarters and remote assembly line, bypassing the intervening craft-stage/region occurs. The latter is typical of the electronics industry, for example, but not the motor-vehicle industry which retains a threefold division, or, for example, some clothing and footwear industries[13] which may retain a division of labour concentrated in local space (Massey and Meegan, 1979; Massey, 1980).

This explanation of uneven regional development as an outcome of changing spatial relations contingent upon the actions of capitalists main-taining accumulation and control of production through restructuring its organization, has much to commend it in the terms with which we are here concerned. It avoids the functionalism of similar, preceding formulations such as that of Lipietz, because it does not rely on the unequal exchange mechanism to explain regional inequality. By contrast to the core-periphery determinism which is there implied, spatial divisions of labour can exist which do not involve unevenness of that kind of intensity. This means there is no essential spatial equilibrium or disequilibrium being postulated and towards which the system is necessarily tending, although in the present phase of capitalist development the contradictions of concentration in some sectors and spatial decentralization in others are observable effects of varying accumulation strategies. The stress upon the variability of spatial outcome sector-by-sector is precisely the theoretical result of rejecting the temptations of employing idealist or rationalist formulations such as ecological association or structural determination and deriving an explan-ation of spatial processes from an understanding of the effects upon the organization of production of accumulation imperatives. This is not to say that there are not points of criticism to be made of this approach, as will be seen, but rather that it provides a good example of materialist analysis and theorization.

One problem is a tendency towards economic reductionism, whereby the logic of accumulation does seem to drag class relations, state action, and regional restructuring along behind it. However, this is remedied somewhat in the recognition that class resistance is a significant modifier of accumula-tion imperatives (Massey, 1980, p. 2). Even so this introduces a further inclination to subsume certain socio-cultural factors, such as low female activity rates in heavy industry regions, solely to relations of production. A larger problem, though, concerns the theorization of the state's role in assisting the recomposition of spatial divisions of labour. It tends to be viewed as adopting a responsive posture, mainly towards capital, in supply-ing conditions for accumulation, while at other times meeting labour's local demands for alternative job opportunities through regional policy, in a relatively passive, unreflective way. A functionalist interpretation is thus avoided mainly at the expense of rendering state-involvement in capitalist development somewhat ephemeral; this is, ironically, a feature even of the detailed study of the restructuring of the electronics industry in Britain for which the state, through the Industrial Reorganization Corporation, was directly responsible (Massey and Meegan, 1979).

To conclude this somewhat lengthy chapter, it is important to pick out those elements from the many theories of development processes which we have considered which are going to be of most assistance in our attempt at producing a materialist framework for overcoming the separation between theorizing planning on the one hand, and theorizing development on the other. The first point to be made is that it is clearly possible to conceptualize the connections, especially at the urban level, between development and planning without simply assimilating them. Thus we can agree with Castells's argument that urban planning is inserted in the relation between capital and labour whose contradictions dynamize the development process, although not with his delimitation of that involvement principally to consumption issues. The main problem here lies in the structuralist editing of both the nature of 'the urban' and the form of the state. Better theorizations of the development of the former are available in Scott's and Harvey's work but only at the expense of worse theorizations of the latter. Of particular value is the concept of the urban area as a site of production, consumption and circulation (exchange) space with planning acting as a mediator to all three from a location between the state and civil society, although Scott does not theorize either of the latter adequately, and his dismissal of production relations as central to class struggle is a mistake. Harvey's analysis of the role of the built environment in capital accumulation improves once the under-consumption thesis is jettisoned, especially in regard to the contradiction between the hypermobility of capital and the inertia of labour giving rise to localized struggles, with implications for uneven state action. These insights begin to point away from any monolithic theory of development and state planning and towards more localized complexes of factors which produce different developmental effects over space.

At the broader, regional to international level, much of the available theory can be seen to be overdependent upon the developmental effects of inequality in the sphere of exchange to provide fully satisfactory accounts. Nevertheless, the cultural dimension in Hechter's study constitutes a sphere of protest and struggle, not necessarily reflective of class relations, which cannot be ignored in considering forms of development and state intervention which occur differentially over space. The core-periphery metaphor which structures the latter analysis is given a much-needed flexibility in Wallerstein's formulation of 'the semi-periphery', a concept which is not inconsistent with certain of Lipietz's and Massey's, less macroscopic, ideas about changing regional fortunes as a representation of changing spatial divisions of labour, and one which Mingione (1981, p. 193) sees as important to explaining the forms taken by sub-national divisions of labour. However, we have seen that it is crucially important to begin the analysis of the processes which produce differentiated spatial divisions of labour with the study of capital accumulation, a task which necessarily focuses attention upon the changing strategies of capital at the point of production. The contest between classes around this focus would appear to be fundamental in setting constraints for other struggles whether over consumption services, for cultural reasons, or issues centring upon gender or race which may directly or indirectly be stimulated by, or reacted to, the planning system. It is for this reason that theories which treat exchange as the dominant source of exploitation have been found inadequate. However, it has also been seen that a focus on production requirements and accumulation imperatives to the exclusion of exchange relations (actions occurring in the sphere of circulation) tend to be closely associated with an inappropriate economic reductionism. This was a problem in the work of Carney *et al.* (1977; 1980) despite the otherwise useful analysis of the contradictory requirements of the components of capital, which shared similarities to Harvey's later findings.

The barest outlines for further progress thus seem to be encompassed in certain of the features of recent materialist analyses of the development process. However, most of the theorizations are inadequate as they stand in full, for reasons which have to do with varying degrees of functionalism, rationalism, idealism, essentialism and abstractionism. The elements to which it seems worthwhile paying closer attention include: the effect of accumulation imperatives upon relations of production and vice versa; the spatially diverse forms of unevenness in development which are representative of the local, sectoral manifestation of contradictions between capital and labour; the ways in which spatial concentrations of development differentially and indeterminately accommodate those contradictions; the extent to which variations in the spatial division of labour constitute solutions to different levels of contradiction from the international to the local; the extent to which such solutions are overdetermined by contradictions located outside the relations of production in civil society; and the precise ways in which state planning connects with the distinctive components of capital, and key points on the circuit of capital accumulation, that is production, distribution, exchange and consumption. To set about fulfilling the last task involves more detailed discussion of theories of the state, and, more particularly, theories of those branches of the central, regional and local state relating most closely to development planning. It is to a consideration of these matters in terms, once again, of the evaluative criteria which must guide our choice, that the following chapter is devoted.

8 The state, the local state and development planning

We have seen so far that materialist theories of development tend to incorporate a highly functionalist and reductionist theorization of the state's involvement in the development process. This occurs even where theorizations of other aspects of development avoid such problems to a large extent. In none of the accounts which have been discussed does the state appear as anything other than a kind of reserve power of the capitalist class which is triggered into action on demand or by virtue of a special expertise in pre-visioning what those demands are likely to be. The important constraints which are imposed upon state action by the existence of a class society, and indeed, the limitations upon what a dominant class can itself achieve are assumed away. The problems of its antagonistic relationship with a subordinate class which, nevertheless, is not powerless with regard to the operation of means of production, are obliterated by the determinations of space, exchange or the logic of capital accumulation. Moreover, the possibility of important variations in the relationship between state and capital, or more accurately branches of capital (industrial versus financial; industrial producers versus industrial consumers; banks versus other institutionalized finance capital), and their spatial representation in development processes is not explored. Finally, the question of levels and specificities within the overall apparatus of the state, the extent to which conflicts on an intra-state basis affect the development process, and where the planning of development sits in relation to class and non-class interests as these impinge on the state, are similarly underemphasized.

It seems, therefore, that to the extent that recent progress can be said to have occurred in the theorization of processes of development, due to the new and deeper awareness of underlying spatial tendencies associated with capital accumulation, such advances may be being simultaneously undermined by a failure to theorize these dialectically. That is, by focusing upon a fundamentally linear idea of capital accumulation to which the remainder of the complex determinations of capitalist society, state, classes, culture, ideology, are conceptually subordinated, a large slice of material reality which, for part of the time at least, exists in opposition to accumulation imperatives, and modifies their spatial manifestations, remains untheorized. While this remains the case, understanding of capitalist development will be unnecessarily distorted. As a partial remedy to that problem this chapter is devoted to a discussion and critical evaluation of recent developments in the theory of the capitalist state (for good general treatments see Jessop, 1977; 1982; Holloway and Picciotto, 1977; 1978). However, while it will be important to take account of the strengths and weaknesses of these theories as they refer to explanations of state form and content in themselves, our main concern remains with the state in relation to development in cities and regions. For that reason we will seek to gauge the relevance of theorizations of the state at the more local and, where they exist, regional levels than is customary in giving accounts of state theory. The chapter begins, therefore, with a somewhat cursory account of the main macro-theoretic lines of development. This is followed by a more detailed discussion of theories of the local state, and the chapter concludes with some ideas about the differentiation of levels at which urban and regional planning operates within the state, and the extent to which class and popular struggles have determined its hierarchization.

Theories of the state

In this section we will briefly consider three kinds of state theory in the light, once more, of the evaluative criteria outlined in chapter seven. There, it will be recalled, it was concluded that major weaknesses in the theorization of planning and other social processes stemmed from their rationalism, essentialism, idealism, functionalism and abstractionism, and that superior theories would have to avoid these characteristics. However, we have subsequently seen that these criteria are by no means to be understood as mechanically distinguishing traditional theory from more radical formulations. Much work which carefully criticizes traditional development theory, for example, shares many of its faults where alternatives are proposed despite its Ricardian, Marxian or Weberian credentials. We intend to show that much the same can be said for a good deal of recent state theory too. Three sets of theories will be outlined and criticized, the first of these we will refer to as *class-theories* of the state, the second as *crisis-theories* of the state, and the third as *capital-theories* of the state.

Class-theories

Class-theories of the state may be defined in terms of their identification of the nature of state actions with a particular political role in which the state's central problem is to resolve class conflict. The two best known (and most recycled and criticized) of these are represented in the apparently mutually exclusive theories of Miliband (1969; 1973; 1977) and Poulantzas (1973; 1976; 1978). Despite their dissimilarity in, for example, method of approach – individualist in the former case, structuralist in the latter, or degrees of freedom ascribed to the state – an instrument of the dominant class for Miliband; relatively autonomous for Poulantzas, the fact that both start by taking the state as in principle analysable in abstraction from capital accumulation and social relations of production is a unifying bond. This is not to say that the material base of political classes is totally neglected in either account, rather that it is treated as a static backcloth to the centre stage political action. Miliband's class-theory of the state depends on the assertion that the ruling class in a capitalist society (by definition the capitalist class) shares cultural affinities with the elite which manages the state's affairs: higher civil servants, judges, generals and the like. Because of this the state acts as the willing instrument of the ruling class, reproducing an imbalanced distribution of income and wealth and preserving the dominance of capitalist ideology and political power.

Poulantzas criticizes this view of the state as an instrument on a number of grounds. He rejects the emphasis on shared cultural and ideological affinities between subjects inside and outside the state, arguing instead that the state is objectively capitalist due to its relationship with the underlying mode of production. Next, he dismisses the idea that the state simply responds automatically to the requirements of the ruling class and advances the notion of the state itself being internally structured by the contending class interests of both labour and capital. Finally, he argues that Miliband is wrong to conceive the ruling class as a monolithic and harmonious category, and that, rather, it should be seen as itself subject to contradictions which the state helps to resolve. He promotes a class-theory of his own in which the state is first and foremost to be understood as a distillate of the relations between the struggling classes of capital and labour. Hence, the state may, on occasion, not act instrumentally for the dominant class but against it, if only to preserve its long-term dominance. So, for example, the public provision of certain goods and services can be explained by Poulantzas's theory. However, because of the restrictions of instrumentalism, such can only be the case following Miliband's theory if resort is made to circular explanation. This would show working-class gains to be ultimately in the interests of capitalists due to the improved quality of worker which results from the greater expenditure on better housing and health services. It is because the class struggle is reproduced within the state that it can act to maintain the cohesion of a class-riven society by making concessions to the dominated class at strategic moments. But to secure the capitalist nature of the society in question, the state must help to organize the contradictory interests of the ruling class into political coherence, while disorganizing working-class efforts at forming a powerful political movement. The state ensures that this happens by providing the conditions for a power bloc to exist, which is composed of fractions of the dominant class, and which acts under the overall hegemonic control of the interests of monopoly capital. The latter point sits rather uncomfortably with the one which stresses the relative autonomy of the state from being a simple instrument of the power bloc (Jessop, 1977, p. 358).

Numerous problems have been identified in both of these theories. It has been pointed out that both theorists, in failing to relate political conflict between classes to the social imbalances entailed by surplus value production, rely upon inadequate abstractions upon which to build a systematic state theory (Holloway and Picciotto, 1977; 1978). Both have also been shown to be reductionist, albeit for different reasons. Miliband's instrumentalist theory of the state reduces state action to that of a mere appendage of the dominant class, rather as tends to happen in neo-Ricardian theories of development as we saw in the work of Scott in the previous chapter. Poulantzas, by contrast, reduces relations rooted in surplus value production to a political struggle between classes defined by their technical function in the productive structure. Both theorists thus operate with a distributional theory of class structure; Miliband, as we have seen, conceives the task of the state as the maintenance of the wealth and income of the ruling class, Poulantzas as the maintenance of overall social cohesion between distributional classes. Each thus imposes, rationalistically, a logic of conflict which is reflective of distributional inequality, but which contains no concept of the mechanisms which can explain why it is that the stakes of that conflict relationship can change and intensify (Clarke, 1977, pp. 3, 14). It is important to note, also, that in postulating the content of state action as either maintaining ruling-class dominance (Miliband) or the cohesion of the social formation (Poulantzas), both adopt essentialist positions which, first, make it difficult to explain exceptions other than in a circular way, and second, imply little prospect of change occurring in social relations other than through gradual evolution.

The latter point leads to the major criticism which has been made of these theories of the state, which is that they are inherently functionalist. Poulantzas's assertion that the state is functional for maintaining overall cohesion within a capitalist social formation

. . . in the sense of the cohesion of the ensemble of the levels of a complex unity, *and as the regulating factor of its global equilibrium as a system*. (Poulantzas, 1973, pp. 44–5)

might have been taken straight from the pages of Talcott Parsons's work, and its remarkable effect is to cause all factors making for cohesion (including the family and trade unions) part of the apparatus of the state, a conception which, as well as being functionalist, seems also to be somewhat chaotic. The functionalism of Miliband's account derives far more straightforwardly from the concept of an instrumental state whose actions are unlimited by incapacities intrinsic to a state in *capitalist*, surplus-value producing, society. Both theories, finally, share a certain idealistic quality although both struggle against this somewhat. Poulantzas clearly adheres to the ideal categories of Althusserian structuralism especially in his early writings, much as Castells did, but the simultaneous attempts to argue that class struggle rather than structural determination underlay the functioning of the state clearly rests uneasily with the systems-language of Althusserianism (Saunders, 1981, pp. 190–1). The idealism in Miliband's state-theory represents an inadequate distancing on his part from the traditional sociological notion that shared norms explain social interaction, in this case between ruling-class and state-elite. Hence, in Miliband's position, the emphasis upon cultural affinities connects together both the idealist and the functionalist characteristics which, combined with others which we have discussed, make his thesis less than satisfactory for our purposes.

Crisis theories

Many of the problems which have been identified with class-theories of the state recur in theories which derive the form and content of the state action from its relation with aspects of social, political, ideological and economic breakdowns in late capitalism. We will briefly discuss the work of the three writers who contribute to what may be termed *crisis-theories* of the state: Habermas (1976); Offe (1972; 1975); Offe and Ronge (1975), and O'Connor (1973). The basic ideas of these theorists have become quite well known, especially as they have been adapted in various ways in analyses of urban problems (Alcaly and Mermelstein, 1977; Friedland, Fox Piven and Alford, 1978; Hill, 1977, 1978; Tabb, 1978; Gough, 1979; Saunders, 1979, 1981), due in part to the empirical immediacy of the crisis tendencies of capitalism which are the subject of their theoretical labours.

Habermas identifies a number of crisis tendencies which are entailed by the state's expansion of functions. These are consequent upon its incorporation of increased economic, administrative and ideological control within its scope in the interests of sustaining private accumulation. First, there are crises which traditionally remained expressed at the level of market relations but which now have been displaced into the state. These reflect the absorption of a large segment of economic activity, especially that which involves sustaining conditions for private accumulation and reproducing labour power. The politicization of these areas involves increased expenditure and the prospect of deficits with attendant problems of breakdown in provision. Next, there are crises associated with the state's capacity rationally to administer the policies by means of which surplus-value production is maintained through demand management, budgetary and monetary manipulations and so on. Then there is the prospect of the legitimacy of a system of socialized management of privately appropriated wealth being brought into question, especially to the extent that crises in the economic and administrative functions of the state produce lower levels of growth and increased unemployment. Finally, the methods by which the legitimacy crisis is overcome, which involve infringing such privatistic norms as individual property rights or self-help in welfare, may lead to a crisis of motivation on the part of individuals.

In discussing the ways in which the state fails to overcome these crisis tendencies, and thus remains a capitalist rather than some form of post-capitalist state, Habermas gives a central position to various constraints operating upon capitalist planning. To do this he constrasts modes of planning and participation drawn from mainstream planning theory, identifying four types. The first of these, *non-participatory incrementalism* is characterized by strong procedural formality and the subjugation of controversy. The second, *non-participatory comprehensive planning*, involves the systematic exclusion of political debate and reliance upon authoritative centralist, technical, systems-guidance towards strategic goals. The third, *pluralist-incrementalism* in which piecemeal change is subject to formal democratic negotiation, is then contrasted with the fourth, *pluralist-comprehensive planning* in which strategy is subject to democratic debate before being delegated to technical control in implementation.[1] He argues that it is the rejection of the non-participatory modes, despite attempts to establish them by the state, which has prevented complete crisis management from being achieved. This has only been possible because, so far, the statements of power holders do not go unchallenged by reasoning individuals. Habermas concludes that for this capacity to be preserved and for domination of the individual by political and ideological manipulation, planning must be the object of an enhanced participatory mode of decision-making. But because pluralist-incrementalism would pose unbearable strains for the continued functioning of the system he asserts that

. . . this procedure of normative genesis must, of course, be connected to the systems-theoretic approach if it is to contribute to a suitable theory of evolution. (Habermas, 1976, p. 140)

In other words he argues that the technicist, bureaucratic structures of the state will gain legitimacy only to the extent that they are thoroughly accountable to *popular* democratic control.

This positive note is countered in the work of one of Habermas's former close associates, Offe, who has been concerned less with the analysis of crisis tendencies themselves, and more with the ways in which the state in capitalist society has developed means of dealing with them, albeit unsuccessfully in the long run. First of all he identifies the means by which the state mobilizes bias against non-capitalist influences being exerted on the policy-making process. This involves the activation of a number of *internal selective mechanisms*; a negative one excludes state policies hostile to capitalist interests from the agenda, a positive one limits policies to those favouring general rather than individual capitalist interests, while a third functions to disguise the class nature of state policy by presenting it as being in everyone's interest. There are also various procedural, ideological and repressive back-up powers which may be invoked to structure choices correctly. These mechanisms become more vital to the state's management of capitalist interests as its role has shifted from being primarily regulative, whereby rights and privileges at the state's disposal were authoritatively allocated, to being more deeply engaged in productive activity, investing in fixed constant capital and variable capital to sustain private accumulation. This is because the old, bureaucratic rules for allocating entitlements are in conflict with the rationality of market forces. One alternative is for the state to engage in rational planning to meet the global needs of private capital. However, this is inappropriate because while the market sets and corrects the goals of private production, state production is not subject to that discipline and is inefficient in consequence. The other alternative is for the state to follow the line advocated by Habermas by adopting decentralized, democratic partici-pation for policy-formation processes. This, though, contains the obvious weakness that as well as reflecting class and popular conflicts, it would also create further ones by inviting more demands than could be accommodated by a capitalist state. In other words, the fundamental contradictions entailed by increasing state involvement in the accumulation process are irremedi-able, and ultimately crisis-inducing.

More recently Offe has been concerned to analyse the conditions under which corporatism[2] comes to be a major mode by means of which the state ensures crisis avoidance (Offe and Wiesenthal, 1980). The process is con-ceived as an effect of a double dependency characteristic of capitalist society. The first of these is based on the inherent inequality between capital and labour. The objectives of the former are clearly signalled by market forces and its class-power rests on individual ownership of means of pro-duction. For labour, by contrast, objectives have to be established against the dominant structures of liberal democracy which atomize class-based interests (see also Esping-Anderson, Friedland and Wright, 1976, pp. 190–1), and power has to be rooted in collective action and organization which is much more vulnerable to disorganization. The second dependency is that of the state upon the power of capital to refuse to invest and accumulate capital. The working class, by contrast, possesses no equivalent external guarantor to assist the furtherance of its interests through state institutions. Two important results flow from this: first, communication between the representatives of capital's interests and the state is inconspicuous because it can be confined to technical issues within a shared framework of under-standing. However, union representation must normally be conspicuous because communication consists of claims which transcend established norms. These claims are also made in the context of a breakdown of consensus and the offensive use of power. Second, because of the pressure to which trade unions are subject they may either find liberal-democratic modes of interest-aggregation imposed upon them (secret ballots, incomes policies, social contracts) or they may *opportunistically* limit their own action to the patterns of the liberal 'interest-group', underwritten by the state. The latter strategy appears rational in terms of achieving short-term success, but suffers its own rationality crisis when legitimacy is removed by the state or by union members critical of an incorporated leadership. Corporatism is therefore an unstable solution to the continuing crises of accumulation, tending to be a temporary basis for short-term gains by labour and capital under social democratic governments.

Aspects of the foregoing crisis-theories of the state are criticized by the proponent of a third and closely-related one by O'Connor (1981). In particular, the work of Habermas on the legitimation crisis, while being praised for identifying the increasing integration between economics, politics and culture within the apparatus of the state which undermines previous simplistic, economistic crisis-theory, is criticized for its 'radicalized Durkheimian approach'. The argument is that despite distinguishing importantly between the ways in which crises in the integration of the macro-systems of capitalism, and crises in the ways in which social integration operate, with the latter not reducible to the former, he has to rely on structural functionalism to explain both processes. In other words Habermas explains crisis in terms of the breakdown of normative consensus in social relations and the failure of individuals to perform allotted functions. Ultimately the integration of systems functions is impaired. But if systems integration falters, for reasons of supply or demand shortages in the economy, for example, social integration need not be impaired, and a crisis need not occur. The weakness is that this approach only points, rationalistically, to alternative logical outcomes. It is thus capable of only a loose specification of crisis tendencies as these are formed through consciously combative struggles by labour against the accumulation prerogatives of capital. Although O'Connor does not mention Offe's research in this critique, clearly to the extent that Offe also works with a theory in which the state's crisis tendencies are reflections of systemic contradictions in the logic of capitalism, a point which seems to be further underlined in his portrayal of state and labour as cripplingly dependent upon capital most recently, he is open to the same strictures. There is, therefore, a one-sided abstraction in both accounts which is neglectful of the dualistic class relationship of capitalism and what that may imply for crisis formation. This is further complicated in Habermas's case by a heavy emphasis upon the idealist notion that the state legitimizes private accumulation by predisposing individual subjects to accept its consequent inequalities. But this is to ignore the possibility that acceptance of private property relations is a matter of conscious consent on the part of workers in exchange for certain securities, for example, that wage increases will be based on the level of profit earned by their firm in the previous year (Przeworski, 1980a).

However, perhaps the most interesting feature of O'Connor's (1981) paper is that it marks at least a partial autocritique of his own influential theory of the fiscal crisis of the state. The latter is conceived as an effect of the state's involvement in overcoming the underconsumption of commodities in monopoly capitalism. The monopoly sector dominates the private market due to its overwhelming control of capital and technology, leaving a small but expanding small business sector to mop up the victims of technological redundancy and to supply the monopolies with cheap product inputs. A third, partially autonomous sector of the economy is occupied by the state's productive functions. Its autonomy stems from economic inefficiency associated with the absence of a market discipline. This is revealed in low productivity, inflationary wage-costs and budgetary incrementalism. This economic structure provides the distributional basis for a class structure in which the middle-class of all three sectors enjoy similar incomes; the working-class in the monopoly sector is relatively affluent; and the working-class in the state and competitive sectors is poor. Class struggles do not occur within the economic sphere but are displaced into the realm of political conflict within the state.

State expenditure reflects the respective needs of capital and labour by being divided into *social capital* expenditure and *social expenses*. These latter are unproductive, being devoted to poverty relief and state repressive functions (police, military). The former are indirectly productive, being divided between subsidies to capital in the form of *social investment*, and to labour in the form of *social consumption*. Capital subsidies may be *complementary* to private sector investments by supplying physical infrastructure, transport services and derelict land reclamation, or they may be *discretionary* in which case an element of risk is taken in order to stimulate accumulation. Labour subsidies are broken down into *collective consumption* services (housing, urban renewal, welfare facilities) and *social security* expenditure (unemployment benefits, pensions, disability allowances). The requirements of the monopolies are for increased complementary capital subsidies and social consumption because the first reduces the costs of constant capital while the second reduces the costs of variable capital and stimulates demand. The fiscal crisis of the state arises from the displacement of distributional class struggle into the state. This forces up state expenditure, hence taxation, but the expenditure is mainly indirectly productive, it is privately appropriated, and the tax base does not expand. As the state is increasingly seen to be sustaining private accumulation, there are taxpayers' revolts, increased consumerism and citizen protest which widen the structural gap between socialized revenue and privatized accumulation. The fiscal crisis turns into a legitimation crisis as the state's accumulation function comes into contradiction with its function of legitimizing the existing system.

There are clearly at least two theories of planning contained within O'Connor's thesis. On the one hand, planning is a direct instrument of big firms in meeting the vast expenditures necessary on infrastructural and circulation investment if scale economies are to be secured by them. These are gained at the direct and intensifying expense of labour which supplies socialized revenues for ultimately private appropriation. Demands for greater participation in the planning process are thus explained as attempts to gain greater accountability from the state in its spending patterns. On the other hand, planning is a state response to the demands for social consumption expenditure from the poorest sections of the working class, some of whom the state directly employs, and the monopoly sector working class for improved housing and welfare facilities. This has contradictory effects for the monopoly sector because it involves partly unproductive expenditure to workers in small businesses, the state sector itself, and the unemployed, which reduces the total of indirectly productive capital flowing to the monopolies. However, in helping depress wage claims in the monopoly sector, planning has a partly functional role for large capital. Generally, planning is conceived as being disfunctional for small businesses because their employees divert capital away from the monopolies and help to create the structural gap which leads to fiscal crisis.

Despite the usefulness of some of these insights, perhaps most of all with regard to the relationship between planning and small businesses, there are clearly problems with this theory overall. It, too, has been shown to be functionalist, although we would not agree with Saunders (1981, p. 245) in arguing that it is functionalist in that investment, consumption and expenses are *all* explained in terms of their contribution to the interests of monopoly capital. Its method of abstraction is inadequate in placing the location of class struggle at the point of distribution, as indeed is its definition of classes in terms of relationship to the market, both of which reflect the neo-Ricardian flaw of ignoring social relations of production. It is also, clearly, a rationalistic creation in that it imposes a conceptually derived framework on to reality with unnecessarily complicating effects. Thus education is classified as social investment whereas from O'Connor's viewpoint, dominated by exchange rather than production, it could equally be justified as social consumption. Finally, in sharing with Habermas the concept of a state legitimation function it is equally subject to the problem of idealism since it reduces human consciousness to prescribed states of mind structured solely by a dominant ideology promulgated through the state. It is perhaps these and related problems which O'Connor is referring to when he talks of the necessity for a conception of crisis which is not founded on social disintegration but social struggle (O'Connor, 1981, p. 325). Crisis-theory which rests upon the systemic contradictions of capitalism means that:

. . . only *logical* possibilities present themselves. For example, fiscal deficits may or may not activate motivation or legitimation deficits. Profits deficits may or may not activate fiscal shortages. Reduced capacities for administrative rationality or economic steering may or may not reinforce fiscal and profits shortages. And so on. (O'Connor, 1981, p. 332, emphasis added)

Capital theories

It was partly in opposition to the problems associated with crisis-theories of the state that the major strand of *capital theory* of the state was advanced (Müller and Neusüss, 1978; Hirsch, 1978; Blanke, Jürgens and Kastendiek, 1978). Despite this, the notion of the accumulation crisis plays a crucial role in these state-theories, especially that of Hirsch, although crisis is not the main determinant of state action as it appears to be in the work we have just discussed. Space does not permit the detailed discussion of the distinctiveness of the various contributions in the detail which they deserve, although useful critical analyses of the main variants of *state derivation theory* have emerged of late (Jessop, 1977, 1982; Holloway and Picciotto, 1978; Urry, 1981a). It is somewhat ironical that Hirsch's version of state derivation theory, which, especially in Hirsch (1981), contains a sustained analysis of the relationship between the state and the urban development process of great relevance to the theorization of planning and the local state, contains features which are less appropriate for the kind of theorization which is being aimed for in this book than those which are to be found in the work of Müller and Neusüss, and Blanke *et al.* The principal reason for this, which will be developed below, is that while Hirsch concentrates on the ways in which the state functions to reproduce capitalist social relations in a relatively direct and unmediated way, the others focus on the ways in which struggle between the main contending classes are fought over the conditions, especially legal rights, on the basis of which wage labour can be secured so as to be at the disposal of capital.

Müller and Neusüss immediately reject any connotations of instrumentalism in the relationship between state and capital by questioning the implication that state action need recognize no limits in pursuing ruling class interests. If this were so, then the state ought logically to be able to remove any obstacle which was not assisting the process of surplus value production, and, conversely, when the state was under the control of socialist parties it ought to be able to proceed rapidly to the abolition of capitalism. That neither of these events ensues implies that the state is formed according to certain contingent constraints which are expressed in political practices. These practices, which are themselves expressions of different class and interest-group positions formed in civil society - separate from the state – force upon the state the functions of law-giver, adjudicator, supervisor and administrator of private property relations. In this way, legal individuals or citizens can engage in associational behaviour to protect and fight to extend rights which are not utterly at variance with the maintenance of capitalist social relations, which are themselves rooted in private property relations.

Thus where capital promises to destroy the individual members of society who form the basis of capitalist society, the state steps in to supervise capital. However, the way in which Müller and Neusüss present this seems to diverge from their earlier idea of state action being prompted by struggle, they see social policy as a functional prerequisite for the maintenance of class society, brought into being paternalistically by the state. In this way the illusion of a neutral state, capable of implementing social reforms and even of being used for transcending capitalist social relations, is created despite the fact that the latter are, in fact, safeguarded by the implementation of the former.

With the exception of the tendency towards explaining social policy in functionalist terms this account avoids most of the problems which we have so far identified with most theories of planning, development and the state. By showing that the logic of capital does not directly produce the response in the state of parallel institutional functions it avoids being rationalistic, and by specifying the mechanism by means of which the state stands aloof from relations formed in civil society as *struggles* which in themselves assist the formation of classes as political actors (as well as objective categories constituted by the relations of production), it avoids idealism. The indeterminacy associated with contingent outcomes of class and interest-group contestation means that no essential function is being postulated for the state. This is despite the fact that the authors themselves see the enhanced capacity for successful struggle on the part of dominated interests *tending* towards the ultimate victory of the latter. For as Urry (1981a, p. 90) points out they fail to show how reformism would be translated into socialism, and thus, at the level of theory, produce a non-essentialist account, perhaps by default. Finally, the problems associated with inadequate abstraction are minimized by the correct derivation of categories and mechanisms from analysis rooted in the social relations of production rather than those of distribution, exchange or consumption.

Hirsch, too, is clear about the centrality of the *capital relation*, as he terms the basic class relationship between capital and labour, to the analysis of the changing forms taken by the state in capitalist society. Because of the necessity for all social relations to be established on the basis of individual freedom it is vital for capital to have at its disposal some means of securing wage labour since, in principle, free workers need not sell their labour power to capitalists if they choose not to. Similarly all capitalists must be free to compete with each other so that coercive power cannot be monopolized within any economic enterprise. However, because of the twin pressures of competition, on the one hand, and struggle for greater shares of the product by the contending classes at the point of production, on the other, accumulation is threatened by the tendency for the rate of profit to decline. This accelerates as capitalists seek to replace workers with machines because the source of profit, namely living labour, is thus expelled from the production process. The state is, therefore, increasingly forced to step in to maintain the preconditions for its own existence, changing its forms in so doing, and to develop the functions it fulfils as a result. These include reproducing capitalist social relations by reorganizing them in ways which penetrate more deeply into previously private spheres of life, reproducing capital itself through the expenditure of devalorized capital (the familiar infrastructural and consumption capital), and engaging in global economic management of a countercyclical nature. All of these and other associated functions constitute counter-tendencies which are mobilized reactively to overcome the crises which occur in the accumulation process due to the tendential decline in the rate of profit, but their effect is to aggravate rather than solve the crisis-tendencies to which capitalism is prone.

Hence, for Hirsch class struggle is conducted by economic classes with direct effects upon state action, so much so that as different segments of the respective classes, especially of the capitalist class, come into their own conflicting relationships, different parts of the state's apparatus themselves come into conflict with each other. This enables the state to function as guarantor for the overall maintenance of capitalist social relations. He thus extends in a rationalistic way a certain conceptual logic which is formed in the analysis of economic relations directly into the sphere of the state. This is done without consideration either of the capacity of the state to meet the needs of all the different fractions of capital involved, rather than only selected ones, or of the extent to which other social pressures force the state to limit its attempts to keep its own activities to those which are functional for capital accumulation. The abstraction is, therefore, not so much incoherent as incomplete; it does display strong overtones of essentialism in postulating an overriding purpose for the state which is to maintain conditions suitable for accumulation above all else; but it is neither idealist, because it, too, specifies the material mechanism of struggle within the capital relation rather than any disembodied *telos* as the source of capitalist development, nor, for all its reference to the functions of the state *vis-à-vis* capital, is it functional*ist* since Hirsch argues that the more the state intervenes the worse the contradictions of the capital relation become.

The reductionism of Hirsch's account of the state is overcome in the work of Blanke *et al.* (1978) who, as has already been suggested, explain the formation of the state under capitalism in terms of struggles over the coercive rights, mainly legal, which in themselves enable capitalist social relations, individual citizenship, private property relations, wage labour etc. to be secured. The framing of laws is conceived as varying according to the level of development of the mode of production and civil society, with direct, but non-functionalist, implications for the state. The laws which eventuate result in certain advantages for both capital and labour being possible, albeit within a structural relationship of overall asymmetry favouring the capacity of the former to appropriate surplus value. Blanke *et al.*

differ from Hirsch, also, in pinpointing the importance of class conflicts within not only, or always mainly, the relations of production, but also those linked to relations of exchange (circulation) and relations of reproduction (consumption) in determining the form taken by the state. Exchange and reproduction relations are predicated on the existence of wage-labour in the form of a commodity for which money is exchanged, which in turn acts as the basis for the reproduction of labour power. As capitalist development gets under way, conflicts around the relations of exchange are predominant in the earlier historic periods. These then give way to the predominance of conflicts over the reproduction of labour power as legal rights to citizenship, representation and association become generalized. However, as Urry (1981a, p. 111) indicates, having made these important points they fail to show how these conflicts themselves come to shape the continuing functioning of the state because they do not clearly perceive their interlinked nature. Thus, the extent to which these conflicts are first formed within civil society, and only then come to activate the development of the state and the system of law in ways which reproduce the basis for further struggle remains unclear.

The problems which remain to be overcome in this latter approach are twofold. First, there is a still inadequate distancing from the idea that the logic of capital accumulation determines the logic of state action, although this rationalistic residue is not as pronounced as it is in Hirsch's theorization of the state. In other words while the state is conceived as more than a simple appendage of capital in both accounts, for Blanke *et al.* its functions are considerably modified by the struggles of at least three different kinds: production, exchange, and reproduction struggles. For Hirsch, by contrast, the modifications are overwhelmingly the product of struggles located within production relations. However, neither theorization gets as near as Müller and Neusüss to specifying a separate sphere, outside the economic sphere, in which the private, associational and class relations of popular existence are formed. Thus the second problem is the failure to develop the important abstractions, by means of which a state theory is derived from production relations, to the point where the relationship between political struggles and economic struggles is seen to be crucially mediated by the sphere of civil society.

However, in three different ways these *capital theoretic* approaches point to interesting possibilities for grounding the link between planning and the development process in material relationships. First, because a space is opened up between the state, as a theoretical object, and the capital relation, it is possible to conceptualize class struggles as being formed on the basis of different combinations of social relations in the spheres of production, exchange and reproduction as these are articulated in civil society. Second, the variability in levels of class-consciousness, class-organization and class-action that is implied by the uneven development of the different combinations of spheres of struggle, and the unevenness of capitalist development itself, *enables a theorization of levels within the state to be constructed from the local to the central state*. This further allows the contradictions between urban and regional planning to be related to those which exist between local and central state. Third, it is also possible to explain the many struggles which form around planning, especially in the local state, which reflect the formation of popular movements (across class lines on occasions), and which can be understood as antagonisms on a 'people' versus 'officialdom' basis in which the central-state–local-state contradiction is important (Jessop, 1980, p. 65).

Theories of the local state

In order to develop the linkage between planning and development theory further, it is important to analyse the relationship between central and local state levels to establish the extent to which the functions in which each engages differ due to the internal differentiation of the state apparatus itself, or due to differentiation in the external pressures placed upon them, or some combination of internal and external factors. There is a growing literature on the subject of the local state, much of it of direct relevance to planning and development theory; crudely, it can be divided along the lines of the debate on the state in general which has just been discussed. The *class-theoretic* version is best represented in Cockburn (1977), the *crisis-theory* of the local state is clearest in Saunders (1979; 1981) and Cawson and Saunders (1981), although with some *class-theory* overtones, and also Dear and Clark (1980), and the *capital-theoretic* approach is contained in Hirsch (1981), Duncan and Goodwin (1982) and Cooke (1982b). Many other theorizations of the local state make use of concepts drawn from state-theory in a relatively undifferentiated way and perhaps the best way to pick out the salient points is to examine them against the background of three criteria which seem to be necessary for a valid theory of the local state to be derived. The first of these refers to the issue of local state autonomy, that is can the local state be specified in ways distinct from the central state, and to what extent do theories of the local state achieve this specificity. The second criterion concerns the extent to which the local state is theorized in the terms which were employed by the most convincing state-theory discussed earlier, namely as a form of social relation rather than an object or set of institutions. Finally, the third criterion involves the extent to which local state theories account for different spheres of struggle – production, circulation, reproduction – in discussing what is done in the name of the local state.

Specificity and autonomy

There seem to be broadly three positions identifiable in respect of the degree of autonomy experienced by the local state in relation to the central state. The first of these is most clearly stated by Cockburn (1977) who conceives the local state as the agent for the central state, subject to its mandate and sharing its burden of administration. Although the local state performs services such as providing housing, planning land use, and allocating certain personal welfare entitlements, it does so as part of the state's general task of providing the basis upon which private accumulation may continue. In this, the emphasis is heavily upon the side of social reproduction and the control of the working class. The local state thus has little autonomy and no specificity because it is simply part of the whole state system, an interpretation which means that the designation 'local state' is of little more than descriptive value. For rather different reasons Dear and Clark (1980) also present the local state as having a number of functions thrust upon it by the central state, and thus having relatively little scope for autonomy. The local state has a functional relationship for the central state whereby:

It is only via the local state system that social and ideological control of a spatially extensive and heterogeneous jurisdiction becomes possible. In this manner, local needs are anticipated and answered, and state legitimacy ensured. While the existence of a local state is functional for capitalism, it is also in keeping with the highest principles of local self-determination in democracy. (Dear and Clark, 1980, p. 5)

To this end the local state acts as the receptacle for a policy of regionalization and localization of crisis in the fiscal, legitimation and rationality functions of the central state which are controlled in the interests of capital. The local state has negligible autonomy but some specificity though it is mainly engaged in legitimizing exercises which hoodwink the public.[3]

At the other extreme Saunders (1981) and Cawson and Saunders (1981) argue that the local state does have autonomy from the central state. This is possible because the latter is responsible for production-related issues and policies while the former discharges functions connected with the reproduction of labour power, that is, issues of consumption rather than production. Such bifurcation has occurred due to the decline in the power of representative politics within the central state consequent upon the growth of corporatist[4] relations between capital, labour and the state. These are situated at the level of the central state because their prime rationale is the resolution of conflicts in the sphere of production relations. Class struggle is thus a central state rather than a local state phenomenon. However, pluralistic, interest-group politics and democratic representation are still to be found operating within the local state. Hence, this is the level at which conflicts over non-production issues are conducted, between competing groups rather than struggling classes, over the allocation of consumption goods and services. Not only does this relative autonomy of the local state give it specificity, it also gives a particular specificity to 'the urban' as against 'the regional' or national levels of resolution, hence making the study of 'urban' sociology or politics a valid disciplinary exercise.

The third position to be discussed here diverges from both of these extremes by seeking to show that the local state has a theoretical specificity and may at certain times experience autonomy from the central state but is mainly constrained to varying degrees by the limits which capitalist social relations set for the state. In Hirsch's (1981) theorization of the contribution of local administrations within the state's strategic obligation to assist capital to restructure, a number of important points are made. The first of these is that restructuring brings about a necessary diminution in the autonomy of the local state. This is because the central state, in stimulating the restructuring process in response to the declining profitability of private capital, is forced to alter the balance of expenditure from a declining budget so that capital subsidization takes precedence over social policy expenditure.

The second, and related, point is that this process helps to underline a certain specific function for the local and regional state apparatuses. This function is precisely that of diversifying conflicts which are transmitted into the central state from the economy. As the crisis tendencies of capitalism increase so the burden of legitimizing the state-induced effects of restructuring is transferred to the local state which acts as 'a filter and buffer against the demands of reproduction' (Hirsch, 1981, p. 603). The latter function is fulfilled through the processes of local politics which 'take on the character of a symbolic conflict-processing mechanism' (Hirsch, 1981, p. 604). However, the third and most valuable point is that these processes of administrative centralization provoke counter-reactions from alienated interests. These reject the destruction of the natural and social environment, the bureaucratization and centralization of political parties, and the narrow representation of class relations as production relations which go hand-in-hand with state crisis management strategies. Instead they pursue decentralized, diffuse, mainly reproduction-related interests via a growing 'grass roots' movement. This frequently has a heterogeneous class basis due to its strong connection with such issues as environmental protection and opposition to industrial location or transport developments. Here the main antagonism is between the state (either central or local depending upon the issue) and the people rather than between classes. Such movements are easily isolated, and even criminalized, by their (illegitimate) head-on confrontations with the state rather than attempting to work through (legitimate) political parties. Also their focus on relations of reproduction isolates them from the cosy, corporatist heights of the central state where issues relating to production are processed in conditions of stability.

The concern with process in conceptualizing the content of local state activity is what mainly distinguishes what he has to say from what we have considered so far. This allows the question of autonomy to be decided historically and empirically rather than establishing its presence or absence as a definitional *sine qua non*. Thus the apparently contradictory lessening of autonomy and increasing importance for crisis diversification occurring simultaneously can be logically accommodated. This is because it is the fragmentation which is possible due to the spatial diffuseness of the local state that provides it with its main factor of specificity. Having said this, however, there are clearly problems with this treatment of the local state which are also found in the others we have discussed, notably problems of functionalism in the separation of the levels of the state between production at the centre and reproduction locally, and rationalism in reducing the state's functions to those which can be derived from the logic of capital accumulation. While Hirsch is less mechanistic about the functional exclusivity of levels than Saunders, his failure to conceptualize the sphere of civil society as having a crucial mediating role between state and economy weakens the latter part of his analysis considerably. Thus popular protest over typical planning issues is only conceived of as having any political force to the extent that it penetrates into the production sphere through the corporatist structures of the central state apparatus. The fact that the latter is the means of isolating production from reproduction issues in Hirsch's (and Saunders's) account clearly makes such penetration unlikely. This is unfortunate for, as Hirsch himself shows, there is evidence of important inter-penetration of reproduction and production relations through the agency of the central state in the form, for example, of environmental protection legislation which has been perceived as negatively and directly affecting surplus value production (Hirsch, 1981, p. 601; Metzgar, 1981, pp. 15–29). Similarly, surplus value production was negatively affected by union introduction of reproduction issues into collective bargaining in the Italian motor vehicle industry from 1969 onwards with important implications for spatial restructuring (Arcangeli *et al.*, 1980; Mingione, 1981). We would conclude that functional separation of this kind, in which one set of social relations is conceived as being represented at one level of the state and another appears elsewhere, is both empirically and theoretically mistaken since it produces a mis-specification of the local state and a reductionist view of class relations.

This leads us briefly to consider an attempt to specify the local state in terms which consciously reject the artificial functional exclusivity of levels. In opposition to such a hierarchization it assesses the extent to which specificity can be derived from social relations rather than structural relationships (Duncan and Goodwin, 1982). The conclusion is that it is only by theorizing the state as a form of the relations between capital and labour that specificity can be given to the concept at all. The state is the manifestation of the separation between the social and political relations of capitalism; the former are class relations (and ethnic, gender and religious relations) while the latter are individualized. Individual relations are secured in the form of legal categories such as citizenship or contract and are represented politically by the franchise and representative democracy. The local state gains its specificity because it is vulnerable to pressures from locally powerful class organizations (principally working class) which can make it, temporarily, autonomous from both the central state and the individuation of bourgeois class dominance. Such autonomy is a reflection of locally-formed consciousness which the local state may both, on occasion, augment as well as, more commonly, undermine.

The major problems with the latter formulation, which is clearly an advance on the functionalism and determinism of the *class-theoretic* versions of the theory of the local state, and the institutionalism and reductionism of *crisis-theoretic* approaches, are that it does not adequately explain the material basis of 'consciousness', tending to treat it idealistically, and it gives undue attention to the constitution of the individual through the law in the process of exchange and insufficient attention to the coercive dimension of law in respect of production and reproduction relations. On the first point, it is the lack of a concept of civil society in which struggles and practices can be fixed in relation to material processes in the spheres of production, reproduction, exchange and distribution (or combining the last two spheres, circulation) that supplies a materialist grounding for the otherwise floating concept of 'consciousness'. On the second point, while it is clearly important to identify law as a basic condition over which struggle occurs to alter the capital relation, and one which individuates class and other social relations to disorganize opposition to bourgeois forms, the coercive underpinnings to the exchange relations of autonomous, apparently equal individuals are crucial. This explains why it is that when individuation is subordinated in the ways the authors describe as occurring in Clay Cross and Poplar (Duncan and Goodwin, 1982, pp. 33–5) the local state has, in fact, *become separate from the state* because it is not reproducing capitalist hegemony. In other words the members of civil society have withdrawn their consent to reproduce labour power by socializing the young to work, or by paying economic rents, and this may, through local politics, result in a bridging of the separation between civil society and political society (the state) which the law sustains. But since bourgeois law is a combination of consent and coercion, the latter dimension must be invoked as the dominant class struggles to restore its hegemony through the re-imposition of the state form of capitalist relations (Gramsci, 1971, pp. 227, 258; Przeworski, 1980a, p. 58).

Social relations

Clearly, from what has just been written, the local state is conceived as a social relation only in the last two theorizations considered. In the class-theoretic and crisis-theoretic versions the local state is conceived functionally as the part of the state's apparatus where concessions gained through class struggle in the central state are administered and allocated

(Cockburn), or as the site of legitimation exercises which conceal the central and local state's ultimate function of meeting capital's needs (Dear and Clark), or as a pluralistic arena of popular struggles over consumption goods, the broad allocations of which are delineated as a result of relatively harmonious class 'struggle' conducted at the highest levels of a corporatist central state (Saunders). Since we have already shown that the division between production and reproduction relations which is supposed to specify the content of central and local state activity is erroneous for the former level, and by extension (local production of the built environment; equity-sharing in office and industrial development) for the latter level too, then it seems that for the *class* and *crisis* local state theories there is no specificity and thus can be no theory of the local state, only a descriptive category.

For the *capital-theoretic* approaches, that is, those which seek to derive the state as a form of the capital relation, there is variation in the manner and extent of the theoretical scope given to class relations in grounding the local state as a theoretical object. On the one side is the argument that the state in general is to be understood as a form taken by the capital-labour relation. Struggles within the sphere of production lead to failures in the continuity of production. This process extends crises throughout the range of socio-economic relations, especially those concerning the reproduction of labour power. Such problems take on a particularly sharp form in cities because these are the fundamental concentrations of population, means of production and reproduction, and the restructuring strains are felt very acutely as a consequence. The impact of the crisis mechanism in the sphere of production is to accelerate the expansion of labour productivity and to transform the labour process thus bringing about new concentrations of economic activity at points spatially polarized from older industrial and rural areas. The old social relations which pertained in these areas are thus reconstituted. Spatial segregation is enhanced down to fine levels of detail within urban concentrations as differential land rents are exploited, and social marginalization of redundant labour is an increasingly urban phenomenon for which, however, social expenditure is hopelessly inadequate. The increased commodification of use values in urban centres as financial and commercial capital become dominant signals the increasingly commodity-like nature of urban social relations under late capitalism. An important effect of these changes is that the form and course of social and economic confrontations no longer coincide with traditional notions of class struggle. Rather, because the local state is increasingly the particular locus for conflict diversification strategies by the central state, popular struggles versus the state are typical as against class struggles within the state (Hirsch, 1981).

The limitation of the concept of struggle to issues forming at the point of production is plainly problematic here, tending to obscure important non-production relations, such as the commodification of individual relationships, which is clearly an important instance of relations of circulation set by the commodity form of bourgeois law rather than directly by relations of production. Moreover, as was suggested earlier, the point of identifying important non-class relations of reproduction is lost because of the failure to establish their relationship to social relations which are themselves characteristic of civil society rather than the workplace. To reiterate the fundamental problem with Hirsch's approach, it is that relations which may be constrained by, but do not derive directly from the class antagonisms inherent in capitalist production, are too readily reduced to a rationalistic conception of the logic of accumulation. In this way useful insights are undermined by economistic reductionism.

This problem is partially avoided by Duncan and Goodwin who, however, also lack a theory of civil society within which to ground an otherwise important conceptualization of the centrality of local social relations (and, by inference, local class structures) to the theory of the local state (see also Urry, 1981b; Cooke, 1982a; 1982b). The argument in support of the salience of local class relations is partly an historical one and partly theoretical analogy. It is shown how the existing local state was unable to manage the functions which the emergent capitalist mode of production demanded of it: the local state was often outside the state in the Gramscian sense discussed above (Foster, 1974; Williams, 1978). Various new laws were passed in response to pressure from the class which was in the process of acceding to power, industrial capitalists, to control 'outlaw' local states, partly through extending suffrage. These local variations were themselves patchy expressions of the uneven capitalist development process that was under way in the early nineteenth century. The theoretical analogy is drawn between local state relations and local workplace relations, both of which vary according to the degree of asymmetry in the power relations between the contending local classes. These, in turn, are the resultant of many determining forces involving many aspects of production relations such as the dominance of particular sectors in the local economy, the level of world competition in the relevant sectors, the impact of historical forces upon the organization of the labour process, the level and intensity of unionization in the labour force, and the interrelationships between the organizations of labour in the workplace and those which represent their interests in the state.

We would not fundamentally disagree with this derivation of the specificity of the local state from the uniqueness of local class relations except in so far as it tends to limit that uniqueness to the effects of struggles in the sphere of production relations. That is, it would seem important to express the impact of other forms of struggle upon the formation of local class relations in addition to those which are located in the workplace. Nevertheless, it is crucial to recognize that over the long term the latter exert constraint upon the shape taken by struggles in other spheres, notably circulation and reproduction, which occur in civil society, and those which occur at the boundary between civil society and the state, taking the form of popular protests and challenges against the state's form of implementing policies. The struggles in the popular sphere, which may have relatively little recognizable class content, are nevertheless important in contributing to the element of local consciousness within (and even across) local class relations. This is for three reasons: first, because the issue around which the local struggle may form often reconstitutes the locality as a category in opposition to the nation, or 'the national interest' with which the central state is associated. Second, such struggles increase the level of consciousness of the true nature of the state as a form of class relation which processes the consent of the governed in definite ways, '. . . not generic and vague as it is expressed in the instant of elections' (Gramsci, 1971, p. 259), to correspond with the interests of capital. This may either politicize or alienate the governed, but the important thing is that state hegemony has been penetrated. Finally, popular democratic struggles assist in the process of undermining the individuation which bourgeois law helps to form between members of classes, they demonstrate the organizational capacities of working people to each other and to members of adjacent sub-classes, and they help sustain certain spatial differences between local class relations. We have in mind here the kind of distinction made in the following:

. . . in the countryside the intellectual (priest, lawyer, notary, teacher, doctor, etc.), has on the whole a higher or at least a different living standard from that of the average peasant and consequently represents a social model for the peasant to look to in his aspiration to escape from or improve his condition. . . . With the urban intellectuals it is another matter. Factory technicians do not exercise any political function over the instrumental masses, or at least this is a phase that has been superseded. Sometimes, rather, the contrary takes place, and the instrumental masses, at least in the person of their own organic intellectuals, exercise a political influence on the technicians. (Gramsci, 1971, pp. 14–15)

This argument, despite an element of apparent spatial determinism which requires relaxing under the more complex socio-spatial relations of contemporary capitalism, nevertheless suggests important qualitative differences regarding the class alignments of local civil society which may be expressed in distinctive ways both within and against the prevailing structure of local political society, of which the local state is a specific form. Certain implications of spatially differentiated class structures and class relations, their connections to the spatial division of labour through differential labour markets, and the contradictions these pose for central and local state development planning are considered in the chapter which follows. For the moment it is necessary to return briefly to a discussion of the relevance of the different spheres of struggle to the specification of the local state.

Spheres of struggle and the local state

As we have seen to some extent already, most theorists of the local state link it to class conflict in some way, and most separate out certain kinds of conflict, giving precedence to one or other as a sphere for which the local state is functionally responsible. Thus Cockburn (1977) sees the functions of the local state lying in the reproduction of the labour force and also, in line with the state's general repressive disposition, the reproduction of capitalist social relations. The techniques by means of which the local state furthers ruling class interests include the imposition of business management ideas on the internal workings of the local state, and undermining the capacity of workers and their allies to control the local state by establishing corporatist mechanisms for absorbing protest which bypass normal popular democratic channels. In this way struggles in the sphere of reproduction take place on the state's terms, although repression of this kind is vulnerable to disengagement by dominated groups who may revert to a more radicalized form of popular democratic struggle. In this respect, formerly fragmented ethnic, gender and cultural interests may regroup to continue more informed struggle in the sphere of reproduction.

A rather different emphasis is placed on the reproduction relations with which the local state is involved by Markusen (1976; 1978). Writing about the local state in the US from a crisis-theory perspective, she points to the historic change from substantial all-round autonomy in American cities to a position in which the separate production and reproduction requirements of the contending classes have produced a massively fragmented local state structure. The local state has expressed the competitive struggle between capitalists on the one hand, and between capital and labour on the other. The former struggle resulted in plant relocation to new, suburban administrative units while the latter produced class segmentation over space, mainly as a reflection of differential reproduction costs. The local state is thus engaged in struggles both in the sphere of production and that of reproduction, though the crisis posed for central city communities deprived of a substantial tax base, and opposition from suburban residents to industrialization and growth, is leading to calls for the planning of productive inputs on a scale larger than that of the fragmented, suburban neighbourhoods.

In another analysis from the *crisis-theoretic* perspective the local state in the US is also seen as having important functions in the spheres of production and reproduction (Friedland, Fox Piven and Alford, 1977). They argue that the decentralization, of which Markusen also speaks, is functional for deflecting political crises in the American government system (thus anticipating Hirsch's similar argument). However, because the local state is structured to respond to production struggles and reproduction struggles, it stores up potential fiscal crises for the future. These arise due to the budgetary incrementalism (see Chapter 3) which is associated with fragmentary decision-making, and which is the effect of pressures from workers for improved social services on top of those from capitalists for improved spatial efficiency in the urban structure. The separation of the political and economic functions of the local state in order to facilitate the legitimation of private accumulation is another part of the conflict-deflection strategy. Agencies which respond to problems in the sphere of production tend to be only indirectly accountable democratically, while those charged with reproduction functions are subject both to participatory pressure from recipients and close scrutiny from budget managers. The budget is most likely to be cut first in the event of local state fiscal crisis.

Other theories of the local state exclude production relations from the level of local politics and state activity altogether (Saunders, 1981; Cawson and Saunders, 1981), arguing that consumption struggles alone are resolved locally as a result of popular democratic participation of a pluralistic kind rather than class conflict. On the other hand, in the analysis provided by Hirsch (1981), popular democratic struggles and those related to the allocation of consumption services tend to be seen as having an expressly urban basis because cities are the concentrated centres of production. However, issues centring upon the reproduction of labour power are contingent in that they arise in response to central state initiatives towards restructuring production relations. They appear as local state concerns principally because of the conflict-diversification strategy adopted by the central state to mitigate crisis tendencies emanating from the sphere of production relations. In somewhat similar vein, although from a more structural-functional perspective, Dear and Clark (1980) see the local state inducing popular democratic participation in the devolved reproduction issues as a kind of pulse-taking function. This allows the central state to formulate enhanced conflict-diversification strategies for the future as a means of heading off further crises.

Only Duncan and Goodwin (1980) seek to derive the local state in terms of the social relations of production and reproduction rather than in terms of the functions it may perform with regard to either the production needs of capital or the demands from labour for improved collective consumption services. They stress the inter-linked nature of relations of production and reproduction in developing the argument that local class relations, forged in particular local workplace and community experiences, give expression to the content of local state action. It has been suggested already that this approach to the derivation of the local state is to be preferred because it avoids the functionalism, rationalism, idealism, abstractionism and essentialism of other approaches. However, it can be shown that further development is necessary if the relationship of the local state to the various spheres of struggle which can be identified is to be specified clearly. The key questions which Duncan and Goodwin do not examine are those concerning civil society, circulation, popular democratic struggles, and the precise relationship between the state, civil society and the sphere of production relations.

If we discuss the latter question first and phrase it so as to ask how and in what ways production relations connect to the local state, it will assist in the location of possible answers to the associated questions. The first and crucial point to be made about the relationship of 'the political' and 'the economic' in capitalist societies is that it is one of separation. It is precisely because of this that the local state theories we have discussed have difficulty in linking the sphere of production relations to that of the state, other than in terms of the latter providing infrastructural investments, most of which are jointly used by capital and labour. However, it is also crucial to recognize that 'the economic' itself cannot simply be understood as a homogeneous area of activity. It was argued in the preceding chapter that some theories of the development process focus on the processes of exchange while others analyse the process of production in order to identify the source of socio-spatial exploitation, and that while the latter is prior it does not thereby relegate the former to insignificance. We can explain this more clearly now. The distinction between production and exchange rests on the nature of the commodity form which only finally releases the surplus value it contains when that value has been realized on the market. Surplus value is 'injected' into the commodity at the point of production by the nature of the relation between capital and labour. Workers receive less than the value of the commodity which they socially produce, in the form of payment for their labour power. The latter payment is made in the sphere of exchange, the sphere of apparent individualistic freedom, equality and utility-maximiz-ation which undermines the asymmetrical class relations of the workplace. The precise sphere of production relations *per se* is an area into which the state, either central or local, has the greatest difficulty in intervening.

Because of this double separation between state and economy, and between production and exchange, when the state does respond to pressure from capital for assistance in maintaining accumulation it does so, both centrally and locally (although in different ways) in the sphere of circulation, of which exchange is a part. Furthermore, it is normal for intervention in the sphere of circulation to be circumscribed by the framework of law which, it will be recalled, individuates those subject to its constraints in similar manner to the relationship of exchange. These two equivalencies come together with important effects where the commodity which is the subject of exchange is labour power. It is in the labour market that labour power is exchanged for the cost of its reproduction and that of its dependants. It is in the labour market, therefore, that capitalists obtain the key resource for commodity, and hence, surplus value, production. Thereafter, the money for which labour power is exchanged is both essential for the realization of the value of commodities for consumption and for the reproduction of labour power. We shall return to a consideration of the labour market, and especially its local, spatial variations which derive from the layers of different spatial divisions of labour, in the next chapter, but the crucial point to make here is that the individuated relationships which emerge from the exchange relations of the sphere of circulation are fundamental constituents of civil society. With respect to the location of the sphere of circulation in *civil society*, of which the labour market is a primary component, it is possible both to locate the other spheres, with their associated modes of class struggle (Esping Anderson, Friedland and Wright, 1976), and specify the nature of local social relations and the local state more clearly.

Civil society is thus to be understood as being both beside and outside the state, locally and centrally, and the relations of production. It is important to clarify this point because in the work of Gramsci, the foremost theoretician of the relationship between state and civil society, it is sometimes unclear. This is because he sometimes refers to civil society as bearing the relationship of a series of outer trenches protecting the state as the coercive core of capitalist social relations, while at other times implying that the reverse is the case, or even that they are the same. It becomes clear from more detailed analysis that the differentiation of relationship is part of its dynamic development and that where the institutions of civil society are strong they can re-exert the coercive hegemony of the state, even if the state has been conquered by anti-bourgeois interests, and thus restore the normal functions of the state. In other words, although the state may temporarily cease to stand beside and outside civil society, the situation in which that occurs is anomalous, and because coercive force resides there it must ultimately come to the aid of the dominant class. However, that does not necessarily imply that it is not possible for the dominant class to be itself radically recomposed.

The extent to which such recomposition is effected is reliant upon the success of the political parties and other organs of popular struggle in gaining the support of individual subjects in civil society who may mobilize around a variety of collective interests and bases of identification such as: status; occupation; gender; religion; language; region; ethnicity or nationality (Przeworski, 1977, pp. 383, 387; Urry, 1981a, pp. 32, 70) as well as class relations of production. Clearly, the likelihood of there being evenly spread intersections of these collective bases over space is remote, a factor which enhances the likelihood of local variation in the intensity of struggles within local civil society. The very heterogeneity of local civil society, local labour markets within civil society, and the demands placed on the local state, are of central importance in differentiating the local from the central state, and explaining why the latter is the repository of coercive, neutralizing legal powers which homogenize socio-spatial diversity by individuating all its subjects. The two other main spheres of struggle in civil society apart from the sphere of circulation are both expressive of the attempts of individuals to find bases of collective identification which are not co-terminous with their position in the relations of production. The first of these is concened with the reproduction of labour power, and concerns those areas, many of which are the subject of planned local state provision, described by most local state theorists in terms of collective consumption services. The second, which is frequently the least class-related, relates to the sphere of popular struggle versus the state and is also, though less directly, concerned with reproduction issues too. These include cultural, ethnic or linguistic reproduction, as well as both production and circulation issues such as female or ethnic employment and/or wage levels, and regional struggles for reduced employment- or income-disparities.

Our conclusion to this section on the local state is that it must be conceived as standing beside and outside civil society and that civil society must be seen as standing between the state and production relations. Within local civil society, a great many bases for collective identification exist which are not simply class relations. One of the most important of these, which is significantly structured by class relations, is the local labour market. The latter will vary in composition according to the complexity of the accretions of spatial divisions of labour in local space. Other markets, such as those concerned with money, ordinary consumption, luxury consumption and so on will also assist the general structuring of the local sphere of circulation. In addition local civil society will vary according to the class and popular alignments occurring in the spheres of reproduction and struggle against the state. Finally it is important to identify the key media of exchange between the three main dimensions of the framework both of which have the effect of undermining the class reality of the basic social relations of capitalist society. The link between the local state and civil society is mainly provided through the medium of law enacted by the central state, while the medium of exchange between the sphere of production and local civil society is money (Urry, 1981a, p. 116).

Levels of planning and spheres of struggle

The next and final task in this chapter is to consider the interrelationships between the central and local state as we have theorized them so far, through the lens of urban and regional planning. One of the first points to be recalled is that we have argued that there is no space for state intervention directly in the sphere of production, hence there is no involvement of state planning in this sphere. However, this does not mean that there is no planning performed in production, the opposite is in fact the case except that the planning which is done, and which is highly rational, carefully controlled and monitored, is private. That is, it is conceived and executed by the representatives of the interests of capital largely against the interests of labour. This was clear in the nineteenth century:

. . . . Engels emphasized that the increasing rationality of capitalist production within each firm is accompanied, and must be accompanied, by the chaos and anarchy of production at the societal scale. (Przeworski, 1980a, p. 47)

and it is as a response to the 'chaos and anarchy' outside the individual workplace that the state apparatuses are mobilized, not only to rationalize the external physical configuration of production, but to sustain the new form of social relations that have developed:

In reality, the State must be conceived of as an 'educator', in as much as it tends precisely to create a new type or level of civilization. . . . It operates according to a plan, urges, incites, solicits and 'punishes'; for, once the conditions are created in which a certain way of life is 'possible', then 'criminal action or omission' must have a punitive sanction, with moral implications, and not merely be judged generically as 'dangerous'. The Law is the repressive and negative aspect of the entire positive, civilizing activity undertaken by the State. (Gramsci, 1971, p. 247)

It is this civilizing process, performed by the state through the medium of law upon civil society, in which we shall seek to locate the primary activities of urban and regional planning. While these will clearly be interconnected in terms of planning practices and effects we can examine them analytically according to the categories discussed at the end of the previous section. This may be carried out with reference to central state and local state functions with a view to identifying instances of contradiction through which local versus central antagonisms are expressed.

Sphere of circulation

Planned central state intervention in the spatial development processes of capitalism have taken the form of administrative acts conditioned by precise legal instruments which, however, only allow for changes in the organization of production to be a possible, indirect effect of changes implemented in the sphere of circulation. The clearest examples of this are those aspects of policy which can be broadly included under the heading of *regional assistance*. We can consider four main kinds of regional assistance here, discussion of which will be amplified in the final chapter, these are: regional capital incentives; regional labour incentives; selective capital incentives; agency assistance.

Regional capital incentives are the well-known tax reliefs, capital grants on plant and machinery, and preferential loan arrangements each of which performs the function of easing the levels of exchange between productive units and the markets with which they are connected in civil society. It may be argued that tax reliefs and rates reductions represent links between productive units and the state but their effect is to make more money capital available for advance by individual capitals. Also the tax system is to be understood more as a loop on the circulation arc of the circuit of capital than a separate sphere, though its scale clearly varies according to the effects of struggles in production and civil society reacting back into the state. The money form of these incentives thus leaves open to individual capitalists the decision as to whether or not advantage may be gained, in terms of accumulation prospects, by accepting the assistance which is the entitlement of capital in general (primary to tertiary sectors) which locates in specified regional and local space.

Regional labour incentives are also, in fact, aids to capital but are of a different kind from those just discussed. They also take the form of transfers of money capital to individual capitals according to the level of employment maintained by those parts of their operations located in assisted areas. One interesting feature which differentiates such incentives is their relative transience as compared to capital incentives. But most importantly they represent a more direct response to the reproduction demands of labour. They demonstrate that in the real world the separation between circulation and reproduction is blurred. This is shown by the example of the Regional Employment Premium (REP) which operated in assisted regions of Britain in the 1960s and 1970s. At the general level it can be argued that all regional policy represents a heightened relative dominance of struggles in the sphere of reproduction over those in the sphere of circulation (this argument will be developed and elaborated in the next chapter). However, periodically there will be tactical shifts towards one of the other spheres of struggle in civil society depending upon the success with which interests strongly associated with the different spheres represent their interests in political society (the state). Such a shift occurred in the 1960s with the development of a coalition of interests in the national state in favour of state-induced centralization of ownership of the more advanced sections of British capital, and diversification of the economies of the heavy-industry regions. The surplus population generated by earlier concentration of heavy industry into the most productive units would be absorbed by decentralizing the labour-intensive parts of the advanced manufacturing enterprises (motor vehicles, electrical and electronic sectors of production) to problem regions (Massey and Meegan, 1979). As a concession to labour (especially the mining, steel and ship-related unions who co-operated with a Labour government in this attempt at restructuring) REP was introduced to assist firms to employ more workers than their new investments really warranted. Hence, following a shift in favour of capital in the sphere of circulation there was a return towards meeting labour's interests albeit on terms which were not disadvantageous to accumulation.

Selective incentives represent a form of capital subsidy which is directed more overtly to the resolution of struggles in the sphere of circulation than reproduction and, within circulation to those capitals which have strategic importance for the accumulation of capital. With respect to the latter point these may either be large, complex concerns which are in need of *hospitalization*, or smaller units where for reasons of technological sophistication, more *precocious* capitals may be considered to warrant state aid in development. The crucial feature of selective incentives is that they only contain elements of relevance to the struggle in the sphere of reproduction to the extent that pressure is successfully brought to bear by representatives of the labour interest that specific industries in specific locations are vital to their capacity to defend reproduction space. In other words, their prime link is in assisting individual capitals to continue or to accelerate the accumulation process by some form of restructuring. Where the individual capital supports large sections of the national labour market and commodity markets (components, maintenance services etc.) as with the Chrysler Corporation in the USA, BL in Britain or Alfa in Italy, then cross-class alignments may make it impossible for the state to resist enacting or activating legislation to hospitalize and/or nationalize weak enterprises. For advanced capitals it is more likely that selective incentives are a direct response to certain industrial and financial capital interests seeking protective support for precocious enterprises, or, perhaps, for precocious aspects of longer established activities. The key spatial effect here is that the general reproduction aims associated with state regional assistance are subordinated to the specific circulation requirements of particular capitals which may be located in areas not suffering from the traditionally understood regional problem.

This leads to consideration of a different form of state regional and sectoral intervention which overlaps functionally with the category of selective assistance to some extent but which is intrinsically structured on a model closer to that of the firm than that of the typical state bureaucracy. Development agencies are a recent state form widely found in capitalist economies (Goodman, 1979; Dulong, 1978; Mingione, 1981; Wickham, 1980; Wickham and Murray, 1981). There is considerable variation in the scope of their activities but one feature which is shared by most is the capacity to act in the sphere of circulation in a highly *discretionary manner* (Cooke, 1980). In other words, in addition to making more normal state reliefs and allocations which are the entitlements of certain kinds of industry and/or region by law, development agencies are normally not, in principle, disallowed from engaging in exchanges with whomsoever they may consider it desirable, subject to certain principles of capitalist rationality. The major one of these is normally that the development agency should be able to show that its activities have either resulted in the agency itself showing a profit in its financial dealings, or where the profit criterion is not applied, that it is responsible for a substantial advantage in terms of employment and/or private capital investment in the area for which it has administrative responsibility. It is normal for such agencies to be unencumbered by the direct involvement of the spatial or sectoral concerns of labour in their decision-making, with one result being that spatial location patterns for new development are strongly influenced by the decision-criteria of private enterprise (proximity to transport links, location in rural or semi-rural areas). Finally, development agencies can and do target specific kinds of industry, usually high-technology manufacturing industry, in which they may take equity-capital, make loans to, or, in the case of new small firms, own completely for a short period. They may also form partnerships with private financial institutions in order to augment sources of investment capital. In these and other respects they mark an important shift away from the traditional inter-penetration of the spheres of circulation and reproduction in the sense that the latter tended to determine, often quite precisely, the locations in which firms were entitled to grants and reliefs. Nevertheless, to the extent that development agencies are established for regions characterized by higher than average unemployment they manage to retain a vaguer relevance to reproduction demands.

Before we pass on to consider the involvement of the local state in the sphere of circulation it is important to mention three other central state forms of planning intervention which are frequently of marked pertinence to the continued accumulation of capital but which also, to varying degrees, constitute policies influenced by broader issues of regional and local repro-duction. The first of these relates to the substantial section of nationalized industries, especially in Britain, France and Italy. While there is little space to discuss their variations between countries it is clear that state ownership gives these industries a huge importance in the spatial development of capitalist economies. Whether this involves large-scale closure, as with the French steel industry in Lorraine, the British coal industry in Durham and South Wales, or the British steel industry in the latter areas plus Scotland, North Wales and the East Midlands; or, by contrast, expansion or relocation of the French steel industry to Dunkirk and Fos-sur-mer, or parts of the Italian motor industry to the Mezzogiorno, it is clearly of structural import-ance to struggles in the sphere of reproduction. It must be added, however, that such investments are normally made in ways which produce advantages to the non-nationalized sections of the respective economies by supplying cheap, subsidized inputs to private industrial capital.

The second important intervention by the state at national level in the sphere of circulation concerns investment in the transportation system, whether through the nationalized rail industry, where this is in public ownership, or by rationally planning the national motorway network. This has a threefold impact upon the sphere of circulation: first, it speeds up and makes more efficient the process of exchange in the labour and commodity markets; second, it stimulates demand from the private sector for con-struction equipment and motor transport; and third, it cheapens the general costs of production and thus enhances accumulation. The third important state intervention to be mentioned in this general context is the range of expenditures from military to agricultural, which often have an uneven regional impact and thus assist problem regions to maintain employment and consumer demand.

Local state intervention in the sphere of circulation occurs mainly through the medium of exchange of the law rather than that of money although the latter is by no means excluded. We can summarize much of this activity under the heading of *zoning* of land. By this we mean the legally authoritative process of designating land for diverse uses even though that land is not itself in the ownership of the local state. Two important points require to be made regarding this fundamental activity of the local state in respect of planning. First, the degree of precision with which different parcels of land are legally delimited in the zoning process varies over time in tune with certain dominant characteristics in the spheres of production and reproduction, and, to a lesser extent, the sphere of popular struggle. Second, zoning is an intervention in the sphere of circulation primarily, because it has the direct effect of conferring a change in use value, and therefore (in a capitalist economy) in the exchange value, of the land which is designated for a particular use if it is different from that to which it is currently put. To state it rather differently, land which has no value in the absence of labour, gains an enhanced differential rent according to the relative scarcity value of the new designation which it receives. This extra rent can be conceived as having a status not dissimilar from that of the extra value an object gains from the *interest* it generates, the latter representing a measure of its scarcity value – money capital generates a variable rate of interest, land designated for office development in Central London a different rate of interest, and paintings by Velasquez an, again, different rate of interest. What is common to them is that each has an interest rate which is determined by its value in exchange, in turn a reflection of scarcity rather than the application of increased labour power to its content.

Clearly, the impact of land-use designations, though universal, varies in intensity according to the scale of demand upon the particular local incidence of that space. This in turn is determined by the degree of concentration of the built environment, the distribution of local income and the local forms of the spatial division of labour. Where the latter coincide around a domination of low-income, labour-intensive, productive-manual activity in relatively formless semi-urban space such as is found in many areas in which the peak of accumulation was associated with competitive capitalism in industries with low capital to labour ratios, land rents for all uses tend to be low. Where, by contrast, they coincide towards the domination of middle and upper income occupational groupings, labour-intensive, productive-manual activity in centripetally structured space, land rents for all uses tend to be high. The social division of labour, and its effect on the spatial variations between local labour markets, have marked constraining effects, both upon the impact which zoning has upon the sphere of circulation, and the kind of zoning activity which the local state planning apparatus can successfully undertake. But the fact that law enabling these effects to occur exists, a factor reflecting the differential scarcity of land due to the manner of its deployment in space, hence differential rent, is a source of recurring contradiction between, in particular, the sphere of circulation and the sphere of reproduction in civil society. This is because exchange value gains resulting from socialized planning action can be privately appropriated rather than returning to the community for socialized consumption.

On many occasions the contradictory nature of the zoning gain to private appropriation is doubled and redoubled by the action of the local state in the sphere of circulation. This occurs when, having designated land for a particular purpose, the local state is called upon to activate its legal entitlement to assemble land into marketable aggregations through its use of compulsory purchase powers. Often this is made necessary by the local state having formed a contractual relationship with a single capital or a group of individual capitals, themselves normally active in the sphere of circulation, to develop the land which has been the subject of the compulsory purchase order. The major, if not the sole beneficiary of this kind of activity tends to be large, non-local, circulation capital interests (banks, pension funds, property developers) which operate over a substantially wider sphere of circulation than local capital interests, and for whom the local state planning apparatuses throughout a given nation-state provide an important mechanism for the appropriation, though not the production, of surplus value. In its circulation aspect the local state tends, quite markedly, to assist large capital at the expense of local capital (Lojkine, 1977). Moreover, it should be noted that this tendency can be further underlined by local state investments to improve the quality of local circulation space, normally to feed into the national transport networks which themselves speed up the circulation time of capital and hence stimulate accumulation for those interests which operate at an inter-regional scale in the sphere of circulation. Benefits, however, may also accrue to local capital to some extent from transport improvements except in so far as parts of it are already in competition with more efficient large, non-local capital. Needless to say, there is little or no direct advantage gained by labour from these investments since new jobs created may only be substitutes for those lost, local taxes may have to be raised to subsidize local state investments (which are, in any case, unlikely to be in the profitable parts of joint ventures), and locally generated profits may contribute to unequal exchange rather than being locally consumed.

Before completing this discussion of the local state and the sphere of circulation it is important to mention changes which occur in the legal form of the zoning designations. In Britain, at least, there has been a progressive diminution in their detail during the post-war era. This has to be linked to changes in the material conditions upon which zoning operates. It seems likely that tight zoning restrictions are initiated under conditions in which the sphere of reproduction and the struggle to direct development away from centres of accumulation towards centres of underaccumulation is strongest. As growth slackens in the former centres, for whatever reason, there is a shift towards the dominance of struggles by various capitalist interests and a relaxation of the micro-detail of zoning. If that is unsuccessful the various minor constraints which local state planning law imposes upon the development process may come under further, sustained, pressure for complete abolition as the struggle in the sphere of circulation moves towards complete domination by capital of labour's interests within that sphere, and in particular, domination by capital of labour's interests in the sphere of reproduction.

Finally, it is important to comment upon the nature of the contradictions which may be seen to operate between the local state and the central state with respect to planning in the sphere of circulation. There are, briefly, three which deserve mention here. The first of these involves the two principal branches of capital: industrial and financial, with, as we have seen, central state regional assistance being devoted largely (though not entirely) to subsidizing the former while the local state makes its main contribution to the latter. In the process, industrial inward investors are forced to pay higher rents upon land which is designated for industrial purposes rather than, say, being able to buy land at an agricultural value to be used for industrial purposes (as happened before zoning was introduced). The second contradiction concerns the location of industry which, for the central state should (increasingly) be in the kind of areas which the local state has traditionally zoned for non-industrial purposes in line with (central state!) green belt and conservation guidelines. The third contradiction concerns the general question of investment in the built environment. This is built fairly uniformly *in situ* with local state sanction because each locality is a centre of added value and hence tax income due to the rent-increase effect of zoning. However the main impact of central state regional assistance may best be described as *peripheral concentration*, especially in respect of the planning connection made between regional assistance and transportation investment.

Sphere of reproduction

Reproduction struggles are logically subsequent to circulation struggles because they develop after workers have organized successfully to resist the efforts of capitalists to raise absolute surplus value (by extending the working day etc.). The earlier circulation struggle contains reproduction elements which are subsequently extended into that area of daily life *outside* the workplace. Because the move towards raising relative surplus value also increases the dependency of capital upon labour due to the mechanized processes introduced, early struggles effectively reduce the asymmetry in power relations between capital and labour. This is for three reasons: first the concentration of ownership also concentrates the labour force, making organization easier; second, the reduction in small, fragmentary, productive units diminishes the capacity of capital for paternalistic control of the labour process[5]; and third, the deskilling effect, which follows from mechanization, massifies the workforce and further assists class organization. So, accumulation becomes threatened as profits are diverted into more profitable sectors, and new previously underindustrialized regions become centres of accumulation. The absence of unionized labour in such regions offers a key condition for accelerated accumulation to occur (Cooke, 1982a).

It is the effect of such shifts upon previously industrialized regions which helps redirect the focus of working-class struggle towards social reproduction and away from circulation issues. But because capital cannot solve the reproduction problem which it has helped to create, even if it inverts the direction of capital flows and invests in sectors of low or negative accumulation again, because to do so would be to undermine its own existence, the reproduction struggle must be orchestrated through the state. Regional policy, therefore, has its reproduction dimension too, to the extent that it assists in the maintenance of a productive basis upon which reproduction of labour power may continue. This is only one, relatively minor, central state intervention which involves responding to the interests of labour to defend its reproduction space in local areas tied closely to local labour markets for which demand has collapsed. With hindsight, such intervention can be seen to have been of long-term value for accumulation (reserve army of labour, low reproduction costs, low wage costs) although initially, by fixing labour spatially, it contradicts capital's short-term labour-supply and capital-expenditure requirements, which lie elsewhere.

Three other central state strategies can be identified as representing outcomes of class conflicts in the sphere of reproduction which take the form of urban and regional development planning. First of all, there is policy for planning complete new environments which would include the development of New Towns and expanded towns, the designation and removal of slum housing areas and the formulation of new residential development targets. More recently, the establishment of partnership schemes with the local state for the redevelopment of inner city areas and the replacement of New Town Corporations by Urban Development Corporations which are, similarly, devoted to renewing obsolete inner-city areas would have to be added. We can make a broad division here between what may be called *instrumental planning* where the agency conducting the planning action is the direct agent of the central state, as in the case of development corporations, whether for New Towns or inner cities, and *delegated planning* where the central state is the source of law which requires the local state to comply with certain conditions which are themselves set as the outcome of struggles in the sphere of reproduction.

Second, there is policy for improving and renovating the existing built environment, especially with regard to residential space, which is a form of *delegated planning*. Here the local state is required to designate and invest in areas the use value of which is deemed to be above average. As one effect of this kind of intervention (which concerns housing action areas, general improvement areas, conservation areas, areas of scenic worth and so on), a rise in the exchange value of the land and property which is the object of this legislation and action is likely to follow. In this respect the outcome from struggle in the sphere of reproduction can transfer value within the sphere of circulation which, in turn, may result in modification or rejection of the enabling legislation.

Finally, the state engages in planning action which is itself quasi-judicial in that it is the responsibility of the central state apparatus to examine, approve and adjudicate on the plans and policies which are produced under *delegated planning* legislation and *instrumental planning* legislation. That is, it has ultimate responsibility in law for controlling most of the development associated with the sphere of reproduction which is planned to occur in local space. This includes adopting or rejecting strategic plans and policies produced by the local state regarding the disposition of activities which may be undertaken in local space. It also, importantly, involves adjudicating where there are conflicts of interest over changes proposed to approved strategic plans or where there are conflicts over substantial developments which may be acceptable in strategic and legal terms but which nevertheless attract high levels of opposition. The public inquiry and the examination in public of structure plan proposals constitute the nearest equivalent in the planning of spatial development to the interpretative activities of the judiciary in civil and criminal law. Indeed, the institution of planning law has as its next level of resolution, in the event of disagreement following a public inquiry, precisely the normal civil law procedures of the judicial system.

To conclude this outline of the relationship between the central state and the sphere of reproduction, we deduce that it is contingent upon the legal nexus, which, it will be recalled, is the principal medium of exchange between the state and civil society, to a greater extent than the cash nexus which links production to civil society. In other words, the sphere of reproduction, and the struggles with which it is associated, are located in that area of civil society which most readily translates struggle in civil society into struggle in the state or political society because it involves the control of the coercive power of law. While this is partly true also of the sphere of circulation, nevertheless, its coercive power is ultimately less the law than money, and, as a consequence the sphere of circulation is located more closely to the sphere of production with the state mediating at a further remove than in the sphere of reproduction. (See Figure 2, p. 265.)

Local state planning, therefore, is *delegated planning*, the factor which defines its lack of autonomy as the general rule. However, it will be recalled that, though normally lacking autonomy, the local state nevertheless derives specificity from the form of its local social relations; the complex combination of its local civil society as structured by its local labour market, which in turn derives from the local impact of the spatial division of labour nationally and internationally. If this were not the case then *delegated planning* would result in a certain homogeneity in the built environment. This would reflect the application of a homogeneous law over the whole territory of the nation-state. Clearly, despite impressionistic evidence of a decline in the heterogeneity of local building styles, cultural variations and productive specialization during the post-war era (which coincides with the existence of a centralized and codified planning law), marked variations of a temporal and spatial nature continue to characterize the content of local state activity.

Rather than seek to summarize such variations according to the level of appearances which differentiates local and sub-national formations we shall confine our comments to the varying bases of collective identification which connect in the sphere of reproduction and which may be expected to exert an impact upon the strategies pursued in the local state. First, the local class relations in the sphere of reproduction will have a dominant influence upon the form taken by the built environment in the first place and, subsequently, upon the priorities adopted in subsequent local state development planning. Variations in the local incidence and control exerted over the local state apparatus by the bourgeoisie *vis-à-vis* labour may be expected to influence the balance of local state support for public versus private emphases in transport, housing, local state employment, leisure, social services and educational provision. The effects of class composition will be modified by cultural factors where, for example, a dominant bourgeoisie nevertheless places value upon high levels of public educational expenditure, for linguistic reasons as in Wales, Quebec or parts of Spain. Alternatively, a progressive labour administration might press for high expenditure on integrating ethnic minorities or subsidizing cultural pluralism, while a reactionary one might not. Similar kinds of divisions might be found with regard to the provision of facilities which meet the demands of women for equality of opportunity. Finally, regional (non-linguistic) identification which cuts across class alignments could be expected to have some bearing upon the level of resources available for expenditure in the local state: it is well known, for example, that the national regions of the UK receive higher than average per capita transfer payments for some categories of expenditure (Cooke, 1980b). Variations in religious affiliation may exert yet another overlaying non-class dimension to the inputs and outputs of the local state's service delivery, and hence the shape of its development planning within the constraints set by the law through which planning is controlled. Local state plans will thus reflect the specificity given to the local state by local bases of identification in civil society, and the results of political struggles which take place within the local state to reproduce wage labour and its dependants. The very heterogeneity of local civil society contradicts the homogeneity of the state's national, legislative writ as a basic, though not always active, principle.

Sphere of popular struggle

In this third sphere of conflict in civil society we are concerned to account for those antagonisms which occur primarily not along class lines but, rather, which tend to be constituted as oppositions between the state – especially in its guise as the embodiment of 'officialdom' – and either those non-class groupings which were mentioned in the preceding section; regional, cultural, ethnic, gender or religious collectivities, or wholly new, possibly temporary groupings which form alliances in order to try to prevent the state, as the coercive form of capitalist class relations, from acting counter to their interests. As we have seen already there is considerable interest expressed in this dimension of struggle by certain state theorists, mainly those who have rejected earlier functionalist and reductionist state-theories (Laclau, 1977; Jessop, 1977, 1980; Hirsch, 1981; Urry, 1981a). However, it is not simply because those struggles, which were previously squeezed uncomfortably into class analyses of social conflict or ignored altogether, have now been provided with a theoretical *imprimatur* that we wish to discuss them here. The reason is that such struggles tend to have focused, quite noticeably in recent history, around the strategies of central and local states with regard to aspects of development planning (Castells, 1977b, 1978; Lojkine, 1977; Dunleavy, 1980; Cooke, 1982b). This fact may help us, provisionally at this point, to identify some explanatory outlines for the emergence of this kind of protest. The first point of note is that it is linked with struggle in the sphere of reproduction in the final analysis, but is characterized by its defensive, non-class basis rather than the more traditional offensive, class-based political struggle in the sphere of reproduction. For the moment we will advance three reasons for non-class popular struggle along the lines of *state versus people*.

The first consideration here is that the basis upon which the state, and more particularly the local state, expresses the asymmetrical social relations of capitalist society, has become inadequate because the class structure of late capitalist society has changed. In other words, there is no longer, if there ever was, a clear-cut division between capital and its interests and labour and its interests. Rather, there has been a massive recomposition of the working class in ways which have both brought more of its members (notably women) into waged work and consequently enabled a greater proportion of the population to have a stronger stake in their reproduction space, which they are more likely to own and to have invested greater personal identity in than was hitherto the case. This means that if the local state seeks to plan a more rational form of production, reproduction and circulation space, the traditional[6] middle-classes and the traditional working-classes will now share interests to a greater extent than when their relationship in the sphere of reproduction was that of landlord and tenant.

The second reason is related to the previous one, namely, that as struggles in the sphere of reproduction have been progressively more successful, with the result that the scope of the state has grown *vis-à-vis* the lives of its citizens, greater numbers of people of all classes have a stake in retaining the services which the state provides even though they may not have been the class members for whom the services were initially intended. This is an interesting reflection of the homogeneity of law once again, the fact that because it articulates with individuated subjects rather than class members it cannot differentiate between the different class gradations of society. The latter distinction tends to be made, to the extent that it does occur, by bureaucraic allocative regulations rather than by the law *per se*, a factor which inspired the interest some time ago in the practices of urban managers in allocating resources to collective consumers (Pahl, 1975). Thus, when, because of fiscal crisis considerations planned provision of services is withdrawn it is more likely to be opposed by individual consumers acting in collective ways than simply by class organizations. The latter, especially parties, will clearly be active in such campaigns and may succeed in 'interpellating', that is appealing to new class members as a result of such activities. However, it need not be the case that class organizations are the first to respond to such changes in circumstances.

Finally, the nature of state procedure in meeting opposition in ways which seem to belie the basic, common-sense notion of *democracy* as the possibility of gaining some positive response from authority, may assist the activation of precisely 'people' versus 'officialdom' movements. Thus, once the state threatens some action which is inconsistent with the interests of citizens, the ensuing attempts to bring influence to bear through normal democratic channels may fail. This may be for reasons such as the issue being spatially confined, therefore politically particular rather than general, or because political representatives find themselves as outsiders to a bipartisan policy agreed by party leaderships, or for other reasons. The call for greater participation by citizens which may follow such rejection is normally either refused or carried out by officialdom meeting the people, with democratic representation being bypassed. In the latter case the element of rigidity which formally governs official behaviour can be enhanced by the use of exclusionary devices such as those described by Offe (1972, 1974). One effect may be to further alienate popular opinion from the workings of the state, inducing a recalcitrant position with regard to local democratic institutions, or, for a minority it may lead to political radicalization on non-class lines. These effects are contradictory to central state *instrumentality* especially where this is tied to the rationality of large capital which is inconsistent with democratic 'wrangling'.

In this wide-ranging chapter we have argued that, of the variety of theorizations of the state and local state which are now available, many are inadequate to the project which is being undertaken in this book. This is because they contain degrees of idealism, rationalism, functionalism, essentialism and abstractionism which we have argued provide an inadequate basis for theory. However, among the group of theories which seek to derive the state from certain properties of the social relations of production in capitalist society, some pointed towards a more adequate basis for theorizing the link between state planning and the processes of spatial development. In particular those theories which allow for the theorization of social relations in the spheres of production, in the state, and most importantly in civil society, were considered to be the most appropriate. We derived from this theoretical approach a theorization of planning which situated the different levels of planning within the state (central and local) according to their relationship with three spheres of struggle in civil society: circulation; reproduction; and popular. Furthermore, it proved possible to specify the local state as an important source of the heterogeneity in social relations of capitalist society which is mitigated to some extent by the homogenizing effect of bourgeois law. Aspects of planning were found to be more closely related to the sphere of circulation where their main medium of exchange was that of money directed towards productive capital. Conversely, those aspects of state activity linked to the sphere of reproduction derived their power from being constituted by the law, primarily. The latter connects the state with civil society as a medium of exchange comparable to money *vis-à-vis* production. Finally, a sphere of popular struggle was designated which is defined by relations of antagonism between the state and an increasingly individuated popular base. The latter seems particularly well-represented as a non-class basis of identification constituted by the state's increased penetration of aspects of formerly private activity. In the following chapter we will examine aspects of the changes which have taken place in the spatial class-basis of capitalist society, and in particular, the impact of development, planning and labour market transformations upon class.

9 Labour markets, local classes and development planning

We have argued the following four propositions thus far:

1 the key mechanism to be explained if spatial transformations are to be understood is the way in which accumulation imperatives affect the geographical reorganization of the division of labour;
2 the conditions which are necessary if accumulation, and hence development, are to continue, are substantially modified by the capacity of capital and labour to further their interests and their share of the product through struggles in the sphere of production;
3 these conditions are further modified when, after the main focus of struggle shifts from the sphere of circulation towards the sphere of reproduction, the capacity of labour to defend its territory against the mobility of capital is enhanced through state development planning;
4 the importance of struggles involving planning is that they may express the heterogeneity of local civil society and the local class relations which give specificity to the local state. In so doing they create tensions and contradictions within the state as a whole because of its prevailing disposition to secure wage-labour for capital by legally constituting homogeneous subjects. These tensions may be expressed in non-class struggles between people and planners.

At a general level these points do not yet fully interlock, however, as it is not clear precisely how changes in the production process of, say, a multi-national company are signalled to the planning system, or whether, indeed, the relationship may more often be the reverse one whereby the company is made aware of certain benefits which are mediated by the planning system. Furthermore, it is unclear whether such differences of approach are influenced by changes in the level of dominance of the different spheres of struggle, and if so, in what ways. More importantly, we neither have a clear picture of the factors making for differentiation in the capacity of local classes to defend their reproduction space, nor knowledge of the extent to which the relative success of certain localities rests on complicity with officialdom rather than antagonism towards it. Finally, the ways in which the double contradiction between capital and labour, on the one hand, and the planning of development in the central versus the local state, on the other, is at least temporarily resolved in the interests of capital, remain poorly understood from our discussion so far. It is to these and related questions that we turn in this chapter. In order to do this it will be advantageous to evaluate, briefly, two bodies of theoretical literature, the first relating to labour market differentiation, the second to class, with some attention being paid to local classes. From these discussions it will be possible to show how the planning system both creates and solves (temporarily) certain contradictions in the development process.

Theories of labour market differentiation

If, as we have argued, the development process produces, and is in turn stimulated to reproduce, spatially diverse divisions of labour in which some areas display concentrations of prestigious, well-paid jobs for which a substantial level of qualification is a prerequisite, while others tend to display the inverse of these qualities, then it is necessary to posit some mechanism which gives rise to this effect. We will look first at the kinds of supply and demand relationships which modern productive enterprise generates with regard to labour power, and, since the latter is expressed in terms of the structure of the market for labour power and the work conditions attending the spaces allocated by the productive process, the labour markets of advanced capitalist economies should at least describe that mechanism. The focus on labour markets, defined as mechanisms in which the exchange of labour power for money capital is transacted, is selected in the recognition that although the sphere of circulation is secondary to that of production in determining the pace and rate of accumulation, labour power is a special commodity, the particularity of which gives it central relevance to the capacity of capital to reproduce itself, and for accumulation thus to occur. The point was made in a rather different way in the previous chapter but it can be briefly restated in the following form. For accumulation to occur capital requires labour power, but it does not control the production of labour power as a commodity, unlike that of other commodities. Labour power is produced and reproduced outside the workplace, a factor which makes the relationship between capital and labour one of double dependence. Labour requires capital in order to subsist but capital needs labour power in order to reproduce itself. Hence, the cost of labour power, unlike that of other commodities, is subject to less direct control by capital than that of other commodities; it may be forced up to a level higher than that which is in the short-term interest of capital but the price will have to be paid or accumulation is impossible. This is particularly the case once class consciousness develops among workers. This tends to stop them competing individualistically and thus limits the capacity of capital to increase absolute surplus value by intensifying the pace of work and/or extending the length of the working day. In other words the exchange relationship between capital and labour penetrates deeply into the production relations which they conduct in the workplace, beyond the sphere of circulation and the rhythms of civil society.

The theories of the labour market which will help us to analyse structural inequalities and opportunities influencing the pace and direction of development are threefold: theories of dual labour markets; theories of segmented labour markets; and theories of discontinuous labour markets. We consciously do not consider neo-classical labour market theory because of its idealistic and rationalistic overtones and also because it makes unwarranted and erroneous assumptions about the capacity of workers to impersonate 'rational economic man' in choosing an occupation (Blackburn and Mann, 1979, p. 15). Hence the first theory of labour markets to be considered is that which pictures those in capitalist economies as characteristically divided into *primary and secondary sections* (Doeringer and Piore, 1971; Bosanquet and Doeringer, 1973; Piore, 1973). This theory was derived from an attempt to explain the persistence of marked differences in income between workers having no evident economic reason for being unequally recompensed. These include groups such as ethnic minorities, women and migrant workers. In addition, and as a partial means of explaining labour market discrimination, this theory also incorporates an explanation for the growth of the *internal labour market*, that is, the arrangement whereby firms acquire labour from within their own organization rather than recruiting predominantly from the open market.

The primary section of the labour market is dominated by large multi-regional or multinational firms which are capital-intensive, technologically advanced and highly profitable. Workers in the primary sector earn high wages and display a high degree of unionization, factors which reflect, as well as helping to strengthen, the internalized nature of the labour market. The latter system arises because of the need in large corporations for high levels of stability in their labour forces. This arises for two reasons: first, their concentrated power gives them a large measure of control over their product markets, the effect of which is to reduce market fluctuations and increase their reliance upon stability and loyalty on the part of labour. Second, the high levels of capital-intensivity associated with technically-advanced production processes, reduce the level of skill required in the labour force but increase the degree of experience and responsibility required of machine handlers. Internal promotions on the basis of seniority secure the requirement of stability and diminish the extent of uncertainty within the labour market. The fundamental aim on the part of monopoly enterprises of the kind which generates internal labour markets is the achievement of continuity of production. To that end a variety of fringe benefits linked to length of service is made available to the primary section of the labour force.

It might be expected that as monopolies increase their share of product markets there would occur a corresponding decline in the number of small businesses in a given economy. The reverse is, however, the case, for the growth in monopoly market share is accompanied by the numerical growth of small businesses. These firms provide the basis for the secondary section of the labour market. The key characteristic here is instability of employment: there is no call for stable work patterns, wages are low with fringe benefits non-existent, unionization is poorly developed, and production is concentrated in simple, labour-intensive processes aimed at supplying output cheaply on to competitive markets. The latter feature tends to imply that instability of employment is a necessary part of secondary labour markets owing to the constant process of adjustment to the oscillations of competitive markets. As a result an unstable workforce, inured to redundancy, and composed of women, ethnic minorities, disabled persons and otherwise docile categories, such as socially marginal people, dominates the secondary section. In certain instances it appears that a relationship of interdependence arises between primary and secondary productive units since the latter can be used by the former to depress wages and weaken union control of the labour process in the monopolies. Hence, components hitherto produced by large corporations may be sub-contracted out to legally independent but economically dependent small firms operating in competitive markets.

While there are features of interest to our general argument in dual labour market theory, there are problems with this particular version which require mentioning. The first of these is its rationalist mode of explanation which seems to have a good deal in common with the concepts of 'core' and 'periphery' which were discussed in Chapter 7. That is, a dualistic concept of dominance and dependence is derived as a logical conception and mechanically superimposed on to the massive complexity of the advanced capitalist labour market. For this to work the theory seems to require that each section of the labour market is sealed off from the other such that labour market inequality is systematically built into this sphere of exchange. This problem is recognized by the identification of points of entry from external labour markets to internal labour markets which are reserved for the lowest level manual labourers often in branch plants or subsidiaries, but this seems to be a somewhat limited recognition of the model's need for a topping-up device rather than being grounded in real processes. We are left wondering whether inequalities in labour markets derive from the structure of industry, or more realistically, from social structure. And this is the other main problem with dual labour market theory which is that it rests on an economic reductionist argument whereby big firms, paying good wages give rise to one stratum of the working (and middle) class, whereas small firms, paying poor wages create another. But this is clearly to abstract in a one-sided fashion the class stratification of capitalist societies from the distributional outcomes of different managerial strategies. It leaves no room for explaining class formation as a resultant of many complex forces operating in the spheres of production, reproduction, in civil and political society. Dual labour market theory is, in other words, a chaotic conception.

One theory which attempts to move beyond some of these and other limitations of dual labour market theory is that which postulates the existence of *labour market segmentation*. In this model there is less reliance upon a simple, dualistic notion of stratification, although that does not mean that such a division is rejected *tout court*. Rather, it is proposed that segmentation is a process which divides the labour market into sub-markets which may cut horizontally or vertically across the occupational hierarchy (Reich, Gordon and Edwards, 1973, p. 359). More specifically, they propose that within the asymmetrical relations which characterize the main class alignment between capital and labour, there are other asymmetries such as that within primary labour markets between *subordinate primary jobs* and *independent primary jobs*. The latter comprise decision-making, problem-solving, essentially conceptual, work characteristically subject to high levels of motivation, employment turnover and rewards for the relevant personnel. The former, which occur in both service and manufac-turing employment, are routinized, disciplined and rule-governed jobs allocated to functionaries in the primary section in conformity with the plans formulated by *independent* workers. The category of secondary labour market is retained although there is little attempt to differentiate strata within this section; rather it is suggested that there are vertical divisions which allocate jobs according to non-economic criteria, such as in terms of gender, race and degree of marginality. In descriptive terms, therefore, this theory marks only a limited advance on pure dual labour market theory except for the following important point. It is proposed that the explanation for the development of segmented labour markets is to be found in the strategy of the capitalist class to divide and rule the working class to prevent the latter from forming the alliances which would threaten the hegemony of capital. Furthermore, once a privileged segment of the working class has been included in subordinate primary employment, hierarchical divisions are introduced as elaborate social control devices associated with loyalty- and seniority-based fringe benefits which 'incorporate' the leading segments of the working class into the internal labour market. The latter effect allows monopoly capitalism to flourish at the expense of the working class as a whole (for similar arguments see O'Connor, 1973; Stone, 1974).

Although this theory presents a slight elaboration of the previous theory of the labour market it does not fundamentally shift the terrain of the debate. In other words, it does not progress beyond the basic rationalism of dual labour market theory, merely proposing a subcategorization within the latter. Nor does it supply adequate grounds for convincing us of the necessity of segmentation for the maintenance of capitalist social relations. Indeed, the latter point is one of the weakest in this approach to the analysis of segmentation for it is clearly functionalist in its presentation of capitalists as cleverly fragmenting a passive working class on the principle of 'anticipated reactions'. As a further echo of this functionalism it is perhaps noteworthy, too, that more attention is devoted to the primary section (bosses and subordinates) than to the secondary section (ultra-subordinates), suggesting an inclination to view the structure of the labour market as to be understood in terms of the economic requirements of capital rather than a product of struggles between capital and labour and, indeed, within the latter. Segmented labour market theory is an advance in terms of elaboration but is unnecessarily limited by its reliance on functional and economistic explanations.

More recent work has made good some of the omissions and crudities of dual and segmented labour market theory, although with some considerable variation in the depth of analysis adduced in support of the relevant elaborations. The important point which seems to unite both the smaller and the greater advancements is the aim of moving away from the rather mechanistic rigidities of the earlier work without falling into the neo-classical trap of conceiving a smooth continuity, governed by supply and demand for scarce resources (skills), as characterizing the profile of capitalist labour markets. This involves seeking a theoretically useful balance between the important idea of systematic fragmentation into sub-markets which are relatively self-contained, on the one hand, and the recognition that labour markets express degrees of gradation and overlap, on the other hand. The result is a variety of attempts to represent modern labour markets as characteristically *discontinuous*, and it is to a discussion of some of the key elements which seek to explain that discontinuity that we now turn.

An important first step in undermining the rigidities of the received wisdom regarding the structure of labour markets is represented in Blackburn and Mann's (1979) detailed British case study centred upon Peterborough. They concluded that the working class (the prime object of their study) operates within a hierarchical structure in the labour markets they studied, which were predominantly *internal labour markets*. However, there are no significant barriers to mobility between unskilled and skilled status other than those associated with seniority and unionization. In other words, most working-class manual work is homogeneous in spite of its hierarchization – 85 per cent of manual workers could perform all but 5 per cent of manual jobs, including 'skilled' ones, and most of these are less difficult than driving a car to work. The key division is between men and women who are seldom in competition for the same employment, with the result that women occupy the bottom positions in the hierarchy, receiving low pay in exchange for long hours, job insecurity and bad working conditions. At the other end of the manual occupational hierarchy there is some distinction between skilled workers who have undergone apprenticeships and 'skilled' workers whose position has been negotiated by their trade union. The main basis of distinction here is that the former are more autonomous *vis-à-vis* management because their skills are more marketable outside their present occupation. Within internal labour markets, therefore, Blackburn and Mann seem to identify a relatively undifferentiated primary labour market with males predominating in manual occupations. Women manual workers have difficulty entering primary internal labour markets, and thus:

. . . are probably a 'secondary' labour force in the sense of the dual and radical labour market theories. The internal labour market and other defences against insecurity exist on the backs of a secondary labour force, and in this country, that means largely on the backs of women. (Blackburn and Mann, 1979, p. 284)

In conclusion, therefore, they seem to postulate a semi-discontinuous labour market with little differentiation between skilled and unskilled segments in the primary sector, and little class distinctiveness between internal and external labour markets. The main distinction to be drawn in the latter case is one based upon gender, with women being concentrated in the small manufacturing and service industries. The strongest distinction, though not constituting an impassable boundary, is that between the fairly homogeneous manual, internal labour markets and the non-manual stratum of the same corporate structures.

Clearly, these findings present an interesting, albeit limited, challenge to the patterned pictures presented by dual and segmented labour market theorists. Of particular interest is the observation that the actions of workers themselves, especially through trade unions, may be influential in giving basically homogeneous employment a hierarchical veneer, within which seniority rules may determine which individuals receive an allocation from the scarce quota of good jobs. This suggests that it is at least partly as a result of struggles around internal labour markets that organized labour manages to impose whatever degree of orderliness is to be found within them – an argument directly counter to that proposed by Stone (1974) who saw job hierarchies as a device of management to divide the workforce against itself.[1] The former line of argument, namely that the structuration of labour markets is the result of a process aimed at derandomizing and thus reducing the level of uncertainty attending the contractual relations of employment, is developed by Berger and Piore (1980). Of especial interest in this work are the ways in which it attempts to accommodate the elements of discontinuity which we have been discussing with a reformulated dual labour market theory, and the emphasis placed upon the concept of the division of labour in reaching a solution to this theoretical dilemma.

Realizing that there were problems with the original dualistic and segmented labour market theories, Berger and Piore now argue that there is a *qualitative* difference about different sub-markets within the overall labour market which expresses their discontinuity even though there may be a degree of mobility between different market segments. These qualitative differences are represented in two dimensions: in the horizontal plane it is proposed that there are now three strata in the primary section of the labour market: an upper tier of professional and managerial employment; a lower tier of manual and non-manual occupations; and a middle stratum of skilled craft occupations. The secondary section is the same as in earlier theories, unskilled, unstable, underpaid and marginal. In the vertical plane the qualitative variations between the strata are given in terms of the division of labour in late capitalism and, specifically, in terms of the kinds of cognitive skills or ways of thinking which characterize different locations within the division of labour. The presence or absence of unionization is ascribed a determinant influence upon the degree of stability, rule-governed behaviour and customary procedures present in the lower tier primary section and missing from the secondary section. There is, clearly, a marked similarity here with Blackburn and Mann's account.

However, Berger and Piore's explanation for these social inequalities takes us a little closer to the kind of analysis of *spatial* inequality which Massey and others have developed. For it is argued that the fundamental difference between those who occupy positions of ultimate control in the productive process and those who do not is given by the difference between *abstract* and *concrete* learning. The former, which is typified by classroom learning in which rational deduction from concepts is the means of performing tasks, is characteristic of upper-tier occupations, while the latter, which involves memorizing sequences of operations, predominates in lower-tier occupations. The latter type of learning is supplied by on-the-job training and, in practice, involves routinized responses to cues or signals which may be given by, for example, the arrival of a sub-assembly on the production line, or a bulb lighting on a wiring circuit, or a customer seeking attention in a shop or office. The social relations of concrete learning, and work derived from it, are of key importance in giving coherence and comprehensibility to the tasks being performed in the lower tiers, and for internal labour markets the discussion, negotiation and bargaining over the organization of task performance are central factors in the emergence and persistence of unionization, especially for craft workers. In the secondary sector, where diverse products may be required from day to day and the source of conception may be hierarchically and geographically remote, workers are heavily dependent upon supervisors for their direction, and the social forces which stimulate unionization are consequently far weaker.

Nevertheless, despite making these interesting points Berger and Piore display a marked neo-Smithian[2] tendency towards explaining the underlying changes in the division of labour as being largely a product of technological change, stimulated by capital in order to overcome uncertainty in the product market-place, rather than being in direct response to labour's struggles to increase their degree of control in the sphere of production and their share of the product in the sphere of circulation. Moreover, they go on

214   *Theories of Planning and Spatial Development*

to argue that primary, lower-tier labour becomes like capital and exploits the secondary section in like manner, a conclusion which demonstrates the inadequacies of a rationalistic insistence upon maintaining the essential notion of dualism within the reworked theory. For no explanation is offered in support of the idea of an alliance between internal labour markets versus external labour markets other than that both sections within the internal labour market share the aim of reducing uncertainty, and achieve this aim at the expense of external labour markets. While this desire to reduce uncertainty may be common to all tiers of the labour market, Berger and Piore fail to recognize that for labour to remove the uncertainty in its contractual relations with capital it must transcend capitalist social relations, so that to reduce uncertainty must logically imply action contrary to the interests of capital.[3] Ironically, in discussing empirical instances of dualism, notably in Italy, they describe how precisely this kind of pressure by labour resulted in capital transferring production to the secondary sector in order to bypass the gains made in reducing uncertainty by lower-tier, primary section, occupational groups.

The underlying reason for these weaknesses is the reluctance of Berger and Piore to dispense with a theory of stratification. By the latter we mean a theory which designates spaces, or strata, in a society, which are themselves given largely by differential levels of income and into which are slotted human subjects in the form of passive agents. Reliance upon a stratification model in labour market theory has been roundly criticized for ignoring the negotiated nature of social structure and the centrality of power relations to the outcomes of those negotiations (Kreckel, 1980). The division of labour is precisely the major outcome of the asymmetrical relations between capital and labour, on the one hand, and within labour, on the other. Thus it is to further consideration of the mechanisms which make for discontinuities within the overall division of labour that we now turn. We are, therefore, rejecting the particular analytical usage of the concept of the division of labour introduced by Berger and Piore because it is unduly technicist and economically reductionist for the purposes with which we are concerned.

The biggest step forward in identifying mechanisms making for substantial inequality between manual workers is undertaken by Offe and Hinrichs (1977) who, unlike any of the previous theorists considered here, focus on the secondary section and its discontinuities rather than the primary section. They ask why it is occupied primarily by marginal or 'problem' groups of workers and consider the conventional idea that these comprise an easily manoeuvrable mass of unresistant and readily exploited labour, functional for the needs of corporate capital. But they reject the functionalism inherent in that explanation, arguing that reality does not reflect corporate interests in such simplistic ways. Rather they argue that the theorist must seek out those forces which are *resistant* to corporate interests, and also the reasons for a lack of *resistance* in certain quarters. They offer three reasons why secondary section workers are unresistant: first, they are composed largely of people who can gain subsistence outside the labour market: wives, pensioners, the disabled, part-time farmers; second, they do not conform to the image of the normal worker held by trade union functionaries, so they lack bargaining strength in relation to capital because of a lack of qualifications and marketability and in relation to labour because they cannot gain representation of their interests. Thus only those secondary section workers who are non-stigmatized by marginality gain 'normal' union recognition and protection, the remaining bulk of secondary workers have only the law to protect their minimal rights.

Building upon this concept of *exclusion* Kreckel (1980) identifies five mechanisms which structure the contemporary private sector labour market into an eightfold discontinuity. These mechanisms are: *demarcation, exclusion, solidarism, inclusion* and *exposure*. They operate as follows. In the normal capitalist labour market, which is characterized by a primary asymmetry in the relations between capital and labour, favouring the former, there is a secondary asymmetry which systematically underlines the primary one. This operates by virtue of the existence of the five mechanisms. Only *solidarism* primarily works to further the interests of labour for the reasons given in the analysis (discussed in Chapter 8) which Offe and Wiesenthal (1980) have advanced, namely that it is only by *associating* that workers can compensate for the great power advantage enjoyed by capital due to its ownership of the means of production. The point about such ownership is that it represents a unified, legally separate and thus alienable, concentration of disembodied labour power which can be liquidated, transformed into money capital, and re-invested elsewhere. Such power can only be constrained to the extent that *solidarism* amongst workers, either directly or through the state and the law, threatens this capacity by withholding the vital ingredient for surplus value production, the living labour power of individual workers. The four remaining mechanisms represent, to varying degrees, interruptions to the constraining influence of *solidarism*. *Demarcation*, which can express the interest of both certain parts of labour, and capital, for a degree of occupational exclusiveness, will tend to work against forces leading towards *solidarism*. Craft unionism is the strongest source of demarcation, and one which capital is prepared to comply with while productivity increases are given a lower priority than continuous production. But demarcation is markedly weakened as a divide-and-rule strategy for both capital and skilled labour, as competition drives out skilled work from the production process in many industries and the demands of rising productivity replace rigid demarcation with flexible working practices.

However, while *demarcation* along the horizontal axis, between similar occupational groupings, becomes less important, *exclusion*, applied in the vertical axis becomes of major importance. This is the means whereby increasingly homogeneous, semi-skilled, workforces protect their positions in employment at the expense of weakening the position of other groups. The obvious instances here, include young people, many of whom are *excluded* from the labour market because older, especially male, workers are able to retain employment through union-negotiated transfers within internal labour markets. Others particularly affected by *exclusion* are women and ethnic minorities, the former because they are concentrated in a labour market sub-section which acts as a buffer zone betweeen 'normal' male workers and marginals, and the latter because they do not have union representation precisely as a result of their marginal status. Lastly *inclusion* and *exposure* are mechanisms closely associated with strategies by capital to control labour markets in their own interests. *Inclusion* occurs where, for example, a skilled sub-market is artificially 'encircled' within a corporation by being given special status or even corporation-specific qualifications. The effect is to reduce the bargaining strength of such occupational groupings by delimiting the capacity of workers to acquire equivalent status elsewhere. *Exposure* works in a rather similar way but at the bottom end of the labour market where unskilled workers are made aware that they are easily replaced by unemployed or marginal workers. Where this is accompanied by *exclusion* from union representation too, such groups may be locked into a bargaining vacuum.

Finally, Kreckel constructs a discontinuous labour market structure in which occupational inequalities are conditioned by these mechanisms into eight levels. At the lowest end of what is, for purposes of illustration, still referred to as the secondary section, are the heavily *exposed* and *excluded* workers who have no legal rights because they are illegal immigrants, or are in some other way criminalized. Next to this group come the 'stigmatized' marginal, unskilled or deskilled workers who cannot develop *solidaristic* associations, are *excluded* and *exposed*, but do have some legal and thus welfare status (such as guest workers). Moving on to the next group we see the upper secondary section workers identified as 'normal' unskilled by Offe and Hinrichs, who may thus be *solidaristic*. Then on the boundary between the secondary and primary sections are found the specialized or corporate-qualified workers who have been the subjects of *inclusion* by capital and for whom *demarcation* is important. Above this group is another, vulnerable to *inclusion*, but for whom *demarcation* is endangered by deskilling, and thus the threat of *exposure* is heightened. This is the group whose skills or qualifications are devaluing. A more secure skilled group is that which is easily able to market its qualifications outside the particular internal labour market in which it currently is found. Typically these workers will be craft-unionized and thus predisposed towards a strategy of *exclusion*, exclusive *solidarism* and *demarcation*. At a level above this are those occupations on the borderline between subordinate and independent primary section labour markets which, because of *solidaristic* and *exclusive* strategies in technologically sensitive services (for example air traffic controllers, power engineers) experience revaluation of skills and qualifications. Finally, the most *exclusive* area of the labour market is occupied by those possessing academic, managerial or professional qualifications which confer the strongest bargaining rights upon its occupants even to the extent of minimizing the 'market' aspect of the relationship between employer and employee in favour of more discretionary forms of appointment.

This seems quite a useful categorization although as Kreckel himself makes clear it can only be used for assisting in the framing of research questions rather than supplying answers. It will be modified by:

Racial, sexual or age distinctions . . . on all levels, regional imbalances, the rural–urban division, variations between industries or cyclical influences . . . as well as the differentiating impact of unions, employers' organizations and state interventionism. . . . (Kreckel, 1980, p. 545)

To which, Kreckel notes, must be added, variants in labour market structure found in: state employment, self-employment, and as affected by variations in the extent of unpaid labour, notably in the domestic sphere. Before we go on to consider work which has sought to analyse the spatial dimension of labour market differentiation it is worth pointing to two criticisms of the typology developed by Kreckel. The first is that, although he is aware that the argument that occupational inequality arises because the positions which require the highest qualifications are scarce, is functionalist (Kreckel, 1980, p. 531) he is prone to employ the same argument himself in explaining relative positions in the labour market in terms of the presence or absence of those qualities either in individuals (qualifications) or unions (capacity to *exclude*) which fit them to better positions in the hierarchy. The second point of criticism is that the resulting hierarchization pays relatively little attention to the homogenization factor which Blackburn and Mann discuss and which, in the process of deskilling workers and upgrading unskilled ones to semi-skilled status reduces the capacity of *exclusive* craft-unions to resist more widespread entry into occupations which may once have been thought to be their preserve. In other words, Kreckel is a little too rationalist in his conceptualization of real-world processes, a problem which derives from insufficient attention being paid to the changes in production methods, the labour process and production relations, and the implications of these for the mechanisms making for occupational inequality which he has identified.

Spatially differentiated labour markets

One of the general criticisms that can be made of all the labour market theories we have considered is that, rather as with much neo-classical economic analysis, the processes described appear to occur on the head of a pin. The lack of a spatial dimension in the analysis is surprising, especially in those theories which postulate segregation between labour markets, since *a priori* it seems reasonable to expect that space would exert some such effect upon the relationships between sub-markets. In what follows we shall consider three different approaches to introducing the spatial dimension into labour market studies, each of which makes interesting use of the idea that the spatial development of capitalism is in some way changed by local and/or regional class relations, in particular as indicated by the degree of unionization in local areas. The first of these can be referred to as *the neo-dualism thesis* which is found extensively in work on spatial development in Italy (Paci, 1973; Bagnasco, 1977, 1981; Arcangeli *et al.*, 1979; Mingione, 1978, 1981; Brusco, 1982; for a summary of some of this work see Berger and Piore, 1980).

The original duality in the developing capitalist economy is that which is based on the urban–rural dichotomy. The reserve army of unemployed and underemployed workers is found in low productivity agricultural activity whereas in the urban centres industry develops and concentrates, so increasing the demand for labour. The latter is both attracted away from the countryside by higher real wages in the towns but also by being 'released' from an agriculture which is itself becoming more mechanized as the urban markets for its output become enlarged. However, as concentration continues and competition between firms, rather than with agriculture, sets wage levels, a new dualism emerges which consists of large, advanced, monopoly corporations concentrated in a specific region and the rest of the national territory being devoted to more or less dependent status *vis-à-vis* the primate industrial region. The latter involves industrial dependence in that there are small businesses which, though independent, are tied to the monopolies as suppliers. Also, there are large capital-intensive units which have been located in depressed regions with state assistance. These 'cathedrals in the desert' do not, however, generate local linkages and self-sustained regional growth. Finally, there are the bloated, tertiarized, public sector occupations which absorb some of the urban unemployed, again mainly in depressed regions (Mingione, 1981).

As it stands this is fairly crudely put, but of some considerable interest is the spatial ordering which seems, empirically, to have emerged on the basis of this dualistic economic structure and, more to the point, the effect which struggles in the spheres of production, circulation, reproduction and popular democracy have exerted upon this structure. For, in effect, it seems that Italy has become something of a microcosm of Wallerstein's *world system* with a core in the Piedmont around Turin and Milan, a periphery in the Mezzogiorno, and a semi-periphery between the industrial core and Rome. The semi-periphery is of considerable interest since it is ascribed in part to the effects of the 'hot autumn' of 1969 and subsequent years when core-region workers (notably in Fiat in Turin) fought not only for improved wages but also for greater control of the labour process and gains in the sphere of reproduction. Their success is described in the following:

. . . Fiat was forced to agree to a contract which committed it to policies for transportation, housing, and regional development which affected groups of workers extending well beyond its own employees. Unions here have, moreover, pressed for things seldom demanded by American unions: escalator clauses tying all wages to price indices; wage differentials; unified wage setting procedures and lines of career advance for blue and white collar jobs. (Berger and Piore, 1980, p. 30)

Capital's reply to this shift in the balance of class forces is widely interpreted as taking two forms: the first involved attempts to regain control within the workplace by intensified introduction of automated assembly processes (robotization) and restructuring the labour process so as to reduce the autonomy of worker's councils; the second involved *productive decentralization*. That is, sub-contracting parts of the production process to small, often family, firms located in predominantly rural areas at a distance from the centres of strong unionization. This has the effect of cheapening inputs and keeping wages down while disciplining the core labour force (Bagnasco, 1977, 1981; Arcangeli *et al.*, 1980). Put differently, accumulation imperatives are fulfilled against efforts by workers to reduce the power imbalances which they entail, by a conscious strategy of spatial diversification on the part of capital.

A rather different spatial analysis of the role of the labour market in capitalist development is provided by Friedman (1977). He rejects dual and segmented labour market theory for their reliance upon the notion of stratification as a new and rigidifying feature of contemporary labour markets, and for the functionalism inherent in presenting this stratification as a conscious strategy by capital. Rather, he makes the important point, which accords with our general argument, that *resistance* is:

a force . . . which is *differentially* distributed among workers, and which capitalists and top managers often accommodate and attempt to co-opt. (Friedman, 1977, p. 114; emphasis in original)

However, despite making this point Friedman makes exaggerated use of a *core-periphery* model by means of which to differentiate not only workers, but intra-firm relations, firms, regions and countries. The problems of employing this rationalistic device are replicated in ways which have the unfortunate effect of obscuring what is often a penetrative historical and theoretical account of the impact of class struggle upon capitalist spatial development. Thus, having criticized segmentation theorists for conceiving segmentation as a function of managerial strategies Friedman himself presents peripheral firms as being maintained by the conscious strategies of management to secure a functional means of absorbing fluctuations and maintaining stability. Hence, whereas segmentation theorists present workers as passive agents of capital, Friedman tends to do the same for the managers of small businesses and, by implication, *their* employees.

Despite this problem Friedman makes a number of useful arguments which prefigure the points made about the mechanisms associated with occupational inequality by Kreckel. *Excluded* groups of workers are seen as being differently managed from those who either themselves possess *exclusivity* or *inclusivity*. The former are subject to *direct control* of their labour process whereas the latter tend to be allowed to exercise greater degrees of *responsible autonomy* either because they occupy important places in the technical division of labour or possibly because of the power of less-skilled workers to threaten continuity of production through collective means. Those subject to direct control (peripheral workers) tend to be the ones made redundant first in times of recession: they are defined in terms of their relative dispensability to a firm's productive capacity and consist of those groups demonstrating the lowest levels of *solidarism*; women, immigrants and ethnic minorities. As we have seen inter-firm relations between primary (core) and secondary (periphery) sections of the labour market are characterized by the latter's exploitation by the former. But the most interesting spatial dimension of the core-periphery relationship is revealed in the proposition that the ability of large firms to survive is dependent first, on their capacity to find a peripheral labour market to offset fluctuations of a cyclical nature, and second upon shifts in location of the main sites of production:

The very nature of the centre-periphery pattern creates conditions which lead top managers eventually to try to destroy the pattern and recreate it elsewhere. (Friedman, 1977, p. 139)

Thus Friedman envisages a long-term *rotation* of regions which will be economically relatively buoyant – the coalfields and textile centres in the nineteenth century, the motor vehicle and domestic appliance centres of the mid-twentieth century, and a gradual dispersal of the remnants of the latter industries out to the assisted areas of the UK contemporarily – prompted by the success of workers in the spheres of production and circulation struggle. The point at which *rotation* initiatives begin (see also Goodman, 1979) is associated with the intersection of two factors. First, the relative success by labour in struggles within the central state to establish assisted area status, and, second, a decline in those same areas of the strength of labour organizations, relative wage-rates, and property values, a process which can take a few generations. Where worker resistance is weak, established industries tend not to need to *rotate* in the fashion described. Thus Friedman agrees with an earlier conclusion drawn by Beynon (1975) regarding the motivation for industrial relocation, at least in the car industry:

The reasons which influenced the Ford Motor Company's move to Halewood were the same as those that led it to establish a plant at Genk in the underdeveloped Limsburg region of Belgium. Unemployment means low wages and a vulnerable labour force. . . . In Britain expansion away from traditional areas of manufacture created the possibility for the motor employers to organize the production of motor cars free from the job control that had built up in the old factories. Ford's moves to Liverpool and Swansea were paralleled by Vauxhall's move to Ellesmere Port on Merseyside and the opening of a Rootes (Chrysler) plant at Linwood. (Beynon, 1975, p. 65)

However, it seems likely that the traditions of unionization and struggle which these regions had developed in earlier rounds of capitalist development meant that the advantage to capital from locating there was short-lived.

Hence, two similar responses (by motor-vehicle manufacturers) to class pressure seem to be identified in both *neo-dualism* and *core-periphery* theories. On the one hand, both postulate and provide evidence that large firms exist in a symbiotic relationship of interdependence with small suppliers and that this can have implications for spatial development through *productive decentralization* at the regional scale (Italy) and the intra-regional scale (UK). On the other hand, both identify relocation of large-scale productive plant away from areas of strong union organization and into areas characterized by high unemployment. Moreover, both register some perceived willingness on the part of workers to take low wages. Whereas in Italy this does not seem to be necessarily accompanied by a *rotation* strategy on the part of capital, it is argued that this is likely in the UK (although empirically the pattern looks identical to that in Italy with assembly plants tending to be 'cathedrals in the desert' too). To the extent that restructuring does involve shifts in the centres of production it may be better characterized as the development of *multinucleated centres* based on multiple sourcing and the internationalization of production. At the theoretical level, however, both of these approaches, while providing valuable explanations of the role of struggle in spatial development, tend to be over-constrained by the use of unnecessarily rationalistic conceptual frameworks.

The last approaches to this subject to be considered here make no attempt to fit processes to rationalist conceptualizations but rather try to derive explanations of spatially uneven development from rather more strongly class-based analyses of the variation between local labour markets (Urry, 1981b; Massey, 1980; Cooke, 1981, 1982a). The main difference between these analyses and the others discussed in this section is the way they each come to the important conclusion that classes, and thus labour markets, cannot be satisfactorily conceptualized in rationalist and functionalist terms such as 'core' and 'periphery'. Rather they are to be understood as under-going a permanent, dynamic process of recomposition or reconstitution in relation to the developing antagonism between accumulation imperatives and worker resistance. In this precise respect they come closest to the position taken by Blackburn and Mann (1979):

Thus the long-term expansion of capitalism appears to generate a continuous process of intra-working class division and reconstitution, a process which could only stop with the integration of the world's population into the labour force of capitalism. (Blackburn and Mann, 1979, p. 301)

The important difference is that none of the three authors mentioned would see recomposition *ending* with capitalist integration; each views it as one of the key defining characteristics of precisely that mode of production, the ending of which could only, implicitly, be conceived with the *disappearance* of capitalism.

Creating this recomposition effect in the local class structure is the process whereby the spatial division of labour is restructured on an increasingly international scale. New and more highly differentiated local labour markets come into existence because of the ways in which the production process in large corporate organizations is decomposed or fragmented in ways which take advantage of the size, skills and level of unionization of local labour markets. This works to the advantage of capital on the whole because it fragments the inter-regional solidarity of a working class organized on a functional or sectoral basis rather than a territorial one (Urry, 1981b, p. 24). Moreover, it leads to inter-regional competition by organized labour and local capital to create conditions in which the central and/or regional state can offer inward-investing capital a corporatist package of labour market incentives, notably responsible industrial relations practices on the part of labour (Cooke, 1982a, p. 23). Finally, and most importantly, it expresses an increase in the expulsion of male working class members from waged work, especially in 'traditional' heavy industry areas (the 'normal' unionized workers after Offe and Hinrichs) and the corresponding insertion of women in both the new, decentralized production units and in service industry, both state and private sector. In consequence, both the means of resistance and the quality of work in traditional local labour markets are diminished by the process of recomposition which follows the changing spatial division of labour (Massey, 1980, p. 9).

What, if anything, can be said which helps to fix, at least conceptually, the main outlines of the categories which enable these and other writers to continue to think of labour markets as being structured in some way rather than simply being a *melange*. Moreover, to what extent do the factors which make for discontinuity (and inequality) within the overall labour market gain expression in the spatial dimension? Clearly, detailed responses to this question are a matter for empirical research, however, Table 1 gives a rather bare territorial typology[4] of socially differentiated labour markets based on the following studies (Kreckel, 1980; Urry, 1981b; Cooke, 1981). The point of doing this is to attempt to give indications of the kind of jobs which may be expected to be found in various types of area, the reasons why, and the extent to which the interests of employees in such areas can converge across the recomposition effect of contemporary capitalism to be reconstituted not simply as local, but rather as aspatial, class interests. To clarify the meaning and discuss certain problems with the question of class interests we will turn to a brief discussion of theories of class structure and class relations in the next section of this chapter.

Table 1 *A classification for spatially discontinuous labour markets*

Predominant labour market	Main determinants	Primary class interest	Predominant location
(i) *Marginalized*			
Illegal immigrants, criminalized, male and female non-citizens	Demand for 'sweated' labour, growth of informal or 'black' economy	Latent proletarian due to only having labour power to sell, but non-solidaristic	Regional-metropolitan and primate city ethnic enclaves, 'inner city'
(ii) *Underclass*			
Unemployed, redundant or deskilled citizens, labour-reserves	Technological restructuring, 'runaway industries', excessive wage costs, anti-union closures	Latent proletarian because labour-power not in demand, basis for solidarism fragmented	State-assisted areas, regional-metropolitan and primate inner-city ethnic and indigenous enclaves or 'traditional communities'
(iii) *Precarious*			
Guestworkers, part-time workers, limited-contract and seasonal workers male and female	Fluctuating demand for labour in unstable occupations. Inadequate non-work sources of income	Latent proletarian because labour power insufficiently in demand to ensure reproduction. Excluded from solidaristic organizations	Rural and various urban centres of labour-intensive employment, males in agricultural and construction work, females in miscellaneous services

Table 1 – *continued*

Predominant labour market	Main determinants	Primary class interest	Predominant location
(iv) *Selective*			
Temporary workers, periodic workers male and female	Constant demand in tight labour markets, aggravated by employment protection law	Proletarian because only have labour-power to sell, are not employers, and may be unionized	Regional-metropolitan and primate service centres, female secretarial/commercial, male/female periodic teachers, legal assistants, clerical
(v) *Feminized*			
Full-time, service-sector workers, predominantly female	Growth of state and private service sectors, routinized secretarial, data-processing etc. work	Proletarian because only have labour-power to sell, and likely to be unionized	Regional-metropolitan (and some smaller) administrative centres, with substantial retailing and commercial functions
(vi) *'Normal' compliant*			
Small, independent businesses, subcontractors, mainly unskilled, male employment	Components-suppliers to corporate enterprise, objects of 'productive de-centralization', competitive, low-wage, under-unionized	Latent proletarian due to anti-unionism of small employers, and advantages gained thereby for large firms	Periphery of industrial conurbations, semi-rural areas, possibly near branch-plants

(vii) *'Normal' resistant*

Large, manufacturing firms, semi-skilled male employment, substantial female minority, especially in branch plants	Economies of scale, industrial monopoly, advanced mechanization, strong internal labour markets, training, benefits	Proletarian because only have labour-power to sell and unionization vital to worker security	Industrial conurbations, branch plants in and near to assisted areas

(viii) *Crafts* (devaluing)

Skilled, manual employment, mainly in large manufacturing firms, predominantly male	Scarcity, monopoly of expertise, exclusivity, or if deskilling is occurring, inclusivity	Proletarian because only have labour-power to sell, high solidarity, unionization, demarcation	Industrial conurbations, centres of metal manufacturing, mechanical and electrical engineering

(ix) *Crafts* (revaluing)

Skilled, manual employment, specialized manufacturing and services. Small and medium sized firms. Male and some female	Scarcity, new skills or those which have been enhanced by technical change	Weakly proletarian because of potential for self-employment, Solidaristic, exclusive, trade unionism	Mainly periphery of primate or large industrial cities, e.g. airports, power stations, R & D offices

(x) *Self-employed*

Small to medium-sized independent businesses, subcontractors, suppliers, primary, extractive producers	Traditional petty-bourgeoisie, past and emergent demand for supplies to large firms	Capitalist due to purchasing labour-power and producing surplus value	Periphery of industrial conurbations, semi-rural areas, suburbia, specialist inner-city 'quarters'

Table 1 – *continued*

Predominant labour market	Main determinants	Primary class interest	Predominant location
(xi) *Subordinate functionaries*			
Lower-order state and private sector administration, management and professional occupations	Growth of subordinate technical and administrative functions as complexity of division of labour increases	Capitalist where production is of or for surplus value. Proletarian where labour power is sold to meet social needs	Regional-metropolitan centres, primate-city centres, local administrative centres
(xii) *Independent functionaries*			
Higher-order state and private sector administration, management and professional occupations	Increased separation of conception and decision taking in production, financing and administration of national and international capital and state functions	Capitalist because main interest is in reproducing national and international conditions for surplus value production	Primate region or specialized centres of government, finance or production

A few brief comments are necessary before we move on to examine the dynamic relations between the categories in Table 1 in terms of class relations, and their implications for development planning. The first point to be made is that this listing does not by any means represent a rigid hierarchy, rather a set of overlapping, in some instances (such as *self-employed* and *'normal' compliant*, or *feminized* and both sets of *functionaries*) conterminous, and, in other instances (such as *'normal' resistant* and *crafts*), parallel, categories. The second point to be made is that the primary class interest of the different groups is defined objectively, that is, in terms of the relationship of the members of each category to the basic relations of production. This is a binary choice between those who are owners of means of production, purchasers of labour power and whose aim is surplus value production or to facilitate it, and those who have only their labour power to sell in the market-place: the division between capitalists and proletarians (Carchedi, 1975).

The third point, which can only be outlined here, is that it may be hypothesized that capitalist development will seek out certain spatial labour market directions in which to proceed. Crudely, this will be away from locations where *'normal'* resistance and, possibly, *crafts* labour markets are predominant and towards any of the following labour market locations in descending order of priority: close to *underclass* labour reserves; to *'normal' compliant, self-employed* areas; to *precarious* and *marginalized* labour markets. The tendency has been for moves towards the first two of these kinds of location up to the recent past (Fothergill and Gudgin, 1979; Keeble, 1980) but conditions are being brought about (partly by state inducements such as finance and aid to small firms, enterprise zones, urban development corporations) which are likely to result in a continuation of *productive decentralization* to non-metropolitan areas on the one hand, and *productive recentralization* on the other. Both of the latter processes will be dominated by the continued growth of independent subcontracting rather than the incorporation or relocation of corporately-owned sub-units. This is because the latter process tends to produce productivity stagnation and stable unit costs whereas the former allows substantial corporate productivity increases and reduced corporate unit costs as a consequence of lower labour costs, less *solidarism* and greater *exposure* in the independent small businesses (Arcangeli *et al.*, 1980; Berger and Piore, 1980; Mingione, 1981; Cross, 1981).

The last point of importance about this typology of discontinuous labour markets is that a marked degree of discontinuity is supplied by the spatial dimension. This, of course, is something which most theorists who posit a dual or segmented structure to labour markets overlook. But it is clearly of some importance when differences between, for example, *'normal' compliant* and *'normal' resistant*, *precarious* and *selective* part-time work or those between *marginalized* and *underclass* labour markets are being considered. Plainly, we are not saying that these categories are hermetically sealed from one another over space, rather that capitalism's tendency to recompose the class structure takes on a distinctively spatial aspect at certain points.[5] In other instances space may be far less relevant in differentiating sub-markets than, say, gender, as in *feminized* labour markets, or ethnicity, which is what contributes to the spatial segregation characteristic of *marginalized* labour markets.

Having made these points, a further qualification must be added, which is that by no means will apparently similar labour markets display homogeneity with regard to the pursuit of their objective class interests: to assume so would be absurdly reductionist, essentialist, functionalist and rationalistic in respect of class consciousness. It is to a consideration of factors which may help understanding of spatial and temporal variations in class organization and action within broadly homogeneous labour markets that we turn in the following section.

Class structure and class relations

There are basically two positions taken within Marxist theories of class which can help us delimit the range of possible arguments about the relationship between the objective, economically-determined places which people occupy in the class structure, the extent of their class consciousness, and the nature of their political action. We shall briefly outline these positions and offer criticisms before moving on to identify a third theory which is consistent with the argument we developed in the preceding chapter. It will be recalled that this stressed the centrality of the local dimension of civil society, the state and class relations to an understanding of the general trend of spatial development under capitalism. This will then enable us to conclude the chapter with an analysis of the interaction between local classes, spatial development and urban and regional planning measures.

The first approach to theorizing class structure involves the systematic analysis of the economic positions which people occupy, beginning with the primary bifurcation between capitalists and workers, rather as class interests were allocated in the typology of labour markets discussed earlier. It will be recalled that in the latter case the particular class interest associated with labour market position was defined in terms of production relations. Put simply, this was according to whether specific categories only sold their labour power, on the one hand, or aimed for the production of (or for) surplus value, on the other. The distinction between production 'of (or for)' expresses the difference between industrial capitalists, who control and organize the labour process with the direct view in mind of generating surplus value, and financial capitalists, along with state functionaries, who make their contribution largely in the sphere of circulation by advancing money capital for the ultimate purpose of surplus value production. They do not themselves directly engage in the process of surplus value production. While the dualism of this division is helpful it is not subtle enough to capture an important intermediate position in the class structure of advanced capitalism, which has exercised the minds of leading class theorists a great deal recently. This refers to the variously termed 'new middle class' (Urry, 1973; Carchedi, 1977); 'professional-managerial class' (Ehrenreich and Ehrenreich, 1979); 'new petty bourgeoisie' (Poulantzas, 1975); or the occupants of 'contradictory class locations' (Wright, 1978; for a good review of this literature see Wright, 1980).

The important point which is added to the analysis of class structure by this debate is that there are certain economic positions which cannot *objectively* be neatly slotted into one or other of the two fundamental classes. Such groups include: managers and supervisors whose subordinate functions mean they do not have decisive control over investment and labour process decisions; small employers who do employ labour power but may work alongside them; and semi-autonomous employees who sell their labour power but may exert some control over their own labour process (Wright, 1980, p. 330). Put differently, they are non-owners of the means of production and non-producers of surplus value, but who may be powerful, may hire labour and have high status, and include managers, professionals, clerks and foremen (Urry, 1973, p. 183). Or put yet again differently, those who are excluded from economic ownership of the means of production, but who assist the global function of capital (control and surveillance of the labour process) and the function of the collective worker (participation in the labour process) comprise the new middle class, mainly managers and supervisors from larger firms, augmented by small employers (Carchedi, 1977).

Having performed these analyses of the various class positions of the working population (waged work) in terms of the basic social relations of capitalist society, theorists of this class-theoretic predisposition are then able to make certain deductions about the relative aggregate balance of class forces in concrete instances. Not all of them do this to the same extent as Wright (1978, 1980) who has estimated the size of the US working class, as modified by each of the various theoretical definitions of the new middle class. This varies from between 20 per cent and 40 per cent for those approaches which postulate an intervening new petty bourgeoisie (Poulantzas), up to 60 per cent for those simply excluding the professional-managerial class (Ehrenreich and Ehrenreich), while for those such as Wright and Carchedi who identify contradictory or ambiguous class positions for the new middle class, the estimate is 42 per cent and 52 per cent respectively, the latter figure being considered the most realistic. However, the main deductions drawn from either the kind of empirical analysis performed by Wright or the more theoretical analysis of Carchedi refer to the implications of aggregate class strength for the prospects of class struggle. Wright's main argument is that the contradictory class locations are the ones potentially most open to influence by class struggle though he offers no support for this assertion. Carchedi, with a more dynamically grounded theory, argues that the new middle classes are increasingly proletarianized by the reduction of the skill content of their work. This is due to the fragmentation of tasks and the introduction of new production techniques as capital seeks to raise the level of productivity in the face of competition and the declining profit rate.

These analyses are clearly of the first importance to the production of knowledge about the changing size and structure of classes as capitalist development proceeds, although Carchedi's is the best in terms of identifying the mechanism which brings part of that change about. This is seen to be deskilling, consequent upon labour process restructuring. They share the desire to derive class categories non-idealistically and non-rationalistically and do so from the conceptually coherent basis of social relations of production. However, there are certain problems implicit in this approach given the aims which these theorists set themselves. These are to identify the nature and scale of class positions and to make deductions about the respective political strength of the two main contending classes, capital and labour. The first problem is the inherent functionalism which is entailed in the analyses made. Carchedi is particularly prone to this fault but so to varying degrees are others we have considered: these are indeed, as Wright notes, theories of 'empty places' (1980, p. 370) whose occupants have their roles largely determined for them. Hence, the possibility that such places have been formed, with varying degrees of success, and with spatial and temporal variations, as outcomes of contending class strategies is overlooked. The introduction of the category of contradictory class positions seems to be little more than a device for dealing with the problem of indeterminacy, albeit in a plainly functionalist way (also, for criticism of deskilling theory, see Wood (1982)).

The second problem is related to the previous one and concerns the heavy overtones of economism and reductionism involved in deriving classes simply from occupational structures. This is too simplistic a way of dealing with the complexities of class formation and class organization which are a prelude to and an expression of social relationships formed in spheres other than that of production. It is probable, with regard to this criticism, that the problem rests on an overambition to extend the important theoretical and empirical findings made with respect to class stucture into the field of class struggle without making the crucial intervening connections, a point which Wright (1980) seems to recognize when he draws attention to Przeworski's argument that there is no necessary correspondence between economic places and organized classes (Przeworski, 1977). We would also add a third problem with this kind of approach in general, which is that it seems to postulate an essential evenness across national territory regarding the relations of antagonism between capital and labour, and, that by piecing together the fragments, real class forces are revealed. However, the defining feature of capitalist development is, we have argued, its lack of a single essence, its general unevenness, indeterminacy and capacity to take advantage of spatially differentiated class strengths, sub-nationally and internationally, as it develops. Other factors than aggregate occupational categories have to be taken into account before the very useful work of defining the class structures of advanced capitalism can be used to help in the understanding of the processes of class recomposition, development of class consciousness, organization and resistance which are of significance to the pace and direction of spatial development.

One approach to the analysis of class organization and its associated political action, which is the polar opposite to the one discussed above, is to argue that there is no link between economically-defined class position and the position taken in political class struggle. In other words, there is a necessary non-correspondence between the sphere of production and the ways in which classes are represented in the political society of the state. This argument is developed most fully by Hirst (1977). The argument is put in this way in a perfectly reasonable attempt to overcome the economic reduction-ism which follows from employing the notion that whatever occurs in the economic 'base' is reflected in the political and ideological 'superstructure' of capitalist society. Hirst argues that social relations which are formed in the sphere of production cannot be represented unproblematically in other spheres of social existence. This is because, as the means by which they are represented in the different spheres are themselves different, this difference comes to dominate what it is that is being represented. In other words, a base-superstructure mechanism is a practical impossibility because once such a distinction is admitted then so is the idea of some degree of autonomy, and it is the latter which distorts the connections between the different levels at which social relations exist.

This theory of class, arguing as it does for a complete hiatus between social relations of production and political classes, certainly overcomes the tendency towards economic reductionism but in the process throws out the baby with the bathwater. For by arguing, not unreasonably, that political struggles consist of elements other than the content of class antagonisms at the point of production, Hirst stretches too far when arguing that they are devoid of economic content. We seem to be confronted here by another example of the mechanistic division of real processes according to a ration-alist logic, similar in kind to that which is characteristic of writers who differentiate monolithic 'places' into which consumption and production separately fit. Both suffer from the illusion that reality is a reflection of tidy conceptual schemes.

In Hirst's case he overlooks the important point that economic relations are interpenetrated by political relations and vice versa, as Urry (1981a) and Hall (1977) have shown theoretically in discussion of the ways in which struggles within political society (the state) change from being dominated by one set of issues (circulation) to domination by another (reproduction) as capitalist development itself crosses certain thresholds. In particular, this can be seen in the present conjuncture where the economic difficulties of British capitalism channel political action and debate back towards ways of aiding capital at the expense of reductions in past gains made in the sphere of reproduction. We conclude, therefore, that there cannot be a satis-factory analysis of political classes based on the notion of a necessary non-correspondence between classes at the economic and political levels, nor can there be if it is assumed that there is a necessary correspondence. Rather, our argument so far would favour an interpretation of the relationship which echoes Hall's (1977) solution to the problem, namely that it is one in which there is no necessary correspondence between the two class determinations. This is because such a formulation retains the possibility for non-economic struggles to occur within politics while maintaining the constraining effects imposed upon political struggles by the historical and, we would argue, spatial, stages of capitalist development.

Such a conclusion returns us to a consideration of the relationships between regional and/or local class structure, class organization and spatial development. This is because implicit in what has been said thus far is the idea that it is mistaken to seek explanations for the uneven nature of capitalist development by assuming that, to the extent that this is influenced by class relations, classes should themselves be conceived as somehow spatially invariant. To do this is to ascribe the determinants of capitalist development to one class, the owners of means of production, seeking out locations in terms of an undifferentiated comparative advantage. We have argued, by contrast, that spatial development is significantly conditioned by the spatial division of labour and the resulting differentiations between labour markets which, in turn, express the composition of local class structures. The question now is what mechanisms activate particular local class structures into positions which threaten the accumulation process, and which may, in turn, induce a relocation of capital or some form of *in situ* capital restructuring, either of which represents a small part of the larger process of capitalist development. This is, to say the least, a difficult question to respond to, but it is one towards which our general argument so far offers some pointers. In order to sketch the outlines of a theoretical answer and try to provide a means of framing the empirical questions which need to be asked of the range of sectors, spatial units, and relevant historic periods, with which future research must be concerned, we will return briefly to Przeworski's (1977) analysis of the processes of class formation.

It will be recalled that, following Gramsci, Przeworski proposed that in order to understand the link between economic classes and political classes it was necessary to develop a theory of civil society. This was precisely because classes could not be thought of as being uniquely set in motion as a result of being assigned places in the social structure, rather they were to be conceived as the effects of struggles in which production relations were not the sole determinants. The import of this observation is that classes do not exist until they have been formed in situations of struggle, *the occupants of the empty places are not, therefore, classes*. Nevertheless, the conflicts which occur are constrained by the stage of development and so each round of capitalist development provides the condition for struggles out of which different kinds of working class, intermediate class or capitalist class will be formed. Similarly, spatial unevenness in the development process will aid the formation of different kinds of class in different regions and localities (to the extent that they are dominated by different labour markets). From this point it becomes important to ask why some local classes develop solidarism and class consciousness in certain instances, why others do not, why those that do nevertheless lose these characteristics on occasions, and whether class organization bears a clear relationship to particular labour markets (or sets of economic places). This places the emphasis on the interaction between production relations and the realm in which individuals are capable of becoming conscious of a certain commonality of experience with others, which is local civil society. Here, meanings and cultural forms relating to experience in different spheres of struggle and in different units within the sphere of production (factories, mines, offices) and in different localities are exchanged. This is the precise field of class organization in its political-ideological sense, where parties which have defined certain interests are in operation to actively bring about the formation of classes. Once active, these parties may begin to change the form of the state because by articulating grievances and challenging previous political relations they set in train the process of undermining them.

To understand how this process develops it is useful to consider, with illustrations where these are available, the content of the four spheres of struggle, one in production, the others in civil society, which were introduced in the previous chapter. In particular, we shall make distinctions within each sphere and suggest ways in which, at a theoretical level as well as the empirical level, certain combinations of these distinctions can provide conditions for spatially uneven class mobilization. In this there will be occasional reference back to some of the earlier discussion in this chapter on labour market discontinuity.

If we look at the sphere of production first, it can be postulated that there are at least three main points of conflict around which new bases for the common experience of grievance can arise, which are of fundamental importance to the development of class consciousness within and beyond the workplace. The first of these refers to a conflict between capital and labour over the organization of the labour process. This involves questions of the relative autonomy which workers themselves enjoy in the detailed distribution of given tasks, the extent of supervision by agents of capital *vis-à-vis* those of labour, and the relative power of labour to resist attempts to increase the level of discipline exerted by capital in the process of production. The second involves a distinct, though often related, conflict between capital and labour over the question of increased mechanization of the labour process and the consequent expulsion of skilled labour from the production process which is often entailed thereby. There is an important difference between these two conflicts since the latter is nearly always resolved in the interests of capital, while the former, to the extent that it occurs in the absence of intensified mechanization, often has a less determinate outcome, at least in the short term. The third conflict occurs within labour, between craft and general workers and their unions. Craft workers are classically the leading, solidaristic component of the labour force, especially in emergent industries, as Bologna (1976) shows with regard to German machinists in 1918, Cooke (1982a) shows for steelworkers in nineteenth-century Wales, and Humphrey (1980/81) shows for contemporary Brazilian autoworkers. However, it is in the interest of both capital[6] and unskilled labour to reduce the control and relatively high value of labour power which craft-workers can command in the labour process. Deskilling thus puts the former in a position to increase surplus value by increasing productivity, while the latter gain in status, relative autonomy and bargaining strength as the responsibilities of semi-skilled work increase.

As capitalism is an especially dynamic mode of production which depends upon discovering new ways of keeping up the level of accumulation for its existence, there is a tendency inherent in its various labour processes towards the constant recomposition of its workforce either by substituting workers with other workers, workers with machines, or skills with other skills. It is in this context that workers develop consciousness of the politics of the workplace and the capacity through struggle to prevent their individual and collective recomposition at the behest of capital. This develops first among craft unions, then among unorganized underhands or general workers who become more important to production as deskilling weakens skilled groups. The key spatial and sectoral indeterminacy is the extent to which craft unions are able to resist the encroachments of both capital and general unions. Where the latter become the dominant force in the representation of workers' interests, as in the recent history of motor-vehicle production, coal-mining but not in steel-making or the construction industry, for example, there will exist a tendency towards greater negotiating strength and preparedness to take militant action on an organized basis. This is assisted where skilled workers have materially more to lose by, for example, plant closure, because their chances of skill transfer may be limited, whereas unskilled or semi-skilled workers neither have a great investment of time in their present skills nor, ultimately, the same fear of exposure to unemployment and possible re-employment in a different industry. There are two caveats to this argument: one is that in times of general economic recession the *exposure* factor is markedly heightened and exerts a disciplining effect upon general unions; the other is that where semi-skilled production work is *feminized* there will tend to be a lower preparedness to take militant action, although this may only be a temporary phenomenon due to the relative newness of many women to waged work, and their past *exclusion* by male-dominated trade unions.

Moving to the sphere of circulation and focusing upon the important

points of conflict, three can be identified. The first of these involves fluctuations in real-wage levels. That is, in industries which are characterized by a
relationship with the market in which demand and supply levels themselves
fluctuate markedly, with the result that wages are affected, it may be
anticipated that struggles to minimize the sense of grievance and hardship
entailed will ensue. The nature of the fluctuation will vary by sector and
historic time period such that in industries dominated by semi-skilled and
unskilled work it may take the form of sliding-scale arrangements, whereby
wages are tied to price in the market-place or it may involve temporary
lay-offs or short-time working. However, where, as in the steel industry in
the past, reductions in orders, and thus demand for labour power, could be
absorbed through the laying-off of poorly unionized underhands, thus
keeping industrial strife at a low level by protecting stronger craft unions,
such fluctuations need not result in struggles to change the system. By
contrast, in the coal industry – especially in South Wales where it was more
closely tied to export markets than in other coalfields – dockwork, and the
pre-war motor industry which were respectively characterized by casual
working and seasonal fluctuations in demand, and increasing domination by
general unions, struggles to iron out the fluctuations by arranging more
rational systems of working did ensue (Wilkinson, 1977; Elbaum and
Wilkinson, 1979; Exell, 1980; Zeitlin, 1980).

The second point of conflict in the sphere of circulation concerns variations in wage differentials on an intersectoral basis. The comparison of
wage rates between industries is an important means by which unions
negotiate with capital in defence of living standards and when, as occurred
most clearly in the coal industry in the early 1970s, it becomes clear that the
valorization process (the means by which capital seeks out the best sources
of surplus value) involves capital shifts towards more profitable sectors and
associated relative wage decreases for workers in the less profitable sectors,
it may provide the basis for strategies of resistance. That this need not
happen is shown by the parallel experience of steelworkers in the 1970s who
slipped down the wages league without serious, organized resistance being
forthcoming. The third, and more explosive point of conflict concerns
intrasectoral change in wage differentials. In particular the differentials
between skilled and unskilled workers show a long-term tendency to
diminution precisely as the intended effect of increased mechanization of
production and its associated deskilling of the workforce. Where craft
unions are under threat in this way some of the most serious, often plant-
based and therefore spatially concentrated, inter-union struggle occurs.
Much of the content of the Donovan Commission Report of 1969 focused on
the increased incidence of unofficial strikes of this kind and it singled out the
steel industry (hitherto a quiescent industry), coal, docks, shipbuilding and
motor vehicles as suffering particularly badly at that period from the
conflicts between skilled and unskilled workers consequent upon the

modernization strategies which had been undertaken in those industries. The important tendency to be identified from the existence of these points of conflict in the sphere of circulation is that there will be a higher incidence of grievance-related resistance to the depression of real wages in sectors (and regions dominated by sectors) in which any and/or all of the conflict points are activated. A key variable would seem to be the relative strength of craft unions to resist the encroachment of general union members into what they consider to be their occupational and income preserves, and that of general unions to take advantage of capital's deskilling strategy against craft workers. An important caveat is the existence, in areas where these are issues, of a substantial labour reserve, either of redundant workers or women who may not previously have been involved in waged work. The effect of this factor is to increase the *exposure* of workers to unemployment because of the relative ease with which capital can substitute them from the reserve.

If we turn our attention to the sphere of reproduction we see first of all that it has three dimensions, two of which relate primarily, though by no means exclusively, to furthering the interests of capital, and one of which is mainly in the direct interest of labour while being of vital indirect interest to capital. They concern respectively, the reproduction of capital, the reproduction of capitalist social relations, and the reproduction of labour power. Each of these becomes relatively more important, historically, as the later stages of capitalist development have been reached. This occurs when circulation issues, though still important, are no longer the paramount source of struggle since certain major and basic gains such as unionization, representation and enfranchisement will have been made already. The main point of conflict with regard to the reproduction of capital is that between the twin imperatives of valorization and accumulation. The former involves the decision as to whether or not it is necessary for capital to be shifted out of one branch of capital (for example shipbuilding, motor-cycle manufacture) and into another (foreign manufacturing, domestic growth sectors), while the latter involves the decision as to whether capital can continue to be reproduced if there is a restructuring of the production process and the relations of production (possibly involving spatial shifts) within a single branch of industrial sector (Palloix, 1976). The resolution of such a conflict will normally involve the state to the extent that it facilitates conditions for capital reproduction in one or other of these ways. Because the state is subject to pressure from the labour side of the basic class division of capitalism to help to resist the heightened level of *exposure* which can be entailed by a valorization strategy, there will tend to be a greater pressure for capital reproduction to follow the accumulation strategy with state assistance. This will, of course, include the range of development planning incentives for the period during which the sphere of reproduction dominates civil society and the state. When the accumulation strategy no longer ensures capital reproduction, there may be a shift towards a valorization strategy with the state responding less to general reproduction demands as it moves back under the burgeoning dominance of the sphere of circulation to overcome the accumulation crisis.

Both valorization and accumulation strategies are likely to have been provoked in part by the capacity for resistance and *solidarism* developed in struggles fought around the various points of conflict in the spheres of production and circulation. They will therefore be likely to incorporate a spatial dimension as capital seeks to escape locations which exert unbearable constraints upon its reproductive capacities. Of central importance to this kind of solution is the existence of areas where resistance is likely to be lower. In the absence of pre-capitalist formations (such as regions dominated by a peasant economy) it is necessary for capital to relocate in areas where capitalist social relations can be reproduced to the advantage of continued accumulation. This can be achieved in three main ways: first, by capital of one stage of development relinquishing an area, creating a labour reserve, and capital of a later stage of development taking advantage of the lower resistance among the workforce which is one result of capital flight. A second way is for capital to bypass the redundant labour reserves but to seek out new sub-markets, notably the female labour force in pockets where low female activity rates pertain. Lastly, there may be a combination of the first two strategies overlain by intensive state intervention in basic industries and the welfare state whose effect is markedly to increase individual consumption levels by improving wage levels (for example associated with nationalization) and supplying improved welfare facilities. The latter undermines the self-help schemes and informal, family-centred 'welfare' system typical of basic-industry regions, helping to integrate such communities more fully into a high consumption culture (Clarke, 1979; Cooke, 1982a).

The latter point ties in closely with the third dimension of the sphere of reproduction, which concerns the reproduction of labour power. A number of characteristics may be identified with regard to struggles in this part of the sphere of reproduction, notably that the state is heavily involved, that a range of social groupings makes demands thus blurring the economic class basis of struggle, and that state responses tend to substitute commodified (that is market) allocations with non-commodified ones (Esping-Andersen, Friedland and Wright, 1976; Urry, 1981a). The import of this for capitalist development is that because non-commodified welfare provisions place a disproportionate cost on capital it will tend to shift to areas with low reproduction costs, other things being equal. Even though various strategies to reproduce capitalist social relations may have been followed in resistant areas, it is likely that they continue to offer certain advantages to capital in the short-to-medium term, especially if location is near to, but not actually within, the labour reserve areas. Nevertheless, older industrial areas may continue to prove attractive to relocating capital. For those firms pursuing an accumulation strategy, decomposing the labour intensive parts of the production process to low labour power reproduction-cost areas remains advantageous. This is because of lower than average taxes and wage costs due to the existence of a cheap and ready-made built environment from previous rounds of investment.

Finally, it is important to note that the sphere of popular-democratic struggle which, from the previous paragraph, is found within the part of reproduction concerned mostly with labour power, although without a specifically economic-class base, may be both a source of pressure upon capital to relocate to low labour power reproduction cost areas, and a growing constraint upon its capacity to sustain accumulation once it has relocated. The first point, which repeats the argument of the previous chapter to some extent, is that popular democratic struggle is very largely organized in relation to the state's actions in the sphere of reproduction, including housing, transfer payments, and environmental improvement. This implies that, to the extent that such struggle is itself organized through political parties (though, of course, it need not be) it is an important source of 'the relative autonomy of the political' (from the economic). Hence, the difference, in part at least, between those forces in civil society which come to represent the interests of specific groups of workers, especially around the crucial cash medium of exchange between production and circulation, *the unions*, and those which must represent wider social groupings and their specific interests within the state, *the political parties*. That there is an organic link between the unions and the Labour party in Britain, for example, is undeniable but that they are not the same thing is equally so. This is the primary reason why the outcomes of class or popular democratic pressure upon the state, separately or in concert, cannot directly reflect the demands which were originally articulated. It is because there must always be an element of 'double-determination' about state policy, such that interests contrary to those of capital are respected without those of capital being obliterated and *vice versa* that accumulation is able to resume its rhythmic, spatially uneven, although increasingly constrained progress.

Development planning and socio-spatial recomposition

The important task now remains of indicating the ways in which the state, through its urban and regional development planning system, connects to the rhythms of socio-spatial recomposition of classes in labour markets. We have shown already in the preceding chapter the main links between the planning system and the spheres of struggle within civil society, so now the question is to establish the extent to which the overall effect of spatial *rotation* can be understood as the outcome of rational decision-making. The tentative answer which we shall offer initially to that question is that, on balance, there is a degree of rational control of the development process exercised through state planning at central and then local level, but that there are counter-tendencies which make such planning often appear ambiguous and internally contradictory. The reason for the latter contradictions are twofold: first there are such contradictions as we have already identified between demands upon the state to intervene in the spheres of circulation on the one hand and reproduction (especially of labour power, communities, existing built environments) on the other. These sometimes manifest themselves as central-local state antagonisms of a general kind. But the second source of contradiction comes from the problem that is caused by many different parts of, for example, the central state apparatus having functions which contribute in some way to development planning. This is also a problem in the local state but not to the same extent. In what follows an attempt will be made to defend the tentative positive answer to the question of the extent to which spatial recomposition is planned through the state.

The premise with which this defence begins may sound somewhat functionalist although it merely proposes that planning has taken on a key function, which could be performed in other ways, and historically has been, without which capitalism becomes non-viable. The planning system brings together land and labour power, without which capital cannot be set to work to accumulate and valorize. Clearly, this has occurred without the intervention of the state planning system in the past, during the era when the sphere of circulation was the dominant focus of struggle, and when the absence of exchange equality between individuals as legal subjects, as well as political constituents, allowed the costs of making that land-labour power connection to be borne by wage-labour. But it is as a result of the gradual success of labour in the sphere of circulation and the consequent rise to dominance of the sphere of reproduction as the primary focus of political conflict (with all that is thereby implied for state action, including planning) that the state, through its planning apparatus, has been obliged to develop the function of assisting capital accumulation (and to some extent valorization, though less so) by responding to the reproduction demands of labour. This is clearly not by any means a straightforward task and it is fraught with contradictions, but to the extent that state planning agencies alone are obliged to discharge this land-labour power linkage they have a certain level of power to influence the development process.

We are not arguing that planners necessarily possess clairvoyant powers, rather that the planning system is expected to, and to a degree does, pick up developmental signals and helps to structure the locational opportunities for mobile capital, modify the spatial discontinuities in the labour market and *rotate* or recycle the built environments which are the sites for the reproduction of relevant labour power. The developmental signals which the state development planning system receives are relayed to it as an unavoidable aspect of the state's intermediate position between capital, land use, and the supply of, and demand for, labour power in the era of dominance of the sphere of reproduction. The range of signals is from the very largest inward investment proposal, through regional demands for assistance, down to the smallest local planning application, each of which, to varying degrees, signifies potential or actual locally-pertinent conditions for development. It should be added that these signals are often substantially modified by, as well as exerting a modifying effect upon, the level and intensity of exchange in the land market which, as we have seen previously, is closely interlocked with planning policy.

But what the state, through its planning system, is obliged to undertake under the conditions of late capitalism is to enable capital to take advantage of inherited patterns of uneven development. These patterns themselves become deeply inscribed into the territorial settlement pattern where labour successfully defends its reproduction space. This process entails the planning system in laying the foundations for long-term, and occasionally rapid, social and spatial recomposition, the reproduction of capitalist social relations, the restructuring of local labour markets, and the maintenance of capitalism as the dominant mode of production in the national territory. Because of this there is an underlying tendency for the state planning system to favour those branches and sizes of capital which are themselves most at ease operating within a framework of spatially homogeneous legal and territorial constraints. Inevitably this tends to be large, non-local capital whose markets are easily enlarged by its command over financial, legal and technological resources, at the expense of weaker, local capital which is often constrained to pursue development policies by the unitary system of planning law at odds with its limited command over financial, legal and technological expertise.

In the remainder of this chapter we wish to outline five 'strategies'[7] by means of which development planning meets a fundamental obligation of the state *vis-à-vis* capital, which is to supply it with appropriately composed wage-labour under conditions in which it is not possible for this to occur automatically. The 'strategies' to be discussed are respecively: *concentration*; *decentralization*; *containment*; *semi-peripheralization*; and *recycling*.

Concentration

This 'strategy' involves regional level re-organization of the productive base in ways which concentrate productive capacity into what, by comparison with previous patterns, can be considered as supercentres. It is not to be confused with the process of spatial centralization of activities across a wide range into, for example, large conurbations or metropolitan centres. Rather, it involves removing a scattered or fragmented distribution of small capitals and replacing them in a different, though related, location within broadly the same geographical area. This concentration 'strategy' has been employed on at least two occasions in post-war Britain and is described for France in Castells's (1977; and Godard, 1974) studies of 'Monopolville', and Bleitrach and Chenu's (1981) study of Fos-sur-Mer. In Britain the concentration 'strategy' was dominant in the heavy-industry regions immediately following the Second World War. It was by no means initiated by the conventional planning system although it caused the latter to respond to initiatives operating within and through the state, in particular around those interests supporting nationalization of basic industries. The class forces which moved into alignment to enable the nationalization of steel,[8] in particular, provide a useful insight into the process of *transmutation* by means of which:

changes produced by popular pressure are transmuted into something less acceptable to those popular forces. . . . Many of the changes produced in this manner within capitalist societies satisfy none of the major classes in such societies. (Urry, 1981a, p. 147)

Post-war reconstruction was heavily influenced by the dominance which the USA had achieved in the international economy as a result of its own stable growth in wartime, and the destruction of its competitors' economies. Of key importance in setting the reconstructed economies off in directions favourable to the consumerist trend which had revived American capitalism, was Marshall Aid. A substantial portion of this was allocated to steel industry reconstruction, in particular with a view to redirecting steel production towards the growth sectors of motor vehicles and domestic appliances which consumed sheet steel. However, the traditional, private, producers were unwilling to reconstruct substantially to supply this new market, preferring to remain in the specialized and protected export market, largely con-terminous with empire. For this reason there emerged a coincidence of interests in favour of introducing new, American, strip-mill technology under a nationalized programme which involved the steel unions (who had established nationalization as a priority in the inter-war depression), the Labour government, and the more advanced steel-consuming industries. This power bloc was crucial in defeating the opposition of private steel-makers to nationalization. The effect of the latter was to concentrate steel production in locations close to nationalized coal supplies but, for technical reasons, at a little distance from the coalfields themselves.

This process, which occurred in most of the steel-producing regions, required substantial diversion of resources in the sphere of reproduction (housing, education etc.) away from coalfield communities and towards the new, modernized (usually coastal) steel plant locations, and the gradual disappearance of the traditional, fragmented steel-mills with their relatively high workforce skill-content. One effect of such reconstructions upon the traditional working-class culture of such regions is described below:

Concentration and centralization as well as the policies of large-scale companies often involve shifts in the geographical distribution of capital – shifts which must be understood in an international as well as a regional and national framework. Localities that suffer the sudden withdrawal of capital also suffer major disruptions in their patterns of social and cultural life. Cultural forms that have developed, for instance, in a close connection with the original division of labour, may lose their very rationale. From the point of view of capital, its mobility requires the mobility of labour. It therefore also requires the fractioning of the local and more fixed patterns of reproduction: it specifically requires the destruction of locality as a major form through which working people experience their social life. The resistance of locally bound labour to capital's migration has, in turn, produced state policies that seek a greater conformity – here in the form of industrial grants to tempt capital to move to pools of labour, there in the form of mobility and redundancy payments to encourage labourers to pursue capital. (Clarke, 1979, p. 239)

It seems to be very largely unavoidable that the state's compromises between capital and labour should produce disenchanted workers, consumerist consolations, managerial cynicism and economic inefficiency, since neither side fulfils its ambitions. Despite this, in Britain's second post-war reconstruction period under the Wilson government even more grandiose concentration 'strategies' were advocated in the estuarine regions such as Humberside and Severnside. These were never fulfilled, primarily because the end of the post-war boom was already in sight, and other 'strategies' were becoming more favourable to capital restructuring.

Decentralization

In some ways this 'strategy' has identical origins to that which characterizes the *concentration* 'strategy', but it emerges, in the shape of outcomes, with markedly different effects. The similarity lies in the fact that both respond to the tendency for competition between capital units to lead to the aggrandisement of certain of those units. This tendency is aggravated when competition takes on an increasingly internationalized scope. However, whereas the tendency leads to spatial concentration where heavy industry (or the production of means of production) is concerned, largely because of production technology but also because of defensive pressure from labour, it has led to spatial decentralization in light industry (production of means of consumption). This bifurcation reflects a fundamental difference in capital: labour ratios in the two departments of production; a greater capital concentration in the former, a greater labour concentration in the latter.

There is thus some degree of coincidence of interests between pressure from labour in declining heavy industry areas for planning measures which will sustain the capacity for such areas to reproduce labour power, measures which, for a time at least, favour labour intensive investment, and pressure upon the state from capital to provide conditions which stimulate accumulation in consumer industries, while keeping valorization as an option for surplus productive capital (Massey, 1981, p. 205). This occurred most obviously in Britain in the 1960s when there was substantial state regional and sectoral intervention in the sphere of circulation, which, most observers seem to agree, was accompanied by a shift in location of manufacturing industry away from traditional locations in the conurbations and towards the assisted regions. The twin employment effects of this 'strategy' from the viewpoint of capital are a reduction in the overall numbers employed in specific sectors, and a reduction in the skill level of the labour force as new branch plants in assisted areas can be more highly mechanized and thus employ semi-skilled and quickly trained labour.

The main burden of decentralization policy has applied to manufacturing industry under the influence of central state regional policy, industrial restructuring policy and, at the detailed level, industrial zoning and limited infrastructural provision by local states. However, in the 1960s and 1970s *decentralization* policy also began to apply in the tertiary industries following the introduction of restrictions on office development. In the private sector substantial tertiary employment imbalance was emerging, as were labour-supply shortages in centres of heavy office work concentration (notably London, Paris). This also occurred in a context of pressure from labour upon the state for redistribution of government employment to regions suffering from high unemployment. Once more, this was predominantly a *central* state measure for planned *decentralization*, although, unlike comparable measures in the manufacturing sector, its relative effectiveness derived less from intervention in the sphere of circulation (although assistance for service-sector job creation was available) and more from quasi-legal withholding of development licences, a certain degree of propaganda, and, most importantly, auto-decentralization of parts of the state's own sub-system within the sphere of circulation (administration, taxation, pensions).

The recomposition of labour markets associated with *decentralization* 'strategies' is clear to see. With regard to manufacturing labour, *decentralization* facilitates the deskilling process which, we have argued, is of central importance to the reduction of labour costs, and also, to the extent that relocation is accompanied by rationalization or even closures in traditional centres of production, it enables substantial reductions in the total cost of variable capital to be effected. In the areas in which new investment occurs a double advantage is provided for capital. First, for a period, labour will be 'green' and disorganized so that work practices unacceptable in strongly unionized plants can be introduced without opposition. But second, as labour does become organized, and a learning process develops between representatives of old and new plants such that pressure may emerge for homogeneous work practices, peripheral plants find they are in a relatively weak bargaining position. This is due to the existence of large local labour reserves and, more importantly, the capacity of corporate capital to threaten closure in areas of high unemployment. In this way, development planning helps to provide important conditions for securing continuous production and sustained accumulation. By responding to reproduction demands from labour the state creates conditions in which good labour relations may be found in development areas. By contrast, tertiarization of the *decentralist* kind seems to be more a means of responding to demands from non-metropolitan areas for service employment in a context of severe labour shortages in centres of service sector concentration. The kind of work which tends to be *decentralized* is that which demands the least skilled or qualified workers who are readily available in the regions but in heavy demand, and thus higher cost, in, for example, capital cities such as London or Paris (Lipietz, 1980b; Cooke, 1981). The recomposition effect here is contra-dictory, in that it may incorporate working-class women and youth (the dominant labour supply sought) into white-collar, 'embourgeoisement' patterns of identification while also raising consciousness of the process of proletarianization due to the increased mechanization and deskilling found in modern 'office-factories', as Lipietz refers to such units.

Containment

This 'strategy' is one in which the principal outlines are set by central state planning measures but in which the details are administered, often with substantial latitude, by the local state planning machinery. It is at its strongest when the sphere of reproduction is dominant over the sphere of circulation and is most clearly illustrated in British planning policy during the 1950s and 1960s, as described by Hall *et al.* (1973). The complexities of the *containment* 'strategy' cannot be encompassed in a brief outline such as this, but two main dimensions can be picked out, each of which has special relevance to the theoretical perspective on planning and labour markets with which we are here concerned. The first of these refers to the element of constriction upon metropolitan and conurban growth which the broad *con-tainment* 'strategy' displays. This has the effect of building up enormous developmental tensions during a period when, as in post-war Britain, repro-duction issues such as slum clearance, inner-city renewal and comprehensive environmental improvement (for example smoke control) are dominant. For, unless peripheral conurbation land is made available to rehouse slum dwellers, such reproduction planning must involve massive inner-area redevelopment which effectively obliterates previous rounds of investment in the total built environment, including all but the largest productive, industrial investments. The economic impact of such redevelopment favours big capital against small capital in two main ways. First, the scale of repro-duction requires large-scale construction capital to be centrally involved in the process, and, while this also entails substantial growth for small, subcontracting firms, it destabilizes them by tying them closely to the activities of the corporate construction sector for the limit of a contract-period. Second, the destruction of built environments, in which fairly fragile small capitals have found a niche, perhaps connected with the proximity of a large corporate enterprise capable of resisting wholesale spatial restructuring, poses obvious problems for the self-employed, *'normal'* compliant and *marginalized* labour markets which may dry up locally overnight. Now, it need not be the case that small firms go out of business – they may be provided with alternative accommodation, as in the 'flatted factories' (high-rise small business units) solution or nursery units – but the associated tendencies, such as higher residential rents for workers leading to higher wage demands, higher business rents, increased taxes to pay for redevelopment, corporate policy to reduce dependence on independent suppliers, and so on, produce a cumulative pressure resulting in closure and/or relocation. This may, finally, occur due to the artificial speeding up of the devaluation and depreciation of fixed capital in the inner-city, brought about by re-development, but which would have happened in any case as large and small capital sought out new locations of fresh labour power in which to invest (Gripaios, 1977; Dennis, 1978; Cross, 1981).

The second dimension of *containment* policy having a bearing upon local labour market recomposition involves the corollary planning measure of new or expanded town development. While it may be thought that the view in which new towns policy 'involved a direct intervention in the productive system' to exert social control (Castells, 1977, p. 280), is somewhat extreme, it is difficult to avoid the conclusion that the policy both supplied capital with 'green' labour in 'green field' locations while responding to demands from labour for improved reproduction conditions. Some of the most buoyant sectors of British industry were thus supplied with ready-made semi-skilled labour markets of, first, the *'normal'* compliant, later the *'normal'* resistant kinds, without having to bear the agglomeration diseconomies of metropolitan or conurban locations. Much the same can be said for those firms which located in the expanded towns developed by conurban and metropolitan local states to house their overspill population. But *containment* policy also created pressure for the local state to find loopholes in the constrictive aspects of the policy to allow capital to expand without relocating at a substantial distance from base. As Hall *et al.* (1973) describe, this pressure lay at the basis of widespread local state compliance with some local small and medium capital to avoid Industrial Development Certificate (licences to expand locally) restrictions by zoning new industrial estates and turning a blind eye to industrial expansion in disused airfields, and the like. When, in any case, the massive fluctuations in the application of stringent IDC control are also considered it does not seem unreasonable to postulate a policy of counter-planning by the Board of Trade (later the Department of Industry), to give its constituency, *'normal'* compliant, local, small and medium capital, the sites it wanted, in suburban and small-town locations (Pickvance, 1981).

Semi-peripheralization

The latter policy 'undercurrent' has clearly become a more blatant 'strategy' in that both the Industry Department and local states in relatively pros-perous regions have, increasingly, responded to the demands of small to medium capital for new locations. These are, ideally, sufficiently close to conurbations in which large corporate manufacturing consumers are located, but sufficiently distant from them to be relatively unaffected by the higher labour costs entailed by proximity to *'normal' resistant* labour markets. In this respect, the pattern of manufacturing employment growth in the rural fringe of the large British conurbations, associated with employment decline in the conurbations themselves, may well signify a process of 'productive decentralization' to the semi-periphery similar to that being observed in contemporary Italy (Fothergill and Gudgin, 1979; Keeble, 1980; Mingione, 1981). In the British context it seems likely that such locations offer precisely the kind of rural (or semi-rural), possibly female-dominated, labour pools in reasonable proximity to product markets, that help the upper reaches of the secondary section of the labour market, notably *'normal' compliant* and *self-employed* sub-markets, to function. In certain locations, too, extra state assistance may bring areas which would normally be ascribed the status of peripheral sub-regions into the orbit of a conurban semi-periphery. This would apply in the areas administered by the Highlands and Islands Development Board, part of whose designated area is adjacent to West-Central Scotland conurbation, and the Development Board for Rural Wales, similarly placed *vis-à-vis* the Birmingham conurbation. Both rural areas have registered high percentage increases (from negligible base points) in manufacturing employment in the 1960s and 1970s.

The key question concerns the ways in which *semi-peripheralization* occurs. The first of these has already been touched upon. It involves the diffused designation of land for industrial purposes in city and county development and structure plans and the establishment of firms on this land or on purpose-built industrial estates in a context where IDC control is as slack as is noted below:

Firstly, a Department of Environment survey in 1976 of firms in the South East failed to uncover a single case where the system had acted as a deterrent. Secondly . . . the force of the deterrence argument depends on the rate of refusals being very high. But this is the reverse of the truth: as the Department of Environment states 'most applications for IDCs in the South East are in fact granted'. (Pickvance, 1981, p. 237)

The second way in which semi-peripheralization can occur is when a local state planning policy may oppose industrialization of a location, but where this is disputed by the central state, perhaps committed to industrializaion for wider, strategic reasons. Even though local planning applications may be rejected at local state level they can be overturned on appeal by the relevant minister with whom final authority for planning approval resides. A third way involves particular kinds of planning permission, for example for warehousing, being granted and a subsequent change of use application for industrial purposes being approved where there is some initial restriction upon industrialization. It seems reasonable to postulate that as the difficulties of profitability for capital have increased, containment constraints have been relaxed *de facto*, and that this is registered in *semi-peripheral* employment growth, and a sustained decline in the stringency of IDC control as the crisis has deepened.

Recycling

The final 'strategy' to be discussed here is the most recent, and effectively points to a policy shift towards reconnecting the *marginalized* and *underclass* labour markets with waged work to the extent that the former, debatably, and the latter, by definition, constitute slack labour markets. At a theoretical level, it can be postulated that as the *semi-periphery* and even, to a lesser extent, the locations favoured by *decentralist* strategy, begin to lose a certain competitive edge consequent upon negotiated wage increases, other kinds of low-cost location will be sought out by capital, with the assistance of the state. It may well be that the involvement of the latter will, initially, be in response to criteria of a more socially responsible nature, as for instance in the inner-city ethnic enclaves or areas of severe deindustrialization. The important difference between contemporary and previous initiatives in such areas is that policy-measures are seen to require strong elements of aid to capital if reproduction goals are to be fulfilled as distinct from being based upon transfer payments in the sphere of reproduction to stimulate local demand. Furthermore, there is an important difference betwen *recycling* and *decentralization* 'strategies'. Whereas the latter is principally characterized by a two-tier, central-local state 'strategy' which, first, designates assisted areas largely according to levels of unemployment, but, second, plans development to occur in growth points within commuting distance but, essentially, in locations *separate* from unemployment blackspots (for example valley mouths in South Wales; away from D-villages in North East England), the former focuses directly upon stress areas.

As 'strategic' planning emphasis has slipped away from being dominated by the sphere of reproduction and back towards domination by struggle in the sphere of circulation, so the central state, in particular, has developed policies which are aimed at *recycling* the subemployed and unemployed in ways which assist the recapitalization of capitalism (Miller, 1978; 1980). The main features of this process involve a three-pronged central state set of initiatives which have latterly come to be taken up in modified and limited form by some local states. The most striking central state initiative (albeit 'administered' locally) is the Enterprise Zone idea. This takes the very weakest and poorest areas of the inner-city and deregulates them in a multiplicity of ways ranging from local derating and minimization of taxation, to exception from much of the employment protection, equality of opportunity and safety at work law which pertains in the rest of the state's jurisdiction. It appeals overtly to the hyper-exploitative self-employed labour market which connects directly with the *marginalized* and *underclass* labour markets in which the 'black' or informal economy can be found. The second initiative, which is aimed directly at similar areas, is the inner-city regeneration measure which is administered by Urban Development Corporations such as the London Docklands scheme. Here, a strongly privatistic planning approach reliant upon 'buying-in' expertise from private planning consultants, managed by entrepreneural spirits untrammelled by local democratic pressures, and responsible to the central state, seeks to recycle the redundant inner-city labour force back into productive activity through a mixture of notoriously exploitative service employment (tourism, catering, entertainment etc.) and the ubiquitous small businesses. The third initiative is that found, especially in former steel towns, where massive deindustrialization has occurred. Here a combination of Development Agencies (English Industrial Estates Corporation, Scottish Development Agency, Welsh Development Agency, British Steel Corporation (Industry) Ltd.) are involved in redeveloping former steelworks and building concentrations of advance factories, small nursery units, workshops etc., as well as providing assistance and finance to the small firm sector which is aimed at reseeding such areas with private enterprise. Latterly this tendency has become popular within the local state as *local economic initiatives* grow into local enterprise agencies, local development corporations and local centres of trade and industry (Boddy and Barrett, 1980; Bramley *et al.*, 1979; Townroe, 1979; Underwood and Stewart, 1978; Lawless, 1979; Storey and Robinson, 1981; Muller and Bruce, 1981).

The important element in common between *recycling* and the other four development planning 'strategies' is that they are each responses, but also guides, to capital's diverse approaches, in turn affected by capital scale, to keep up accumulation. More recently, with the move towards small businesses, a stronger tendency can be identified towards the pursuit of a valorization 'strategy'. Whether following the first or the second route, it is of some considerable importance that the planning system can direct capital towards appropriately prepared markets where wage-labour is available. The key advantage lies in its preparedness to be connected with means of production in ways which maximize the continuity of production by minimizing the propensity to strike. At various stages in the development of the post-war planning system one, or a combination, of the possible spatial development 'strategies' which we have discussed has been available. They are formed on the basis of the development signals which the central and local state planning machinery receives from capital and labour, and increasingly, popular-democratic forces. It is in this way that the uneven development of capitalism, which is one of its most characteristic features, is exploited and reproduced in a not entirely accidental fashion.

Uneven development is itself an expression of the changing division of labour by means of which capitals survive against internal and external competition and the pressure also exerted upon the profit rate by the systematic conflicts of a class society. The planning system in the central and local state expresses the dynamism of these conflicts in policies which normally contain elements of relevance to both of the main contending classes, especially at the level of the central state. At local state level, the specificity of local labour markets, past struggles, and the degrees of resistance, compliance and defeat which local classes have experienced *vis-à-vis* capital, produce variations in the emphasis which is given to development planning in local space. It remains now, in the final chapter, to bring together, in as coherent a fashion as possible, the various levels and dimensions of planning action which we have discussed, to clarify, finally, the relationship between development planning and its external determinants, on the one hand, and the implications of changes in these determinants upon the *internal* organization of planning strategies, on the other.

10 Planning and spatial development: some deductions and connections

In this concluding chapter it is intended that the rather disparate deductions made about the planning of urban and regional development should be drawn together into a more formal conceptual framework. This will show the principal categories and connections through which the planning system helps to enhance the accumulation process by assisting in the social and spatial recomposition of labour power. The relevant boxes and links which represent this fundamental relationship can be shown relatively straight-forwardly. However, it is less easy to represent the dynamic aspects which we have argued are fundamental to the working out of these relationships in reality. Attempts will thus be made in textual commentary to give some flavour of the variable emphases that are brought to bear on the planning system, and which are, in turn, of influence upon the spatial division of labour over time.

Having made these introductory points, it is important that another, more substantial point is understood about the status of the framework to be discussed. This is that it does not seek to represent any *general* theory of planning, such has occasionally been the aim of planning theorists at other times. What has been discussed is an attempt at explanation of certain important characteristics of the planning process under conditions of advanced capitalism in the post-war years (largely, though not exclusively, in the UK). Certain broad deductions, or pointers about the near future can be taken from what we have argued. But these cannot in any detailed way be taken as predictions about the form of the planning system of the future. This is because although it seems likely that the weakness of British industry will constrain expenditure in the area of labour power reproduction to levels below those of the early 1970s in real terms, this very likelihood will bring forth forces which may tend to push it above the levels experienced in the early 1980s. It is precisely this relative indeterminacy, albeit within broad constraints set within the sphere of production, that makes any attempt at meaningful, general theorizing vulnerable in the extreme. The best, we feel, that can be done *vis-à-vis* this problem is to have outlined certain relevant, *general* tendencies in capitalist development and show how these link to the forms and strategic emphases of development planning. However, if as seems possible from currently visible tendencies in the restructuring of production relations, labour power in advanced economies enters a prolonged period of over-supply, at least as far as larger internationally competitive capital is concerned, the implications for development planning cannot be clearly deduced, although some extension of the social control function may be implied.

Some deductions for planning

It is worth briefly considering three (among many) possibilities here. First, as we have stressed, the planning system is important in bringing together land and labour in ways which are constructive for capital (as a general rule). But when a point is reached where this can, once again, be done more or less automatically because demand for labour by the large corporations both diminishes substantially and becomes more specialized, then development planning may become focused on social control of labour reserves rather than connecting them to work opportunities. To some extent this process has already begun under the aegis of the Manpower Services Commission. It has been shown to be far more disposed towards socializing young people into retaining positive attitudes towards work than supplying them with the advanced skills which certain labour markets are thought to require (Lawless, 1981a; Solomos, 1981). Moreover, manpower planning has begun to be seen as a key local state obligation, too, in the Greater London Council and other metropolitan administrations. It may be, therefore, that a one-dimensional planning approach to the problem of segmented (by age) labour reserves will involve targeted financial outlays and associated policies which aim to reproduce surplus population through *decommodified* work and/or leisure programmes. The aspect of 'decommodification' refers to ways in which the profit motive has been replaced by the concept of social need as the criterion determining the nature of relations of exchange, as for example in 'wages' paid under MSC or other state welfare schemes.

Second, it is probable that in a context where 'normal' resistant labour markets display demand-side deficiencies and firms show an increasing disposition towards substituting large internal labour markets with 'normal' compliant, self-employed and even marginalized ones, then a more two-dimensional planning policy might be conceived. Instead of, as in the past, undermining the productive units of the secondary labour market sectors, either through urban renewal projects or the more day-to-day enforcement of the law on land-use control in the shape of the General Development Order and Use Classes Order, it may be that planning will involve connecting known secondary labour sub-markets with local labour reserves. This would not simply duplicate central state administration of the job-finding process, but rather, involve local state planning agencies in generating more detailed information from analyses of local economic structure, then feeding into training and local manpower planning services in ways responsive to demand and supply mis-matches in local labour sub-markets.

Clearly, this would be all but impossible for marginalized sub-markets especially in view of the continuing statutory obligations of local planning administrations to use legal force to control land-use patterns. However, the heightened level of discretion allowed to local planning administrations in the most recent planning legislation (DoE, 1980) makes it more rather than less likely that non-conforming land-uses will be placed under less pressure than hitherto.

But a third possible alternative path for planning in the local state to proceed would involve a three-dimensional planning policy which linked together the local manpower planning activity, the local labour market analyses, and the burgeoning local enterprise board or development agency activities. In other words, it is probable that the problems of accumulation have already posed insurmountable difficulties for the continuation of conventional development planning through the medium of structure plans, local plans and the detailed instruments of land-use control. Such a context is giving rise to solutions within the spheres of production and circulation that make almost the opposite kinds of demand upon the planning system to those which have been normal in the past. Instead of planning administrations having to allocate land for expanding and/or migrating productive units at the expense of smaller, non-conforming land uses, they may now be expected to provide a context in which a minimal level of official controls is exerted. This is clearly foreshadowed in the Enterprise Zone idea which, so far, in the UK has been saddled with the image of recycling in areas which are fairly unattractive to capital, both environmentally and in labour market terms.[1] However, if as has been discussed in the USA, such zones are established in pleasant suburbs or the semi-periphery then a large part of planning philosophy comes directly under attack. In order to survive increasing central state administrative authority, which is plainly reducing local state autonomy (though by no means its specificity) to a historically low level, and which can easily be invoked by parliamentary legislative *fiat*, it seems likely that the local state planning apparatus will necessarily fight back with the weapon which must elude the central state by definition, namely, knowledge of, and capacity to respond to, pressures in local space.

So far, each of the three dimensions: local manpower initiatives, local labour markets and local economic initiatives, tend to function independently of each other. There seems to be little prospect of central state activities being capable of interlinking down to the level of complex detail at which local labour markets operate. As we have suggested, the MSC seems less than adequate as an agency for fitting skill-supplies to skill-demands; the Departments of Employment and Industry cannot make serious and thorough-going inroads upon the diffuse problems of spatially and socially segmented surplus population, and even regional development agencies have difficulty in relating inward investment to available, sectoral expertise. The point may soon be reached when even that state expenditure now leaning increasingly towards the sphere of circulation, is exposed to the scrutiny of monetarist logic. In such circumstances the local state may be induced further towards planning the conditions for recapitalizing local capitalism by undertaking aspects of local economic midwifery which bring together the supply and demand sides of the market equation. The latter will involve identifying local economic demands and filling gaps, especially in terms of labour-supply, financial, infrastructural and even technical-managerial services. This is shown to a large extent in the work of some of the more successful job-creation agency schemes such as the BSC (Industry) Clyde and South Wales Workshops *inter alia*, or the Clerkenwell and St Helens Trust schemes, as well as being implicit in the EEC's 'mobilization of indigenous potential' initiative (Dineen, 1981; Ewers and Wettman, 1980).

In pointing to certain prospects for future planning it must be stressed, once again, that these appear to be implied by tendencies currently visible in state and capital responses to sustained crisis. It seems, frankly, unlikely that the sort of coherent planning of labour supply and economic development that we have just discussed, can work as more than a temporary expedient under the dominance of market relations, and that sub-optimal versions of the one- and two-dimensional policies will probably eventuate. This is mainly because the kind of information which would be needed by the local (or for that matter, central) state to enable firms to plan their detailed labour, training and skills requirements could not be forthcoming in a competitive regime. To remove the element of uncertainty which labour must endure is precisely to undermine one area which systematically biases the basic relation between labour and capital in favour of the latter. The state, secretive though it is, cannot be as discreet about likely future labour demand as firms have to be if they are to take advantage of competitive market conditions. This is, of course, because of the constraints of democracy, constraints which do not hamper business decision-making.

We seem, in pointing to certain requirements which capital has, yet the state cannot fulfil, to have reached the same dividing line between capitalist and socialist social relations as that identified by Broadbent (1977). Referring to the 'cleft stick' or 'catch 22' dilemma for the state he says that the state's activities can only grow so far if capitalist social relations are to be maintained:

. . . even in the most 'socialist' of Western economies the size of the state is far lower than in the most 'capitalist' of the planned economies. The gap to be bridged between these two systems is far wider than the differences which exist *within* the systems, and this symbolizes the 'untouchable' area into which the state cannot expand, without changing the whole nature of the market economy. (Broadbent, 1977, p. 30)

This widely accepted view, which has a good deal of historical empirical support, seems to echo Gramsci's analysis of the ultimately coercive nature of the capitalist state, that is that the capital relation reasserts itself in the form of force where capitalist hegemony has been breached. Such force may even temporarily reside in civil society, outside the actual apparatus of the state when the latter, for an instant, comes under the control of interests hostile to capitalism. However, the crucial point of Gramsci's analysis, which cannot be encompassed in the widely-held, but functionalist, notion that the capitalist state is unshakeable unless by violent means, is its acceptance of the indeterminacy which acompanies democratic struggle. That is, while recognizing the difficulty of transforming the state through a static strategy of resistance or *war of position* (Gramsci, 1971, pp. 228–39), he insisted that pressure could be, and as we have seen, has frequently been put upon the state to bring about a diminution of the power asymmetry between capital and labour. We have argued that planning measures are one expression of this pressure, so are certain legal and welfare measures.

Nevertheless, a problem which confronts progressive forces in planning as in other state activities derives from one important effect of gains made by labour within the state. This is that they frequently take an administrative and allocative form which apes the undemocratic command structures of the capitalist business enterprise. We are referring to a further dimension of the process of *transmutation* whereby political struggles result in both state structures and policies that satisfy none of the contending interests concerned. This is clearly a more substantial point than that which says all government policy inevitably represents some degree of compromise, or indeed, that all collective action does so (Olson, 1965). The latter tends to be employed as a rationale for the superiority of individualistic modes of action at the expense of collective modes. Such a rationale is of only limited pertinence to a discussion of the contradictions posed by the co-existence and interdependence of individualist and collectivist logics of action in contemporary capitalism. However, even the limited argument that individuals suffer substantial constraints in the degree to which their objectives can be fulfilled if they engage in collective action does point towards the vaguer outlines of the problem of transmutation. This is because it expresses the notion that however good the intentions of political parties, pressure groups, and the like, in seeking to establish state apparatuses aimed at correcting distributional imbalances, their legalistic, and hence, coercive, basis turns them into instruments which appear to further oppress rather than assist the proposed beneficiaries.

We are referring here to the problem of *statism*.[2] This syndrome consists of five characteristic elements:

1 it derives from social democratic commitments to tackle social evils by means of a centralized bureaucracy. The standard mode of service-delivery involves a distinctive combination of paternalism and patronization;

2 it involves substantial chains of decision and command being established

between the state as 'patron' and beneficiaries. Such a system of remote control divorces and objectifies the perceived experiences of proposed beneficiaries from their actually-experienced conditions;

3 it is dependent upon a specific form of representation of class and popular interests in which beneficiaries are deemed to delegate the definition of their needs to experts and are in return passive recipients of services;

4 an important effect of such systems of service delivery is that denying beneficiaries reasonable direct influence over the form and content of their entitlements while, nevertheless, continuing to deliver a service, permits social control to be widely exercised via the state;

5 the fundamental weakness of statism as a strategy is that it provides a space for anti-socialist forces to equate statism with socialism and to identify freedom, liberty and individuality with anti-socialism. This can occur in the face of arguments that the welfare state is aimed precisely at freeing individuals from poverty, disease and ignorance, because it confirms the everyday experience of the practices of state bureaucracies for most people.

This analysis is derived in part from the work of Johnson (1972), who develops certain ideas about authoritarianism and social distance in state agencies. These are discussed under the heading of *state-mediated* systems of control of the relationship between the professional and his or her client. The other part derives from more recent work by Hall (1979, 1980, 1981). In the latter contributions the concept of *statism* is used as a means of expressing the particular kind of solution to the antagonisms of capital and labour formed by the conjunction of Keynesian economic management and the principles of the welfare state as enunciated by Beveridge. It is to be clearly separated from a considerably wider usage often found in French work on the state, such as that of Lefebvre (1976) who writes of a state mode of production having come into existence such that *statism* penetrates all aspects of human existence in advanced societies. Also, Poulantzas (1978) ties the concept to certain dictatorial strains he identifies in some modern European political systems in the form of *authoritarian statism*. The problem with both of these formulations is that they generalize what may be temporary phenomena as definite stages in the ineluctable passage of history out of capitalism and into socialism. Hall, by contrast, is considerably less confident that the more narrowly-defined statism which we have discussed is more than a temporary solution to class conflict which has already outlived its usefulness to both capital and labour.

From the more general analysis of the relationship between the forms of planning which emerged in the post-war period when the sphere of reproduction was a dominant influence upon the patterns of spatial development, we would deduce that *statism*, in the way we have analysed it above, is an expression precisely of the dominance of reproduction issues, especially those concerning the reproduction of labour power. We would further deduce that it is currently undergoing certain kinds of modification with some features which were previously rather well-subordinated coming to the forefront while others are themselves being relegated to less significant positions. Of particular interest here is the emergence to prominence of *discretionary* modes of decision-making in those areas of state activity which are closely linked with economic revival. As has been shown this began at central state level, but has begun to filter down in quite a diffused fashion into the local state through varieties of local economic initiatives (Cooke, 1980a; Lawless, 1981b, pp. 59–87). It does not seem unreasonable to equate this with a rise to dominance of the sphere of circulation, in particular expressing the present dominance of capital over labour in the workplace, civil society and the state, encapsulated most emblematically in the doctrine of *monetarism* as practised in the UK, for example, since 1976 under both Labour and Conservative governments.[3]

Planning of socially-useful production

The important question for those who care to see planning as a progressive movement, assisting in the process of social change yet not artificially divorced from the practices of the state, is the extent to which *statism* can be overcome. That is, to what extent is it possible for urban and regional development planning in the immediate future to transcend the 'people' versus 'officialdom' contradiction? The more important question of the extent to which planning can help overcome the capital versus labour contradiction is not posed because it represents an obvious absurdity. For, while we have argued that development planning has its uses for capital and labour, it cannot be pretended that its institutions preside over commanding power *vis-à-vis* either the institutions of capital or those of labour, in the final analysis.

In recent years interest in the more widespread use of planning thought and expertise has developed at the popular level in important ways. As is well known, it began in the sphere of labour power reproduction with the disaffection of popular groupings precisely against the planning by official-dom of residential environments. We have described some of the planning theories which emerged to give coherence and a positive emphasis to the social energy which was being released and dissipated in protest and 'par-ticipation' in earlier chapters, notably in the work of Davidoff and subse-quent pluralist apologists. Nevertheless, despite the transparent weaknesses of the advocacy model of circumventing *statism* (for example, as described by Fox Piven, 1970) this movement of popular protest and counter-planning represented a provisional critique of standard bureaucratic planning approaches. More recently, in the UK, signs have appeared of a movement towards popular planning, not in the sphere of reproduction, but in the sphere of production. We are referring here *not* to the relatively familiar incidence of workers' co-operatives which occasionally emerge in the aftermath of a failure by capital to avoid business failure. Rather, we are pointing to the appearance of *workers' plans* for the manufacture of socially useful products.

Clearly, we can do no more in a book of this nature than outline the main features and principles of the movement towards the production of workers' plans (for fuller descriptions the following should be consulted: Coates, 1978; Elliott, 1977; Cooley, 1980; Cooley and Wainwright, 1981). The best known is the Lucas Aerospace combine committee's corporate plan although a similar one was produced by workers at Vickers[4] (Beynon and Wainwright, 1979). The principles and objectives of the workers' planning model to be described below are derived from the Lucas Aerospace plan not because its detailed proposals on production are necessarily superior to the Vickers plan, but due to its wider scope and more far-reaching suggestions for linking action across a range of organizational levels.

At the first, and most general level, it is recognized that the workers' plans movement depends to a large extent upon the existence of a favourable climate within political and civil society. This means that the state apparatus would have to be under the control of a government sympathetic to the general interests of labour. In addition, those parts of the state directly related to the sphere of circulation, notably the Departments of Employment, Industry and, probably, Environment, would preferably be controlled by Ministers particularly sympathetic to the idea and practice of production for use as an alternative to production solely for exchange. Moreover, a climate of the kind described would offer the possibility that local states which were themselves politically dominated by interests similarly sympathetic to progressive, needs-based planning of production could supply both technical and financial assistance to new ventures or groups taking over redundant, medium-sized productive plant. What the workers' plans movement calls for is a *non-statist* industrial strategy capable of stimulating production for use in an economy which, transitionally at least, would remain under the hegemony of production for exchange, albeit substantially state-managed.

Second, the production of workers' plans represents an important aspect of the struggle by shopfloor workers to undermine the element of 'statism' experienced within their own trade unions. Of particular importance here is opposition to corporatism at the national and local scales, whereby ordinary workers can find themselves striving, for example, to keep plants open against a coalition formed between capital and the representatives of labour in the workplace, who have themselves become remote from their members. This involves building connections between unions, and between the same unions in different plants, at fairly low, that is shop steward and/or convener, levels, and developing multi-union organizations; for example, the Lucas Aerospace combine committee which was composed of thirty-five shop stewards from seventeen different locations. Such a process which moves beyond rigid structures of demarcation and isolationism is a key part of the development of activism and political consciousness. It can combine class identities across the manual–mental labour divide and link the different skills and expertise of shopfloor and office personnel in ways not wholly dissimilar from those envisaged by Gramsci (1971, p. 15) when he spoke of technicians coming under the influence of the *organic intellectuals* of the shopfloor.

The third principle and objective of workers' plans is that they should only be devoted to the identification of products and methods of producing them according to the criterion of social usefulness. That is, they reject the corner-stone of capitalist production that only those commodities which have the capacity for short-term profit-maximization should be produced. Such myopia is replaced with a more prescient vision of the advantages of long-term 'social profit'. Thus in a context where, for example, a private business, planning on the basis of profitability in a competitive environment, lays off workers temporarily, or makes them permanently redundant, thereby increasing spare productive capacity and social waste, one possibility would be that the spare capacity could be turned to socially productive use. Products which could be manufactured would clearly have to be capable of being made with available machinery and skills. However, the range of possible products could be large – the Lucas Aerospace combine committee identified 150 possible products. Many of these were potentially of direct value to the medical profession, such as artificial-kidney machines, which could be made using technology then being employed to produce rocketry and other defence equipment. To health-related products could be added a wide range of energy-conserving equipment such as lighter railway vehicles, coal-to-gas/oil conversion equipment, efficient generators and pumps for industrial and domestic use, and so on. Production of this kind, as well as being more socially useful than artificially 'profitable' defence equipment, most of which is invisibly subsidized by the state to massive levels (Thompson, 1980), is, plainly, infinitely more socially useful than the enforced idleness and waste of unemployment.

But the fourth important feature of production of this kind is that it involves a commitment not only to the manufacture of socially-useful products but also to establishing the labour process as a less socially degrading and socially wasteful arrangement of activities. With respect to the degradation of work, particularly in regard to the ways in which modern production methods deskill the labour process (for discussions see Braverman, 1974; Clawson, 1980; Zimbalist, 1979; Wood, 1982), the Lucas plan aimed to restore control of the detailed labour process to the worker as described below:

. . . the combine committee proposed means of production which enhanced rather than destroyed human skills. One example is telechiric devices (literally meaning 'hands at a distance'). Telechiric devices are capable of mimicking in real time the actions of a skilled worker. When the worker stops the system stops, and the worker is in control all the time. The system does not 'absorb' or 'objectivise' human knowledge. It merely responds to it. It is therefore possible to link advanced technology with human skill to provide for human-centred equipment – rather than deskill, control or even displace the human being. (Cooley and Wainwright, 1981, p. 14)

However, as well as conceiving more humanistic methods of production this approach also proposes more socially-useful means of conserving and recycling energy and materials used in the production process. But most important of all it embodies a rejection of the wasteful treatment of labour itself in the modern business enterprise, as represented by the ways in which labour power is systematically reduced to its lowest common denominator of unreflective muscle-power.

Finally, penetration of the hegemonic structures of the market system, which the intellectual and practical processes of conception, organization and persuasion associated with planning socially-useful production entails, brings related benefits and realizations. The process of establishing multi-union combines demonstrates to workers the importance of communication and mutual assistance across sectoral divisions. Moreover, it provides experience of the potential for power which workers organized in class, rather than sectional, terms may be capable of exercising as a means to effecting social change. It shows how multi-union combines, perhaps operating through local trades councils, may gain the support of public sector trade unions and how the latter may, constitutionally, influence the political parties with which they identify to develop more progressive policies for deployment by the local state. In this way it is not inconceivable that local planning policy, already increasingly disposed towards *discretionary* intervention in the local sphere of circulation to revive local capital, might, in certain areas, be tailored to suit local workers' plans for socially-useful production. Furthermore, the experience of assisting worker control of new or revived production, itself dependent upon the development of horizontal organizational links between unions, might profitably dispose the local state towards greater degrees of popular control in the sphere of reproduction. Examples would include tenants control of local authority housing estates and/or wider powers for neighbourhood control of local use values, such as environmental quality, open space, community facilities, and so on. In every case the plan can form the basis for negotiation and bargaining between popular interests in whichever sphere of struggle they exist, and the respective power structures prevailing within those spheres.

It will be apparent that in discussing the workers' plans movement and its potential for penetrating both the hegemony of the market and the *statism* which helps to sustain it, an argument has been advanced which runs the risk of being rejected for reasons discussed in Chapter 3 of this book. That is, it may look as though a kind of radical pluralism is being advocated. It is therefore important to show why what has just been discussed represents a substantial improvement upon the liberal, pluralistic planning which became popular in the 1960s and 1970s. There are three reasons for this. First, the workers' plans approach is clearly rooted in the ongoing struggles between capital and labour in the sphere of production. This means that it accepts that there is a basic conflict of interests between the two classes that come together at the point of production, and that the system of production which pertains is inferior to production for use and so must be replaced. However, it also recognizes that in order for that to happen labour must be prepared to forge links which overcome divisions and then work through and within the state to achieve gains. This is clearly superior to merely organizing protest, pressure and plans from outside the state[5] and treating the latter as somehow above and outside of political struggle. Second, it differs from old-style pluralism because it envisages planning in the workplace, and beyond, not as a defensive act by popular and working-class interests, but rather as part of an offensive position. The latter is seen as being brought to bear in situations where power holders are negotiating across the table in the process of collective bargaining, whether in the workplace or, conceivably, in the community as, for example, over rents and housing conditions. And third, and most importantly, it represents above all a strategy of *linkage* rather than one in which groups which may merely come together temporarily to fight for some particular local cause and then evaporate. The notion of popular planning activated through the existing and permanent structures of the organized working-class, but in ways which are conscious of the corporatist tendencies at the upper levels of those structures, is potentially much more resilient than the inevitably transient formations which are represented in the concept of advocacy planning.

We have arrived at these fairly tentative proposals for a new and challenging contribution from the planning profession from theory. It is recommended that progressive planners begin turning their expertise towards assisting workers to develop socially-useful methods and kinds of production. This comes as a deduction of what is possible given tendencies that can already be inferred from the ways in which the planning of spatial development is presently moving. It is recognized that in a capitalist society the overwhelming tendency will be for even left-controlled local authorities to incline towards the familiar option of allowing management to manage. This will apply even where the local state may be instrumental in bringing new small firms into existence through, for example, the local enterprise board idea. But a danger lies wherever this kind of initiative either enhances the growth of the kind of low wage, often unsafe work and exploitative production relations of the typical small capitalist enterprise, or the manufacture of junk products by transient 'entrepreneurs' who exploit consumers too. The chances of this occurring seem *a priori* less likely where production itself is not rooted in an underlying principle of exploitation. For it is that principle which tends to make even more enlightened capitalistic enterprise seek to maintain alienating work practices in the pursuit of profit.

Recent theories of planning

We consider that it is primarily because our analysis of the relationship between planning and the development process exists in a framework which expresses the basically exploitative nature of capitalism, on the one hand, while refusing to conceive of the institutions of capitalist society as being functional for capital *ad infinitum*, on the other, that it is superior to certain other attempts to theorize planning hitherto. In order to exemplify the reasoning behind this statement it will be useful briefly to evaluate three alternative theorizations of the planning process (Faludi, 1973b; Camhis, 1978, 1979; Scott and Roweis, 1977; Scott, 1980) before reiterating the main features of the conceptual framework which has been developed in the latter parts of this book.

In Faludi's theory of planning there are three reasons why it is impossible for the theory which is developed to act as a useful explanatory guide either to planners within the state or to those outside it. This is despite the objective of the book in question to generate a 'meta-theory of planning' (a theory of how to plan the planning process – a general theory). The first reason for failure is the conscious separation of the concepts of planning, on the one hand, and spatial development on the other. This false dichotomy results in an idealized and rationalistic conceptual logic being elaborated whereby, irrespective of location, time or organizational context, only limited variants on a basically rationalist model of decision-making are derived. In particular, the assumption that goals are both capable of generating widespread public support and remaining meaningful would seem to need correction in the light of, first, the contradictions which the capital-labour conflict pose for planning at the level of theory and, second, the conflict to which official planning often gives rise *vis-à-vis* class and other groupings in civil society.

The second problem is that it conceives planning as an activity standing above and outside even pluralistic social forces. This means that the planning system is ascribed a functional role, the purpose of which is to objectively derive optimal, or occasionally second-best, solutions to problems. The latter are not seen as perhaps being expressions of irreconcilable tensions between diametrically opposed interests but rather the effect of some impediment standing in the way of consensual goal achievement. Such a functionalist conception of the position of planning does have the advantage of showing how the problem of *statism* is sustained, yet simultaneously rationalized, by the apologists of bureaucratic centralism. Finally, this approach is misleading for planners in the local or central state in that it portrays their function as that of something equivalent to an artificial intelligence machine into which messages from 'the environment' are transmitted and out of which emanate solutions to problems. We have already discussed the incoherence of the methodologically individualist equation of the complex organization with human mental processes but it bears reiterating at this point. As an analogy it is bad because it requires that we reduce the complex social forces operating in any human organization to the psychologistic level of the individual brain, thereby removing from the object of analysis precisely the qualities which provide it with its specificity. When such an analogy is then projected back as a model for planners to follow it invites the latter in turn to operate idealistically and individualistically upon problems which are likely to be intractable to such approaches.

A rather similar problem attends the more recent writings of Camhis (1978, 1979) on planning theory. He also adopts the method of arguing by analogy and shows how the four mainstream theories of planning – rational-comprehensive; disjointed-incrementalist; mixed-scanning; and transactive planning – equate to four philosophies of science: hypothetico-deductive (verificationist); hypothetico-deductive (falsificationist); advanced falsificationist; and relativist. We do not wish to comment at length upon the validity of this comparison except in so far as it seems *a priori* somewhat dubious to equate Faludian procedural planning theory with philosophy, and substantive spatial development theory with science and then use these correspondences as a basis for equating planning theory and the philosophy of science. This is because, as we have seen, Faludi's procedural theory is concerned primarily with generating a meta-theory of planning rather than of spatial development. The more correct equation would be one which compared planning theory with the rather bizarre sounding philosophy of philosophy. The tautology implied in the latter seems to cast some doubt on the whole of Camhis's project from the outset. This is somewhat unfortunate because the author shares some of the critical ground on which this book is based, as for example in its attack upon the idealism and rationalism which is contained in procedural planning theory (Camhis, 1978, pp. 45, 46). Despite this awareness, however, Camhis then goes on to 'justify' the equations he makes in such purely idealistic forms as the following:

Both planning and science look for their justification in the same general and abstract notions (themselves related to material relationships) such as 'human happiness', 'objectivity', 'rationality'. . . . Planning seeks both inspiration from, and justification in, 'science' and the 'philosophy of science'. Science is an activity highly respected for its 'objectivity' and 'value-freedom'. Philosophy in general, and philosophy of science in particular, represent not only the justification of science itself, but also a higher more abstract view of the world. . . . Planning, considering itself to be a science, looks to the philosophy of science to find the 'right' scientific method. (Camhis, 1978, p. 46)

The problem here is in some ways similar to that of Faludi in that material processes are anthropomorphized into the ideas of a conscious acting subject. The passage strains to keep touch with material reality but is reduced to the following incoherence in desperation:

It is not far from the truth to say that, the more detached from the material relationships an idea appears to be, the more connected it is. (Camhis, 1978, p. 46)

What is lacking in an account of this kind are precisely the material forces which act upon and within the state planning system to stimulate ideological reproduction and justifications for new ideological practices. It would be unfair to suggest that the author is inattentive to these forces in the final analysis, but they do not feature as an integral part of the derivation of theory, tending to be assigned a secondary analytical position to that occupied by ideas *per se*. Moreover, materialist thinking is only seriously introduced to discuss the alternative forms of planning that are open to consideration from a Marxist viewpoint, an approach that leaves the explanation of bourgeois theories of planning, with which the bulk of his work is concerned, suspended over the idealist ground of which the author is so critical.

It is not a weakness of precisely this kind that minimizes the force of the other main approach to planning theory we propose to consider (Scott and Roweis, 1977; Roweis and Scott, 1978, 1981; Scott, 1980). For, while these writers display certain weaknesses which lead them to make erroneous deductions, they are nevertheless conscious of the need to avoid idealism, rationalism and inappropriate abstractionism in theorizing planning. Furthermore, they provide the useful service of identifying precisely such characteristics in more conventional theorizations of planning. However, the fundamental problem with this approach is that in rooting planning in the capitalist mode of production they do not actually penetrate analytically into the productive heart of that mode. Rather, they remain at the superficial analytical level of wages, prices and profit (Scott and Roweis, 1977, p. 1102), or in the sphere of circulation rather than entering the sphere of production. By doing the latter it is then possible to identify more clearly the contingent nature of planning action. Hence, it is in mediating through the form of bourgeois law that the capitalist state (and planning system) supplies temporary solutions to conflicts emanating from the social relations of production. It is not therefore:

. . . precisely out of the intervening tension between the claimants of profits and the claimants of wages that the *capitalist State* progresses . . . as the guardian of a tense and delicate social balance . . . and as a general integrating mechanism of collective survival. (Scott and Roweis, 1977, p. 1102, emphasis in original) but rather as a form of dominance expressing the basic asymmetry of the capital-labour relation *subject to the modifying effects of class and popular struggle in many spheres of conflict.* The implication here is not that the state or, more pertinently, the state planning apparatus is 'functional' for capital by 'guaranteeing' its property relations 'automatically', but that the planning system is itself fraught with the contradictory lines of force found in civil and political society. This means that planning does not simply serve capital, it helps to provide conditions for accumulation or valorization to continue. This is carried out in a context set by resistance to those activities from labour and a variety of ethnic, regional, local, gender, religious and other interest groups. The outcomes of this process are uncertain.

It is because of this functionalist analysis that Scott and Roweis's (1977) prediction that:

. . . urban planning is likely to grow into an ever more insistent element of the capitalist urbanization process. (Scott and Roweis, 1977, p. 1111)

emerges from their analysis tentatively yet erroneously. For, if the state must function to maintain capitalism, an increasingly urbanized system of production, and if, as is argued, the system is in widespread crisis, then such a prediction logically follows. Yet the crisis in the UK and USA has been met by the state being systematically withdrawn from areas which were precisely the prerogative of the urban and regional planning apparatus. In both countries the Enterprise Zone idea strikes at the heart of post-war planning philosophy; in the UK, regional policy has been cut back; in the USA environmental protection is being dismantled, and in both countries public sector budgets for the sphere of reproduction have declined substantially. These events seem to indicate not that planning is an essential part of advanced capitalism, but rather that it is one kind of solution to class struggles, and that its form may change, or disappear, to be replaced by new kinds of solution structured by new legal arrangements. We would conclude, therefore, that it is of key importance that urban and regional development planning under capitalism is conceptualized as a somewhat limited and indeterminate part of an equally indeterminate framework of uneven social relations.

Planning and spatial development: a conceptual framework

This brings us conveniently to the representation, in simplified form, of the conceptual framework towards which the argument of this book has worked in the preceding chapters. A diagram of the principal relationships is shown in Figure 2 and in what follows the reader will be guided through its various components and linkages from top to bottom. The first feature to notice is that the diagram is divided into five separate levels, each of which defines a distinct section of the structure of relationships linking the institutions of

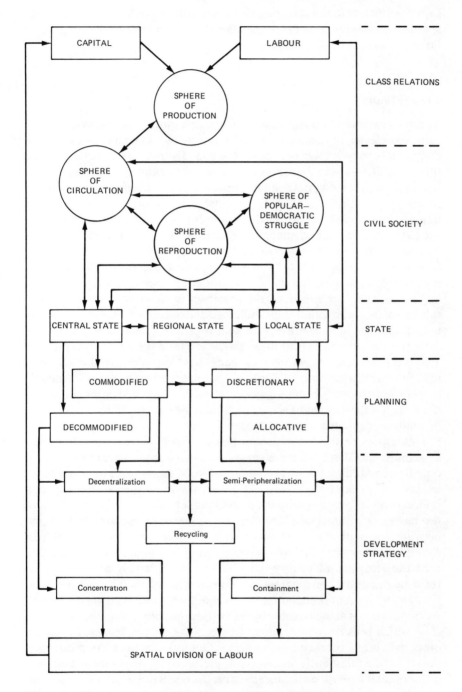

Figure 2 *Planning and spatial development under capitalism*

capitalist society to the state planning apparatus and linking the latter to the spatial development process. Exposition of the framework will be organized on the basis of these five divisions.

Class relations

The most basic relationship in capitalism is that which exists between the two principal classes necessary to its existence as the dominant mode of production in a given society or *social formation*. The reason for introducing the term 'social formation' is important since the social relationships found within a given society, between its various classes and groupings, are by no means simply a reflection of its principal mode of production. There are likely to be remnants of the social relations of a previous mode of production such as feudalism (for example landed aristocracy, peasantry) and possibly of a future mode such as socialism (for example welfare state employees). But these groupings will tend to play a subordinate rather than a determining part in shaping the social relationships of capitalist formations. The key relationship forms around the dominant mode of production. In capitalist societies production is for exchange and only incidentally for its social usefulness. The important feature with regard to exchange is that it is an activity which enables profit to be abstracted from the production process. This is not a necessary feature of exchange in other, non-capitalist societies, nor, of course, need certain kinds of (non-market) exchange (for example neighbours swopping beans for tomatoes) necessarily yield profit. However, if it were not the case that a sphere of exchange existed in which profits could be realized, capitalism could not exist.

The reason for this is that labour power, which, in capitalism, is treated as a commodity that is itself bought and sold in the sphere of exchange, could only be acquired by the will of labour to work for no wage or by force (as in slavery, serfdom etc.). Now, as the possibility of the former occurring is closed-off in capitalism by the systematic separation of the masses from the means of production (land clearances, enclosure movement etc.) and because the latter is inconsistent with the freedom of individuals (for example proto-capitalists) to exploit opportunities for profitable enterprise, then the struggles of history have hitherto been largely concerned with resisting constraints on the freedom of workers to sell their labour power for a wage and entrepreneurs to seek to make profits and accumulate capital. Accumulation is made possible by the two groups coming together as, first, a class which sells its labour power freely to the highest bidder, having no other means of existence since its separation from the means of production (land, farm equipment), and, second, a class which buys labour power in order to set it to work on the means of production which it does possess. The latter's position as owners of means of production in the form of potentially value-attracting *capital* (machines, factories, raw materials, money) designates it as the class of capitalists.

So far we have done little to avoid the possible deduction that profits are created in the sphere of exchange, and it is now necessary to show why this is not so. At a superficial level it can appear as though this is where profit comes from, indeed neo-classical and neo-Ricardian economists assume this to be the case. However, while the market is necessary if the value of commodities is to be realized and, moreover, it is clearly of great importance in determining the variation in profit rate between capitals, that is, the 'laws of supply and demand' do apply to constrain profit levels (Harris, 1980, p. 259), it is not sufficient for that purpose. This is because market constraints are insufficient on their own to determine the relative success of one enterprise over another when both are operating in the same market. While it is possible that one has the edge over the other in terms of product and/or raw material distribution, it is most likely that greater competitiveness has its origin in the ways in which the successful enterprise connects the labour power which has been purchased with the means of production which it owns. In other words, value, which is subsequently realized in the sphere of exchange, is formed in the sphere of production by the particular combination of social relations of production (purchasers and sellers of labour power, owners and non-owners of means of production) and the relevant forces of production. The two categories of relations and forces of production meet in the capitalist labour process, that is, the particular methods of organizing the work performed and the disposition, intensity and range of mechanization available to assist the production of commodities.

The important point about the relationship between relations and forces of production is that it is dialectical, meaning that they are systematically in opposition, with changes in the one tending to be met by counter-changes in the other. However, in the final analysis, the results of developments in technology (forces of production) are dependent for their implementation upon acquiescence by labour in the workplace (relations of production). Moreover, technological development is itself a method of disciplining the workforce (diminishing the mental content of manual labour, thus lessening the workers' control of the labour process). For these two reasons changes in balance between forces and relations of production tend to be brought about by shifts in the power relations between capital and labour to favour the latter. This provokes a response by capital to restore its dominance in the social relations of production. In the context which we are discussing in this book, struggles in the sphere of production around the three main areas of control of the labour process, mechanization and deskilling may have spatial effects where an *in situ* solution is not possible: either a *decentralization* strategy may be adopted, especially with respect to the labour-intensive activities of production, or *semi-peripheralization* and, possibly, *recycling* options may be followed where intra-corporate restructuring is devalued.

Each of these strategies will express in varying degrees the fact that employers seek out locations where two necessary factors are available to them. The first is a relatively disorganized labour force which can fairly readily be set to work in ways which allow increased surplus value to be produced. The second is relatively cheap labour power which gives an added edge to the realization of profit from surplus value when commodities are exchanged.

Civil society

Because wage-labour is purchased as a commodity by capitalists in a manner comparable to but not identical with that in which other, physical or technical, commodities are bought and sold, that is between nominally-free, legally-equal subjects, it is crucial to distinguish the relationships which make this possible from those we have just discussed. In the former case, the basic social relation is one of inequality out of which comes the capacity of capitalists to accumulate further plant, machinery, land, money and so on – it is an exploitative relationship. In the latter case the inequality is less visible, there is formal equality between the participants in exchange although this is, in turn, influenced somewhat by the fact that there is an unequal distribution of resources between say, the average employer and the average labourer, which makes formal exchange equality rather hollow. Nevertheless, in precise terms each transaction is conducted between individuals who have no intrinsic constraints on their capacity to buy and sell their commodities. The connection between the sphere of production and the sphere of circulation (composed of exchange and distribution) is supplied by the cash nexus. Commodities are available on various markets and they are purchased at price levels dictated by their costs of production, on the one hand, and the levels of supply and demand, on the other.

　The struggles which attach to the sphere of circulation are to a considerable extent motivated by the necessity for labour power to reproduce itself. This activity is one which takes place outside of the sphere of production, and that of the state, and forms an important basis for the diverse relationships and conflicts of civil society. The sphere of reproduction is thus dependent upon the sphere of circulation in as much as the latter is the source of wages which make possible the reproduction of the labour force. This occurs, of course, through the purchase of commodities such as food, housing, leisure activities and so on for consumption. The connections between the sphere of circulation and the sphere of reproduction are predominantly conducted through the medium of money, too. However, there is an element of legal interference here too since the state sets minimum wage and welfare benefit standards which result in some levels of income being rather higher than they otherwise would be. By contrast the state legally intervenes to reduce the received income of most workers and employers by means of taxation, although it should be noted that there is some controversy as to whether taxation is a deduction from the income of labour or whether that deduction is actually compensated by wage-levels negotiated in free collective bargaining so that the burden of taxation is really borne only by capital (Gough, 1979; Fine and Harris, 1976). It actually seems to matter relatively little since tax revenue re-enters the sphere of circulation where, whatever class interest is actually in control of the state apparatus, it tends to assist the reproduction of conditions favourable to capital in the long run. Thus it would seem likely that only where the process of reproducing capitalist social relations were to have broken down, due perhaps to the state being under the control of interests favouring expenditure on labour power reproduction to an inordinate extent (such that work was devalued) would the balance shift decisively against the maintenance of capitalism, having presumably shifted significantly against the reproduction of capital itself in the first place.

The latter tendency is to some extent supported by struggle in the third main sphere of activity in civil society. This occurs primarily between popular (non-class or cross-class) interests and the state, or between popular interests, on the one hand, and capital (or even, possibly, organized labour) on the other, mediated by the state. Thus, for example, the ecological lobby has, in numerous liberal democratic societies, been effective in pressing political parties and/or governments to establish new laws which improve the capacity of the population to reproduce itself (clean air, anti-pollution of water, control on dumping of toxic wastes etc.). The effects are either to cause capital to carry the extra cost burden directly, or, if the burden is off-loaded on to consumers, to limit the competitiveness of firms against those less affected by anti-pollution ordinances. As with the spheres of circulation, to a limited extent, and reproduction, to a greater extent, the sphere of popular struggle involves legal connections both to the various levels of the state (especially central state) and the other two spheres of civil society but also exerts financial effects (largely in terms of increased costs) *vis-à-vis* both of the other spheres. Such costs are incurred as a result of pollution legislation, opposition to motorway development, anti-nuclear power protests, wage-equality for women, regionalism, racial equality and the host of other popular campaigns which supplement the traditional class-party basis of democratic politics.

The state

In broad terms the state in capitalist society is here conceived as a form of the domination of capital over labour which, set outside civil society, nevertheless formalizes and sustains its key institutions through the medium of law. Once we start to speak of the state we move on to the terrain upon which urban and regional development planning is located. The latter set of activities represents one part of the complex range of interactions between the state and civil society. These arise as a result of class and popular pressures in civil society being transmitted, primarily through political parties, though by no means exclusively so, into the political society of the state. They re-emerge as relatively homogeneous, individuating laws which provide a framework of constraints and entitlements within which normal social affairs are conducted. Planning is linked to civil society by laws which relate to the spheres of circulation, reproduction and popular struggle but not to the sphere of production, which remains outside civil society. The relevant law is administered through both the apparatus of the central state and that of the local state. However, in many countries (perhaps in most advanced capitalist countries) and to an increasing, but unevenly developed, level in the UK, there is to be found an important intermediate point of intervention represented by the regional state. In the main the central state is involved in supplying various forms of direct subsidy to capital through the sphere of circulation, including regional assistance and large-scale infra-structural investment. But the central state is also heavily involved in con-trolling, either through enlarged investments or expenditure cut-backs and limitations on autonomy, the scale of expenditure in the sphere of repro-duction, most notably with regard to the reproduction of labour power. The relationship of the central state to the sphere of popular struggle is primarily a legal one in that it enacts and administers new laws the origin of which lies within this sphere. However, it is possible that money may become a more important medium of exchange (and control?) if the state extends the concept of legal aid to cover expenses incurred by protesters in campaigning against proposals of which they disapprove.[6]

The local state operates as a specific set of state institutions whose par-ticularity is given by the matrix of uneven development. This contains connotations of local variation in class structure and labour market, and the consequent contradictions which are set up as with local heterogeneity versus national-legal homogeneity, capital mobility versus labour im-mobility, and local state autonomy versus central state control. The local state, in administering central state statutes with respect to the planning of land, provides conditions for the appropriation of surplus value by financial capital, in particular. This occurs through the effects of inducing artificial scarcity and transferring an interest-like capacity to land according to its use designation. By extension, such designations can be to the advantage of large capital to the extent that they provide conditions for the concentration in space of advanced processes of information and managerial exchange which can enhance the speed of the circulation of capital and thus of accumulation (Lojkine, 1977). It is also the local state which is directly involved in the provision of many goods and services which assist the reproduction of labour power. In this respect its interventions are rather more than simple delegations of legal authority from the central state since revenues can be raised and spent locally through local taxation. Thus with regard to both the sphere of circulation (investment in joint property-development schemes with private capital) and that of reproduction (production of housing etc.) the local state interacts through the media of law and money. Finally, in relation to the sphere of popular struggle the local state is frequently the focus precisely of 'people' versus 'officialdom' antagonisms. To the extent that these are granted status by the local state it is normal for the rules and procedures established by law to be the main medium of exchange, although there is clearly often an element of extra-legal interaction involved in protests of this kind (squatting, sit-ins, violent demonstrations etc.).

The regional state apparatus occupies an ambiguous position between the central and local levels, at least in the UK to which the following remarks pertain. It is mainly an administrative arm of the central state with a mainly functional (water, gas, electricity, health services etc.) constituency, although occasionally (Scotland, Wales, Northern Ireland) displaying a territorial rather than a functional constitution. Because it is non-democratic it has often pursued more overtly discretionary forms of intervention *vis-à-vis* both the sphere of circulation, as with development agencies, and reproduction, as with housing investment programmes.[7] This tendency is underlined by the territorial regional state apparatus, in particular, since this has normally been established where economic problems are regionally overdetermined by national-cultural questions in the absence of direct democratic accountability. Moreover, the shift in emphasis from reproduction back to circulation, which the establishment of such agencies implies, further underlines the appropriateness of more selective industrial policy by the regional state. This subsequently grows to prominence in both central and local state industrial policy.

Planning

The kind of planning intervention which regional development agencies have typically made seems to be becoming a dominant mode of operation under conditions in which the revival of capitalism is seen to be a prerequisite. This contrasts with the earlier period (roughly 1945–1975) when reproduction issues dominated state policy. In the earlier period direct central state planning (which was conceptually and administratively separate from urban and regional planning *per se*) took the partial form of *decommodified* intervention. By the latter we mean that it involved the planning of production in industries which had been removed from private ownership and hence were not ruled by the discipline of market relations – they had been taken out of a purely commodity-productive mode and inserted into a mode in which social need (usefulness) was partly substituted. This does not mean that the central state was not involved in planning measures which subsidized *commodified* production as well during this period, rather that this was not the sole, or even at times the largest, source of state expenditure having an impact upon spatial development patterns. Thus private firms were benefiting from regional policy periodically during the years in question but so was the state sector, equally periodically (Cameron, 1979, p. 313).

During the period in question the main planning mode adopted within the local state can be described as *allocative* since the principal tasks of the local state planning machinery were to designate land uses in a coherent and rational manner. The point of this exercise was to control development so that it did not occur in socially wasteful locations which were expensive to service or which degraded the amenity or agricultural value of certain types of land. On the other side of the coin, such action did involve the allocation of land not affected by such criteria for development purposes in accordance with general guidelines and laws originating in parliament and the relevant state bureaucracy. However, there remained (and remains) a degree of *discretion* in the application of such allocative ground-rules in local space. This is an expression of particular local configurations of class-power in local state representation and the degree of linkage existing between key local and central state personnel involved in the development planning process. Thus loopholes can be found to enable some kinds of development which are deemed inappropriate to particular kinds of location to take place there willy-nilly. However, in a period when reproduction dominates circulation this discretionary element will tend to remain relatively well-subordinated.

When, by contrast, serious economic difficulty on a national scale causes priorities to shift away from the reproduction of labour power and towards the reproduction of capital, and circulation more generally, then the local state (like the central and regional state) is thrust into a closer relationship with capital than has hitherto been the case. Whereas the pressure during the peak phases of reproduction expenditure and planning tends to be towards greater democratic control of and participation in the allocative process, the opposite is the case under the dominance of the sphere of circulation. New initiatives for assisting capital are established which have little or no direct democratic accountability; speed of decision and rapid deployment of (albeit small) capital is the order of the day. The result is that considerable discretion is left in the hands of the management boards of local (and central) state development agencies to spend state resources on particular, selected projects and industrial sectors which show signs of earning a higher than average profit-rate. In this respect, the representatives of capital are fairly swift in getting into positions where even relatively small sums of locally-generated capital can be put to profitable use. However, this tendency can also, in principle, be turned to the advantage of progressive interests seeking to establish islands of socially-useful production in local space.

Development 'strategy'

There are at least five distinct development 'strategies' available to the planning system, each of which combines the state's temporary responses to the conflicting pressures of capital and labour by bringing labour and land together in ways which assist capital accumulation. We shall focus on the actions of the regional state first in this exposition because it seems that this level is emerging as the leading state form in supplying important conditions for the maintenance of capitalism under conditions of recession, international competition and industrial restructuring. In this respect it is possible that the observations made some years ago by Markusen (1976, 1978) and Friedland, Fox Piven and Alford (1977) about state subsidies to industry being seen as most appropriately supra-local and indirectly democratically accountable in the USA, are being echoed across the Atlantic. For UK regional development agencies (including BSC (Industry) Ltd in the category) combine commodified and discretionary planning to produce spatial *decentralization* and *semi-peripheralization* in the areas in which they operate as well as increasingly tending to adopt direct labour force *recycling* strategies in areas which have suddenly become centres of surplus population (especially from the steel industry). To clarify, once again, the distinction which we are making between *decentralization* and *semi-peripheralization*, the former involves intra-corporate restructuring and the location of branch plants in or near assisted areas, the latter involves extra-corporate restructuring in which agencies provide infrastructure for small, independent suppliers to emerge, often in rural or semi-rural areas. The process of semi-peripheralization is managed in non-assisted areas by the exercise of greater *discretion* by the local state but the spatial effects are more diffuse, there being a less active growth point strategy being undertaken. The impact of all three 'strategies' is markedly to recompose the spatial division of labour across the national territory.

The central state is also involved in sustaining a decentralist 'strategy' by virtue of its continued support for regional selective and non-selective assistance. However, in the UK, at least, there is some slackening of attachment to such a development 'strategy' by the central state *per se* as the general policy moves more towards a diminution of controls upon location of industry. This is further underlined by the reversal of policy towards the nationalized industries which, in the era of dominance by the sphere of reproduction, were undergoing a process of concentration in specialist regional locations. While these locations have continued as the key centres of production their relative importance as sources of large-scale employment and, hence, internal labour markets, has diminished substantially. This in turn has opened up the possibility for a marked recomposition of these labour markets through *recycling* and limited *decentralization* 'strategies'.

Finally, the local state which, almost irrespective of location was, through the middle post-war years, pursuing a 'strategy' of *containment* under the hegemony of central state planning law, has begun to respond to different priorities. It is unlikely that there will be a return to precisely the conditions which prevailed in the inter-war years, in which mobile capital was given a free hand with respect to industrial and residential location. The results of this freedom were substantial, regionalized (South East and West Midlands of England) growth, but also the accompanying urban sprawl which fore-shadowed *containment* legislation. Rather, it seems that a rediscovery of internal vacant land resources within urban areas, combined with an economic and political environment which stimulates nationalized indus-tries to sell off land-holdings in urban areas will focus attention on the development potential of land in the inner cities, on the one hand, and older, former heavy-industry locations on the other. Nevertheless, for those local states not located in such areas, the apparent relaxation of controls upon development, accompanying the prioritization of circulation issues, will inevitably make the *semi-peripheralization* 'strategy' tempting. This is especially so for growth sector industry and higher-order services, many of which would prefer to locate in semi-rural areas for labour supply and environmental reasons. The resulting spatial division and redivision of labour produced by capital's interaction with the various 'strategies' of development planning thus provides the new basis for class relations in the sphere of production.

The 'strategic' picture is thus somewhat complex at present. From theory it is possible to deduce that there should be a shift away from reproduction expenditure towards circulation expenditure as the problems of industrial survival come into a dominating position with respect to state planning policy. At the empirical level there are clear signs that in the UK the planning system is passing from an emphasis upon containment and concen-tration with decentralization, towards a mixture of 'strategies', increasingly involving the regional and local state, and the central state operating in local space. The clearest tendency is for the state to be assisting capital, in whichever ways it can, to escape from the recent reduction in the power asymmetry between capital and labour. The change in question was expres-sive of a growth in the latter's defensive strength and the failure of the former to compete successfully on an international scale. Such a 'strategy'-complex involves the state, at various levels, providing conditions for profit-able production by bringing together land, subsidies and labour. To the extent that these factors can be supplied in areas dominated by relatively quiescent local class-relations and labour markets then the planning system is enabling capital to take advantage of them. In the process new, more fragmentary and less solidary, labour markets are being formed and others, often in areas which were previously prosperous engines of post-war economic growth, are being left high and dry.

The present seems to be a crucial period for the survival of capitalist social relations. The state planning system remains integral, though by no means critical, to the success of that exercise. We might, however, from a progressive standpoint, paraphrase de Valera's assertion to the effect that Ireland could prosper out of Britain's entanglement in the Great War (among others), by observing that capital's adversity is labour's opportunity too. The point, though, for planners is to change conditions rather than return them to *status quo ante*. Our analysis suggests that an understanding of the connection between planning and spatial development under capitalism is of great importance if planners are to gain a clear picture of their position in the development process. But to bring even relatively small-scale improvements to the communities over which they exercise some control and responsibility, it is likely that planners will have to change their own conditions by moving beyond the limitations of statism and into new forms of institutional relationship with the groups and classes whose interests they share.

Notes

Chapter 1 Introduction

1 Although there is no necessary identity between eternalist and idealist notions in general, in British (and American) planning the ideals of the founding fathers about the unseemliness of full-blooded urbanity and the appropriateness of an alternative, organic synthesis of the urban and rural, in the planned suburb or medium-sized town, for example, have remained dominant. This is far less the case in other fields where such an organicist idealism has predominated, for example, literary criticism, where Leavis's cultural organicism has been thoroughly undermined.

2 For the moment, the term 'structural' is used loosely to designate a general approach to analysis in which the primary focus is not upon individuals, their attributes and behaviour but rather upon the frameworks within which individual and collective actions are constrained and facilitated.

3 By neo-Ricardian is meant work which broadly rejects neo-classical and most Keynesian economics in favour of an approach to political economy established by David Ricardo (1772–1823). Neo-Ricardians, unlike Marxist economists, argue that the determinants of the division of the product into wages and profits reside in the sphere of exchange, not the sphere of production.

Chapter 2 Alternative assumptions of planning theories

1 It should be noted that the belief was shared by other equally important philosophers such as Saint-Simon (1760–1825) and J. S. Mill (1806–1873).

2 The concept of a 'dialectical' relationship expresses the philosophical notion of the unity of opposites. In other words, it expresses a process whereby the opposition between a *thesis* or position, confronted by its *antithesis* or counter-position, is resolved by the formation of a *synthesis* of the two. Thus Hegel, employing dialectical explanation, could represent the process of movement as a synthesis of the opposed attributes of presence and absence from given points (see Connerton (ed.), 1976).

3 Putting the second criticism in a stronger way it seems reasonable to ask of a conventionalist why simply any theory (convention) we might care to invent should not work. Why, in other words, do we usually have so few theories from which to choose in the explanation of a given process or event? I am grateful to Andrew Sayer for this elaboration.

4 This is not to say that realists insist on the dependence of all objects or events since the very existence of indeterminacy of some (many?) outcomes implies some form of independence.

5 The term 'development planning' is preferred to others such as 'physical' and 'land-use' planning, or 'urban and regional planning' (although the latter is sometimes used) because it captures more fully what planning is actively influencing and engaging with, that is the development of economic, political, social and cultural processes over space.

6 Of course, such criticisms remain on the same terrain as that occupied by behavioural analysis. If individualism is rejected *per se* and social action is understood as being determined by structural *social relations* (both external and internal to the individual), then behaviouralism, with its restriction of what is observable to merely individual action is revealed as a somewhat eccentric mode of analysis. For example, it would postulate that the power of an industrial manager or trade-union leader cannot be understood as a property of the structure of social relations and institutions in which such an individual finds himself/herself, which is plainly absurd.

7 Symbolic interactionism is an approach to the study of social relations which involves the interpretation of subjective meanings which inform actions rather than the observation of objective behaviour (see Manis and Meltzer, 1967). Ethnomethodology is a related way of studying social action through, in particular, identifying the common-sense methods by which individuals recognize and structure their social worlds (see, for example, Garfinkel, 1967).

8 The employment of the term 'naturalistic' in this context requires some clarification. Naturalism is a philosophy which argues that there is no fundamental difference between the natural and social worlds and that the methods for studying the former are entirely appropriate to the study of the latter. The usage in the present section is only tenuously linked to the normal philosophical meaning of the term. Here, what is meant is that there is a way of viewing the world in which certain characteristics of a determinate historic period – for example that dominated by the free-market economy – are taken to be permanent, 'natural' features of every period and society. Such a view is often justified by reference to certain parallel features of natural and social phenomena such as the survival of the fittest firms and animal species, for example (see Rowthorn, 1974; Marx, 1976, p. 174 '. . . economists say that present-day relations – the relations of bourgeois production – are natural . . .').

Chapter 3 Marginalist theories of planning

1 It may be that certain secondary system-variables appear capable of being interfered with by those, such as planners, charged with 'system-guidance' (Friedmann, 1973) but if the key, system-forming variables remain the occupants of 'black boxes', such interference may, ultimately, be merely gratuitous.

2 PPBS stands for Plan, Programme Budgeting System.

3 By 'Taylorism' is meant a mode of organizing the labour process according to the principles of scientific management, as introduced by Frederick Taylor. The basic idea is expressed in the following quotation: 'The workman is told minutely just what he is to do and how he is to do it, and any improvement he makes upon the orders given to him is fatal to success' (Taylor, 1906 cited in Cooley, 1981).

4 This is not to say that development planning of the kind with which we are concerned here is a necessary part of Keynesian demand management policies

(although clearly some means of managing the output of the construction industry would seem to be implied). Rather, development planning is a compatible but largely contingent practice which has flourished most in a context of active state intervention in economic affairs, Keynesian or otherwise.

5   These are determined almost exclusively in terms of monetary costs.

6   However, since Downs is a good example of an *instrumentalist* in terms of his methodological approach to the generation of knowledge, he is only interested in predictive outcomes, not in explaining the process by which such outcomes were achieved.

7   'Log-rolling' refers to situations in which politicians vote for outcomes in which they are not especially interested in exchange for similar behaviour from their colleagues on issues in which they *are* deeply interested. The 'pork-barrel' is the public budget, from which politicians may gain advantage for their constituencies if they have something with which to trade, for example a capacity to assist the implementation of a government policy whose universal applicability, rather than its particular relevance for the politicians in question, makes it of greater value to the government. Hence, 'log-rolling' may result in particular political advantages accruing to specific constituencies, and hence to specific politicians, from the 'pork-barrel'. In Britain, a recent example was the Callaghan Governments' granting of Pneumoconiosis Compensation to qualifying former slate-quarrymen, almost all of whom were located in two of the three Plaid Cymru (Welsh Nationalist) constituencies, when the Labour government was dependent upon Plaid Cymru support to remain in office in early 1979. In the General Election of that year the two Plaid Cymru MPs in slate-quarrying constituencies retained their seats, the other did not.

8   This is not to overlook the problem posed for a state which, as in Britain, has been heavily burdened with mitigating the effects of market failure in production, for example nationalization of substantial segments of failed private industry, and consumption, for example necessity of providing adequate universal health and education systems. The criticisms and material weaknesses attending much of state enterprise in Britain bespeaks of the category of *state failure* coming to accompany that, earlier established, concept of market failure. (For a discussion of this in a West German context, see Heinze and Olk, 1982.)

Chapter 4   Planning and consensus: a review of the critics

1   By 'democratic' is here meant the relatively early diffusion of the joint-stock form of enterprise in the USA which meant that relatively low-income shareholders could exist and influence (albeit minimally as individuals) the running of companies. This was largely denied to their European income-group counterparts, but also goes some way to explaining the origins of the 1929 Wall Street crash.

2   The functionalism inherent in Foley's analysis of the nature of planning in Britain and America is discussed in depth in Chapter 5. The main problem, for the moment, derives from his exaggerated stress on the *values* held by planners in explaining the form taken by planning policies in the post-war years. This massively underestimates the economic and political constraints and support for particular kinds of policy in the period of reconstruction.

3   It may seem that an important school of organization theory, the human relations approach, is being ignored in this discussion of early planning theory.
Unfortunately the revolutionizing effect of the prescriptive studies carried out by
Elton Mayo, Lloyd Warner and Kurt Lewin (see Mouzelis, 1975, pp. 97–119)
upon the formalism of Taylor and scientific management was attenuated in the
neo-formalism of Herbert Simon's 'models of man' approach. This relied upon
reductionist, neo-classical economic models of rational decision-making
behaviour. As a consequence the human relations school was relatively unin-
fluential on the development of planning theory.

4   Although the Conservatives' discovery of planning was primarily that of a form
of economic management rather than the more restricted development planning
with which we are concerned, it should not be forgotten that regional policy was
boosted and a minister, Lord Hailsham, was appointed with responsibility for
the planning of development in a single region, North-East England. Also, much
of the groundwork for the changes in development planning which were enacted
in the middle and late 1960s was prepared by the Ministry of Housing and Local
Government under Sir Keith Joseph's period of office in the early 1960s. I am
grateful to Brian McLoughlin for the last point (see also Crossman, 1975).

5   For a fuller discussion of this and related distinctions, see Isajiw (1968).

6   The nature and extent of these class settlements in Britain and the USA have
been explored in Cooke (1982a) while Davis (1980) concentrates on the USA
and Jessop (1980) focuses on Britain.

7   There was an intellectual strand which linked the organicism of Durkheim,
through Le Play (1806–1882), whose Folk, Work, Place syntheses and studies
were influential, to that of Patrick Geddes (1854–1932). This fitted in well with
the more widespread advocacy of the idea of the organic community by
reformers such as Ruskin (1819-1900) and Morris (1834–1896), and practitioners
such as Howard (1850–1928), the Cadburys, Lever Bros and so on (see, for
example, Fletcher (1970); Farmer (1967); Halliday (1968)).

8   See the previous point, note 7.

9   The massive impact of the inter-war agricultural slump on the break-up of the
large landed estates in large areas of Britain, the resulting space which thus
opened up for speculative residential (and, to a lesser extent, industrial)
development on the urban fringe, and the ways in which the landed interests
used the ostensibly inimical town and country planning movement to defend its
position remain largely unexplored by planning historians. Some valuable work
on the link between the slump and urban sprawl is to be found in Hobsbawm
(1968).

10 This interpretation of the nature of Weber's sociology stems from the contradiction between his argument that rationality is what is specifically and essentially
human and his location of the source of the ultimate values which motivate
rational action beyond the natural world (of which humans are, of course,
members). For a fuller account of this argument, see Hindess (1977).

11 For example, the son (or daughter) of a coal-miner who becomes a manager of a
coal-producing company (even if it is nationalized) has clearly moved from
membership of the class which is defined in terms of having to sell its labour
power to survive (working class) to that of the class which purchases labour
power, controls (not necessarily owns) forces of production, and generally

dominates relations of production (capitalist class). His or her income will be concomitantly enlarged as a result of the occupational change from the class position occupied by the family of the coal-miner. Rather less obviously, the coal-miner's son or daughter (or former miner) who becomes an administrator in a hospital may employ labour but not be in a position to control forces or relations of production whether in a private or a public hospital. That individual may objectively have changed position from being a member of the working class to being a member of the 'intermediate', 'managerial', or even 'middle' class, with income enlargement corresponding to the occupational shift. These issues are explored in more detail in Chapter 9.

12   A policy is said to be Pareto optimal when a change in the distribution of rewards to improve the welfare of one member of society cannot be made without decreasing the welfare of at least one other member of society. See, for example, Budd (1978). The term includes a reference to the Italian economist, Vilfredo Pareto (1848–1923).

Chapter 5   The Berkeley school: structural-functional planning theory

1   The contemporaneity of the Berkeley International Urban Research Centre under Kingsley Davis, an advocate of the idea that functionalism *was* sociology, should also be taken into account.

2   This is also noted in a recent book on planning theory although the functionalist connection is not made; see McConnell (1981).

3   But also, for a time at least, large output and employment growth; see Dosi (1981); Rothwell and Zegveld (1982); Duncan, M. (1981). See Mullan (1980) on labour supply problems in high-technology industries in Stevenage New Town.

4   For within the framework of private property relations the variable degrees of freedom experienced by households due to income differences, class and institutional factors, and changing demands upon space and facilities related to stages in the life cycle, act as powerful mechanisms of social segregation rather than social mixing.

5   For a fuller analysis of the internal contradictions of Social Democracy see Miliband (1972), Przeworski (1980b), and Gamble (1981).

6   Although it does not seem unreasonable to employ teleological explanation for a limited project such as accounting for intentional action, which has some purpose in view. On this see Ryan (1970) and Von Wright (1971).

7   As well as the attempt made in this book to re-establish the connections between the spatial and the aspatial, making this link is clearly becoming one of the most exciting research tasks in sociology and geography, as the following existing and forthcoming publications testify: Giddens (1981); Urry (1981b); Massey (forthcoming); Gregory and Urry (eds) (1983); and the new journal entitled *Society and Space*.

8   The division of labour is formed within the sphere of production as it interacts with the complexities of labour markets (national and local) in which labour power is bought and sold. Once the second element (labour market) is recognized then the interaction between the division of labour and aspects of social life which are not directly concerned with production is made conceptually. In Chapters 8, 9 and 10 of this book the ways in which relations operating between

the division of labour, civil society (the sphere in which markets, cultures and everyday life operate) and the state are examined.

Chapter 6   Theories of development processes I

1   In practice systems analysis does not remain limited to homeostatic principles. However, in planning theory the metaphor of the thermostat as an illustration of the function of planning in advanced societies has predominated, explicitly in the work of Faludi (1973b), implicitly in that of Friedmann (1973); McLoughlin (1969) and Chadwick (1971). Kirk (1980) makes the point that this was a singularly inappropriate metaphor given the limited nature of development planning powers in such societies. Broadbent (1977) makes a related point about the detachment of systems theory from practice in planning in accounting for the often obsessive concern with perfecting techniques found in the work of systems planners.

2   This is a necessary but not a sufficient condition for adequate explanation to be capable of being generated. The problem with forming theory either from *a priori* logical or mathematical relationships or as occurs more often in development planning, theorizing socio-spatial relations according to the conceptual logic of certain entities, relations or processes of the natural world such as organisms, gravity, entropy and so on, is normally that a spurious rationality (and hence predicability) is ascribed to socio-spatial processes. This is not to say that such processes may not have a rational basis but that this requires establishing at the level of socio-spatial relations.

3   An example here would be the idea that markets have a natural equilibrium towards which they are constantly tending to move, despite internally and externally imposed 'shocks' caused by large and rapid shifts in demand or supply of some commodity. One of Keynes's notable insights was to show that markets could remain in a state of permanent disequilibrium if left to their own devices (Keynes, 1936, pp. 378, 384).

4   It will be seen in Chapter 7 that many Marxist theorizations of urban and regional development suffer from an inherent functionalism, and are, as a consequence judged unhelpful in the context of this book. For a detailed discussion and critique of Marxist functionalism see Giddens (1981).

5   Alfred Weber was the brother of Max Weber whose contribution to social theory was discussed in Chapter 4.

6   Here the approach taken by Alfred Weber seems to owe a good deal to Max Weber's ideal typical notion of rational action. In particular, the idea that rationality is only part of human action and subject to interference from irrational factors, but that rationality is more susceptible of interpretation and understanding, hence, presumably prediction, seems to have been taken up in Alfred Weber's approach to locational decision-making. I am grateful to John Urry for indicating the importance of this connection. See also Chapter 4, note 10, and Hindess (1977, pp. 24–30) on rationality in Max Weber's work.

7   This is also true of Christaller's (1933) central place theory.

8   A standard objection to this line of criticism is that Lösch did not set out to explain patterns and processes of location as they existed but as they ought to exist in rational world. That is, the theory is normative, rather than positive in

intent. But it is clear from the quotation by Lösch that this is rather an over-simplification. It is clear that there is an intention to use the theory in question to determine the extent to which its rationalist assumptions can explain aspects of real location outcomes. In this respect there is a clear link with the use made of ideal type models by both Weber brothers.

9   It might be objected that there is no teleology in Lösch's equilibrium assumption since the equilibrium is the unintended outcome of numerous individual decisions. However, as Chisolm (1975, p. 139) makes clear Lösch did assume shared purposes between actors in (a) pursuing profit-maximizing goals, and (b) recognizing when social welfare is being maximized (by the presence of the maximum number of independent economic units) and thereafter terminating the struggle for space.

10   This symmetry is also noted by Dunford (1977).

11   Monopsony refers to the situation in which a firm has overall control over the pricing and output of a given sector because it is the dominant purchaser. It can be compared with *monopoly* where a firm has effective control over prices pertaining in a given market because it is the dominant supplier.

Chapter 7   Theories of development processes II

1   Such transparent organicism and functionalism is partly explicable in terms of the migration of concepts from the school of British 'civics sociologists' of which Patrick Geddes was a founder member, and in which a prefigurative human ecology was emerging, to the developing Chicago School of Sociology in the early twentieth century, where ecological studies were intensively undertaken. See Fletcher (1970) and Halliday (1968).

2   It is the case, as Castells (1976a) notes, that the central focus of the early Chicago school writers such as Park, Burgess and McKenzie was on processes of social disorganization and individual maladjustment (they could hardly have over-looked these characteristics of 1920s' Chicago). However, this seems to have been an instrumental focus in that the process which they sought to explain was how, out of disorder, anomie and rapid social change, a new (urban) culture demonstrating orderly characteristics of social integration and cohesion emerges.

3   For a sustained analysis of the concept of 'structuration' see Giddens (1981).

4   The main problem with structuralist rationalism is its substitution of theoretical categories for concrete analyses in the explanation of actual phenomena, for example urban concentrations exist to meet capital's need for the reproduction of labour power. Statements such as this paraphrase of Castells's argument can appear logical in terms of his conceptual framework but it is by no means clear what has been included and extruded from the categories in question. As a consequence it is difficult to know how to test or even illuminate the argument. For fuller discussion of these and related points see Sayer (1979) and Duncan, S. (1981).

5   This is because, in Castells's terminology they have not resulted in 'pertinent effects', that is they have not brought about some significant shift in the balance of class forces. Though recognizing such 'pertinent effects' would seem *a priori* a difficult task, it must be presumed that the formation of permanent class

alliances, across the production/consumption 'divide' would be pertinent for Castells (as indeed it would for most observers of political transformation). See Castells (1977) and Pickvance (1976).

6 The concept is crucial because in its absence analyses of conflicts between labour and capital tend either to be reduced to their economic content (for example Holloway and Picciotto, 1978) or their political content (for example Poulantzas, 1975) in ways which massively underestimate the complexity of class relations while conveying a misleadingly simplistic 'predictive' quality to outcomes of conflict. Much of the indeterminacy of social processes rests on non-economic and non-political social relations as these are formed within civil society. The importance of the concept of civil society is discussed more fully in Chapters 8 and 9.

7 See Humphries (1977) for an extended discussion of this interpretation of the family.

8 The problem here is that the analysis, which purports to be of class relations, actually focuses upon superficial categories (wages, profits, prices) the magnitudes of which are determined by technical market conditions rather than relations of domination and subordination (hence exploitation) operating within production and systematically reproduced socially, politically, culturally and legally.

9 Abstraction of this axiomatic kind allows 'predictions' to be deduced from given premises but in ways which avoid imputing causality. As note 6 (above) suggests, this problem is shared by those who offer reductionist Marxist accounts of social phenomena too.

10 That is, the state performs its *essential* function which is to ensure the continuation, by whatever means necessary, of capital's dominance over labour.

11 This is because the capital to labour ratio (what Marx refers to as the organic composition of capital) of production in peripheral countries is low (labour intensive production being the most common form) while that in core countries tends to be high. Exchanges of commodities are thus carried out on the basis of a greater value content for a lesser so value flows to the centre from the periphery.

12 This should not be understood as a rejection of the idea that exploitation also operates in the sphere of exchange, rather that there is an inadequate consideration of exploitation in the sphere of production due to the stress placed upon exchange in such theories.

13 For a detailed analysis of spatial variations in the restructuring of employment within and between particular industrial sectors, see Massey and Meegan (1982).

Chapter 8 The state, the local state and development planning

1 For a discussion of some problems with Habermas's notion of the pluralistic nature of liberal democracy see Kemp and Cooke (1981).

2 This is the term designating a process in which powerful interest groups (mainly representing large firms and organized labour) negotiate with the government over key aspects of its policy (for example wages, state investment, welfare expenditure) in exchange for securing their members' acquiescence towards its strategy (Jessop, 1979, 1982).

3   Apart from the functionalism inherent in this argument there seem to be at least two major inconsistencies contained within it. First, it is difficult to see how 'social and ideological control' equates with 'local needs' being 'anticipated and answered'. Second, it is equally difficult to see how 'local self-determination' and what is 'functional for capitalism' fit together in the light of, for example, Offe's (1975) careful analysis of their incompatibilities.

4   See note 2 above.

5   Although for a contrasting interpretation, see Urry (1981c).

6   The 'traditional' middle classes may be taken to include, for example, shop-keepers, firm-managers, lawyers, doctors, owner-occupier farmers. The 'traditional' working class includes production workers in factories, mills and mines, transport workers, dockers etc. See discussion in following chapter.

Chapter 9   Labour markets, local classes and development planning

1   A telling instance of an independent action by male trade unionists to effect a discriminating restructuring of an internal labour market to the detriment of women is recorded in the video 'Political Annie's Off Again' by Eileen Smith and Richard Davies shown at CSE Urban and Regional Working Group meeting, Cardiff, May 1982.

2   That is, in the tradition of Adam Smith (1723–1790) author of *The Wealth of Nations* (a text latterly introduced to higher economists in the British civil service by Sir Keith Joseph).

3   Following on from note 1 above the desire of men to ensure retention of their jobs at the expense of women in the factory in question, related to the interests of management in complex ways. On the one hand, division within the workforce would appear to have strengthened management's hand in achieving the desired level of redundancies, but, on the other, cheaper, female labour was being reduced, and the struggle by women to seek to prevent this resulted in a great deal of interrupted production from stoppages, strikes, etc.

4   As a typology what follows is an attempt to indicate some possibly important spatial effects of the multiple processes which help to give direction to the dynamics of local labour markets. By no means is it rooted in any 'general theory' of spatial labour markets largely because a theory which purported to comprehend the complexities of such phenomena without reductionism of some kind would be an impossibility.

5   The spatial aspect has become one of considerable importance of late (primarily during the 1970s) as even relatively moderate-sized firms have begun to inter-nationalize production by locating in low-wage 'platforms' in South-East Asia, Africa and Latin America. However, new foreign direct investment within the developed countries massively outweighs that going to less developed countries. This spatial emphasis has been attributed to a 'crisis of Fordism' in the advanced countries whereby what *appears* to be a problem of under-consumption is in fact a problem caused by an insufficiently high rate of exploit-ation of labour. In less developed countries this exploitation problem is temporarily offset by low wages; in developed countries by increased auto-mation (see Lipietz, 1982).

6   It is sometimes in the interest of capital to increase the level of skill, as the

contemporary complaint about the paucity of electronic engineers in Britain (and elsewhere) testifies.

7 The word 'strategies' is put into quotation marks because it conveys the notion of rational and intended action being translated into concrete effects with misleading clarity. In one case, *containment*, there was a degree of intentionality about the concerted efforts of central and local state planners to manage urban sprawl, although there were plenty of contingent loopholes as Hall *et al*. (1973) make clear. In other cases, notably of *semi-peripheralization* and even *concentration* the 'strategic' element of intentionality was either highly diffused or circumscribed by goals which were less spatial than sectoral. Nevertheless, that certain distinctive spatial effects are expressive of changing periodic emphases in state policies, and that the latter are in some sense intended as coherent interventions seems a not unreasonable proposition, and the word 'strategies' is retained as a means of conveying, perhaps oversimply, that connection.

8 On the politics of steel nationalization, see MacEachern (1979, 1980).

Chapter 10 Planning and spatial development: some deductions and connections

1 In this respect they seem well-entrenched in the tradition of regional assistance with which the state functionaries and politicians are so familiar in Britain.

2 It is more accurate to refer to *statism* of this kind as a characteristic product of social democratic states, that is those in which some combination of Keynesianism and Beveridgism informs large areas of state activity, rather than states *per se*. See Miliband (1972) and Przeworski (1980b).

3 To the extent that monetarist budgetary policy was pressed upon the state in the UK by the extra-state banking agency, the International Monetary Fund, and subsequently applied (albeit in somewhat watered-down form) by the democratically-elected Conservative government against the better judgement of most of the higher economic civil servants within the UK state, it is conceivable that monetarism has represented something of a triumph of (finance) capital over the state. It is the prospect that labour might triumph similarly with some opposed ideology (Bennism?) that seems to have troubled many Conservatives who have been lukewarm or hostile to monetarist policies. See Gamble (1981).

4 And more recently still by British Leyland shop stewards, 'Leyland Vehicles: the Workers' Alternative', Leyland Vehicles Joint Works Committee (1982), CSE Books.

5 As was typically the case with advocacy planning which tended to deflect scarce popular energies into activities which were not directly political. Hence, elaborate plans often foundered due to the lack of political organizations which could articulate them.

6 The prospect of the latter occurring has been made considerably remoter by the decision of Nigel Lawson, Secretary of State for Energy, not to make funds available for the use of opposition groups wishing to appear at the Sizewell Public Inquiry (1982) into the proposal to build Britain's first pressurized water-cooled nuclear power station.

7 Especially in Northern Ireland, see, for example, O'Dowd and Tomlinson (1980) and Parson (1981).

References

Alcaly, R., and Mermelstein, D. (1977) (eds.), *The Fiscal Crisis of American Cities*, New York: Vintage.

Alexander, C. (1968), 'A city is not a tree', *Ekistics*, vol. 139, pp. 344–348.

Alonso, W. (1964), *Location and Land Use: Towards a General Theory of Land Rent*, Cambridge: Harvard University Press.

Althusser, L., and Balibar, E. (1970), *Reading Capital*, London: New Left Books.

Altshuler, A. (1965), *The City Planning Process*, Ithaca: Cornell University Press.

Altshuler, A. (1968), 'New institutions to serve the individual', in W. Ewald (ed.), *Environment and Policy: the next 50 years*, Bloomington: Indiana University Press.

Amin, S. (1976), *Unequal Development*, Brighton: Harvester.

Amin, S. (1978), *The Law of Value and Historical Materialism*, New York: Monthly Review Press.

Anderson, J. (1975), 'The political economy of urbanism: an introduction and bibliography', Architectural Association, London, Department of Urban and Regional Planning.

Anton, T. (1966), *The Politics of State Expenditure in Illinois*, Urbana: University of Illinois Press.

Arcangeli, F., Borzaga, C., and Goglio, S. (1980), 'Patterns of peripheral development in Italian regions, 1964–1977', Paper Presented to 19th European Congress of the Regional Science Association, London.

Bagnasco, A. (1977), *Tre Italie: La Problematica Territoriale dello Sviluppo Italiano*, Bologna: Il Mulino.

Bagnasco, A. (1981), 'Labour market, class structure and regional formations in Italy', *International Journal of Urban and Regional Research*, vol. 5, no. 1, pp. 40–44.

Bailey, J. (1973), *Social Theory for Planning*, London: Routledge and Kegan Paul.

Batey, J., and Breheny, M. (1978), 'Methods in Strategic Planning' (2 parts), *Town Planning Review*, vol. 49, pp. 259–273, 502–518.

Benson, K. (1973), 'The interorganizational network as a political economy', *Administrative Science Quarterly*, vol. 20, pp. 229–249.

Benton, T. (1977), *Philosophical Foundations of the Three Sociologies*, London: Routledge and Kegan Paul.

Berger, S., and Piore, M. (1980), *Dualism and Discontinuity in Industrial Societies*, Cambridge: Cambridge University Press.

Berry, B., and Kasarda, J. (1977), *Contemporary Urban Ecology*, New York: Macmillan.

Beynon, H. (1975), *Working for Ford*, Wakefield: EP Publishing.

Beynon, H., and Wainwright, H. (1979), *The Workers' Report on Vickers*, London: Pluto.

Bhaskar. R. (1975), *A Realist Theory of Science*, Leeds: Alma Press.

Blackburn, R., and Mann, M. (1979), *The Working Class in the Labour Market*, London: Macmillan.

Blanke, B., Jürgens, U., and Kastendiek, H. (1978), 'On the current Marxist discussion on the analysis of form and function of the bourgeois state', in J. Holloway and S. Picciotto (eds.), *State and Capital: a Marxist Debate*, London: Edward Arnold.

Bleitrach, D., and Chenu, A. (1981), 'Modes of domination and everyday life: some notes on recent research', in M. Harloe and E. Lebas (eds.), *City, Class and Capital*, London: Edward Arnold.

Boddy, M., and Barrett, S. (1980), 'Local government and the industrial development process', *Working Paper 6*, School for Advanced Urban Studies, University of Bristol.

Bologna, S. (1976), 'Class composition and the theory of the party at the origin of the Workers Councils Movement', in *The Labour Process and Class Strategies*, Conference of Socialist Economists, London, Stage 1.

Borts, G., and Stein, J. (1968), 'Regional growth and maturity in the United States: a study of regional structural change', in L. Needleman (ed.), *Regional Analysis*, Harmondsworth: Penguin.

Bosanquet, N., and Doeringer, P. (1973), 'Is there a dual labour market in Great Britain?', *The Economic Journal*, vol. 83, pp. 421–435.

Boyce, D., Day, N., and McDonald, C. (1970), 'Metropolitan plan making', *Monograph No. 4*, Cambridge, Mass., Regional Science Institute.

Bramley, G., Stewart, M., and Underwood, J. (1979), 'Local economic initiatives: a review', *Town Planning Review*, vol. 50, no. 2, pp. 131–147.

Braverman, H. (1974), *Labour and Monopoly Capital*, New York: Monthly Review Press.

Braybrooke, D., and Lindblom, C. (1963), *A Strategy of Decision*, New York: Free Press.

Brenner, R. (1977), 'The origins of capitalist development: a critique of neo-Smithian Marxism', *New Left Review*, vol. 104, pp. 25–92.

Breugel, I. (1975), 'The Marxist theory of rent and the contemporary city: a critique of Harvey, in political economy of housing workshop', *Political Economy and the Housing Question*, London, Conference of Socialist Economists.

Brewer, A. (1980), 'On Amin's model of autocentric accumulation', *Capital and Class*, vol. 10, pp. 114–124.

Broadbent, A. (1977), *Planning and Profit in the Urban Economy*, London: Methuen.

Brusco, S. (1982), 'The Emilian model: productive decentralisation and social integration', *Cambridge Journal of Economics*, vol. 6, pp. 167–184.

Budd, A. (1978), *The Politics of Economic Planning*, London: Fontana.

Cameron, G. (1979), 'The national industrial strategy and regional policy', in D. Maclennan and S. Parr (eds.), *Regional Policy: Past Experience and New Directions*, Oxford: Martin Robertson.

Camhis, M. (1978), 'Planning theory and philosophy', *Antipode*, vol. 10, no. 2, pp. 44–63.

Camhis, M. (1979), *Planning Theory and Philosophy*, London: Tavistock.

Carchedi, G. (1975), 'An essay on the economic identification of the new middle class', *Economy and Society*, vol. 4, no. 1, pp. 1–86.

Carchedi, G. (1977), *On the Economic Identification of Social Classes*, London: Routledge and Kegan Paul.

Cardoso, F. (1973), 'Associated-dependent development: theoretical and practical implications', in A. Stepan (ed.), *Authoritarian Brazil*, London: Yale University Press.

Cardoso, F., and Faletto, P. (1979), *Dependency and Development in Latin America*, London: University of California Press.

Carney, J., Hudson, R., and Lewis, J. (1980) (eds.), *Regions in Crisis*, London: Croom Helm.

Carney, J., Hudson, R., Ive, G., and Lewis, J. (1976), 'Regional underdevelopment in late capitalism: a study of the North East of England', in I. Masser (ed.), *Theory and Practice in Regional Science*, London: Pion.

Carney, J., Lewis, J., and Hudson, R. (1977), 'Coal combines and inter-regional uneven development in the UK', in D. Massey and R. Batey (eds.), *London Papers in Regional Science: Alternative Frameworks for Analysis*, London: Pion.

Castells, M. (1976a), 'Theory and ideology in urban sociology', in C. Pickvance (ed.), *Urban Sociology: Critical Essays*, London: Tavistock.

Castells, M. (1976b), 'Theoretical propositions for an experimental study of urban social movements', in C. Pickvance (ed.), *Urban Sociology: Critical Essays*, London: Tavistock.

Castells, M. (1977a), *The Urban Question*, London: Edward Arnold.

Castells, M. (1977b), 'Towards a political urban sociology', in M. Harloe (ed.), *Captive Cities*, London: John Wiley.

Castells, M. (1978), *City, Class and Power*, London: Macmillan.

Castells, M., and Godard, F. (1974), *Monopolville*, Paris: Maspero.

Cawson, R. and Saunders, P. (1981), 'Corporatism, competitive politics and class struggle', Paper Presented at British Sociological Association/Political Studies Association Conference on 'Capital, Ideology and Politics', University of Sheffield, January.

Chadwick, G. (1971), *A Systems View of Planning*, Oxford: Pergamon.

Chapin, F. (1965), *Urban Land Use Planning*, Urbana: Illinois University Press.

Chapin, F. (1968), 'Activity systems and urban structure: a working schema', *Journal of the American Institute of Planners*, vol. 24, no. 1, pp. 11–18.

Chisolm, M. (1975), *Human Geography: Evolution or Revolution?*, Harmondsworth: Penguin.

Christaller, W. (1933), *Central Places in Southern Germany*, Englewood Cliffs: Prentice-Hall.

Clarke, J. (1979), 'Capital and culture: the post-war working class revisited', in J. Clarke, C. Critcher, and R. Johnson (eds.), *Working Class Culture*, London: Hutchinson.

Clarke, S. (1977), 'Marxism, sociology and Poulantzas' theory of the state', *Capital and Class*, vol. 2, pp. 1–31.

Clawson, D. (1980), *Bureaucracy and the Labour Process*, New York: Monthly Review Press.

Coates, K. (1978), *The Right to Useful Work*, Nottingham: Spokesman.

Cockburn, C. (1977), *The Local State*, London: Pluto.

Cohen, P. (1968), *Modern Social Theory*, London: Heinemann.

Cole, J., and Cole, S. (1973), *Social Stratification in Science*, Chicago: University of Chicago Press.

Coleman, J. (1972), *Policy Research in the Social Sciences*, Morristown: General Learning Press.

Connerton, P. (1976) (ed.), *Critical Sociology*, Harmondsworth: Penguin.

Cooke, P. (1980a), 'Discretionary intervention and the Welsh development agency', *Area*, vol. 12, pp. 269–278.

Cooke, P. (1980b), 'Dependent development in UK regions with particular reference to Wales', *Progress Planning*, vol. 15, pp. 1–62.

Cooke, P. (1981), 'Tertiarisation and socio-spatial differentiation in Wales', *Geoforum*, vol. 12, no. 4, pp. 319–330.

Cooke, P. (1982a), 'Class relations and uneven development in Wales', in G. Day and D. Robbins, *Diversity and Decomposition in the Labour Market*, Farnborough: Gower.

Cooke, P. (1982b), 'Class interests, regional restructuring and state formation in Wales', *International Journal of Urban and Regional Research*, vol. 6, no. 2, pp. 187–203.

Cooley, M. (1980), *Architect or Bee?*, Slough: Langley Technical Services.

Cooley, M. (1981), 'The Taylorisation of intellectual work', in L. Levidow and B. Young (eds.), *Science, Technology and the Labour Process*, London: CSE Books.

Cooley, M., and Wainwright, H. (1981), 'The Lucas Plan: its lessons for labour', *New Socialist*, vol. 2, pp. 13–16.

Coser, L. (1965), *The Functions of Social Conflict*, London: Routledge and Kegan Paul.

Coventry City Council (1971), *Coventry–Solihull–Warwickshire: A Strategy for a Sub-Region*, Coventry City Council.

Crecine, J. (1969), *Governmental Problem Solving*, Skokie: Rand-McNally.

Cross, M. (1981), *New Firm Formation and Regional Development*, Farnborough: Gower.

Crossman, R. (1975), *The Diaries of a Cabinet Minister: Volume 1, Minister of Housing 1964–1966*, London: Hamish Hamilton and Jonathan Cape.

Crouch, C. (1979), 'The state, capital and liberal democracy', in C. Crouch (ed.), *State and Economy in Contemporary Capitalism*, London: Croom Helm.

Dahl, R. (1961), *Who Governs?*, New Haven: Yale University Press.

Dahl, R. (1971), *Polyarchy*, New Haven: Yale University Press.

Dahl, R., and Lindblom, C. (1953), *Politics, Economics and Welfare*, Chicago: University of Chicago Press.

Danziger, J. (1976), 'Assessing incrementalism in British municipal budgeting', *British Journal of Political Science*, vol. 6, no. 3, pp. 335–350.

Davidoff, P. (1973), 'Advocacy and pluralism in planning', in A. Faludi (ed.), *A Reader in Planning Theory*, Oxford: Pergamon.

Davidoff, P., and Reiner, T. (1973), 'A choice theory of planning', in A. Faludi (ed.), *A Reader in Planning Theory*, Oxford: Pergamon.

Davis, M. (1980), 'Why the U.S. working class is different', *New Left Review*, vol. 123, pp. 3–46.

Dear, M., and Clark, G. (1980), 'Dimensions of local state autonomy', *Urban Planning Policy Analysis and Administration Discussion Paper D80–12*, John F. Kennedy School of Government, Harvard University, Cambridge, Mass. (also published in *Environment and Planning A*, 13, 10, 1189–1322).

Dearlove, J. (1979), *The Reorganization of British Local Government*, Cambridge: Cambridge University Press.

Dennis, R. (1978), 'The decline of manufacturing employment in Greater London: 1966–1974', *Urban Studies*, vol. 15, pp. 63–73.

Department of the Environment (1967), *Management of Local Government*, London: HMSO.

Department of the Environment (1970), *Development Plans: a Manual on Form and Content*, London: HMSO.

Department of the Environment (1972), *Local Government Reorganization*, London: HMSO.

Department of the Environment (1980), *Local Government, Planning and Land Act*, London: HMSO.

Dicken, P., and Lloyd, P. (1981), *Modern Western Society*, London: Harper & Row.

Dineen, M. (1981), 'Cosmetics for Toxteth', *The Observer*, November 22.

Dobb, M. (1972), 'The trend of modern economics', in E. Hunt and J. Schwartz (eds.), *A Critique of Economic Theory*, Harmondsworth: Penguin.

Doeringer, P., and Piore, M. (1971), *Internal Labour Markets and Manpower Analysis*, Lexington: D. C. Heath.

Donnison, D. (1975), 'The age of innocence is past: some ideas about research and planning', *Urban Studies*, vol. 12, pp. 263–272.

Dos Santos, T. (1970), 'The structure of dependence', *American Economic Review* (Supp.), vol. 60, pp. 231–236.

Dosi, G. (1981), 'Technical change and survival: Europe's semiconductor industry', *Sussex European Papers No. 9*, European Research Centre, University of Sussex.

Downs, A. (1957), *An Economic Theory of Democracy*, New York: Harper & Row.

Downs, A. (1967), *Inside Bureaucracy*, Boston: Little Brown.

Downs, A. (1970), *Urban Problems and Prospects*, Chicago: Markham.

Drake, M. *et al.* (1975), *Aspects of Structure Planning*, CES, Research Paper 20, London: Centre for Environmental Studies.

Dror, Y. (1964), 'Muddling through – science or inertia?', *Public Administration Review*, vol. 24, pp. 153–157.

Dulong, R. (1978), *Les Regions, l'état et la Societé Locale*, Paris: Presses Universitaires de France.

Duncan, M. (1981), 'Microelectronics: five areas of subordination', in L. Levidow and B. Young (eds.), *Science, Technology and the Labour Process*, London: CSE Books.

Duncan, S. (1981), 'Housing policy, the methodology of levels, and urban research: the case of Castells', *International Journal of Urban and Regional Research*, vol. 5, no. 2, pp. 231–254.

Duncan, S., and Goodwin, M. (1982), 'The local state and restructuring social relations: theory and practice', *International Journal of Urban and Regional Research*, vol. 6, no. 2, pp. 157–186.

Dunford, M. (1977), 'The restructuring of industrial space', *International Journal of Urban and Regional Research*, vol. 1, no. 4, pp. 510–520.

Dunford, M. (1979), 'Capital accumulation and regional development in France', *Geoforum*, vol. 10, no. 1, pp. 81–108.

Dunleavy, P. (1977), 'Protest and quiescence in urban politics: a critique of some pluralist and structuralist myths', *International Journal of Urban and Regional Research*, vol. 1, no. 2, pp. 193–218.

Dunleavy, P. (1980), *Urban Political Analysis*, London: Macmillan.

Dunleavy, P. (1981), *The Politics of Mass Housing*, London: Oxford University Press.

Edwards, R., Reich, M., and Gordon, D. (1975), *Labour Market Segmentation*, Lexington: D. C. Heath.

Ehrenreich, B., and Ehrenreich, J. (1979), 'The professional-managerial class', in P. Walker (ed.), *Between Capital and Labour*, Boston: South End Press.

Elbaum, B., and Wilkinson F. (1979), 'Industrial relations and uneven development: a comparative study of the American and British steel industries', *Cambridge Journal of Economics*, vol. 3, pp. 275–303.

Elliott, D. (1977), *The Lucas Aerospace Workers Campaign*, London: Fabian Pamphlet.

Else, P., and Marshall, G. (1979), 'The management of public expenditure', *Policy Studies Institute*, vol. 45, no. 580.

Emmanuel, A. (1972), *Unequal Exchange*, London: New Left Books.

Esping-Andersen, G., Friedland, R., and Wright, E. (1976), 'Modes of class struggle and the capitalist state', *Kapitalistate*, vols. 4/5, pp. 186–220.

Etzioni, A. (1968), *The Active Society*, New York: The Free Press.

Etzioni, A. (1971), 'Policy research', *The American Sociologist*, vol. 6, pp. 8–12.

Etzioni, A. (1973), 'Mixed scanning: a "third" approach to decision-making', in A. Faludi (ed.), *A Reader in Planning Theory*, Oxford: Pergamon.

Etzioni, A. (1976), *Social Problems*, Englewood Cliffs: Prentice-Hall.

Evans, A. (1973), *The Economics of Residential Location*, London: Macmillan.

Evans, A. (1976), 'Economic influences on social mix', *Urban Studies*, vol. 13, pp. 247–260.

Ewers, H., and Wettman, R. (1980), 'Innovation-oriented regional policy', *Regional Studies*, vol. 14, no. 3, pp. 161–180.

Exell, A. (1980), 'Morris motors in the 1940's', *History Workshop Journal*, vol. 9, pp. 90–115.

Faludi, A. (1971), 'Problems with "Problem Solving"', *Journal of the Royal Town Planning Institute*, vol. 57, p. 415.

Faludi, A. (1973a) (ed.), *A Reader in Planning Theory*, Oxford: Pergamon.

Faludi, A. (1973b), *Planning Theory*, Oxford: Pergamon.

Farmer, M. (1967), 'The positivist movement and the development of English sociology', *Sociological Review*, vol. 15, pp. 5–20.

Fenno, R. (1966), *The Power of the Purse*, Boston: Little Brown.

Feyerabend, P. (1973), *Against Method*, London: New Left Books.

Fine, B. (1980), *Economic Theory and Ideology*, London: Edward Arnold.

Fine, B., and Harris, L. (1976), 'State expenditure in advanced capitalism: a critique', *New Left Review*, vol. 98, pp. 97–112.

Fletcher, R. (1970), *The Making of Sociology*, vol. 2, London: Nelson.

Foley, D. (1964), 'An approach to metropolitan spatial structure', in M. Webber (ed.), *Explorations into Urban Structure*, Philadelphia: University of Pennsylvania Press.

Foley, D. (1973), 'British town planning: one ideology or three', in A. Faludi (ed.), *A Reader in Planning Theory*, Oxford: Pergamon.

Foster, J. (1974), *Class Struggle and the Industrial Revolution*, London: Methuen.

Fothergill, S., and Gudgin, G. (1979), 'Regional employment change: a sub-regional explanation', *Progress in Planning*, vol. 12, pp. 155–219.

Fox Piven, F. (1970), 'Whom does the advocate planner serve?', *Social Policy*, May/June, pp. 32–37.

Frank, A. (1967), *Capitalism and Underdevelopment in Latin America*, London: Monthly Press Review.

Frank, A. (1972), *Dependence and Underdevelopment: Latin America's Political Economy*, New York: Doubleday.

Frank, A. (1979), *Dependent Accumulation and Underdevelopment*, London: Macmillan.

Friedland, R., Fox Piven, F., and Alford, R. (1977), 'Political conflict, urban structure and the fiscal crisis', *International Journal of Urban and Regional Research*, vol. 1, pp. 447–471.

Friedman, A. (1977), *Industry and Labour*, London: Macmillan.

Friedman, M. (1970), *The Counter-Revolution in Monetary Theory*, Institute of Economic Affairs, Occasional Paper 33, London: IEA.

Friedmann, J. (1969), 'Notes on societal action', *Journal of the American Institute of Planners*, vol. 35, pp. 311–318.

Friedmann, J. (1973), 'A reply to Altshuler: comprehensive planning as a process', in A. Faludi (ed.), *A Reader in Planning Theory*, Oxford: Pergamon.

Friedmann, J. (1974), *Retracking America: A Theory of Transactive Planning*, New York: Doubleday.

Friend, J., Power, J., and Yewlett, C. (1974), *Public Planning: the Intercorporate Dimension*, London: Tavistock.

Galbraith, J. (1970), *The New Industrial State*, Harmondsworth: Penguin.

Gamble, A. (1981), *Britain in Decline*, London: Macmillan.

Gamble, A., and Walton, P. (1976), *Capitalism in Crisis: Inflation and the State*, London: Macmillan.

Gans, H. (1972), *People and Plans*, Harmondsworth: Penguin.

Garfinkel, H. (1967), *Studies in Ethnomethodology*, Englewood Cliffs: Prentice-Hall.

Giddens, A. (1981), *A Contemporary Critique of Historical Materialism*, London: Macmillan.

Glass, R. (1968), 'Urban sociology in Great Britain', in R. Pahl (ed.), *Readings in Urban Sociology*, Oxford: Pergamon.

Glass, R. (1973), 'The evaluation of planning: some sociological considerations', in A. Faludi (ed.), *A Reader in Planning Theory*, Oxford: Pergamon.

Goodman, R. (1979), *The Last Entrepreneurs: America's Regional Wars for Jobs and Dollars*, New York: Simon & Schuster.

Goldsmith, M. (1980), *Politics, Planning and the City*, London: Hutchinson.

Gough, I. (1979), *The Political Economy of the Welfare State*, London: Macmillan.

Gouldner, A. (1971), *The Coming Crisis of Western Sociology*, London: Heinemann.

Gramsci, A. (1971), *Selections from Prison Notebooks*, London: Lawrence & Wishart.

Gregory, D., and Urry, J. (forthcoming) (eds.), *Social Relations and Spatial Structures*, London: Macmillan.

Gripaios, P. (1977), 'Industrial decline in London: an examination of its causes', *Urban Studies*, vol. 14, pp. 181–189.

Gutch, R. (1972), 'The use of goals', *Journal of the Royal Town Planning Institute*, vol. 58, pp. 264–265.

Habermas, J. (1976), *Legitimation Crisis*, London: Heinemann.

Hague, C., and McCourt, A. (1974), 'Comprehensive planning, public participation and the public interest', *Urban Studies*, vol. 11, pp. 143–155.

Haines, R. (1981), 'The rejection of corporate management in Birmingham in theoretical perspective', *Local Government Studies*, vol. 4, pp. 25–38.

Hall, P., Drewett, R., and Gracey, H. (1973), *The Containment of Urban England*, London: Allen & Unwin.

Hall, S. (1977), 'The "political" and the "economic" in Marx's theory of classes', in A. Hunt (ed.), *Class and Class Structure*, London: Lawrence & Wishart.

Hall, S. (1979), 'The great moving right show', *Marxism Today*, January, pp. 14–20.

Hall, S. (1980), 'Thatcherism – a new stage?', *Marxism Today*, February, pp. 26–28.

Hall, S. (1981), 'Moving right', *Socialist Review*, vol. 55, pp. 113–138.

Halliday, R. (1968), 'The sociological movement, the sociological society and the genesis of academic sociology in Britain', *Sociological Review*, vol. 16, pp. 377–398.

Harloe, M. (1970), 'Review of Milton Keynes Final Report', *Environment & Planning A*, vol. 2, pp. 357–368.

Harloe, M. (1977) (ed.), *Captive Cities*, London: John Wiley.

Harloe, M. (1979), 'Marxism, the state and the urban question: critical notes on two recent French theories', in C. Crouch (ed.), *State and Economy in Contemporary Capitalism*, London: Croom Helm.

Harré, R. (1970), *The Principles of Scientific Thinking*, London: Macmillan.

Harris, B. (1978), 'A note on planning theory', *Environment & Planning A*, vol. 10, pp. 221–224.

Harris, L. (1980), 'The state and the economy: some theoretical problems', in R. Miliband and J. Saville (eds.), *The Socialist Register*, London: Merlin.

Harvey, D. (1973), *Social Justice and the City*, London: Edward Arnold.

Harvey, D. (1974), 'Class monopoly rent, finance capital and the urban revolution', *Regional Studies*, vol. 8, pp. 239–252.

Harvey, D. (1978a), 'The urban process under capitalism: a framework for analysis', *International Journal of Urban and Regional Research*, vol. 2, pp. 101–131.

Harvey, D. (1978b), 'Labour, capital and class struggle around the built environment in advanced capitalist societies', in K. Cox (ed.), *Urbanisation and Conflict in Market Societies*, London: Methuen.

Harvey, D. (1981), 'The space-economy of capitalist production: a Marxian interpretation', Paper Presented at Conference on New Perspectives on the Urban Political Economy, American University, Washington D.C., May.

Healey, P. (1979), 'Networking as a normative principle', *Local Government Studies*, vol. 5, pp. 55–68.

Hechter, M. (1975), *Internal Colonialism: The Celtic Fringe in British National Development, 1536–1966*, London: Routledge & Kegan Paul.

Heinze, R., and Olk, T. (1982), 'Development of the informal economy: a strategy for resolving the crisis of the welfare state', *Futures*, June, pp. 189–204.

Herbert, D., and Johnston, R. (1976) (eds.), *Social Areas in Cities, Vol I: Spatial Processes and Form*, London: John Wiley.

Heydebrand, W. (1977), 'Organizational contradictions in public bureaucracies: towards a Marxian theory of organizations', *The Sociological Quarterly*, vol. 18, pp. 83–107.

Hill, R. (1977), 'State capitalism and the urban fiscal crisis in the United States', *International Journal of Urban and Regional Research*, vol. 1, pp. 76–100.

Hill, R. (1978), 'Fiscal collapse and political struggle in decaying central cities in the United States', in W. Tabb and L. Sawers (eds.), *Marxism and the Metropolis*, New York: Oxford University Press.

Hindess, B. (1977), *Philosophy and Methodology in the Social Sciences*, Brighton: Harvester.

Hirsch, J. (1978), 'The state apparatus and social reproduction: elements of a theory of the bourgeois state', in J. Holloway and S. Picciotto (eds.), *State and Capital: A Marxist Debate*, London: Edward Arnold.

Hirsch, J. (1981), 'The apparatus of the state, the reproduction of capital, and urban conflicts', in M. Dear and A. Scott (eds.), *Urbanization and Urban Planning in Capitalist Society*, London: Methuen.

Hirst, P. (1977), 'Economic classes and politics', in A. Hunt (ed.), *Class and Class Structure*, London: Lawrence & Wishart.

Hobsbawm, E. (1968), *Industry and Empire*, London: Weidenfeld and Nicholson.

Holland, S. (1976), *Capital Versus the Regions*, London: Macmillan.

Holloway, J., and Picciotto, S. (1977), 'Capital, crisis and the state', *Capital and Class*, vol. 2, pp. 76–101.

Holloway, J., and Picciotto, S. (1978), *State and Capital: A Marxist Debate*, London: Edward Arnold.

Humphrey, J. (1980–81), 'Labour use and labour control in the Brazilian automobile industry', *Capital and Class*, vol. 12, pp. 43–57.

Humphries, J. (1977), 'Class struggle and the persistence of the working class family', *Cambridge Journal of Economics*, vol. 1, pp. 241–258.

Isajiw, W. (1968), *Causation and Functionalism in Sociology*, London: Routledge & Kegan Paul.

Isard, W., Smith, T. *et al.* (1969), *General Theory: Social, Political, Economic, and Regional*, Cambridge: Massachusetts Institute of Technology Press.

Jacques, M. (1976), 'Consequences of the General Strike', in J. Skelley (ed.), *The General Strike, 1926*, London: Lawrence & Wishart.

Jefferson, R. (1973), 'Planning and the innovation process', *Progress in Planning*, vol. 1, no. 3, pp. 233–310.

Jessop, B. (1977), 'Recent theories of the capitalist state', *Cambridge Journal of Economics*, vol. 1, pp. 353–373.

Jessop, B. (1979), 'Corporatism, parliamentarism and social democracy', in P. Schmitter and G. Lehmbruch (eds.), *Trends Towards Corporatist Intermediation*, London: Sage.

Jessop, B. (1980), 'The political indeterminacy of democracy', in A. Hunt (ed.), *Marxism and Democracy*, London: Lawrence & Wishart.

Jessop, B. (1982), *The Capitalist State*, Oxford: Martin Robertson.

Johnson, T. (1972), *Professions and Power*, London: Macmillan.

Keat, R., and Urry, J. (1975), *Social Theory as Science*, London: Routledge & Kegan Paul.

Keeble, D. (1980), 'Industrial decline, regional policy and the urban-rural manufacturing shift in the United Kingdom', *Environment & Planning A*, vol. 12, pp. 945–962.

Kemp, R., and Cooke, P. (1981), 'The repoliticisation of the public sphere: a reconsideration of Habermas', *Social Praxis*, vol. 8, pp. 125–142.

Keynes, J. (1936), *General Theory of Employment, Interest and Money*, London: Macmillan.

King, A. (1975), 'Overload: problems of governing in the late 1970's', *Political Studies*, vol. 23, pp. 284–296.

Kirk, G. (1980), *Urban Planning in a Capitalist Society*, London: Croom Helm.

Krieger, M. (1974), 'Some new directions for planning theories', *Journal of the American Institute of Planners*, vol. 40, pp. 156–163.

Kreckel, R. (1980), 'Unequal opportunity structure and labour market segmentation', *Sociology*, vol. 14, no. 4, pp. 525–550.

Kuhn, T. (1967), *The Structure of Scientific Revolutions*, Chicago: University of Chicago Press.

Laclau, E. (1977), *Politics and Ideology in Marxist Theory*, London: Verso.

Lambert, J., Paris, C., and Blackaby, B. (1978), *Housing Policy and the State: Allocation, Access and Control*, London: Macmillan.

Lawless, P. (1979), *Urban Deprivation and Government Initiative*, London: Faber.

Lawless, P. (1981a), 'The role of some central government agencies in urban economic regeneration', *Regional Studies*, vol. 15, pp. 1–14.

Lawless, P. (1981b), *Britain's Inner Cities: Problems and Policies*, London: Harper & Row.

Lefebvre, H. (1976), *The Survival of Capitalism*, London: Allison & Busby.

Leicester City and Leicestershire County Councils (1969), *Leicester and Leicestershire Sub-Regional Planning Study*, Leicester-Leicestershire Joint Councils.

Lewis, W. (1955), *The Theory of Economic Growth*, New York: Basic Books.

Lilienfeld, D. (1978), *The Rise of Systems Theory*, London: John Wiley.

Lindblom, C. (1968), *The Policy Making Process*, Englewood Cliffs: Prentice-Hall.

Lindblom, C. (1973), 'The science of "muddling through",' in A. Faludi (ed.), *A Reader in Planning Theory*, Oxford: Pergamon.

Lindblom, C. (1977), *Politics and Markets*, New York: Basic Books.

Lipietz, A. (1977), *Le Capital et Son Éspace*, Paris: Maspero.

Lipietz, A. (1980a), 'Inter-regional polarisation and the tertiarisation of society', Paper Presented to the 19th European Congress of the Regional Science Association, London.

Lipietz, A. (1980b), 'The structuration of space, the problem of land, and spatial policy', in J. Carney *et al.* (eds.), *Regions in Crisis*, London: Croom Helm.

Lipietz, A. (1982), 'Towards global Fordism?', *New Left Review*, vol. 132, pp. 33–47.

Llewelyn Davies, R. Ptnrs. (1968), *Milton Keynes Final Report*, Milton Keynes.

Llewelyn Davies, R. (1972), 'Changing goals in design: the Milton Keynes example', in H. Evans (ed.), *New Towns: the British Experience*, London: Charles Knight.

Lojkine, J. (1977), 'Big firms' strategies, urban policy and urban social movements', in M. Harloe (ed.), *Captive Cities*, London: John Wiley.

Lowi, T. (1969), *The End of Liberalism*, New York: Norton.

Lukes, S. (1974), *Power: a Radical View*, London: Macmillan.

Lukes, S. (1977), 'The new democracy', in S. Lukes (ed.), *Essays in Social Theory*, London: Macmillan.

Mabey, C. (1973), 'Social and ethnic mix in schools and the relationship with attainment of children aged 8 and 11', *CES Research Paper 9*, London: Centre for Environmental Studies.

MacEachern, D. (1979), 'Party government and the class interest of capital: conflict over the steel industry', *Capital and Class*, vol. 8, pp. 125–143.

MacEachern, D. (1980), *A Class Against Itself: Power and the Nationalisation of the British Steel Industry*, Cambridge: Cambridge University Press.

MacPherson, C. (1962), *The Political Theory of Possessive Individualism*, London: Oxford University Press.

MacPherson, C. (1972), 'Post-liberal democracy?', in R. Blackburn (ed.), *Ideology in Social Science*, London: Fontana.

Mandel, E. (1975), *Late Capitalism*, London: Verso.

Manis, J., and Meltzer, B. (1967), *Symbolic Interaction: a Reader in Social Psychology*, Boston: Allyn and Bacon.

March, J., and Simon, H. (1958), *Organizations*, New York: John Wiley.

Markusen, A. (1976), 'Class and urban social expenditures: a local theory of the state', *Kapitalistate*, vols. 4/5, pp. 50–65.

Markusen, A. (1978), 'Class and urban social expenditures: a Marxist theory of metropolitan government', in W. Tabb and L. Sawers (eds.), *Marxism and the Metropolis*, New York: Oxford University Press.

Marx, K. (1973), *Grundrisse*, Harmondsworth: Penguin.

Marx, K. (1976), *Capital, vol. I*, Harmondsworth: Penguin.

Massey, D. (1978), 'Regionalism: some current issues', *Capital and Class*, vol. 6, pp. 106–125.

Massey, D. (1979), 'In what sense a regional problem?', *Regional Studies*, vol. 13, pp. 233–243.

Massey, D. (1980), 'Industrial restructuring as class restructuring: some examples of the implications of industrial change for class structure', *Centre for Environmental Studies Working Note 604*, London: CES.

Massey, D. (1981), 'The UK electrical engineering and electronics industries: the implications of the crisis for the restructuring of capital and locational change', in M. Dear and A. Scott (eds.), *Urbanization and Urban Planning in Capitalist Society*, London: Methuen.

Massey, D. (forthcoming), *Space and Class: Industrial Location, the Regional Problem and British Economic Decline*, London: Macmillan.

Massey, D., and Meegan, R. (1979), 'The geography of industrial reorganization', *Progress in Planning*, vol. 10, pp. 155–237.

Massey, D., and Meegan, R. (1982), *The Anatomy of Job Loss*, London: Methuen.

McConnell, S. (1981), *Theories for Planning*, London: Heinemann.

McLoughlin, B. (1969), *Urban and Regional Planning: A Systems Approach*, London: Faber.

Merton, R. (1968), *Social Theory and Social Structure*, Glencoe: Free Press.

Metzgar, J. (1981), 'Plant shutdowns and worker response: the case of Johnstown, Pa.', *Socialist Review*, vol. 53, pp. 9–50.

Meyerson M., and Banfield, E. (1955), *Politics, Planning and the Public Interest*, Glencoe: Free Press.

Michaels, D. (1974), 'Speculations on future planning process theory', in D. Godschalk (ed.), *Planning in America: Learning from Turbulence*, Washington: American Institute of Planners.

Miliband, R. (1969), *The State in Capitalist Society*, London: Weidenfeld & Nicholson.

Miliband, R. (1972), *Parliamentary Socialism*, London: Merlin.

Miliband, R. (1973), 'Poulantzas and the capitalist state', *New Left Review*, vol. 82, pp. 83–92.

Miliband, R. (1977), *Marxism and Politics*, Oxford: Oxford University Press.

Miller, S. (1978), 'The recapitalization of capitalism', *International Journal of Urban and Regional Research*, vol. 2, no. 2, pp. 202–212.

Miller, S. (1980), 'The eighties and the left: an American view', in R. Miliband and J. Saville (eds.), *The Socialist Register*, London: Merlin.

Mingione, E. (1978), 'Capitalist crisis, neo-dualism and marginalisation', *International Journal of Urban and Regional Research*, vol. 2, no. 2, pp. 213–221.

Mingione, E. (1981), *Social Conflict and the City*, Oxford: Basil Blackwell.

Mitroff, I. (1974), *The Subjective Side of Science*, Amsterdam: Elsevier.

Mouzelis, N. (1975), *Organisation and Bureaucracy*, London: Routledge & Kegan Paul.

Mulkay, M. (1979), *Science and the Sociology of Knowledge*, Allen & Unwin.

Mullan, B. (1980), *Stevenage Ltd: Aspects of the Planning and Politics of Stevenage New Town 1945–1978*, London: Routledge & Kegan Paul.

Muller, R., and Bruce, A. (1981), 'Local government in pursuit of an industrial strategy', *Local Government Studies*, vol. 7, pp. 3–20.

Müller, W., and Neusüss, C. (1978), 'The "welfare-state illusion" and the contradiction between wage labour and capital', in J. Holloway and S. Picciotto (eds.), *State and Capital: A Marxist Debate*, London: Edward Arnold.

Muth, R. (1962), 'The spatial structure of the housing market', *Regional Science Association, Papers and Proceedings*, vol. 7, pp. 207–220.

Myrdal, G. (1957), *Economic Theory and Underdeveloped Regions*, London: Duckworth.

Needham, B. (1971), 'Concrete problems not abstract goals', *Journal of the Royal Town Planning Institute*, vol. 57, pp. 217–319.

Nottinghamshire–Derbyshire Sub-Regional Planning Unit (1969), *Notts–Derby Sub-Regional Study*, Notts–Derbyshire County Councils.

O'Connor, J. (1973), *The Fiscal Crisis of the State*, New York: St. Martins Press.

O'Connor, J. (1981), 'The meaning of crisis', *International Journal of Urban and Regional Research*, vol. 5, no. 3, pp. 301–329.

O'Dowd, L., and Tomlinson, M. (1980), 'Urban politics in Belfast: two case studies', *International Journal of Urban and Regional Research*, vol. 4, no. 1, pp. 72–96.

Offe, C. (1972), 'Political authority and class structures – an analysis of late capitalist societies', *International Journal of Sociology*, vol. 2, pp. 73–108.

Offe, C. (1974), 'Structural problems of the capitalist state', in K. Von Beyme (ed.), *German Political Studies*, vol. 1, London: Sage.

Offe, C. (1975), 'The theory of the capitalist state and the problem of policy formation', in L. Lindberg *et al.* (eds.), *Stress and Contradiction in Modern Capitalism*, Lexington: D. C. Heath.

Offe, C., and Ronge, V. (1975), 'Theses on the theory of the state', *New German Critique*, vol. 6, pp. 137–147.

Offe, C., and Hinrichs, K. (1977), 'Sozialökonomie des Arbeitmarktes und die "benachteiligter" Gruppen von Arbeitnehmern', in C. Offe (ed.), *Opfer des Arbeitsmarktes*, Darmstadt: Luchterhand.

Offe, C., and Wiesenthal, H. (1980), 'Two logics of collective action: theoretical notes on social class and organizational form', *Political Power and Social Theory*, vol. 1, pp. 67–115.

Olson, M. (1965), *The Logic of Collective Action*, Cambridge: Harvard University Press.

Organisation for Economic Development and Co-operation (1979), *The Impact of the Newly Industrialising Countries*, Paris: OECD.

Orlans, H. (1952), *Stevenage: A Sociological Study of a New Town*, London: Routledge & Kegan Paul.

Paci, M. (1973), *Mercato del Lavoro e Classi Sociali in Italia*, Bologna: Il Mulino.

Pahl, R. (1968), *Readings in Urban Sociology*, Oxford: Pergamon.

Pahl, R. (1975), *Whose City?*, Harmondsworth: Penguin.

Paillox, C. (1976), The labour process: from Fordism to neo-Fordism, in 'The labour process and class strategies', *CSE Pamphlet 1*, London: Conference of Socialist Economists.

Park, R., Burgess, E., and McKenzie, R. (1925), *The City*, Chicago: University of Chicago Press.

Parson, D. (1981), 'Urban renewal and housing action areas in Belfast: legitimation and the incorporation of protest', *International Journal of Urban and Regional Research*, vol. 5, no. 2, pp. 218–230.

Parsons, T. (1955), *The Social System*, London: Routledge & Kegan Paul.

Parsons, T., and Shils, E. (1951), *Toward a General Theory of Action*, Cambridge: Harvard University Press.

Pettigrew, A. (1972), 'Information control as a power resource', *Sociology*, vol. 6, no. 1, pp. 187–204.

Pickvance, C. (1976), 'On the study of urban social movements', in C. Pickvance (ed.), *Urban Sociology: Critical Essays*, London: Tavistock.

Pickvance, C. (1981), 'Policies as chameleons: an interpretation of regional policy and office policy in Britain', in M. Dear and A. Scott (eds.), *Urbanization and Urban Planning in Capitalist Society*, London: Methuen.

Piore, M. (1973), on the technological foundations of economic dualism, *Massachusetts Institute of Technology, Working Paper No. 110*, Cambridge: MIT.

Poulantzas, N. (1973), *Political Power and Social Classes*, London: New Left Books.

Poulantzas, N. (1975), *Classes in Contemporary Capitalism*, London: New Left Books.

Poulantzas, N. (1976), 'The capitalist state: a reply to Miliband and Laclau', *New Left Review*, vol. 95, pp. 63–83.

Poulantzas, N. (1978), *State, Power, Socialism*, London: New Left Books.

Przeworski, A. (1977), 'Proletariat into a class: the process of class formation from Karl Kautsky's "The Class Struggle" to recent controversies', *Politics and Society*, vol. 7, no. 4, pp. 343–401.

Przeworski, A. (1980a), 'Material bases of consent: economics and politics in a hegemonic system', *Political Power and Social Theory*, vol. 1, pp. 21–66.

Przeworski, A. (1980b), 'Social democracy as a historical phenomenon', *New Left Review*, vol. 122, pp. 27–58.

Ranney, D. (1969), *Planning and Politics in the Metropolis*, Columbus: Merrill.

Reich, M., Gordon, D., and Edwards, R. (1973), 'A theory of labour market segmentation', *American Economic Review*, vol. 63, no. 2, pp. 359–365.

Rex, J. (1961), *Key Problems in Sociological Theory*, London: Routledge & Kegan Paul.

Richardson, H. (1969), *Regional Economics*, Harmondsworth: Penguin.

Robinson, I. (1973), 'Beyond the middle-range planning bridge', in A. Faludi (ed.), *A Reader in Planning Theory*, Oxford: Pergamon.

Rondinelli, D. (1971), 'Adjunctive planning and urban development policy', *Urban Affairs Quarterly*, pp. 13–39.

Rostow, W. (1963), *The Stages of Economic Growth*, Cambridge: Cambridge University Press.

Rothblatt, D. (1971), 'Rational planning re-examined', *Journal of the American Institute of Planners*, vol. 37, pp. 26–37.

Rothwell, R., and Zegveld, W. (1982), *Innovation and the Small and Medium Sized Firm*, London: Francis Pinter.

Roweis, S., and Scott, A. (1978), 'The urban land question', in K. Cox (ed.), *Urbanization and Conflict in Market Societies*, London: Methuen.

Rowthorn, R. (1974), 'Neo-classicism, neo-Ricardianism and Marxism', *New Left Review*, vol. 86, pp. 63–87.

Ryan, A. (1970), *The Philosophy of the Social Sciences*, London: Macmillan.

Saunders, P. (1979), *Urban Politics: A Sociological Interpretation*, London: Hutchinson.

Saunders, P. (1981), *Social Theory and the Urban Question*, London: Hutchinson.

Saxenian, A. (1981), 'Silicon chips and spatial structure: the industrial basis of urbanization in Santa Clara County, California', Paper Presented at Conference on New Perspectives on the Urban Political Economy, American University, Washington D.C., May.

Sayer, A. (1976), 'A critique of urban and regional modelling', *Progress in Planning*, vol. 6, no. 3, pp. 191–254.

300   *Theories of Planning and Spatial Development*

Sayer, A. (1978), 'Mathematical modelling in regional science and political economy: some comments', *Antipode*, vol. 102, pp. 79–86.

Sayer, A. (1979), 'Theory and empirical research in urban and regional political economy: a sympathetic critique', *Urban and Regional Studies Working Paper 14*, Brighton: Sussex University.

Sayer, A. (1981), 'Abstraction: a realist interpretation', *Radical Philosophy*, Summer, pp. 6–15.

Scott, A. (1980), *The Urban Land Nexus and the State*, London: Pion.

Scott, A., and Roweis, S. (1977), 'Urban planning in theory and practice: a re-appraisal', *Environment and Planning A*, vol. 9, pp. 1097–1119.

Sharkansky, I. (1970), *The Routines of Politics*, New York: Van Nostrand.

Silverman, D. (1970), *The Theory of Organisations*, London: Heinemann.

Simmie, J. (1974), *Citizens in Conflict*, London: Hutchinson.

Simon, H. (1955), 'A behavioural model of rational choice', *Quarterly Journal of Economics*, vol. 69, pp. 99–118.

Skidelsky, R. (1979), 'The decline of Keynesian politics', in C. Crouch (ed.), *State and Economy in Contemporary Capitalism*, London: Croom Helm.

Skjei, S. (1976), 'Urban problems and the theoretical justification of urban planning', *Urban Affairs Quarterly*, vol. 11, no. 3, pp. 323–344.

Solomos, J. (1981), 'Unemployment, the labour market and state policies: some aspects of crisis management in the seventies', Unpublished Paper Presented at CSE Regionalism Group Meeting, London, October.

Solow, R. (1973), 'On equilibrium models of urban location', in E. Parkin (ed.), *Essays in Modern Economics*, London: Longmans.

Stedman Jones, G. (1977), 'The Marxism of the early Lukacs', in *Western Marxism: A Critical Reader*, London: New Left Books.

Stone, K. (1974), 'The origins of job structures in the steel industry', *Review of Radical Political Economics*, vol. 6, pp. 61–97.

Storey, D., and Robinson, F. (1981), 'Local authorities and the attraction of industry – the case of Cleveland County Council', *Local Government Studies*, vol. 4, pp. 21–37.

Sullivan, G. (1972), 'Incremental budget-making in the American states: a test of the Anton Model', *The Journal of Politics*, vol. 34, pp. 639–647.

Tabb, W. (1978), 'The New York City fiscal crisis', in W. Tabb, and L. Sawers (eds.), *Marxism and the Metropolis*, New York: Oxford University Press.

Taylor, F. (1913), *The Principles of Scientific Management*, New York: Harper & Row.

Thompson, E. (1980), 'Notes on exterminism: the last stage of civilization', *New Left Review*, vol. 121, pp. 3–32.

Tilly, C. (1968), 'Race and migration to the American city', in J. Wilson (ed.), *The Metropolitan Enigma*, Cambridge: Harvard University Press.

Tomlinson, J., (1981), 'The economics of politics and public expenditure: a critique', *Economy and Society*, vol. 10, no. 4, pp. 381–402.

Townroe, P. (1979), 'The design of local economic development policies', *Town Planning Review*, vol. 50, no. 2, pp. 148–163.

Toye, P. (1976), 'Economic theories of politics and public finance', *The British Journal of Political Science*, vol. 6, pp. 433–448.

Underwood, J., and Stewart, M. (1978), 'Local economic initiatives by local authorities', *The Planner*, vol. 64, pp. 110–112.

Urry, J. (1973), 'Towards a structural theory of the new middle class', *Acta Sociologica*, vol. 16, pp. 175–187.

Urry, J. (1981a), *The Anatomy of Capitalist Societies*, London: Macmillan.

Urry, J. (1981b), 'Localities, regions and social class', *International Journal of Urban and Regional Research*, vol. 5, no. 4, pp. 455–474.

Urry, J. (1981c), 'Paternalism, management and localities', *Lancaster Regionalism Group Working Paper 2*, University of Lancaster.

Wainwright, H., and Elliott, D. (1982), *The Lucas Plan*, London: Allison & Busby.

Wallerstein, I. (1974), *The Modern World-System: Capitalist Agriculture and the Origins of the European World-Economy in the Sixteenth Century*, New York: Academic Press.

Wallerstein, I. (1979), *The Capitalist World-Economy*, Cambridge: Cambridge University Press.

Webber, M. (1964), 'The urban place and the non-place urban realm', in M. Webber (ed.), *Explorations into Urban Structure*, Philadelphia: University of Pennsylvania Press.

Webber, M. (1968), 'Planning in an environment of change: beyond the industrial age', *Town Planning Review*, vol. 39, pp. 179–195.

Webber, M. (1973), 'Comprehensive planning and social responsibility', in A. Faludi (ed.), *A Reader in Planning Theory*, Oxford: Pergamon.

Weber, M. (1948), 'Politics as a vocation', in H. Gerth and C. Mills (eds.), *From Max Weber: Essays in Sociology*, London: Routledge & Kegan Paul.

White, M., and White, L. (1964), *The Intellectual Versus the City*, New York: Mentor.

Wickham, J. (1980), 'The political preconditions of discretion: the case of the IDA', Unpublished Paper Presented at BSA (Wales) Group Meeting, Gregynog, May.

Wickham, J., and Murray, P. (1981), 'Technocratic ideology and the reproduction of inequality: the electronics industry in the Republic of Ireland', Paper Presented at British Sociological Association Annual Conference, Aberystwyth, April.

Wildavsky, A. (1964), *The Politics of the Budgetary Process*, Boston: Little Brown.

Wildavsky, A. (1973), 'If planning is everything, maybe it's nothing', *Policy Sciences*, vol. 4, pp. 127–153.

Wilkinson, F. (1977), 'Collective bargaining in the steel industry in the 1920's', in A. Briggs and J. Saville (eds.), *Essays in Labour History*, London: Croom Helm.

Williams, G. (1978), *The Merthyr Rising*, London: Croom Helm.

Williams, R. (1973), *The Country and the City*, London: Paladin.

Williams, W. (1971), *Social Policy Research and Analysis: the Experience in the Federal Social Agencies*, New York: Elsevier.

Winkler, J. (1977), 'The corporatist economy: theory and administration', in R. Scase (ed.), *Industrial Society: Class, Cleavage and Control*, London: Allen & Unwin.

Wood, S. (1982) (ed.), *The Degradation of Work?*, London: Hutchinson.

Wright, E. (1978), *Class, Crisis and the State*, London: New Left Books.

Wright, E. (1980), 'Varieties of Marxist conceptions of class structure', *Politics and Society*, vol. 9, pp. 323–370.

von Wright, G. (1971), *Explanation and Understanding*, Ithaca: Cornell University Press.

Wrong, D. (1961), 'The over-socialised conception of man in modern sociology', *American Sociological Review*, vol. 26, no. 2, pp. 183–193.

Zeitlin, J. (1980), 'The emergence of shop steward organisation and job control in the British car industry', *History Workshop Journal*, vol. 10, pp. 119–137.

Zimbalist, A. (1979) (ed.), *Case Studies on the Labour Process*, New York: Monthly Review Press.

Index